THE PLACE OF
ATTACHMENT
IN HUMAN
BEHAVIOR

THE PLACE OF ATTACHMENT IN HUMAN BEHAVIOR

EDITED BY

Colin Murray Parkes

AND

Joan Stevenson-Hinde

Basic Books, Inc., Publishers   New York

Library of Congress Cataloging in Publication Data

Main entry under title:
The place of attachment in human behavior.

Includes bibliographies and index.
1. Attachment behavior. 2. Developmental psychology.
3. Psychology, pathological. I. Parkes, Colin Murray.
II. Stevenson-Hinde, Joan
BF575.A86P55   155.9'24   81-66979
ISBN 0-465-05771-3   AACR2

Contents

PART III

Bonding in Adult Life

PART IV

Disorders in Adult Life

Contributors

KENNETH S. ADAM, M.D. Professor of Psychiatry, McMaster University, Hamilton, Ontario, Canada.

MARY D. SALTER AINSWORTH, Ph.D. Commonwealth Professor of Psychology and Behavioral Medicine and Psychiatry, University of Virginia, Charlottesville, Virginia.

MURIEL BARRETT, Diploma for the Teaching of Maladjusted Children, Institute of Education, University of London. Remedial Teacher and Educational Therapist, Department for Children and Parents, Tavistock Clinic, London.

JOHN BOWLBY, M.D., F.R.C.P., F.R.C. Psych. Honorary Consultant Psychiatrist, Tavistock Clinic, London.

GEORGE W. BROWN, Ph.D. Professor, Department of Sociology, Bedford College, London.

PAULINE P. DELOZIER, Ph.D. Clinical Psychologist, Ross Loos Medical Group, Department of Mental Health, West Covina, California; Research Associate, Child and Family Development Program, Children's Institute International, Los Angeles, California.

DOROTHY H. HEARD, Ph.D. F.R.C.P., F.R.C. Psych. Honorary Lecturer and Consultant, Department of Psychiatry, University of Leeds, St. James's University Hospital, Leeds. Formerly Consultant Child Psychiatrist, Department for Children and Parents, Tavistock Clinic, London.

SCOTT HENDERSON, M.D., F.R.A.C.P. Director, National Health and Medical Research Council, Social Psychiatry Research Unit, The Australian National University, Canberra.

ROBERT A. HINDE, Sc.D., F.R.S. Royal Society Research Professor and Honorary Director, M.R.C. Unit on the Development and Integration of Behaviour, University of Cambridge.

MARY MAIN, Ph.D. Associate Professor of Psychology, University of California, Berkeley, California.

PETER MARRIS, Professor, Graduate School of Architecture and Urban Planning, University of California, Los Angeles, California.

COLIN MURRAY PARKES, M.D., D.P.M., F.R.C. Psych. Senior Lecturer in Psychiatry, The London Hospital Medical College, London.

ANDREA POUND, B.Sc., M. Phil. Principal Clinical Psychologist, Child Guidance Training Centre, London.

BEVERLEY RAPHAEL, M.D. Professor of Psychiatry, Faculty of Medicine, University of Newcastle, Australia.

JOAN STEVENSON-HINDE, Ph.D. Scientific Officer, M.R.C. Unit on the Development and Integration of Behaviour, University of Cambridge.

JUDITH TROWELL, M.R.C. Psych., D.C.H. Consultant Child Psychiatrist, Tavistock Clinic, London.

ROBERT S. WEISS, Ph.D. Professor of Sociology, University of Massachusetts, Boston; Lecturer in Sociology, Laboratory of Community Psychiatry, Massachusetts Mental Health Center, Harvard Medical School.

DONNA R. WESTON, M.A. Doctoral candidate in Psychology, University of California, Berkeley, California; Lecturer, Department of Psychology, San Francisco State University, San Francisco, California.

Preface

Colin Murray Parkes
and Joan Stevenson-Hinde

LOVE may not make the world go round, but there can be no doubt that the child's first attachment to another person (usually his mother[1]) gives rise to expectations and assumptions about the world, the effects of which will be felt throughout his life.

Foremost among those scientists and clinicians who have made us aware of the importance of this observation is John Bowlby. His seminal work, *Attachment and Loss*, which appeared in three volumes in 1969, 1973, and 1980, remains the chief statement of attachment theory and a model for the successful development of a scientific paradigm. The relationship that a child develops with his mother is seen as a complex interweaving of reciprocal expectations and behaviors that forms a starting point for later relationships. To understand the nature of that unique attachment, Bowlby has drawn his ideas from many sources: from the behavioral sciences of ethology, psychology, psychoanalysis, and psychiatry, and from the more abstract realms of cybernetics and information theory. With penetrating logic and a scrupulous regard for scientific method, he has built up a constellation of ideas that makes sense of much that has previously been inexplicable or poorly explained and opens the way to the solution of a range of problems.

Inevitably he has trodden on a few toes. Some of his fellow psychoanalysts have been hurt by his criticisms of metapsychology. Some

1. Here, "his" should be taken as referring to either sex and "mother" as implying the chief person who cares for a child regardless of that person's sex and blood relationship to the child.

members of the women's movement have seen his assertion of the child's need for parenting as a threat to the liberation of women. Some child psychiatrists have seen in his claims of the damaging effects of loss of a mother an assumption that these effects cannot be undone if a satisfactory substitute is found. Bowlby has been quite prepared to answer his critics and, where necessary, to modify his own views. The result, overall, has been a strengthening of confidence in his basic model and a greater willingness within the scientific community to follow the leads he has given.

Bowlby has not started a "school"—his ideas extend too widely to be relevant to a single discipline. He has, rather, opened the door to new ways of thinking about a wide range of important problems. His research seminars at the Tavistock Centre in London have attracted scientists from diverse locations and disciplines whose only common link is an interest in attachment itself. Most of the contributors to this volume are former participants.

It was Ved Varma, consultant psychologist and former educational psychologist to the London borough of Brent, who first initiated the idea of a book that would be both a tribute to John Bowlby and a compilation of recent work influenced by his thinking. Unfortunately it was not possible for Dr. Varma to undertake the project himself and it was the first editor, with the help of John Bowlby and members of his research seminar, who drew up the outline plan.

From the start the book was conceived in four parts, corresponding to the four areas of study most relevant to attachment. First there is work concerned with the nature of child-mother attachments, the various forms these may take, and how they develop under normal conditions. Second, we examine how attachments develop under abnormal conditions and the problems that result. In part III we look at the implications of these childhood attachments for understanding how attachments occur and develop in adult life, and in part IV we consider certain psychiatric disorders in adulthood, the incidence and course of which may be influenced by earlier or current attachments and their consequences.

Because of the diversity of viewpoints involved, it was important for the contributors to meet to develop a common language and frame of reference that would be acceptable to all. This was made possible by the King Edward's Hospital Fund for London, which served to host us at a three-day conference in London where preliminary statements were read and discussed. Although they are not authors of chapters in the book, other researchers who shared their thoughts with us at the conference include John Byng-Hall, Hamish Cameron, Marion Mac-kenzie, Janet Mattinson, Dennis Scott, Ian Sinclair, and Anthony Stevens. We are most grateful for their contributions.

The book that emerged follows the original outline with the addition of an epilogue by John Bowlby. Bowlby was present at the conference, and his comments on many of the draft chapters indicate his continuing contribution to the development of the field. He continues to teach and to meet regularly with fellow workers, to stimulate new ideas, and to develop the wider ramifications of his research.

On the topic of infant-mother attachment, Mary Ainsworth is an unquestioned authority. Her strange-situation test has become the research instrument by which attachment is measured in early childhood. By exposing children to a standard unfamiliar situation and observing how they react when mother leaves, while she is away, and when she returns, Ainsworth has developed sophisticated measures of attachment behavior. Her observations reveal interesting differences in the ways children respond in these standard situations and are described in chapter 1.

Out of Ainsworth's research comes a surprising finding: that certain children, in the strange situation, do not show attachment behavior—rather, they avoid their mothers. This has been further investigated by Mary Main and Donna Weston who, in chapter 2, describe the sequence of experiments by which they have studied and explained this potentially ominous finding.

Part I concludes with an insightful chapter by Robert Hinde, whose own studies of attachment behavior in primates have led him to reappraise the conceptual basis of attachment theory and argue that data language and theory language must be kept separate. The simple evolutionary model that was adequate for initial generalizations about infant-mother interactions becomes inadequate when individual differences are examined.

Throughout the book we have tried to be consistent in our use of central terms. Attachment behavior can best be defined in John Bowlby's words as

Any form of behaviour that results in a person attaining or retaining proximity to some other differentiated and preferred individual, usually conceived as stronger and/or wiser. As such the behaviour includes following, clinging, crying, calling, greeting, smiling, and other more sophisticated forms. It is developing during the second trimester of life and is evident from six months onward when an infant shows by his behaviour that he discriminates sharply between his mother-figure, a few other familiar people, and everyone else. In the company of his mother he is cheerful, re-laxed, and inclined to explore and play. When alone with strangers he is apt to become acutely distressed: he protests his mother's absence and strives to regain contact with her. These responses are at a maximum during the second and third years of life and then diminish slowly. (Thenceforward, although attachment behaviour is less evident in both the frequency of its occurrence and its intensity, it nonetheless persists as an important part of man's behavioural equipment, not only during later childhood but during adolescence and adult life as well. In adults it is especially evident when a person is distressed, ill, or afraid. (1975, p. 292)

Further discussion of this and related terms may be found in chapter 3. On other central issues we have not reached a clear consensus. One such area concerns the plurality of attachment figures. Bowlby argues that by the end of the first year of life the child has usually more than one attachment figure, but these figures "are not treated as the equivalents of one another" (1969, p. 304). For most children attachment figures may be arranged in a hierarchical order of preference, with a "principal attachment figure" at the top. This refers not to a figure who is preferred for all sorts of social interactions, but rather to one who is preferred when the attachment behavior system may be assumed to be aroused, as when the child is frightened, hungry, tired, or ill. Studies relevant to the concept of a hierarchy are reviewed by Ainsworth in chapter 1. However, she emphasizes the need for further research into the role of parents and other individuals as principal attachment figures.

A related issue concerns the *quality* of attachment to different figures. Recent findings have shown that knowing the category of attachment to one parent does not help to predict the category to the other parent (e.g., Main and Weston, 1981), although there may be an "effect of relationship upon relationship" (see chapter 1 herein, p. 20). However, of eighty children assessed in the strange-situation test with mother and at a different time with father, only one was "especially securely attached" (i.e., category B3, see Ainsworth et al., 1978) to *both* parents.[2] The implication is that it is difficult to form a really secure attachment with more than one person.

In part II we consider the effects on attachment behavior of various kinds of obstetric management (chapter 4), child abuse (chapter 5), maternal depression (chapter 6), and the death of a parent (chapter 7). In each of these areas important work has been conducted in recent years, work which enables us to understand how impairment of at-

2. Mary Main, personal communication.

tachment can damage the developing child. Thus, the bond between mother and child which develops at or shortly after birth, seems to be particularly easily impaired if the circumstances of birth are not right. This observation must cause obstetricians and midwives to reexamine their ways of managing childbirth.[3]

The very thought of child abuse is distressing, and it is not made less so by the recognition that abused children tend to become abusing parents. Thus the damage is passed from generation to generation. If we are to break this cycle we need a clear and precise understanding of attachment behavior and the particular forms which predispose to abuse.

The problem of depression in mothers is linked to this problem and has even wider implications. Whether or not a depressed mother seeks medical help, it is unlikely that a member of the caring professions will recognize the effect of her depression on her children or offer help to her. Similarly there has been little attention paid to the needs of bereaved children aside from whatever support may be offered to their parents.

In chapters 4, 5, 6, and 7, each contributor describes her own recent research, reviews the work of others, and discusses its implications in the light of attachment theory. This section ends with a chapter that knits together theory and practice by describing therapeutic work with families in which a child has become severely retarded in reading.

The divide between sociology and psychology, two disciplines whose subject matter is people but whose proponents are too often blind to each other's points of view, is crossed in part III. Here two sociologists, Robert Weiss and Peter Marris, show unusual breadth of vision in extending our understanding of attachments from childhood to adult life and from the small social unit of the child-mother relationship to that of the whole family and to other social units as well. Weiss's analysis of attachment bonds in adult life forms an effective link between the subject matter of the first two parts of the book and that of the last two.

As in childhood, a "principal attachment figure" may be found in adulthood. Weiss argues that attachment to one figure is competitive with forming other attachments. "Unique relationships" in adulthood are further discussed in chapter 10 by Marris, who postulates a hierarchy of priorities.

3. James Thurber's neoscience "psycho-babycraft" may need to be taken seriously after all.

To quote Bowlby, "attachment behaviour does not disappear with childhood but persists throughout life" (1969, p. 350). Weiss suggests that child-parent attachment is similar to adult-adult attachment, and that in adolescence child-parent attachment normally weakens, enabling new attachments to be formed. Indeed, parallels between reactions to loss of an attachment figure in childhood and in adulthood are striking (e.g., Parkes, 1972; Bowlby, 1980). Still later in life, attachment behavior, as well as the opportunity to form "new" attachments, may decrease (see chapter 13).

However, we still need to know much more about the time course of attachment behavior: How does it change over childhood, adolescence, and adulthood? Bowlby's (1969) description of attachment behavior suggests a gradual development, with the formation of a "goal-corrected partnership" at about four years of age. But once this has developed, how are attachments relinquished, if they are, and how are new attachments formed? Weiss suggests that relinquishing attachment involves a "switching off." Thus any increase or decrease in adult attachment may be the result of attachment behavior being switched on or off for longer and longer periods, rather than any gradual increase or decrease in strength.

Marris extends our horizons in an exciting and important chapter in which he contrasts the depth of meaning that derives from the unique and irreplaceable attachments in our lives with the failure of attempts to find meaning by repudiating personal attachments and seeking for technological and scientific control of our world and its people. Whereas the functions that people perform for each other are replaceable, the people are not.

In part IV the relationship between attachment and mental illness is studied from four perspectives. Scott Henderson (chapter 11) describes some of his own research into the ways in which a person's current social relationships are perceived and how these increase or decrease his vulnerability to neurosis. His data support the view that "it is not the supportiveness of the actual social environment, but the way it is construed that is likely to be causally powerful" (p. 228).

George Brown (chapter 12) examines the role that loss of mother before the age of eleven can play in increasing the vulnerability of women to depression in later life. This vulnerability leads, apparently, to a decreased tolerance of life events—"strange-situations" emerging in the lives of adults that act as provoking factors in the depressions that follow. Brown's work is of considerable importance to psychiatry and, not surprisingly, has evoked controversy. In his chapter he answers his critics and provides fresh data to support his major claims.

Further grounds for regarding attachment problems as potentially pathogenic come from the work of Ken Adam, who in chapter 13 reviews the literature and describes his own studies of the relationship between loss of a parent in childhood and the mental states that predispose to suicide in adult life. He disagrees with other workers who have regarded actual suicide as a different class of event from attempted suicide and suggests that "attempted suicide and actual suicide may not represent different but overlapping groups, as has been suggested by the epidemiological data, but rather the same group on different points of a developmental continuum of attachment" (p. 290).

Having established that certain types of insecure attachment, of loss, and of life events can interact to increase the risk of psychiatric disorders, it remains to be determined how this outcome might be prevented. This topic is considered in chapter 14, where Colin Parkes reviews recent work which indicates that, in some areas of service, successful prevention has already been achieved.

In his epilogue, John Bowlby considers why it can take a long time for a body of knowledge to have an effective impact on clinical practice. He sees this book as the "first fruits" of a harvest yet to come and emphasizes that attachment theory is a growing field. Yet as Hinde (chapter 3) cautions, it would be detrimental if we put attachment theory on a pedestal, to be proved or disproved. This echoes Mary Ainsworth's view that:

> Attachment theory might be described as "programmatic" and open-ended. It does not purport to be a tight network of propositions on the basis of which hypotheses may be formulated, any one of which, in the event of an adequate but unsuccessful test, could invalidate the theory as a whole. Instead, this is an explanatory theory—a guide to understanding data already at our disposal and a guide to further research. (Ainsworth et al., 1978, p. 4)

Rather than a "theory" of attachment, we are developing a "conceptual framework" (Bowlby, 1980, p. 441). Within such a framework, familiar scenes may be viewed in a new light, some in perfect focus and others as yet "glimpsed through a glass, darkly."

REFERENCES

Ainsworth, M. D. S.; Blehar, M. C.; Waters, E.; and Wall, S. 1978. *Patterns of attachment: A psychological study of the strange-situation.* New Jersey: Lawrence Erlbaum Associates.

Bowlby, J. 1969. *Attachment and loss. Vol. 1: Attachment.* New York: Basic Books.

————— 1973. *Attachment and loss. Vol. 2: Separation: Anxiety and anger.* New York: Basic Books.

————— 1975. Attachment theory, separation anxiety, and mourning. In *American handbook of psychiatry. Vol. 6: New psychiatric frontiers,* ed. D. A. Hamburg and H. K. M. Brodie. New York: Basic Books.

————— 1980. *Attachment and loss. Vol. 3: Loss: Sadness and depression.* New York: Basic Books.

Main, M. and Weston, D. R. 1981. The quality of the toddler's relationship to mother and to father: Related to conflict behavior and the readiness to establish new relationships. *Child Development* 52:932–940.

Parkes, C. M. 1972. *Bereavement: Studies of grief in adult life.* New York: International Universities Press and London: Pelican.

PART I

Infant–Mother Attachment

1

Mary D. Salter Ainsworth

ATTACHMENT: RETROSPECT AND PROSPECT

DURING the last decade or so a massive amount of research relevant to attachment has accumulated. It is not my intention here to review it comprehensively. Although much has been learned about attachment, much more is still unknown or very imperfectly known, especially about attachments beyond infancy and to figures other than the mother. Therefore, this is a highly selective review, emphasizing findings that in my opinion form a promising foundation for future research and focusing for the most part on research that has stemmed from a concept of attachment compatible with the paradigm formulated by Bowlby (1969). Research that is already well known may be referred to, but the emphasis will be placed on recent research; however, few details can be given. Eight main themes provide the framework for the review, and in regard to each prospects for future research will be considered.

The eight themes are as follows: (1) behavioral systems and the interplay among systems; (2) the importance of organized patterns of behavior as a basis for identifying patterns of infant-mother attachment; (3) developmental changes in the attachment of child to mother; (4) other changes not attributable to normative developmental processes; (5) maternal behavior as related to infant attachment; (6) further consideration of patterns of infant behavior; (7) evidence perti-

This paper is adapted from the author's presidential address to the Society for Research in Child Development at its biennial meeting at San Francisco, March 16, 1979.

nent to the hypothesis of a hierarchy of attachments to caregiving figures in infancy; and (8) other types of attachments.

Behavioral Systems and the Interplay among Systems

One aspect of attachment theory that is particularly useful as an aid to understanding the complexity of attachment behavior is the notion that the behavioral system is but one among a number of behavioral systems, such as exploratory, fear/wariness, affiliative, food seeking, etc. For each of these systems there is a set of conditions under which the system is activated. If a behavioral system is activated at low intensity, it is entirely likely that another system will be activated at higher intensity, and this will determine the actual behavior to be displayed. This concept is relevant to the phenomenon of a baby using his mother as a secure base from which to explore (Ainsworth, 1967). Novelty, within certain limits, activates his exploratory behavioral system. If his mother is present and if he is rested, healthy, and not hungry, his attachment system is likely to be inactive or activated at low intensity. If his environment is a relatively rich one, containing novel objects or complex objects with novel aspects, his exploratory system is likely to be activated at higher intensity than the attachment system, and he will be content to leave his mother in order to explore. For a while one will see little or no attachment behavior—perhaps only the occasional glance at his mother, perhaps a smile or a vocalization. However, Bowlby's (1969) concept of "set-goal" is relevant here. If the baby strays too far from his mother or stays away too long, his set-goal for proximity to her is exceeded, the attachment system is activated at higher intensity, and he tends to return to his mother. But this return reduces the intensity of activation of the attachment system, so that the exploratory system is again in the ascendant and he moves off to explore again. Should his mother move off or disappear, the child's attachment behavior would be activated again and at much higher intensity than before, perhaps overriding the exploratory system altogether. Exploration would be abandoned, and the child would be likely to expend every effort toward reaching his mother or signaling her to return to him. The balance between the two systems in the individual child at that particular time and in that particular context determines what he will do.

On the other hand, it is well known that the strange or unfamiliar is not only novel and provocative of exploration but that it may also activate wary or fearful behavior. At the same time attachment behavior is likely to be intensified. Consequently, in an unfamiliar environment there is interplay among three systems. If a stranger is present, still a fourth system is involved, for a baby tends to be friendly and sociable with other human beings as well as to be wary/fearful of the stranger *qua* strange. It is suggested that much of the apparently conflicting evidence in the literature about infant response to strangers can be clarified through examining the interplay of these four behavioral systems—attachment, wariness/fear, affiliation or sociability, and exploration (Bretherton and Ainsworth, 1974).

Closely related to the notion of interplay among behavioral systems is context—both behavioral and environmental. Behavioral context refers to the relative intensity of activation of the relevant systems. Environmental context has much to do with what systems are activated and at what intensity. Obviously the investigation of the interplay among behavioral systems in different situations and at different ages has only begun. Without pointing to specific research that especially cries out to be done, this approach can be recommended as useful in the design of research situations and in the analysis of findings.

Patterns of Attachment

Although it has been useful to examine various attachment behaviors, such as smiling and crying, one at a time, tracing their early development, it is now more important for attachment research to deal with organized patterns of behavior than with separate, discrete ones. In his initial formulation of an evolutionary-ethological approach to the origins of a child's tie to his mother, Bowlby (1958) drew attention to a few species-characteristic behaviors that had evolved because they promoted proximity between mother and infant and thus served the biological function of protecting the infant during his early and most vulnerable years. When I was reporting my findings of the development of attachment among infants in Uganda (Ainsworth, 1967), I searched my records for behaviors that could help identify whether and when a baby had become attached to his mother. I found sixteen such behaviors. In the course of my much more intensive and system-

5

atic study of Baltimore mother-infant dyads, I searched for additional criterion behaviors, but the new study added little or nothing to the roster of attachment behaviors identified among the Ganda.

More important, it became clear that little additional understanding of attachment was gained by tracing the development of these specific attachment behaviors beyond the first six months or so. By the last half of the first year, as Bowlby (1969) suggested, the baby becomes capable of organizing his behavior on a goal-corrected basis. (Or, in Piaget's [1952] terminology, the baby has become capable of true intention, because he can distinguish between means and ends. His schemata are no longer embedded in their original sensorimotor contexts but have become mobile and useful as means toward ends in many contexts.) From this point onward, what is important is not the separate attachment behaviors but the way in which they—together with other behaviors—become organized toward the attachment figure. This is a flexible sort of organization[1] that finds different behavioral expression in different contexts. Any of several means of promoting proximity may be selected by the infant in different situations and at different times.

Indeed, research findings should discourage future investigators from considering discrete attachment behaviors—for example, smiling, vocalization, crying, approach, and touching—as separate behavioral measures independent of their environmental and behavioral contexts. A number of investigators, including Maccoby and Feldman (1972); Coates, Anderson, and Hartup (1972*a,b*); and Waters (1978) have reported that these show little stability either from one situation to another or across time. Nor do these behaviors predict important aspects of social and emotional behavior in other settings, according to a study by Main (1973). In contrast, *patterns* of behavior have been found to have remarkable stability over time.

A useful instrument for the study of patterns of attachment is the "strange-situation" technique. An infant and mother are brought into a comfortable laboratory room; a stranger enters and sits talking to the mother and then to the infant; the mother leaves the room unobtrusively; the mother returns and the stranger leaves them together; the mother leaves the infant alone in the room; the stranger returns; the

1. A goal-corrected organization is not the only way in which behavior may be organized. Bowlby (1969) identified two other organizational modes—chaining and a "causal hierarchy"—either or both of which may be operative in organisms incapable of goal-corrected behavior. Before he becomes capable of goal-corrected organization (i.e., organization according to a "plan hierarchy"), a human infant's behavior is nevertheless organized, presumably in simpler but less flexible modes.

mother returns once more. Each of these seven episodes lasts three minutes unless the infant is more than mildly distressed. Measures of behavior reflecting the nature of the attachment relationship can thus be obtained under standardized conditions.

In referring to the pattern of organization of an infant's behavior toward his mother, we are not limited only to attachment behaviors. On the contrary, a major discovery in our strange-situation work (e.g., Ainsworth et al., 1978) is that the organization of the infant's attachment to his mother cannot be understood by attending only to attachment behaviors. In some infants behaviors antithetical to proximity promotion appear in addition to or even in lieu of attachment behavior—specifically, avoidant or resistant behaviors. Thus, for example, one pattern of behavior displayed toward the mother in the reunion episodes of the strange situation mingles proximity/contact seeking and angry, resistant behavior (Group C). In another pattern avoidant behavior is conspicuous, perhaps mingled with proximity seeking (Group A). Still a third pattern features various modes of proximity/contact seeking with little or no avoidance or resistance (Group B). Infants behaved differently in the preseparation and separation episodes than in the reunion episodes, and yet those displaying a given pattern in the reunion episodes differed from other infants also in the patterning of behavior in the other episodes. More details of the three sets of patterns are given in a later section entitled "Patterns of Infant Behavior" and in chapter 2. Suffice it to say here that, using the strange-situation procedure, most infants can be classified as *securely* (Group B) or *anxiously* (Groups A and C) attached to their mothers, and that the anxiously attached infants can be further classified as *avoidant* (Group A) or *ambivalent* (Group C).

Both Connell (1976) and Waters (1978) have observed infants in the strange situation at twelve and again at eighteen months. Over 80 percent of the infants in Connell's sample and 96 percent of the infants in Waters's sample showed the same pattern of behavior toward the mother at both times. Note again that the strength or incidence of discrete attachment behaviors in the strange situation is not stable; however, organization does tend to be stable.[2]

2. It is my view that the pattern of attachment an infant displays toward his mother reflects an inner organization, presumably represented in the central nervous system (Ainsworth, 1972). It is reasonable to suppose that this central organization has been built up gradually in the course of interaction with the mother, and that the better established it becomes, the more it tends to resist the influences exerted in any specific situation. An important component of the central organization underlying infant-mother attachment is a central representation or "working model" of the mother herself

The way in which a baby organizes his behavior to his mother in a twenty-minute laboratory situation would be of little significance if it did not reflect a more general organization across a variety of situations. My associates and I (Ainsworth et al., 1978) examined this issue and reported clear evidence that patterns of strange-situation behavior are linked to patterns of behavior manifested at home. We also cited evidence from investigators who observed other samples of infants in other situations. Some were concerned with the contemporaneous relationship of strange-situation behavior to behavior in other types of situations. Thus S. M. Bell (unpublished ms.) found that strange-situation patterns shown by disadvantaged black infants were significantly related to affect displayed by both infant and mother in their interaction in a free-play situation. Rosenberg (1975), also using a free-play situation, found that the infant in dyads showing much mutual ignoring had been judged anxious and avoidant in his strange-situation behavior, whereas the infant in dyads showing much mutual attentiveness had been judged to be securely attached.

Other investigators undertook prospective studies, comparing strange-situation patterns in one-year-olds with patterns of behavior in other situations some months—or even years—later. Their findings are particularly exciting. In general, they show continuities between the way a one-year-old has organized his attachment to his mother and the way he organizes his behavior to her *or* to other persons later on. Bell's secure black babies and their mothers continued to display positive affect in interaction with each other in play sessions throughout the baby's second and third years, whereas her anxiously attached infants and their mothers continued to display more negative affect. Main (1973, in press; Londerville and Main, 1981) found that at twenty-two months securely attached babies had become cooperative toddlers—both with the mother and an adult playmate in a laboratory play session, and with the examiner in a Bayley test.

Matas, Arendt, and Sroufe (1978) observed two-year-olds with their mothers in a problem-solving situation. Those who had been judged to

---

(Bowlby, 1969). If the mother's behavior in any given situation is at variance with the expectations an infant has built up, his behavior will nevertheless be determined in large part by his working model of her and not wholly by her actual behavior in that specific situation. Over time, however, a baby's central representation of his mother is open to revision, should the nature of her behavior in interaction with him change substantially. Therefore, the tendency of patterns of attachment to be stable over time implies both stability in the nature of the mother's behavior in interaction with the infant and stability in the infant's own inner organization of his attachment to her.

be securely attached six months earlier both sought and accepted their mothers' help with a problem they otherwise could not have solved. Those who were anxiously attached and avoidant neither sought nor accepted their mothers' help, and indeed were more likely to turn to the experimenter. Those who were anxiously attached and ambivalent gave up easily, clearly distressed. Arendt, Gove, and Sroufe (1979) observed the same sample at age five and found that those who had been judged secure as one-year-olds were more "ego resilient" as kindergarteners—more able to adapt resourcefully to changing personal and environmental circumstances—than were other children. Finally, Waters, Wippman, and Sroufe (1979) classified the children of Bronson's (1968) sample as securely or anxiously attached to their mothers on the basis of their behavior in an adaptation of the strange-situation test at fifteen months, and found that these assessments were related to Bronson's Q-sort analyses of interpersonal and personal competence in a nursery school peer group at three-and-one-half years. Specifically, two years later the securely attached infants had become more self-directed, more curious, more sought by other children, less withdrawn, more likely to be leaders, and more sympathetic to the distress of peers.

Thus there now is a considerable body of evidence of continuity linking the organization of attachment to the mother at one year and the organization of social-emotional behavior up to at least five years. Obviously the continuity reported by these studies implies developmental transformations in the way that behavior is organized rather than continuities of specific (discrete) behaviors across situations and across time. Both Maccoby and Feldman (1972) and Lewis and Ban (1971) suggested that continuity might be found in transformations, with the younger child emphasizing "proximal behaviors" in relation to his mother and the older child more frequently manifesting "distal behaviors" (implying a shift from proximity and touch to looking, smiling, vocalization, and eventually speech). That some such shift takes place is not to be doubted, but the continuity is not to be discovered if one focuses on discrete behavioral measures; it can only be discovered if one focuses on patterns of organization of behavior.[3]

---

3. The specific pattern of behavior in one situation at a given age cannot be expected to recur in the same form in either the same or other situations at later ages. Thus Sroufe (1979) emphasized that a pattern of behavior at a given age may be "coherent with" another pattern of behavior at a later age. The salient methodological consideration is to select at each age point age-appropriate situations, each of which elicits a range of behavior patterns that are more or less adaptive for that age.

Research to date has elucidated only a few of the ways in which the organization of an infant's attachment to his mother may influence his later development and his behavior in other situations. Since longitudinal research is difficult, and short-term longitudinal studies seem much more feasible than long-term studies, it seems very important that research with each age group be linked somehow with what is known about the same children at earlier ages. In this context it has been suggested that the strange-situation procedure might serve for a time as a "marker" instrument. If used in a standardized way with many different samples of one-year-olds, it would facilitate the integration of findings of diverse studies intended to explore how infant-mother attachment may affect later development. Through such research so many correlates of strange-situation patterns are likely to be found that the result should be a variety of methods of assessment of attachment throughout the range of early childhood.

Developmental Changes in a Child's Attachment to His Mother

Even during the first year there are developmental changes in an infant's relationship with his mother (Ainsworth, 1967; Bowlby, 1969; Schaffer and Emerson, 1964; Yarrow, 1967). Here, however, we are concerned with the developmental changes that take place later. Among children aged two to four, distress in the brief separation episodes of the strange situation decreases with increasing age (Maccoby and Feldman, 1972; Marvin, 1977). Upon reunion the two-year-old may be content with mere proximity to his mother rather than requiring the close bodily contact a one-year-old seeks, and later he is likely to be content merely with reestablishing interaction with her from a distance.

Marvin (e.g., 1977), following some hypotheses suggested by Bowlby (1969), demonstrated links between age-related shifts of attachment behavior and cognitive acquisitions. Both Marvin and Bowlby attributed the major shift to the emergence of conceptual perspective taking—to becoming able to understand something of the mother's perspective, plans, and set-goals. Marvin's research has indicated that the first evidence of an ability to take another's conceptual perspective occurs some time between a child's third and fourth birthdays. Like Bowlby, Marvin also emphasized the child's elaboration of "working models" of the mother and the role of improved communication attributable to the development of language. Marvin and his associates (Marvin and Greenberg, unpublished ms.; Marvin, Mossler, and VanDevender, unpublished ms.) have assembled evidence that age-related shifts in strange-situation behavior are associated with the ability of the child to reach or attempt to reach shared plans with his mother through verbal communication.[4]

Attachment to the mother does not disappear when the preschool years have ended, even though it becomes somewhat attenuated. Increasing involvement with other children and with other adults, such as teachers, suggests that the relationship with the mother—indeed with parents—does not penetrate[5] as many aspects of the child's life as it does in infancy. Nevertheless, children, adolescents, and young adults are likely to rely on their parents, at least when they experience disappointments, illness, or other crises. Parents continue to be especially important to many people even after they marry and have children of their own. Systematic studies of attachment to parents beyond the infancy period are much needed.

Other Changes in Child-Mother Attachment

Here we are concerned with changes in the nature of a child's attachment to his mother that may be attributed to changes in his interaction with her, not to mere developmental changes. Earlier, evidence was presented of the stability of the patterning of an infant's attachment to his mother; here we are concerned with the inevitable exceptions to a general tendency toward stability and continuity.

Earlier work on the effect of major separations, lasting for weeks or even years, suggested that these may substantially change a child's

4. Although Marvin found the strange-situation procedure useful in highlighting developmental changes, it seems clear that beyond age two the classificatory system through which the attachment patterns of one-year-olds may be assessed (Ainsworth et al., 1978) is no longer appropriate. Some researchers (e.g., Main, Sroufe, and Waters) have found it useful at eighteen months, but beyond that age it is clear that a modified classificatory system would be desirable for the valid identification of attachment patterns.

5. In Hinde's (1976) system for describing relationships, the variable of "penetration" seems to me to be more useful than a global concept of strength of attachment to describe the so-called attenuation of child-parent attachment that takes place increasingly after infancy.

working model of his mother from that of an accessible and responsive person to that of a person inaccessible and unresponsive, with consequent damage to the security and trust previously implicit in the relationship. Indeed, in the case of a child already anxious in his attachment, such an experience can confirm his previous inner representation of his mother as untrustworthy. Bowlby, who was among the first to emphasize the effect of major separation experiences, especially if they occur in depriving environments, implied in 1973 that threats of separation may be equally devastating—explicit threats of abandonment or parental suicide, implications that parental illness is somehow due to the child's misbehavior, or indeed disharmonies between parents that are interpreted by the child to forecast possible separation from or permanent loss of one or both parents. He suggested that such threats lead the child to be anxious in his attachment to his parent or parents. Bowlby linked this in turn to a variety of subsequent pathological manifestations including so-called school phobia in children and "agoraphobia" in adults. Recently, DeLozier (1979 and chapter 5 herein) has assembled evidence that such threats are conspicuous in the histories of mothers who abuse their children and that these women, as adults, were found to be especially anxious about even very minor separations.

It is clear that Bowlby (1973) does not believe that early infant–mother interaction sets the pattern of an infant's attachment for all time; he reported evidence that events occurring throughout childhood may have a profound effect on the anxiety versus security of relationships experienced with attachment figures. In the third volume of his *Attachment and Loss* series (1980), Bowlby turned to reactions to permanent loss of attachment figures—to grief and mourning and the eventual resolution of mourning. Major separations of this sort have a profound effect on everyone, regardless of age, but the processes of readjustment to the loss seem clearly related to the security-anxiety dimension of earlier attachments. Those whose earlier relationships were secure tend, after a period of mourning, to be able to resume normal life and to find new attachment figures. Those whose earlier relationships were anxious are more likely to manifest pathological variations of the mourning process and to find it difficult to resume an intimate relationship with another later on.

Even in infancy, major changes in the kind of interaction an infant has with his mother may be reflected in the organization of his attachment to her. In turn, such major changes may be contingent upon changes in the mother's basic life situation. It is easy to conceive of a variety of stresses that might affect a mother, making her less responsive to infant communications than she had previously been. It is easy to conceive also that relief from stresses may permit her to become more responsive. In our own longitudinal study (e.g., Ainsworth, 1979) we found evidence of the impact of such changes, despite the fact that most mothers were stable in their behavior, whether for better or for worse. The baby's reaction, in terms of the way he organized his attachment, seemed to reflect both kinds of experience with his mother—experience during the crisis period and experience before or after the crisis.

Evidence that various life stresses may effect changes in the way an infant organizes his attachment to his mother are reported by Vaughn and associates (1979). These authors are assembling a large sample of mother-infant dyads of low socioeconomic status (SES) as a contrast group for the middle-class dyads with which most previous attachment research has been concerned. The continuity of the attachment organization is less in this low-SES sample than Waters (1978) previously reported for a middle-class sample, presumably because of their more stressful life circumstances and the greater likelihood of shifts in degree of stress.

In short, attachment theory does not imply that the nature of the original infant-mother attachment sets the continuing pattern of that relationship without consideration of subsequent events that may alter or disrupt the relationship for better or worse. Systematic research pertinent to such changes is sparse to date; much more is needed.

Maternal Behavior and Infant Attachment

Here we are concerned with the relationship between maternal behavior and the way in which an infant's attachment to his mother becomes organized and in which his behavior toward her becomes patterned. In terms of practical implications, this is the aspect of our attachment research that has produced the richest yield. I began with an assumption that different mothers would prefer different modes of interaction with their babies—some stressing physical contact; some interacting chiefly on a visual basis of eye-to-eye contact, smiles, and gestures; and others relying largely on auditory-vocal interaction. Three scales were devised to measure the amount of interaction in each of these modes, together with nineteen other scales devised to measure maternal behavior in the baby's first quarter year. It had been expected that the three different modes of interaction would be independent of one another and equally effective. However, they were found to be very highly correlated with one another, and indeed with most of the other nineteen measures. Many kinds of maternal behaviors that would be judged to be desirable tended to co-occur. There was no use in undertaking a factor analysis; obviously one factor would account for nearly all the variance.

In the meantime coding had begun of records of approximately seventy-two hours of observation of the behavior of each of twenty-six mother-infant pairs—an onerous task that has occupied years. As each major task of coding was completed, it became apparent that in each there was at least one main dimension of maternal behavior that was especially related to infant behavior—the mother's degree of sensitivity in responding to infant signals and communications. The relationship held for sensitivity to infant signals relevant to feeding (Ainsworth and Bell, 1969), responsiveness to infant crying (Bell and Ainsworth, 1972), pacing in face-to-face interaction contingent upon infant behavioral cues (Blehar, Lieberman, and Ainsworth, 1977), and similar contingent responsiveness to infant cues in the context of close bodily contact (Blehar, Ainsworth, and Main, unpublished ms.). Sensitivity to infant signals was undoubtedly a key dimension in maternal behavior during the baby's first year, and the one that undoubtedly accounted for the very high correlations in our previous analysis.

This variable tends to obscure perception of the effect of individual differences in infant behavior upon maternal behavior, for the mother who is sensitively responsive to infant cues gears her behavior to the cues of this particular infant. It also tends to obscure the fact that maternal behavior alters in response to infant developmental changes, for she gears her behavior to his changing behavior.

Obviously, this sensitivity-insensitivity dimension, important though it is, is only one dimension in terms of which we may describe the vast and complex individual differences among mothers. In a small sample it is difficult to tease out more than a few dimensions. It was found, however, that mothers who were highly sensitive to infant signals were very similar in their behavior, whereas insensitive mothers were insensitive in a variety of different ways. Of these, three dimensions were identified—rejection, interference, and ignoring. Rejection is of particular interest since it is linked especially to one of the patterns of organization of infant attachment.

14

The original measure of rejection featured the extent to which the mother's loving feelings toward her baby were on occasion overwhelmed by feelings of impatience, irritation, and resentment. These angry feelings were linked to a perception of the demands of the baby as interfering with the mother's other interests and activities. The assessment was facilitated by the fact that most of these mothers made negative and critical comments about their babies or expressed regret that they had had the baby.

Mary Main initiated and carried out a reanalysis of all our raw data to flesh out the picture of what might be called "the rejection syndrome" (in Blehar, Ainsworth, and Main, unpublished ms.). All of the rejecting mothers were found to have a deep aversion to close bodily contact. It was assumed that this aversion would be communicated to the baby in the form of rebuffs when he initiated contact and, more important in the earliest weeks, by failing to respond adequately with close bodily contact at the very times when a baby most wants it— when his attachment behavior is activated at such high intensity that only close contact will calm him. Main also found that rejecting mothers tended to have less mobility of emotional expression than other mothers, which can be interpreted as an effort to control expression of frequent resentment and irritation. Finally, the rejecting mothers tended to be rigid and compulsive, some even classically obsessive-compulsive. Earlier (Ainsworth, 1979), I reported that some of the mothers in this sample varied in their responsiveness to their babies over the course of the first year, seemingly in response to various critical life events. This was not the case with rejecting mothers; their pattern seemed deep-seated and unchanging.

The identification of patterns of maternal behavior has both intrinsic interest and implications for applied research into primary prevention and early intervention. These implications may be envisaged more clearly after further consideration of patterns of infant attachment and their association with maternal patterns.

Patterns of Infant Behavior

Let us discuss in more detail the patterns of infant behavior referred to on page 7 and show how these patterns relate to two dimensions of ternal behavior—insensitivity and rejection.[6] When three main groups of infants were first tentatively identified on the basis of their strange-situation behavior, they were labeled A, B, and C, to avoid premature descriptive labels (Ainsworth and Wittig, 1969).

Group B proved to be the largest and normative group comprising 66 percent of a sample of 106 (Ainsworth et al., 1978). Infants in this group behaved in the strange situation just as one-year-olds were expected to behave when the procedure was designed. When they were alone with their mothers, they explored actively, showing very little attachment behavior. Most of them were upset in the separation episodes and explored little. All of them responded strongly to the mother's return in the reunion episodes, the majority seeking close bodily contact with her, and all at least displaying keen interest in interacting with her.

Group C was the smallest group, comprising 12 percent of the sample. These children were anxious even in the preseparation episodes. All were very upset by separation. In the reunion episodes they wanted close bodily contact with their mothers, but they also resisted contact and interaction with her, whereas Group B babies had shown little or no resistance of this sort.

Finally, Group A babies, comprising approximately 20 percent of the sample, did not behave at all as expected. In particular, they showed little or no distress in the separation episodes and, most important, they avoided contact, proximity, or even interaction with the mother in the reunion episodes. Some steadfastly ignored their mother, refusing to approach or even look when she coaxed the child to come. Others mingled attachment behavior with avoidance.

The first clue to the significance of these three patterns of behavior came from a factor analysis of the behavior the twenty-six infants in our longitudinal sample showed at home in the fourth quarter of the first year (Stayton and Ainsworth, 1973). Two main factors emerged. The first was clearly identifiable as a security-anxiety dimension, whereas the second pertained to behavior relevant to close bodily contact. A comparison of the infants' behavior at home and in the strange situation enabled us to give descriptive labels to our three strange-situation groups (e.g., Ainsworth et al., 1978). *Group B infants* could be

6. The dimension of sensitivity-insensitivity may be considered superordinate to the dimension of rejection or, indeed, the dimensions of interference or ignoring, in that sensitive responsiveness to infant signals is incompatible with rejecting, interfering, or ignoring behavior. Insensitivity to signals may, however, be combined with a greater or lesser degree of rejection, interference, and/or ignoring.

16

identified as *securely attached* to their mothers. At home, in comparison with Group A and C babies, they showed less separation anxiety in little everyday separations; they cried less in general; they more often greeted their mothers positively after an absence; and they were more content to be put down after having been held. All of these behaviors are characteristic of the secure pole of the security-anxiety dimension. With regard to the second dimension, they responded more positively to being held, were more easily soothed by close bodily contact, initiated being picked up more often, and sought less often to be put down. The mothers of these securely attached infants, significantly more frequently than other mothers, displayed all of the behaviors reflecting sensitive responsiveness to infant signals and all of the behaviors reflecting positive response to the baby in the context of close bodily contact.

The implication is clearly that Groups A and C could be distinguished from Group B in terms of both the security-anxiety and the bodily-contact dimensions. They showed more distress in little, everyday situations; generally cried more and cried more often in greeting their mothers after an absence; and responded more negatively both to physical contact and to its cessation. Their mothers were less sensitive to infant signals across all contexts. Both the avoidant *Group A* and the ambivalent *Group C* babies were thus identified as *anxiously attached* to their mothers.

In our small sample it was difficult to pinpoint the differences between these two anxiously attached groups in terms of our original home behavioral variables, but significant differences were found in regard to two of the variables Mary Main had assessed. Group A babies less frequently than Group C babies "sank in" to their mothers when held—relaxing and obviously molding their bodies to that of the mother. Even more conspicuously, A babies were more often angry than C babies—although both were significantly more angry than B babies.

The distinction is sharper in regard to maternal behavior. The mothers of the Group A babies were those who had displayed the rejection syndrome mentioned earlier—they had an aversion to close bodily contact, were angry, had relatively wooden facial expressions, and were compulsive. The mothers of the C babies were a diverse group, but they were not rejecting. They seemed to enjoy close bodily contact, but they were all highly insensitive.

Ainsworth and associates (1978) have offered an interpretation of the differences between Groups A and C, which can only be summarized here. Both A and C babies have experienced conflict about close bodily contact with their mothers. The conflict of the C babies is a simple one—between wanting close bodily contact and being angry because their mothers do not consistently pick them up when they want to be held or hold them for as long as they want. Because their mothers are insensitive to their signals, C babies lack confidence in their responsiveness. Thus when the attachment system is highly activated, C babies are doubly upset because they have learned to expect to be frustrated rather than comforted.

The conflict experienced by the A babies is more complex. Like all infants, they want close bodily contact whenever the attachment system is activated at high intensity, but they have also come to avoid closeness with their mothers because of rebuffs. Therefore they have a classic approach-avoidance conflict, which is especially highlighted by the stresses of the strange situation. How this conflict gives rise to the behavior in question is the topic of the next chapter.

There are many promising avenues for future research. Perhaps the most pressing need is for replication of the measures of both infant and maternal behavior in the natural environment of the home throughout the first year, in order to put the antecedents of the strange-situation patterns on the firmer basis that would be provided by a larger sample and independent assessments. It would also be good to pool the strange-situation data collected by different investigators who have used the same procedure. Thus a sample could be built up large enough for a discriminant analysis of the various subgroups into which the three major groups are divided (Ainsworth et al., 1978). This would be a first step in the identification of which further dimensions could define individual differences in infant-mother attachment. The next necessary step would be further studies comparing strange-situation classification with mother-child interaction in other situations, either antecedent, contemporaneous, or at later ages, in order to give meaning to the dimensions identified in the discriminant analysis.

Assessment of attachment of special groups of infants might add greatly to our understanding of anomalies of attachment. Thus, for example, George and Main (1979) have found that young abused children show both aggression and avoidance similar to "normal-range" Group A babies, but to an exaggerated degree. Further, it is to be hoped that through a study of the correlates of the strange-situation classifications a simplified procedure might be devised for more accurate screening of infants and young children at risk of developing

anomalies of attachment. Finally, the information about maternal behavior associated with different patterns of infant attachment offers
useful leads for intervention (e.g., Andrews et al., 1975).

A Hierarchy of Attachment Figures?

In his original 1958 paper, Bowlby proposed that a child is biased to
attach himself especially to one figure, and he referred to this as
"monotropy." Now, obviously, a child can be attached to more than
one person. Indeed Bowlby (1969) made it clear that he meant that a
child is likely to be especially attached to one principal figure, and
that the other persons to whom he is attached are subsidiary or secondary attachment figures. Thus the implication is of a hierarchy of
attachment figures. There are many circumstances in which attachment figures, whether principal or secondary, seem fairly well interchangeable; this has been demonstrated by several investigators who
have observed infants or young children with both fathers and mothers in unfamiliar laboratory situations (Cohen and Campos, 1974; Feldman and Ingham, 1975; Kotelchuck, 1972; Lamb, 1978; Willemsen et
al., 1974). Bowlby argued, however, that when a child is tired, ill, or
distressed he tends to seek his principal attachment figure rather than
secondary figures, if he has any choice in the matter. Furthermore, the
child would tolerate *major* separations from susidiary figures with less
distress than comparable separations from the principal attachment
figure. Nor could the presence of several attachment figures altogether
compensate for the loss of the principal attachment figure.

Infant responses to brief, everyday separations in the familiar home
environment do not give the observer grounds for distinguishing the
principal attachment figure from other attachment figures. I (Ainsworth, 1967) reported that Ganda infants who ordinarily cried when
the mother left the room did not do so when left with another attachment figure. Clarke-Stewart (1978) found no difference in attachment,
separation, or greeting behavior directed to mother and father in the
home. Lamb (e.g., 1976a, 1977), on the other hand, reported from observations both at home and in the laboratory that when an infant is
distressed he tends to seek the mother rather than the father when
both are equally available. This latter finding supports Bowlby's hypothesis of a hierarchy of attachment figures, although Lamb himself

19

(1976*b*) argued that fathers' and mothers' roles are equally important but different. Marvin and associates (1977), in a study of the polymatric Hausa of Nigeria, reported that a majority of infants in their sample had a principal attachment figure among the two to four caregivers to whom they were attached, although the principal figure was by no means always the mother. More research is needed. Simple preference as shown by frequency of either signaling or approach behavior directed toward one figure in comparison with another does not enable us to identify the principal attachment figure, except under conditions of stress, distress, or discomfort; it is no simple matter to achieve an adequate data base of preference under such conditions.

Freud (1938) claimed that the relationship between an infant and his mother was not only the most important "object relation" but also the prototype of all subsequent love relations. Undoubtedly it has occurred to many, however, that a good relationship with the father might compensate for a poor relationship with the mother, or indeed vice versa. Both Lamb (1977) and Main and Weston (1981) have repeated our strange-situation procedure so that the baby is accompanied to the laboratory once by the mother and at another time by the father. Neither investigator found a relationship between patterns of behavior displayed with mother and with father; that is, a baby judged securely attached to the mother was equally likely to be securely or anxiously attached to the father. In the Main and Weston study infants were observed again in the strange situation with the mother, and the pattern of behavior displayed was stable, as previously shown by Connell (1976) and Waters (1978). Several infants found anxious-avoidant with the mother but securely attached to the father were nonetheless exceptionally upset at the father's leavetaking, screaming and wrapping their arms around his knees to prevent it. Using separate assessments of the behavior of both parents, the investigators interpret these findings as evidence for an "effect of relationship upon relationship."

These findings are important for several additional reasons. First, they help us see the infant as an active being who forms different relationships with different persons. Second, they counteract a natural suspicion that might be aroused by the stability findings cited earlier—the suspicion that strange-situation behavior, being stable with respect to the same individual, is simply a matter of infant temperament. Main and Weston's findings suggest that strange-situation classifications reflect established patterns of interaction—with father as well as with mother. Assuming this to be the case, joint classifications are extremely useful. Using play sessions, Main and Weston found evidence of actual disturbance (i.e., stereotypes, inappropriate affect, and "odd" behavior) in almost every baby judged to be anxiously attached to but avoidant with both parents, but none in babies securely attached to just one parent, either mother or father. Main, Weston, and Wakeling (1979) have engaged in a study of infant precursors to empathic reactions at twelve and at eighteen months. So far in this study, every infant judged securely attached to both parents—and not one infant judged avoidant of both parents—responded with concerned attention to the crying of an adult actor.

There is a dearth of published research into others as possible attachment figures, except for the father. What of all the substitute caregivers who have been highlighted as important in the new life styles in our society? Do these substitute caregivers become attachment figures? Where do they fit into a baby's hierarchy of attachment figures? To my present knowledge only five studies seem relevant. Fox (1977) compared the responses of Israeli kibbutz-reared infants to mother and *metapelet* (who cares for these infants during most of each day) in Kotelchuck's version of a strange situation and found that the *metapelet* could serve much as the mother did as an attachment figure. Fleener (1973) reported an experimental study of substitute caregiving, in which infants had long, intensive interaction with a caregiver for several successive days. At the end of this time the infants showed less approach and separation distress to the caregiver than to an unfamiliar person, but when the tests were repeated to compare responses to the mother and caregiver, it was clear that the mother was the preferred attachment figure. Ricciuti (1974) compared infant affective responses to mother, day-caregiver, and stranger in an unfamiliar environment, focusing on responses to separation and reunion. His findings could be interpreted to indicate that among babies old enough to have become attached to their mothers, the day-caregiver had also become an attachment figure but subsidiary to the mother. Farran and Ramey (1977) reported that mothers were preferred to day-caregivers, and indeed that the latter were not preferred to strangers in terms of proximity-seeking and interaction measures. Cummings (1980) compared infant responses to the mother and to two day-caregivers, one stable (i.e., who had been present often when the infant was present) and the other unstable (i.e., present less often), both in an unfamiliar situation and in the familiar day-care environment. As expected, the mother emerged as the principal attachment figure. Although children seemed to accept substitute caregivers in the day-care setting, it was not clear that they became attached to specific day-caregivers.

21

Some efforts have been directed toward assessing the effect of various forms of substitute care on the infant's attachment to his mother (e.g., Blanchard and Main, 1979; Blehar, 1974; Caldwell et al., 1970; Hock, 1976), and surely more research of this kind is needed in order to sort out the effects of type of day care, age of child upon beginning day care, and previous patterns of infant-mother relationships, to name only three relevant variables. What is extraordinary, however, is that there has been so little research into the role of substitute caregivers as possible attachment figures in the caregiving setting itself, and how such relationships compare with and/or supplement attachments to parents. A beginning has been made by Ricciuti and by Cummings, but just a beginning.

Other Attachments, Other Bonds, Other Relationships

So far I have dealt only with a baby's attachment to his mother, his father, and possibly a few subsidiary attachment figures, and I have suggested that parents are likely to continue to be attachment figures, even though they may no longer be as central in the person's life as they were in infancy and early childhood. Surely parents and parent substitutes are not the only attachment figures of significance in a person's lifetime. Harlow and Harlow (1965) wrote of "affectional systems" rather than attachments, and distinguished five of these in the context of their research with rhesus macaques: the relations of infant to mother, of mother to infant, of infant peer to peers, heterosexual relations, and finally the relations of an adult male to infants. In accordance with Bowlby's ethological-evolutionary approach, one should strive to identify the behavioral systems implicit in these relations and their predictable outcomes and biological functions.

Bowlby (1969) identified a maternal behavioral system as complementary to an infant attachment system; both systems have the same predictable outcome (proximity maintenance) and the same biological function (protection of the infant). Presumably paternal behavior has much in common with maternal behavior and may be hypothesized to have the same predictable outcome and the same biological function. What of heterosexual and peer-peer relations? It is by no means clear that they have the same biological function as infant-mother attachment, even though one could make a case that they too involve proximity maintenance. In the epilogue of his most recent volume, Bowlby states that "intimate attachments to other human beings are the hub around which a person's life revolves, not only when he is an infant or a toddler or a schoolchild, but throughout his adolescence and his years of maturity as well, and on into old age." (1980, p. 442). Nevertheless, in 1977 Bowlby implied that an attachment is made to someone who is usually conceived as stronger and/or wiser. Such a criterion would appear to exclude the possibility of identifying as an attachment the bond of parent to child, and to raise the question of criteria of attachments between age peers.

Extrapolating from infant-mother attachment to later relationships, Weiss (chapter 9) suggests three criteria of attachment: (1) that the person wants to be with the attachment figure, especially when he is under stress; (2) that he derives comfort and security from the attachment figure; and (3) that he protests when the attachment figure becomes or threatens to become inaccessible. Applying these criteria, he suggests that some kinds of relationships between adults may be identified as involving an element of attachment: close heterosexual relationships (marriages or quasi-marriages), some cases of "buddies" under stress (e.g., army buddies when in action), and some instances of best friends.

Even among those researchers who have been inspired by Bowlby's attachment paradigm, there is no clear a priori consensus concerning the criteria of attachment (except for the attachment of infants to parent figures). Much further research is needed. Meanwhile, I should like to venture some suggestions in the context of pertinent research already published.

Let us consider first the bond established by a mother with her baby. A number of recent researchers have followed Leiderman (e.g., Leiderman and Seashore, 1975) and Klaus and Kennell (e.g., 1976) in examining conditions under which a mother more or less readily "bonds" to her infant. The latter cite evidence suggesting that immediate postpartum contact with the newborn facilitates rapid bond formation, which in turn is supportive of confident, loving maternal-care behavior that facilitates optimum infant development. Obviously there are many complex variables involved in such bond formation, not all of which have yet been controlled in research on early bonding and its effects on later mother-infant interaction and infant development. Nevertheless, the evidence reported so far suggests that the bonding of mother to infant may take place almost immediately after the infant's birth, provided that conditions are optimum, whereas there is every reason to believe that the attachment of infant to mother develops only gradually during the infant's first six months or so of life. This alone suggests that it is wise to view the bond of mother to infant as distinct from the bond of infant to mother. I am inclined to reserve the term "attachment" for the latter, and to accept Klaus and Kennell's term "bond" for the former. That there is a "relationship" between mother and child, in Hinde's (1979) sense, from the time of the infant's birth onward, and that the nature of this relationship stems from the interaction between them, is not to be gainsaid, but neither the mother-to-infant bond nor the emergent infant-to-mother attachment seems to me to comprehend all important aspects of this relationship. It goes without saying, however, that much further research is needed before the issues implicit in this discussion are clarified.

Even though mother-infant bonding and infant-mother attachment both promote proximity of mother to infant and both may be viewed as performing a protective function, it is clear that the protection is not reciprocal. In terms of Weiss's criteria of attachment, the mother's security is not normally invested in the infant, even though she may wish to be with him and may be made anxious by separation from him. Indeed it is only under unusual circumstances that a mother directs attachment behavior toward her child, instead of normal maternal (caregiving) behavior. Bowlby (1973, 1980) reported such role-reversal as common among parents of children with "school phobia" and implied that this contributed to the child's pathology. DeLozier (1979 and chapter 5 herein) also reported such role-reversal as occurring in abusing parents, as an aspect of their pathology. If "attachment" implies a bond to a person conceived as stronger and/or wiser, then it would seem that attachment is the incorrect term to apply to the normal bonding of a parent to a child.

Parke's (1979) evidence in regard to father-infant interaction may be interpreted to mean that fathers may also become bonded to their infants. Peterson, Mehl, and Leiderman (1979) reported that the father's participation in the baby's birth and his attitude toward the experience were the most important of several pre- and perinatal variables in predicting the nature of his bond to the baby. Clearly more research addressed to the conditions that facilitate and the processes involved in the formation of the father-to-infant bond is required.

Harlow and Suomi (e.g., Harlow and Harlow, 1962; Suomi and Harlow, 1972) have emphasized the role that interaction with age peers can play in facilitating normal social development of infant rhesus macaques who had been reared under grossly depriving circumstances. Recently this has led to active research into the interaction of human infants with their age peers, usually unfamiliar peers. It is by no means clear that attachment to age peers normally occurs in infancy, except perhaps in the case of twins, or that if it does take place it is equivalent to attachment to parent figures. So far the only two clear examples in the literature refer to attachments under abnormal circumstances when no parents or adult parent surrogates were available—the close-knit group of child survivors of Nazi extermination camps reported by Freud and Dann (1951) and Harlow's (1961) "together-together" infant monkeys who had only one another to cling to.

Nonetheless there seems little doubt that interactions with peers of approximately the same age play an important role in a child's social development. The issue is, however, whether children's peer relationships are enduring enough to be identified as bonds or attachments. It seems likely that many of a child's peers are important to him chiefly as playmates. Are playmates more or less interchangeable, so that a loss of or breach in the relationship with one can readily be made good in terms of a relationship with another? If so, the playmate relationship scarcely constitutes an attachment—or a bond. Similarly, among adults, some friends or acquaintances are valued largely as companions either in work or in play—colleagues on the job, golfing companions, bridge partners, and the like. There is no doubt that such companions and the activities shared with them enrich a person's life, but it seems unlikely that they could be viewed as attachment figures as long as loss of or separation from them can be taken in stride, without marked anxiety or grief.

On the other hand, it seems likely that in some instances deep and lasting relationships may be established in childhood, perhaps persisting well into adulthood. Surely these would be with persons who qualify as attachment figures, and so would some children's relationships with siblings. Indeed one could make a case for such attachments having the same biological protective function as bonds between parents and offspring have. I agree with Weiss's suggestion that such reciprocal and mutually protective relationships may, on occasion, be established between same-sex adults, such as army buddies. Research, however, has a long way to go before we have a scientific understanding of bonds between friends. A beginning might be made with more studies of infants and young children interacting with familiar peers, or better still with favorite peers.

The issue of heterosexual bonds is complex, although perhaps more clear-cut than that of same-sex peer bonds. Until recently the social climate effectively inhibited research into heterosexual relations. Now, released from such prohibitions, research into the sexual aspects of heterosexual relationships flourishes, but there has been little attention paid to other than sexual aspects in the context of either marriage or other enduring ties. It seems likely that a more or less enduring heterosexual bond has at least three major components: (1) sexual, (2) attachment, and (3) caregiving. Furthermore, in ethological terms, the biological function of such a bond seems likely to be primarily reproductive. Nevertheless, if indeed there are children as a result of the union, the parent-child bond on the part of each partner tends to cement the union. Where, then, does attachment fit in—if at all? In terms of Bowlby's stronger/wiser criterion for identification of an attachment figure, it seems likely that, in a good marriage, each partner on occasion plays the role of stronger and wiser figure for the other, so that each derives security and comfort from the other, as well as wishing to be with the other and protesting actual or threatened separation.

As attachments to parent figures become less central, and as heterosexual relations become important, it seems likely that a person seeks in a heterosexual bond something of the same kind of security that he or she previously sought from parents. Can this person be counted on to be accessible when needed? Can he or she be relied upon to be responsive to signals and communications? Will this person accept close bodily contact when this is wanted? Surely these considerations enter into heterosexual bonds, as well as the more obvious sexual interests and parental responsibilities.

Finally, it is relevant to consider the recent emphasis on the social network into which a baby is born. Weinraub, Brooks, and Lewis (1977) asserted that the infant-mother relationship is but one of a variety of relationships important for child development. They further implied that the notion of attachment should be supplanted by more general principles applicable to all relationships. Surely there is a need for developing a taxonomy of relationships, as Hinde (e.g., 1979) also suggested. Nevertheless, it seems to me to be more urgent to seek to understand intimate and enduring relationships involving attachment and other bonds than to undertake research into the less enduring relationships with various figures in the social network. As Weiss (chapter 9) points out, a person who has lost or been separated from a spouse is likely to feel very lonely even though friends are available and supportive. Loneliness is an indicator of the need for and absence of attachment; this need is unlikely to be filled by friends, however well intentioned. To extrapolate, "social support systems," unless they involve actual or potential attachment figures, are unlikely to substitute for attachments and other bonds. Or, to rephrase the issue, it seems likely that attachments are a very important part of the social support system—and of the social network.

Conclusions

There is no way to sum up the issues discussed here into a neat set of conclusions. Let me say merely that I consider myself very fortunate to have been at the right place at the right time to engage in attachment research. Because so little relevant research had been done, I decided back in the 1950s to start at the beginning and to examine how it is that a baby becomes attached to his mother. I envisaged such research as a useful steppingstone toward research into later changes in child-mother attachment and relationships with other figures as well. Attachment research focuses on some of the most complex and thorny (and significant) of all the riddles that we face in trying to understand human nature and development. Patience and persistence on the part of many investigators is required before we can incisively sort through the complexities of human attachments, bonds, and other aspects of relationships.

REFERENCES

Ainsworth, M. D. S. 1967. *Infancy in Uganda: Infant care and the growth of love.* Baltimore, Md.: Johns Hopkins Press.
_____. 1972. Attachment and dependency: A comparison. In *Attachment and dependency,* ed. J. L. Gewirtz. Washington, D.C.: V. H. Winston.
_____. 1979. Attachment as related to mother-infant interaction. In *Advances in the study of behavior* (vol. 9); ed. J. S. Rosenblatt, R. A. Hinde, C. Beer, and M. C. Busnel. New York: Academic Press.
_____, and Bell, S. M. 1969. Some contemporary patterns of mother-infant interaction in the feeding situation. In *Stimulation in early infancy,* ed. A. Ambrose. London: Academic Press.
Ainsworth, M. D. S.; Blehar, M. C.; Waters, E.; and Wall, S. 1978. *Patterns of attachment: A psychological study of the strange situation.* Hillsdale, N.J.: Lawrence Erlbaum Associates.

Ainsworth, M. D. S., and Wittig, B. A. 1969. Attachment and exploratory behavior of one-year-olds in a strange situation. In *Determinants of infant behaviour*, ed. B. M. Foss, vol. 4. London: Methuen.

Andrews, S. R.; Blumenthal, J. B.; Bache, W. L., III; and Wiener, G. 1975. Fourth year report: New Orleans Parent-Child Development Center. (Unpublished.)

Arendt, R., Gove, F. L., and Sroufe, L. A. 1979. Continuity of individual adaptation from infancy to kindergarten: A predictive study of ego resiliency and curiosity in preschoolers. *Child Development* 50:950–959.

Bell, S. M. Unpublished manuscript. Cognitive development and mother-child interaction in the first three years of life.

————, and Ainsworth, M. D. S. 1972. Infant crying and maternal responsiveness. *Child Development* 43:1171–1190.

Blanchard, M., and Main, M. 1979. Avoidance of the attachment figure and social-emotional adjustment of day-care infants. *Developmental Psychology* 15:445–446.

Blehar, M. C. 1974. Anxious attachment and defensive reactions associated with day care. *Child Development* 45:683–692.

————, Ainsworth, M. D. S., and Main, M. Unpublished manuscript. *Mother-infant interaction relevant to close bodily contact: A longitudinal study.*

Blehar, M. C., Lieberman, A. F., and Ainsworth, M. D. S. 1977. Early face-to-face interaction and its relation to later infant-mother attachment. *Child Development* 48:182–194.

Bowlby, J. 1958. The nature of a child's tie to his mother. *International Journal of Psychoanalysis* 39:350–373.

————. 1969. *Attachment and loss. Vol. 1: Attachment*. New York: Basic Books.

————. 1973. *Attachment and loss. Vol. 2: Separation: Anxiety and anger*. New York: Basic Books.

————. 1977. The making and breaking of affectional bonds. *British Journal of Psychiatry* 130:201–210.

————. 1980. *Attachment and loss. Vol. 3: Loss: Sadness and depression*. New York: Basic Books.

Bretherton, I., and Ainsworth, M. D. S. 1974. Responses of one-year-olds to a stranger in a strange situation. In *The origins of fear*, ed. M. Lewis and L. A. Rosenblum. New York: Wiley.

Bronson, W. C. 1968. Stable patterns of behavior: The significance of enduring orientation for personality development. In *Minnesota symposia on child psychology*, ed. J. P. Hill, vol. 2. Minneapolis: University of Minnesota Press.

Caldwell, B. M.; Wright, C.; Honig, A.; and Tannenbaum, J. 1970. Infant day care and attachment. *American Journal of Orthopsychiatry* 40:397–412.

Clarke-Stewart, K. A. 1978. And daddy makes three: The father's impact on mother and young child. *Child Development* 49:446–478.

Coates, B., Anderson, E. P., and Hartup, W. W. 1972a. Interrelations in the attachment behavior of human infants. *Developmental Psychology* 6:218–230.

————. 1972b. The stability of attachment behaviors in the human infant. *Developmental Psychology* 6:231–237.

Cohen, L. J., and Campos, J. J. 1974. Father, mother, and stranger as elicitors of attachment behavior in infancy. *Developmental Psychology* 10:146–154.

Connell, D. B. 1976. *Individual differences in attachment: An investigation into stability, implications, and relations to structure of early language development*. Ph.D. dissertation, Syracuse University.

Cummings, E. M. 1980. Caregiver stability and day care. *Developmental Psychology* 16:31–37.

DeLozier, P. 1979. *An application of attachment theory to the study of child abuse*. Ph.D. dissertation, California School of Professional Psychology, Los Angeles.

Farran, D. C., and Ramey, C. T. 1977. Infant day care and attachment behavior towards mothers and teachers. *Child Development* 48:1112–1116.

Feldman, S. S., and Ingham, M. E. 1975. Attachment behavior: A validation study in two age groups. *Child Development* 46:319–330.

Fleener, D. E. 1973. Experimental production of infant-maternal attachment behavior. Paper presented at the meeting of the American Psychological Association, Montreal, August 1973.

28

Fox, N. 1977. Attachment of kibbutz infants to mother and metapelet. *Child Development* 48:1228-1239.

Freud, A., and Dann, S. 1951. An experiment in group upbringing. In *The Psychoanalytic Study of the Child*, ed. R. S. Eissler et al., vol. 6. New York: International Universities Press.

Freud, S. 1938. *An outline of psychoanalysis.* London: Hogarth Press.

George, C., and Main, M. 1979. Social interactions of young abused children: Approach, avoidance, and aggression. *Child Development* 50:306-318.

Harlow, H. F. 1961. The development of affectional patterns in infant monkeys. In *Determinants of infant behavior*, ed. B. M. Foss. New York: Wiley.

Harlow, H. F., and Harlow, M. K. 1962. Social deprivation in monkeys. *Scientific American* 207:136-146.

_____. 1965. The affectional systems. In *Behavior of nonhuman primates*, ed. A. M. Schrier, H. F. Harlow, and F. Stollnitz, vol. 2. New York: Academic Press.

Hinde, R. A. 1976. On describing relationships. *Journal of Child Psychology and Psychiatry* 17:1-19.

_____. 1979. *Towards understanding relationships.* London: Academic Press.

Hock, E. 1976. Alternative approaches to child rearing and their effects on the mother-infant relationship. Final Report to the Office of Child Development, Washington, D.C.

Klaus, M. H., and Kennell, J. H. 1976. *Maternal-infant bonding.* Saint Louis: C. V. Mosby.

Kotelchuck, M. 1972. The nature of a child's tie to his father. Ph.D. dissertation, Harvard University.

Lamb, M. E. 1976a. Twelve-month-olds and their parents: Interaction in a laboratory playroom. *Developmental Psychology* 12:237-244.

_____. 1976b. The role of the father: An overview. In *The role of the father in child development*, ed. M. E. Lamb. New York: Wiley.

_____. 1977. Father-infant and mother-infant interaction in the first year of life. *Child Development* 48:167-181.

_____. 1978. Qualitative aspects of mother- and father-infant attachments. *Infant Behavior and Development* 1:265-275.

Leiderman, P. H., and Seashore, M. J. 1975. Mother-infant neonatal separation: Some delayed consequences. In *Parent-infant interaction*, Ciba Foundation Symposium 33 (new series). Amsterdam: Elsevier.

Lewis, M., and Ban, P. 1971. Stability of attachment behavior: A transformational analysis. Paper presented at the meeting of the Society for Research in Child Development, Minneapolis, March 1971.

Londerville, S., and Main, M. 1981. Security of attachment, compliance, and maternal training methods in the second year of life. *Developmental Psychology* 17:289-299.

Maccoby, E. E., and Feldman, S. S. 1972. *Mother-attachment and stranger-reactions in the third year of life.* Monographs of the Society for Research in Child Development, vol. 37 (Serial no. 146). Chicago: University of Chicago Press.

Main, M. 1973. Exploration, play, and level of cognitive functioning as related to child-mother attachment. Ph. D. dissertation, Johns Hopkins University.

_____. In press. Exploration, play and cognitive functioning as related to security of infant-mother attachment. *Infant Behavior and Development.*

_____, Slaton, S., and Ainsworth, M. D. S. Unpublished manuscript. The development of angry behavior in the first year of life.

_____, and Wakeling, S. 1979. "Concerned attention" to the crying of an adult actor in infancy. Paper presented at the biennial meeting of the Society for Research in Child Development, San Francisco, March 1979.

_____, and Weston, D. R. 1981. Security of attachment to mother and father: Related to conflict behavior and the readiness to form new relationships. *Child Development* 52:932-940.

Marvin, R. S. 1977. An ethological-cognitive model for the attenuation of mother-child attachment behavior. In *Advances in the study of communication and affect. Vol. 3: The development of social attachments*, ed. T. M. Alloway, L. Krames, and P. Pliner. New York: Plenum Press.

29

————, and Greenberg, M. T. Unpublished manuscript. Preschooler's changing conceptions of their mothers: A social-cognitive study of mother-child attachment.

Marvin, R. S., Mossler, D. C., and VanDevender, T. L. Unpublished manuscript. An experimental study of brief separations between mothers and their 4-year-old children.

Marvin, R. S.; VanDevender, T. L.; Iwanaga, M. I.; LeVine; S.; and LeVine, R. A. 1977. Infant-caregiver attachment among the Hausa of Nigeria. In *Ecological factors in human development*, ed. H. McGurk. Amsterdam: North-Holland Publishing Company.

Matas, L., Arend, R. A., and Sroufe, L. A. 1978. Continuity of adaptation in the second year: The relationship between quality of attachment and later competence. *Child Development* 49:547–556.

Parke, R. D. 1979. Perspectives on father-infant interaction. In *Handbook of infant development*, ed. J. D. Osofsky. New York: Wiley.

Peterson, G. H., Mehl, L. E., and Leiderman, P. H. 1979. The role of some birth related variables in father attachment. *American Journal of Orthopsychiatry* 49:330–338.

Piaget, J. 1952. *The origins of intelligence in children*, 2nd ed. New York: International Universities Press. (Originally published 1936.)

Ricciuti, H. N. 1974. Fear and the development of social attachments in the first year of life. In *The origins of fear*, ed. M. Lewis and L. A. Rosenblum. New York: Wiley.

Rosenberg, S. E. 1975. *Individual differences in infant attachment: Relationships to mother, infant and interaction system variables. Dissertation Abstracts International*, vol. 36, p. 1930B (University Microfilms No. 75-22, 954).

Schaffer, H. R., and Emerson, P. E. 1964. *The development of social attachments in infancy.* Monographs of the Society for Research in Child Development, vol. 29 (Serial no. 94). Chicago: University of Chicago Press.

Sroufe, L. A. 1979. The coherence of individual development: Early care, attachment and subsequent developmental issues. *American Psychologist* 34:834–841.

Stayton, D. J., and Ainsworth, M. D. S. 1973. Individual differences in infant responses to brief, everyday separations as related to other infant and maternal behaviors. *Developmental Psychology* 9:226–235.

Suomi, S., and Harlow, H. F. 1972. Social rehabilitation of isolate-reared monkeys. *Developmental Psychology* 6:487–496.

Vaughn, B.; Egeland, B.; Sroufe, L. A.; and Waters, E. 1979. Individual differences in infant-mother attachment at twelve and eighteen months: Stability and change in families under stress. *Child Development* 50:971–975.

Waters, E. 1978. The reliability and stability of individual differences in infant-mother attachment. *Child Development* 49:483–494.

————, Wippman, J., and Sroufe, L. A. 1979. Attachment, positive effect and competence in the peer group: Two studies in construct validation. *Child Development* 50:821–829.

Weinraub, M., Brooks, J., and Lewis, M. 1977. The social network: A reconsideration of the concept of attachment. *Human Development* 20:31–47.

Willemsen, E.; Flaherty, D.; Heaton, C.; and Ritchey, G. 1974. *Attachment behavior of one-year-olds as a function of mother vs. father, sex of child, session, and toys*. Genetic Psychology Monographs, vol. 90, pp. 305–324. Provincetown, MA: The Journal Press.

Yarrow, L. J. 1967. The development of focused relationships during infancy. In *Exceptional Infant*, ed. J. Hellmuth, vol. 1. Seattle: Special Child Publications.

2

Mary Main and Donna R. Weston

AVOIDANCE OF THE ATTACHMENT FIGURE IN INFANCY: DESCRIPTIONS AND INTERPRETATIONS

Introduction

This chapter is divided into three main sections. In the first we describe a pattern of social behavior that has been neglected: active visual, physical, and communicative avoidance. This behavior is surprisingly prevalent in human infants reunited with their attachment figures following long and stressful major separations, and in rejected infants it appears following even very brief separations. Avoidance of the attachment figure presents something of a problem for attachment theorists, simply because it *is* relatively common. Are we to presume

This chapter is an abridged version of a chapter by Mary Main, "Avoidance in the service of attachment: A working paper," appearing in *Behavioral development: The Bielefeld interdisciplinary project*, a publication of Cambridge University Press, New York, 1981.

We are indebted to many for their part in the making of this chapter. First, we are grateful to Mary D. Salter Ainsworth, who made all of her narrative records available for our study. We are grateful to the Grant Foundation of New York which supported much of the work conducted in Berkeley, and to the Institute of Human Development, University of California, Berkeley, which supported the first author and her assistants for several summers. Inge Bretherton, Donelda Stayton, and Everett Waters provided assistance and criticism in our work in Baltimore; Jackie Stadtman, Stewart Wakeling, Judith Solomon, and Loretta Townsend contributed immeasurably to our work in Berkeley.

that the attachment behavior system breaks down so easily that mildly rejected infants regularly avoid rather than approach their mothers?

In the second section we review empirical studies of the correlates of this behavior pattern as it appears in human infants. Here we show how response to separation and reunion relates to both parental and infant behavior observed in other circumstances. In the case of home-reared infants who have never experienced a major separation, avoidance appears following even extremely brief laboratory separations. Observations of infants and mothers in other settings show that in this case avoidance is highly associated with the mother's anger, her emotional inexpressiveness, and her rejection of physical contact with the infant. Avoidance on reunion is also highly predictive of the infant's social and emotional behavior in other situations. Infants who strongly avoid the mother and show no anger following separation are, for example, likely to attack or threaten to attack the mother in other settings.

In the final section we present three interpretations of avoidance. Although these interpretations differ, they are not mutually exclusive, and each may help us to arrive at a coherent explanation of the phenomenon as it appears in human infants. Two of the three explanations are derived from the works of ethologists, who have observed that animals show a limited avoidance of prospective social partners in situations in which it is actually desirable to maintain proximity. Both Tinbergen (1959) and Chance (1962) suggest that avoidance may function paradoxically to permit the partners to maintain proximity in these situations. The third interpretation of avoidance is more psychological in nature. It postulates that avoidance may be a shift in attention that simply functions to help the infant maintain self-control and behavioral organization.

Social Avoidance Behavior

ATTACHMENT BEHAVIOR

Our main intention here is to describe the avoidance of attachment figures and to point out that this pattern appears in circumstances in which it is not expected—following major separations, in association with rejection by the mother, and in response to friendly overtures or even to physical contact with the mother. Before embarking on a study of a pattern deviant from expectation, however, it may be well to describe the norm from which the pattern departs (Medawar, 1967). This leads to a brief description of what is actually expected in such circumstances—that is, attachment behavior—and the reason that it is expected.

Attachment behavior, as we have seen, has the predictable outcome of increasing or maintaining proximity. Signaling (crying, calling), approaching (creeping, reaching, running), and clinging may all be considered attachment behavior. Within an established attachment relationship, however, forms of angry behavior may also be presumed to serve the function of increasing proximity (Bowlby, 1969; see also Trivers, 1974). Thus an infant's tantrum may persuade the mother either to approach him or to permit his approach; in turn, a mother's angry behavior often brings her infant toward her. Anger may serve a similar proximity-promoting function in well-established adult attachment relationships.

When may we expect to see attachment behavior, and what is its function? Bowlby's (1969, 1973) ethological theory of attachment rests upon two related sets of observations. One is that both human and nonhuman primate infants show a strong and even violent concern with maintenance of proximity to attachment figures. The second observation is that, for most nonhuman primate infants and presumably for human infants in the "environment of evolutionary adaptedness," survival is almost entirely dependent upon maintenance of proximity to an attachment figure. The infant separated from his attachment figure(s) has usually lost food, water, warmth, shelter, and protection from predators.

It is presumed that under most rearing conditions the "attachment behavioral system" will develop and insure the maintenance of proximity to protective (parental or attachment) figures. It is presumed, therefore, that almost all human infants will: (1) develop preferences for some persons over others on the basis of social interaction; (2) express these preferences clearly once object permanence is achieved; (3) respond negatively, even angrily, to threats of separation; while (4) seeking increased proximity with the protective figure and even contact in the face of any threats. Thus, threats of separation from the mother, acts of physical rejection by her, and alarming conditions in the environment are presumed to activate the system at particularly high intensities.

AVOIDANCE BEHAVIOR: VARIATIONS IN DEGREE AND APPEARANCE

Social avoidance, the topic of this chapter, refers to movements directed away from a prospective social partner—to, for example, gaze aversion, movements away of head or upper body, turning the back, and moving out of contact or immediate proximity. It also refers to failure to respond to communicative acts of the social partner and even to apparent lack of recognition of a familiar partner.[1]

What does avoidance look like as it occurs in human infants interacting with adult social partners? In a recent work on human children, Tinbergen and Tinbergen (1973) describe a most subtle form of avoidance behavior (which they describe as "the mildest form of rejecting behavior"). This consists of:

> a certain expression of the eyes, which is very difficult to describe but which (as we know for instance from novels) is known to many people. It is often described as an "empty" or "blank" expression, also as "letting the mental shutters down"—it is a vague, expressionless look, often aimed slightly *past* the adult's eyes. . . . This initial response of the child is, *if the observer keeps looking at it,* followed by partial or complete closing of the eyes. This can be, but is not always, very slow; sometimes so slow that one has the impression that "the eyelids have a very long way to go." When closing the eyes is total, the eyelids look completely smoothed out—not even slightly creased, pressed, or "screwed up," as eyes look when closed on other occasions except in sleep. (pp. 179–180)

Tinbergen and Tinbergen refer here to young children responding to strangers. However, in our ongoing Social Development Project at the University of California at Berkeley we have filmed about 400 reunions between infants (twelve to twenty months of age) and parents in a laboratory setting. In this situation the parent calls the infant from outside the door, opens the door, and greets the infant. The *first* response to reunion with the parent in some infants filmed in our laboratory is the blank expression and eye-closing just described.

Gaze aversion is another, perhaps slightly less subtle, form of avoidance. This too is not infrequently the first response to reunion with the parent. But how can looking *away* from someone be distinguished from looking *at* something else? Waters, Matas, and Sroufe (1975) repeatedly reviewed videotapes to distinguish the two behaviors. When gaze truly shifted from one object (a person) to another (possibly an

---

1. The reader interested in obtaining a broad overview of the literature concerning facial and visual avoidance in animals and humans is referred to excellent reviews of facial-visual communication in Vine (1970, 1973) and to a study of human gaze interactions (Argyle and Cook, 1976).

object), an infant often blinked in transition. In the case of gaze aversion, however, blinks rarely occurred in the transition. This suggests a shift in attention in one case, but not in the other. Waters and his colleagues emphasized (as did Tinbergen and Tinbergen) a peculiarly smooth closing movement of the eyelids accompanying real gaze aversion.

However, infants viewing the parent across a distance cannot maintain simple gaze aversion for long. The infant again looks toward and perhaps greets the parent, or turns fully about and moves away, or searches in a rather disorganized way for something to do with his hands. Often he seizes upon a nearby inanimate object. This search for something to do (seize, touch, handle) is striking. A close repeated viewing of films of the apparent "exploratory" behavior that occurs immediately on reunion reveals that the inanimate object generally has far from the infant's full attention. The infant may, for example, turn rather frantically toward a table leg and finger it (but with eyes fixed blankly on the wall ahead), or, in a clumsily decisive move, he may suddenly drop a toy into a box but then (staring straight ahead) close the box on his hand. The general impression is that the infant could not succeed in maintaining his avoidance of the parent without the aid of the seized-upon object.

Studies using telemetry equipment to monitor the infant's heartbeat on reunion support the view that attention to objects at such moments is not complete. Normal exploration of objects is accompanied by heart-rate deceleration, but "exploration" on reunion fails to show this normal decelerating pattern (Sroufe and Waters, 1977). After a few moments (if the parent does not insist on attracting attention) exploration seems to recover its normal pattern. The infant who has avoided his parent in this manner may, however, carefully orient himself with back to the parent for some time longer. In other cases he may (despite the parent's silence) rise and finally approach the parent.

Some infants respond to reunion with the parent with alternating movements of approach and avoidance. Thus we have seen a number of infants start for the parent and, without looking up into the parent's face, veer away immediately and continue to move away at least a short distance. This behavior sequence appears strange. The change from approach to avoidance does not seem related to any changes in the environment, but only to the infant's having reached a certain proximity to the parent. It is our impression that this is usually a distance of about three feet, which is to say just out of the parent's reach. Often we cannot see indications of a moment of decision whether to continue; instead the change from approach to avoidance is smooth, unhesitating, and hence appears almost mechanical.

Finally, we may consider the way in which an infant may avoid the parent when the parent attempts physical contact or even simply a friendly verbal or visual overture. Infants who have strongly avoided the parent on reunion but have nonetheless been picked up generally make clear their desire to be put down in a subtle manner. Thus, rather than struggling in the arms or vocally protesting, such infants subtly bend toward the floor or indicate a wish for an object. If the parent holds such an infant and tries to gaze at or address him, the infant may seemingly attempt to distract the parent's attention by pointing to an object at some distance. Freed and set on the floor, the infant occupies himself with an object. Strongly avoidant infants such as these may appear "deaf" and "blind" if the parent later attempts to attract attention across a distance.

This overview of the essentials of and varations in the behavior pattern has been a summary of informal observations only. In the following section, the reader will see how the behavior is scaled and assessed more formally.

Review of Empirical Studies

AVOIDANCE OF THE ATTACHMENT FIGURE FOLLOWING MAJOR SEPARATIONS

Avoidance of a parent following separations of brief (minutes) duration has been noted only recently; Ainsworth and Bell made their first formal observations of this behavior pattern in 1970. Avoidance of the parent following major[2] separations has, however, long been noted by clinical investigators. The following is a brief review of studies of response to major separations in children between one and three years of age.

An early observation of avoidance of an attachment figure was made by Darwin (1877). He noted that his two-year-old son kept his eyes "slightly averted from mine"—for the first time following his father's ten-day absence from home. In 1944 Burlingham and Freud observed avoidance of an attachment figure in a two-year-old in their war nur-

2. By "major" is meant separation lasting from just over a week to several months.

sery. This child was passionately attached to his nurse, who married and left the nursery. He was described as "completely lost and desperate" after her departure, and yet he

> refused to look at her when she visited him a fortnight later. He turned his head to the other side when she spoke to him, but stared at the door, which had closed behind her, after she had left the room. In the evening he sat up and said: "My very own Mary-Ann! But I don't like her." (p. 63)

Further studies of responses to major separations have been summarized by Bowlby (1973). Children undergoing major separations from parents in environments in which no substitute parental figure is made available (a consistent nurse, etc.) show increasing distress and anger in the separation environment. Over the period of separation, angry behavior is shown increasingly toward objects, adults, and other children without apparent provocation (e.g., Heinicke and Westheimer, 1965). In general, if the parent visits early in the separation, angry behavior (as well as anxious attachment behavior and distress) is readily exhibited. But if the separation lasts long enough, the parent is typically met instead with avoidance.

These changes in reunion behavior are generally preceded by changes in behavior in the separation environment, and Robertson and Bowlby (1952) have described the child as going though three stages of "protest," "despair," and "detachment" within the separation of environment. In the stages of protest and despair, the child's concern is increasingly despairingly centered upon the absent parent. The child takes little or no interest in the (multiple) attendants;[3] and if the parent visits the child shows both angry behavior and attachment. Left longer in the separation environment, the child begins to "settle in" or adapt to it, taking some interest in both the attendants and the toys available. It is in this stage, when behavior has been reorganized as if to accept the new environment, that the child responds with avoidance to visits or reunion. Bowlby and Robertson describe this as the stage of detachment.

A controlled observational study of children undergoing major separations (three to twenty weeks) was conducted by Heinicke and Westheimer (1965). Stable substitute caregivers (assigned to a particular child) were not available. All children had been observed prior to

---

3. The fact that no single *stable* caregiving figure is available during this period may be crucial to the appearance of the syndrome. Robertson and Robertson (1971) kept several infants in their home during major separations. Distress, anger, and anxiety were evident but the infants did not avoid the mother on reunion.

the separation. All were in good health and several had previously enjoyed secure and harmonious relations with the mother. Heinicke and Westheimer observed the moment of reunion for each child and mother:

> At the time of reunion, *all* the separated children were unable to respond affectionately to the mother. In order of frequency, this took the following forms: physical avoidance, remaining present but not responding with affection, and apparent lack of recognition. (p. 280; emphasis added)

The reactions described were seen in relation to the mother and rarely to the father. Some children turned their faces or backs to the mother. "Lack of recognition" seemed not to reflect a failure of memory; rather it seemed to occur with reference to the person to whom the child was most strongly attached—the child would "fail to know" the mother yet greet the father with warmth and familiarity (as seen in Burlingham and Freud, 1944). In fact, in the Heinicke and Westheimer report, nine of the ten children responded with affection to the father.

This initial, "detached" response to reunion with the primary attachment figure generally lasts only a few hours or days. However, rather than being replaced by either a gradual renewal of relationship or a return to previous harmonious interaction patterns, typically it is replaced with a disturbance of a specific nature. This consists of an anxious and clinging concern about the whereabouts of the attachment figure, and sudden and unprovoked (unpredictable or "inexplicable") bouts of hostility and negativism (Heinicke and Westheimer, 1965; Robertson and Robertson, 1971). This disturbance wanes gradually.

Heinicke and Westheimer proposed that the initial avoidant response to reunion could best be understood as serving a defensive function, permitting a child to maintain control over an anger (and probably distress) that has grown too intense to otherwise permit continued behavioral organization. Since anger is one of the emotions the strongly avoidant child does not exhibit on reunion, this must remain as inference. In the Heinicke and Westheimer report the inference is, however, based upon strong correlation between avoidance of the mother on reunion and angry behavior observed in other settings.

CLASSIFICATIONS OF RELATIONSHIPS ON THE BASIS OF RESPONSE TO BRIEF SEPARATIONS IN THE LABORATORY SETTING

The Ainsworth strange-situation test is designed to elicit exploratory behavior in the early episodes and then, through the series of mildly stressful events described in chapter 1, to shift the infant's attention instead to the maintenance of proximity and contact with the parent. Ainsworth's classification of relationships into three major categories (Groups A, B, and C) on p. 7 is based upon infant rather than parental behavior in the strange situation, and behavior in reunion episodes is emphasized. I shall refer to these categories as avoidant (A), secure (B), and ambivalent (C). As this system was devised using a sample of infant-mother dyads, and has to date been used largely with mothers, we shall generally refer to "mother" as the parent in what follows. Our own recent work has shown, however, that the classifications may be used as readily to describe the behavior of infants with their fathers (Main and Weston, 1980). We have found that about 10 percent of the white, middle-class infants seen with father *or* mother are unclassifiable within the Ainsworth system.

Infants are classified as secure in relation to the mother when they actively seek proximity and contact following separation, and when these behaviors appear unmixed with strong anger or avoidance. In the preseparation episodes, securely attached infants may explore the toys and the strange environment. They may or may not be distressed upon separation, but if they are distressed the mother's return readily comforts them and enables them to return either to play or to pleasant interaction with the mother. At the same time, these infants (as opposed to those classified as avoidant) often show anger in the strange situation. This takes the form of clearly angry crying upon separation; "greeting" the mother with an outraged cry on reunion; and irritatedly batting away toys if she tries to entertain the baby rather than to hold him. Angry behavior in all these forms can of course be seen as proximity-promoting (see Bowlby, 1973).

Infants classified as either ambivalent or avoidant are regarded as insecure in relation to the mother. Infants are classified as ambivalent when they both seek proximity and contact upon reunion and yet resist it and seem to find little security in the mother's return or presence. These infants are often distressed even before the first separation, fearful of the stranger, and extremely distressed on separation. In general, they seem immature and their response to the strange situation seems regressive and exaggerated.

Both infants classified as secure and those classified as ambivalent may show some degree of avoidance in one or even both reunion episodes of the strange situation. In fact, while most infants do seek proximity and contact with the parent following separation, analyses of videotaped reunions in our laboratory show that a majority of infants (about 80 percent) show at least brief gaze aversion or blankness immediately upon reunion.

But infants showing strong avoidance of the mother in both reunion episodes are classified as avoidant and generally exhibit a syndrome of associated behaviors. These infants actively avoid and ignore the mother on reunion, even when she seeks their attention. Picked up, they indicate (in an emotionless way) a desire to be put down, often by pointing to a toy or other object as though to distract the mother's attention. They are often markedly more friendly to the stranger than to the mother (which of course makes their treatment of the mother all the more pointed). Throughout the strange situation they generally attend to the toys or the rest of the inanimate environment. Unlike other infants, they show virtually no distress, no fear, and, most important no anger.

Note, that stability of classification is found only when infants are seen in successive strange situations separated by a long time period. Ainsworth and her colleagues (1978) conducted repeated strange situations with children fifty and fifty-two weeks of age. Although scores for avoidance were stable across the sample (i.e., order was preserved), avoidance on the whole diminished significantly and was replaced by distress and proximity seeking. Clearly this second laboratory separation experience following so soon upon the first was highly stressful. Some infants in the sample cried immediately on returning to the same laboratory environment. Not one infant classified as avoidant in the first strange situation could be clearly classified as avoidant in the second. The reader will need to bear these facts in mind when, in the final section, we attempt to develop a coherent explanation of avoidance.

THE AVOIDANCE SCORING SYSTEM

The studies to be reviewed are of whole samples; that is, they include children classified as secure, avoidant, ambivalent, and unclassifiable. As noted earlier, children receiving high scores for avoidance are generally classified as avoidant, but children in other classifications may show low to moderate avoidance. Ainsworth has developed a reliable "interactive scoring system" that assigns infants ratings from 1 to 7 for the degree to which they show avoidance of the mother. The system is unusual in that differences in adult as well as child behavior are taken into account, and it is presumed that several different kinds and/or combinations of behaviors can serve the same goal and indicate activation of similar intensities. The highest score on the scale is given to the baby who fails to greet his mother upon her return and then pays little or no attention to her for an extended period despite her efforts to attract his attention. Moderate scores are given to brief but clear-cut avoidance (the baby may begin to approach, but then turn away and ignore the mother for a period) or persistent low-keyed withdrawal (the baby may greet the mother casually and then return to play with toys in a manner suggestive of most babies in the pre-separation episodes). Low scores are given to very brief delays in responding to the mother's return or brief instances of mild avoidance such as gaze aversion (Ainsworth et al., 1978).

In four independent investigations (conducted in Baltimore; Minneapolis; Bowling Green, Ohio; and Berkeley) avoidance scores have been shown stable: over a two-week period, r (26) = .66 (Ainsworth, et al., 1978); over a six-month period, r (50) = .62 (Waters, 1978; see also Connell, 1976); and over an eight-month period in a sample of mothers *and* of fathers seen at twelve and again at twenty months, r (30) = .59 (Main and Weston, 1980).

These studies show the viability of the Ainsworth scoring system for laboratory observations, but an important further question is whether the behavior observed in the laboratory represents what actually occurs in the field. For this reason, we undertook a study of day-care infants (twelve to twenty-four months). Each was observed on three completely uncontrolled reunions with the parent in the day-care setting and then observed with the same parent in the Ainsworth strange situation. The Ainsworth scoring system was easy to apply to the uncontrolled "field" setting. A person who had no knowledge of the infants' prior behavior in the day-care setting scored strange-situation behavior. Scores for avoidance in day-care center reunions were highly correlated with avoidance scores in the two reunion episodes from the strange situation. Finally, means for the day-care setting and for the laboratory were virtually identical (Blanchard and Main, 1979).

INFANT CHARACTERISTICS ASSOCIATED WITH AVOIDANCE

In this section we will apply the previously discussed 7-point scale to studies that consist of:

1. A sample of thirty-eight infant-mother dyads observed in Baltimore in a videotaped play setting and a Bayley Developmental testing session at twenty-one months, nine months following the strange situation. (This sample is described more fully in Main [1977]; Main, Tomasini, and Tolan [1979]; and Main and Townsend [1982].)

2. The twenty-three mother-infant dyads observed by Ainsworth (also in

41

Baltimore) throughout the first year of life. Each was observed for a total of sixty hours in the home situation and then observed again in the strange situation at twelve months.

3. The sample of twenty-one infants seen in day-care centers in Berkeley that has been described earlier (Blanchard and Main, 1979).

4. A sample of sixty-one infants seen with mother and with father, in the strange-situation test and in other laboratory sessions, in Berkeley (Main and Weston, 1980).

5. A sample of ten battered and ten control children seen in day-care centers in the Bay area of California. This study did not employ the strange situation. However, avoidance of caregivers and of peers making friendly overtures was examined.

Our results were as follows.

First, we determined that avoidance of the mother within the strange situation is *negatively* related to angry behavior toward her (angry crying, hitting, batting away toys, open petulance) observed within the strange situation. However, avoidance of the mother within the strange situation is *positively* related to angry behavior toward the mother seen in other (stress-free) settings. Often it appears out of context.

In the Baltimore sample of thirty-eight infant-mother dyads, avoidance of the mother at twelve months (rated on the 7-point scale) was related to the following behaviors at twenty-one months: the number of (largely unprovoked) attacks and threats of attack upon the mother; number of episodes of "non-exploratory hitting and banging of toys"; the mother's report that the child was "troublesome"; active disobedience in response to maternal commands; and scores for "tantrum" assigned by the Bayley examiner.

These results led to a coding of every episode of angry behavior between nine and twelve months in the Ainsworth records of twenty-three mother-infant dyads. No relation was found between sheer number of anger episodes and avoidance of the mother in the strange situation. However, there was a strong relation between the number of episodes in which the infant physically attacked or threatened to attack the mother in the home and avoidance on reunion in the strange situation. There was also a strong relation between avoidance in the strange situation and the number of "inexplicable" anger episodes in the home situation (that is, the number of well-described episodes for which the coder could find no apparent stimulus). These were often, but not necessarily, related to attacks upon the mother: "The baby is creeping across the floor, smiling. Suddenly he veers toward his mother, strikes her legs, and creeps away."

In an ongoing analysis of the new Berkeley Social Development sample of infants and parents, we are finding an extremely strong relationship ($p<.001$) between active disobedience to the father's commands or prohibitions in a play session and avoidance of the father in the strange situation.

Third, we determined that the infant's avoidance of attachment figures is related to his difficulties in social responsiveness with other adults or friendly overtures and to his readiness to respond positively to new persons attempting to make friends.

Blanchard and Main (1979) observed infants in the day-care setting for one hour and assigned to each infant scores for "social-emotional adjustment." This adjustment was found significantly related negatively to avoidance of the parent (mother *or* father) on reunion in the day-care setting. In addition, in another in-progress study of data from the same sample, avoidance of the parent on reunion in the day-care setting was found positively associated with attacks and threats of attacks on caregivers and with avoidance of caregivers as they made friendly overtures.

In the videotaped play session of the Baltimore study, an adult "playmate" entered the playroom to invite the toddlers to engage in a game of ball. Infants who had strongly avoided their mothers tended not to approach the playmate as she greeted them. Those few who did so approached in a peculiar manner—abortively, only after turning and spinning away, or (in one case) turning a full circle with hands cupped to ears. A microanalysis of the interactive behavior of the most avoidant infant in the sample showed that she approached the playmate to the rear or by turning about and back-stepping.

Scores given for avoidance of the mother at twelve months were positively related to a simple count of instances of gaze aversion and physical avoidance of the playmate. Not surprisingly, given these data, avoidance of the mother also related negatively to the tendency to interact playfully with a test examiner in a separate session (Main, 1973).

Finally, in an analysis of the new Berkeley sample, Main and Weston (1980) report a strong negative relationship between the infant's avoidance of the mother and his apparent readiness to respond positively to adults attempting to make friends in a separate setting.

Fourth, despite the fact that avoidance of the attachment figure is related to avoidance of (or difficulties with) other adults making friendly overtures, we discovered that there is no relationship between a given infant's avoidance of his mother and of his father.

This has been documented in the Main and Weston study of sixty-one infants seen with mother and with father (one parent at twelve months, one at eighteen months). Whereas stability of avoidance of a given parent between twelve and twenty months is high, there is no relationship between scores for avoidance assigned to the infant as he is seen separately with each of the parents (Main and Weston, 1980).

Fifth, we determined that avoidance is related to restrictions in affective responsiveness.

Matas, Arendt, and Sroufe (1978) report significantly less "positive affect" and "enthusiasm" in avoidant, as compared to secure, infants at twenty-four months. Arendt, Gove, and Sroufe (1979) report that infants described as avoidant at eighteen months are described as over-controlled by their kindergarten teachers three years later.

In the Baltimore study, we found avoidance at twelve months negatively related to number of bouts of smiling or laughing about toys (the only affective measure used). Work in preparation using the Berkeley sample indicates a strong negative relation between avoidance of the mother and emotional expressiveness.

Sixth, we find that avoidance is related to indices of conflict or disturbance—to odd behaviors and to stereotypies.

In the Baltimore study, we noted the occurrence of some odd behaviors in strongly avoidant infants. We therefore asked an assistant to provide a tally of "odd" behaviors in the hour-long videotaped play observation. This count included stereotypes, hand flapping, "echoing" of the mother's speech, inexplicable fears (as of small changes in the laboratory room between the time of the Bayley test and the play session), and striking instances of inappropriate behavior. This simple count of odd behaviors was significantly positively related to avoidance.

In the Ainsworth study of infants between nine and twelve months of age, four of the six avoidant infants showed odd behaviors that were shown by hardly any other members of the sample. One baby stared and appeared to be "in a trance" at times, almost to "be autistic." Another avoidant baby rocked repeatedly, had odd vocalizations, his face was "devoid of affect, and he seemed "attached to objects and the environment more than people"—as did another avoidant baby. Clearly here—as, very broadly, in the strange situation—there is some symptomatic link to the cardinal attributes of autism.

In the current Berkeley study, we are looking for conflict behaviors (such as those previously listed) in infants in a situation designed to elicit in sequence apprehension, positive affect, interest in another person, and empathy. Examining behavior at twelve months only, we have found signs of conflict in 75 percent of the infants classified as avoidant of *both* parents, but in only very few of the infants classified as secure with both (8 percent) or just one (15 percent) of the parents.

Finally, we have found there is no evidence that avoidance is associated with either advances or deficits in cognitive or other functioning.

Waters, Vaughn, and Egeland (1980) were unable to find differences between avoidant and secure infants at birth. We have failed to find a significant correlation between avoidance and the Bayley Mental Development scores, or between avoidance and attention span, intensity of interest in objects, or instances of symbolic play at twenty-one months of age. Similar results (comparing avoidant with secure infants) have been reported by other investigators (Connell, 1976; Matas, Arendt, and Sroufe, 1978; Waters, Vaughn, and Egeland, 1980).

MATERNAL CHARACTERISTICS ASSOCIATED WITH AVOIDANCE OF MOTHER

In this area our results were as follows.

First, we found that avoidance of the mother is associated with the mother's apparent aversion to physical contact with the infant.

This supposition (Main, 1977) was first confirmed by an exhaustive review of the Ainsworth records for the entire first year of life. Mothers' apparent aversion to physical contact with the infant (as shown both through statements made to the observer—"I have always hated physical contact"—and through behavior toward the infant) was rated for the child's first three months of life. The mother's aversion to contact was related extremely strongly to avoidance of the mother at the end of his first year. The infant's early "cuddliness," however, had no relation to avoidance. (Waters, Vaughn, and Egeland [1980] have also failed to find a correspondence between differences in neonatal "cuddliness" and later avoidance.)

The mother's attitude toward contact was stable over the first year. Her aversion to contact in the first three months (rated as described earlier) was highly related to coded instances of rejection of the infant's initiations of contact in the fourth quarter [r (23) = .71]. Coded instances of mother's rejection of contact in the home during the fourth quarter—"Don't touch me!"—were also highly related [r (23) = .76] to the infant's avoidance of the mother in the strange situation.

The mother's apparent aversion to physical contact with her infant has also been assessed using videotaped play sessions in both Baltimore (Main, Tomasini, and Tolan, 1979) and Berkeley (Main and Stadtman, 1981). In each sample there is a strong ($r > .60$) relationship to the infant's avoidance of the mother in the strange situation.

Second, we determined that avoidance of the mother is associated with angry and threatening behavior on the part of the mother.

A close examination of the videotapes from our Baltimore sample showed strong differences in maternal "anger," despite the presence of the camera. Mothers of mother-avoidant infants mocked their infants or spoke sarcastically to or about them; some stared them down. One expressed irritation when the infant spilled imaginary tea. Ratings showed a strong association between avoidance and maternal anger in this sample.

George and Main (1979) suggested that, because of these associations between avoidance and maternal anger, the infants of abusing mothers should show a pattern of behavior similar to infants who strongly avoid the mother. In a partial confirmation of this prediction, they found that battered children observed interacting with peers and caregivers in day-care settings behaved (relative to matched controls) as do infants who strongly avoid the mother on reunion in normal samples. Thus they found battered infants more avoidant of peers and caregivers in response to friendly overtures, more likely to assault and threaten to assault them, and more likely to show unpredictable aggressive behavior toward caregivers.

In studies dealing directly with the response of abused children to reunion with the mother in the laboratory (Gaensbauer, Harmon, and Mrazek, 1979) or in the day-care setting (Lewis and Schaeffer, 1979), abused children have, to date, been found typically avoidant.

In our ongoing Berkeley Social Development Project sample of normal, white middle-class dyads, we have observed occasional rough handling of the infant during transport or during disciplinary interventions in a playroom setting. In this brief (eighteen-minute) observation, 45 percent of the mothers whose infants were classified as avoidant of mother on reunion handled the infant roughly on occasion. Only 8 percent of infants judged secure were handled roughly.

Finally, we find that avoidance of the mother is associated with restriction of the mother's affect expression.

While undertaking the analyses of the videotapes collected in Baltimore, it became clear to us that mothers of strongly avoidant infants were restricted in emotional expression. This was not confined to a failure to express pleasure: some mothers showed no change of expression when physically attacked by their infants. In most cases this restriction in affect expression appeared as detachment or "stiffness"

46

rather than as bland unresponsiveness. Actual ratings for maternal inexpressiveness confirmed this association (the study is partially reported in Main, Tomasini, and Tolan, 1979).

Since this association had not been predicted, it seemed possible that it was a chance association particular to our Baltimore study. We therefore undertook a study of the entirety of the Ainsworth narrative data (one year). The mother's inexpressiveness was again strongly related to infant avoidance. This variable has also been assessed in the Berkeley sample. Once more, maternal inexpressiveness in a play setting has been found associated with infant avoidance in the strange situation. (In addition, the father's inexpressiveness is highly associated with infant avoidance of father.)

Interpretations of Avoidance

It is too early to attempt to develop a complete and fully coherent explanation of the phenomenon of infant avoidance. Here we present two interpretations of avoidance as it appears in animals (two ethological interpretations) and a third, more psychologically oriented interpretation that we are currently developing. These three interpretations are presented in more detail in Main (1981). That paper includes a discussion of the power of these explanations to address questions regarding the ontogeny, causation, evolution, and function of avoidant behavior.

ETHOLOGICAL INTERPRETATIONS OF VISUAL AVOIDANCE IN NONHUMAN ANIMALS: DOES AVOIDANCE SERVE PROXIMITY?

Visual avoidance has been studied extensively in birds (particularly gulls and terns) in ethological studies conducted in the 1950s and early 1960s (e.g., Chance, 1962; Cullen, 1957; Moynihan, 1955; Tinbergen and Moynihan, 1952). It has also been observed in encounters between mammals (e.g., Grant and MacKintosh, 1963) including primates (Altmann, 1962; Williams, 1968). It has been observed most often in agonistic encounters, but these include courtship situations (in which tendencies to flee, to attack, and to approach are competing or alternating), as well as situations involving simple questions of submission and dominance. Visual avoidance is often interpreted as indicative of submission or appeasement to a dominant animal (Altmann

47

[1962] describes a careful not-staring that characterizes the subordinate rhesus), although occasionally it is also interpreted as defiance (Williams, 1968).

Ethologists are concerned with the functions of behavior patterns, that is, with the biological (adaptive/survival) function that led to the incorporation of the behavior pattern in the behavioral repertoire of a given species. In the following sections we see that avoidance in the nonhuman animal is considered a social behavior, one that ultimately permits an animal to maintain proximity to a threatening partner.

1. *Avoidance in the service of proximity: the signal function—the effects upon the partner of removing threatening stimuli from view.* Tinbergen (Tinbergen and Moynihan, 1952) suggests an intriguing and peculiar signal function for avoidance. While most communicative movements reveal some particular intention, mood, or state, Tinbergen suggests that avoidance paradoxically serves the "signal" function of concealment. The black-headed gull has developed a facial structure that conspecifics find threatening. In an original analysis of movements of avoidance ("head-flagging") that occur in the black-headed gull, Tinbergen proposes that avoidance is used by the performer to remove the threatening structure from view. Thus, head-flagging seems to have the function of nullifying the effects of threatening gestures and structures; conspicuous structures are concealed rather than displayed.

In a later paper Tinbergen (1959) observes that "facing away" occurs in situations other than courtship. However, he again emphasizes its signal function and the fact that it appears in situations in which the performer would find it desirable to maintain proximity. Facing away seems to inhibit both flight and attack in the partner, by removing the releasing stimuli from view.

2. *Avoidance in the service of proximity: the "cut-off" function—avoidance as an alternative to prospective reactions in the performer.* In a well-known paper written in 1962, M. R. A. Chance draws upon essentially the same kinds of data as Tinbergen, although he reviews some new and extensive analyses of agonistic male-male encounters in the rat. But while Tinbergen sees avoidant movements as inhibiting the release of aggression and withdrawal in the prospective social partner, Chance suggests that the same movements have the same ultimate effect upon aggressive and flight tendencies (tendencies that would interfere with the maintenance of proximity) *in the performing animal itself.* This is because sight of another animal almost always arouses tendencies to flee and to attack. "Cut-off" acts and postures are likely

48

to appear whenever an animal faces a "threatening social partner" because they permit a waning of such tendencies.

Thus Chance too suggests that avoidance serves proximity, but through its consequences for the behavior of the performer rather than through the partner's response. An especially appealing feature of his model is that visual avoidance can be seen as paradoxically reducing the likelihood of flight (as well as aggressive acts) in the performer.

ETHOLOGICAL INTERPRETATIONS OF AVOIDANCE APPLIED TO AVOIDANCE OF THE ATTACHMENT FIGURE IN HUMAN INFANTS

Since, following attachment theory, we must presume that each attached infant needs to maintain proximity to his attachment figure, avoidance of the attachment figure—even in rejected infants—presents a problem. Is it really possible that the attachment behavior system is so easily and frequently rendered inoperative when human infants experience separation and/or rejection? One solution to the problem is to presume that avoidant infants would never have survived in the "environment of evolutionary adaptedness"; that is, to determine that the behavior pattern is an anomaly and has no particular survival value. But as we have seen, both Tinbergen and Chance have provided us a way of seeing avoidance as an evolved pattern that is actually consonant with the working of a proximity-maintaining system. We are now attempting to conceive of avoidance as a conditional or secondary strategy for maintaining proximity under conditions of maternal (separation or) rejection. This means that similar to crying and locomotion, avoidance ultimately—in special circumstances—serves attachment. In what follows we summarize the results of a long argument presented elsewhere (Main, 1981).

Avoidance in the service of proximity: the signal function reconsidered. If avoidance acts as a signal in the service of proximity, it may be a care-eliciting signal that draws the mother to approach and contact her infant. However, close examination of strongly avoidant infants in the strange-situation test simply does not suggest that their avoidance is intended to draw the parent to them—at least not in any simple physical sense that would fit with an "ethological-evolutionary attachment theory" interpretation. This is essentially because the infant who avoids on reunion with the parent also struggles to be put down again when the parent has approached and picked him up.

If avoidance is not a care-eliciting signal, it may still be an appeasement signal enabling the infant to maintain whatever proximity is possible. ("I am turning just a little ways away and ignoring our relationship just a little bit, but please do come and get me.") The rejecting mother's aversion to contact and proximity with her infant could be reinterpreted as a forbidding of the infant's intrusion into her space, and her "anger" could be seen as a threat that occurs when her space or her status relative to the infant is violated. Even the mother's inexpressiveness could be conceived as a kind of signal establishing her dominance (Tronick et al., 1978). In this case the infant's avoidance could be considered some kind of "appeasement" signal made in direct response to the mother's signals of dominance. Avoidance would then be expected whenever a mother in such a mood approached her infant. However, if we take avoidance as an appeasement signal in response to a dominant mother, we are unable to predict avoidance in undominated infants following major separations.

Avoidance in the service of proximity: the effects upon prospective reactions in the performer reconsidered. Can avoidance be seen as functioning primarily to reduce the infant's own tendencies to exhibit behaviors that would interfere with maintenance of proximity to the partner? In this "cut-off" view of avoidance, proximity is maintained by avoidance because blocking sight of the mother reduces the likelihood that the infant will (1) flee from her or (2) show angry behavior toward her. The cut-off view does differ from avoidance as a signal to the partner, in that avoidance is seen as necessary to the infant in order that he may maintain control over flight or aggressive tendencies. Since angry behavior increases observably over periods of major separation, and since rejected infants are expected to experience greater anger than others during even brief separations, we can use this theory to predict avoidance on reunion (due to an increase in anger) in either circumstance. Note that this account also has the advantage of not predicting that the home-reared rejected infant will *continually* avoid the mother (which we doubt that one does), but rather that the infant will avoid her when he simultaneously most needs her and is most angry.

The proposal that avoidance appears as an alternative to angry behavior could be tested in many fashions. We could, for example, examine films of strange-situation behavior to look for extremely subtle facial signals of anger in the avoidant infant. We could also attempt to induce anger toward the mother in secure infants just prior to conducting the strange situation.

Let us now attempt a criticism of this interpretation of avoidance. We can begin by asking whether this theory can deal with the fact that avoidance is replaced by strong proximity-seeking when stress increases still more greatly. It can, because this theory presumes a proximity-maintaining mechanism is continuously active and that that mechanism leads to selection of avoidance as an alternative to angry behavior. In alarming circumstances attachment (proximity-seeking) could simply override anger and hence override avoidance. Thus, since the "danger" that cut-off presumably guards against is simply an exhibition of angry behavior, a display of proximity-seeking in a second strange situation is not a difficulty.[4] On the other hand, if avoidance is overwhelmed by attachment behavior in a second strange situation, why is it not also overwhelmed by attachment behavior following presumably still more stressful major separations?

In addition, in the "cut-off" theory of avoidance, cut-off permits a waning of the proximity-interfering tendencies aroused by sight of the partner. If avoidance functions only to reduce the likelihood of angry behavior upon reunion, why do we not see bouts of avoidance followed by bouts of distress in the strange-situation episodes?

In general, the answer to the question whether avoidance serves proximity must be left open. It *may*, and if it does we have in avoidance a pleasing example of a conditional strategy, an example of avoidance in the service of attachment. Experiments to test this hypothesis in home-reared infants have yet to be conducted. In every strange-situation study conducted to date the infants observed are essentially entrapped within the strange-situation environment. It would be simple to design studies in which the infant has alternatives. Only when the infant is free to leave will we know whether avoidance has ultimately a proximity-maintaining function.

AVOIDANCE AS A MEANS OF MAINTAINING BEHAVIORAL ORGANIZATION: A PSYCHOLOGICAL INTERPRETATION OF AVOIDANCE

Recently we have been considering another and more psychological interpretation of avoidance—the ways in which avoidance permits the infant to maintain organization, control, and even flexibility in behavior. This view of avoidance has also been somewhat anticipated by ethologists, since Chance himself suggests (1962) that a secondary advantage of visual avoidance of a "threatening" partner is consequent maintenance of flexibility in behavior patterns. Thus he makes the

---

4. Note again that infants who avoided in the first strange situation avoided some, though to lesser degree, in the second held in quick succession. To our knowledge there was no accompanying increase in displays of anger.

point that an animal who reduces attention to a partner who has an unwelcome power over its behavior patterns has more freedom for choosing among succeeding behavior patterns than one who does not. Note that here we are no longer necessarily concerned with a proximity-promoting advantage to cut-off—that is, a social advantage for the performer. Retention of flexibility and voluntary control are advantages that could on the whole be called psychological.

This theory of avoidance differs from others in that here avoidance can be seen as an alternative to approach behavior of every kind. The traditional cut-off theory of avoidance logically excluded the possibility that avoidance functions to reduce the likelihood of approach behavior. Avoidance-as-signal allowed for a reduced likelihood of approach, but this was supposed important only insofar as it ultimately increased the likelihood of proximity. If, however, the function of avoidance is to permit continued control, flexibility, and organization in behavior, then we may expect it to occur whenever sight of the mother would threaten an infant with loss of control, of flexibility, and of organization. If approach to or by mother threatens organization, then cut-off could occasionally be used to maintain distance. We could, in short, be seeing real avoidance.

What is "behavioral disorganization"? Behavior can be called disorganized when it vacillates between opposite extremes without reference to changes in the environment or when it appears repeatedly in an environment that does not call for it. Disorganized behavior appears in infants reunited with their mothers while still in the stages of protest or despair (Robertson and Bowlby, 1952), *and* in ambivalent infants in the strange-situation test. Infants in both situations pay little or no attention to toys or other objects. Their whole attention seems distressingly focused upon the parent, whether present or absent. The parent's leavetaking has led to violent distress, but for these infants her return does little to alleviate it. Moreover, when held by the mother the infant clings, then angrily pushes away, then clings, then pushes away, and then clings again. All of this vacillation may be accompanied by unpredictable cries of distress. Observers cannot connect these changes in the infant's behavior to any preceding changes in the mother's. It is as though contact with the mother in itself arouses anger, and then withdrawal, and withdrawal leads again to contact that leads again to anger and withdrawal—a sequence that would seem dependent in its entirety on the alternation of competing systems within the infant. This is highly distressed and disorganized behavior, and it is distressing to witness.

52

If we propose now that avoidant infants are attempting to avoid behavioral disorganization, can we fit the theory (1) to the fact that avoidance appears both in rejected infants following minor separations and in virtually all infants following major separations, and (2) to problems involved in understanding the immediate causation of avoidance? Let us consider first the problems of ontogeny and immediate causation in rejected infants.

Elsewhere (Main, 1977) we have argued that when an attached infant is subjected to threats from an attachment figure who simultaneously rejects physical contact, he is placed in a theoretically irresolvable and indeed self-perpetuating conflict situation. This is because threats of any kind, stemming from any source, arouse tendencies to withdraw from the source of the threat and to approach the mother. If (as is the case with mothers of avoidant infants) the mother is not only threatening but also forbids approach and contact, the conflict is not resolvable. The mere fact that approach is forbidden when it is most necessary should activate still further the attachment behavior system; it should also activate angry behavior; but approach is still not possible; and this should activate still further the system. Thus, on a theoretical level, a kind of positive feedback loop develops. Angry behavior, approach behavior, withdrawal behavior, and conflict behavior should be expected. Indeed, in general we should expect to see the behavior of Ainsworth's ambivalent infants.

Other conflict theories have certainly been proposed to account for the development of disorganization in behavior—for example the "double-bind" theory of schizophrenia originated by Gregory Bateson. They describe, however, a conflict that is less self-perpetuating and far less innately disorganizing than the conflict that here purportedly faces the attached, threatened, and physically rejected infant. Thus in the double-bind theory of schizophrenia the child must deal with two opposing signals from the mother. The mother may, for example, verbally request her child to approach her while nonverbally forbidding him to approach. The child might withdraw in response to her nonverbal behavior and approach in response to her call and find himself at a standstill. However, in this conceptualization, withdrawal would not automatically and in itself lead to approach; what is described is not a self-perpetuating system. Two external and opposing signals are all that keep the child in conflict.

In the case of the rejected attached infant, however, only one signal from the mother is required to place the child in conflict. Withdrawal tendencies arise in response to her threat signal and lead automatically to approach tendencies; the connection between these opposing tendencies is internal to the attached infant and makes no reference to the environment. Because approach is known to be forbidden, the attachment behavior system is still further activated, but approach remains forbidden. Vacillation between approach, avoidance, and angry behavior may be expected. There is no solution to this problem so long as the infant focuses his attention upon the attachment figure. A shift in attention is the only solution.

We have now developed a theory of the ontogeny of avoidance in rejected infants. Avoidance is seen as a necessary shift in attention away from the attachment figure—a shift away from the external stimulus (the mother) that, when paired with the activated attachment behavior system within the infant, brings about the theoretically irresolvable conflict. We need, of course, to understand why the behavior is not exhibited continually—that is, why, according to this theory, it appears at particular times and places. This theory can meet with that requirement since the conflict need not be experienced continually. The mother does not always threaten or block the infant's approach. And, in comfortable situations, attachment behavior is not aroused by the environment. According to this theory the infant should make an effort toward avoidance only when the attachment behavior system is highly activated, since it is at such moments that behavioral disorganization threatens. This should certainly lead to avoidance of the mother in situations such as the strange situation. The only possible solution at such moments is, again, a shift in attention away from everything that is concerned with the mother.

If avoidance is conceived of as necessitated by a threat of disorganization contingent upon attention to the attachment figure, we can explain not only avoidance of the mother but also the suppression of distress during separation, the unusual attention to objects throughout the strange situation, and the desperate-appearing search for an "object of attention" at the moment of reunion. What is being deactivated in this account is the entire attachment behavior system (see Bowlby [1980] for an essentially identical proposal). Here angry behavior may fail to appear not because it would interfere with proximity but because it is ultimately proximity-promoting.

Using this theory of avoidance a very similar account can be drawn from behavior observed during major separations. Concern with the whereabouts of the attachment figure grows extreme; efforts to regain the attachment figure meet with frustration; this leads to angry behavior; and continued frustration leads to still stronger activation of the system. This leads to a disorganizing positive feedback loop, and eventually attention must be shifted away from the attachment figure—toward some other stable caregiving figure if possible (Robertson and Robertson, 1971; Hansen, unpublished manuscript), and if not then toward the inanimate environment. Over a long enough period of separation, distress disappears and the child appears "adapted" to the new environment. But this adaptation is bought at the price of a shift of attention away from the mother. Again we would predict avoidance of the attachment figure on reunion.

This final theory seems satisfactorily to provide a similar account for the two different kinds of experiences that lead to avoidance on reunion with the attachment figure. It deals with the fact that the child who avoids in the strange situation does not always avoid, for the "shift of attention," of which avoidance is a part, is only a strong necessity in the face of strong activation of the attachment behavior system. Since this shift of attention is in fact only an attempt at reorganization or at maintenance of organization, we should also not be surprised that it disappears in rapidly succeeding strange situations. (On the other hand, if the theory is to hold, we would expect disorganized behavior in the avoidant infants in the second strange situation. Since secure infants are organized in their behavior, a simple shift to the secure pattern of behavior would act as disconfirmation of this theory.)

The theory of avoidance as preservation of organization also has other advantages. First, it deals most straightforwardly with the fact that the avoidant infant signals to be put down as soon as he is picked up by the mother. Second, unlike either of the other theories, it provides a single account for differences between avoidant and other children observed in the separation environment. Theories of avoidance as a signal to a partner can hardly prescribe particular patterns of behavior in the absence of all partners. And the theory of avoidance as cut-off of angry behavior is designed to predict only shifts of attention contingent upon the appearance of the partner. It may be that avoidance appears as an alternative to angry behavior or feelings simply because of the ultimate effects of such feelings upon the individual, whether or not the partner is present. Thus avoidance may appear simply because at some point an extreme of anger (and distress) grows psychologically intolerable for the performing individual (a view put forth by John Bowlby, e.g., 1960).

It is only when we conceive of avoidance as part of a more general strategy of shifting attention from the attachment figure that we are able to "predict" that infants who will strongly avoid will first have maintained an "organized" attention to the inanimate environment during the period of separation. No particular pattern of behavior during separation is predicted by the other theories.

Third, avoidance as an organized shift in attention fits pleasingly with plain descriptions of phenomena observed in the strange situation. Most babies who will avoid the mother in the strange situation have a rigidly organized appearance on separation, and, as noted earlier, on the reappearance of the mother they search desperately for something to attend to. Their search for continued self-organization is certainly more obvious than any immediately rising anger tendencies.

Though this interpretation fits with the surface phenomena, it presumes that much is occurring beneath the surface level. Avoidance is still seen as an alternative to attachment behavior and to angry behavior, and it is still seen as a conditional rather than a preferred (or indifferent) infant strategy. Although the avoidant infant may manage to avoid a conflict that is disorganizing and that would otherwise have power to capture his whole attention, the infant is avoiding precisely because of the power held by the attachment figure. At the same time, the child has not lost interest in gaining access to other prospective attachment figures, and may cling to a stranger if one is available. Battered infants are avoidant of the abusive parent but sometimes cry at the leavetaking of the stranger in the strange situation. Hansen (unpublished manuscript) suggests that it is in part the capacity for avoidance that leaves open the possibility of actively searching for a new attachment relation.

If this theory is correct, then avoidance can be conceived as a complex and incomplete shift in attention that certain circumstances render especially necessary. It is necessarily incomplete because, as each observation tells us, infant behavior and infant emotions are organized around the attachment figure no matter what the surface appearance. This is apparent not only in observations of infants responding to separations, but also in the organization of exploration and play and of the infant's response to strangers. It is also evident in the emotional difficulties the infant encounters during major separations when alternative (substitute) "attachment" figures are offered (Robertson and Robertson, 1971).

A shift in attention away from a primary attachment figure then means a blotting out or negation of the image of the parent, who normally would continue to be the central object of attention. Rejected infants and infants experiencing stressful major separations do gradually appear to reorganize their behavior toward the characteristics of the immediate (separation) environment. This is, however, only a surface account of their behavior. In a more complete account, we might better conceive of thought and behavior as becoming actively reorganized *away from* the parent and the memory of the parent. If, as we think, this shift cannot be completely successful inwardly, then we require an effective concept of anti- or negative attention, a concept closely tied to analytic theories of defense. A final test of theory is possible: The theory would predict an active avoidance of all reminders of the mother during her absence.

REFERENCES

Ainsworth, M. D. S., and Bell, S. M. 1970. Attachment, exploration, and separation: Illustrated by the behavior of one-year-olds in a strange situation. *Child Development* 41:49–67.

Ainsworth, M. D. S.; Blehar, M. C.; Waters, E.; and Wall, S. 1978. *Patterns of attachment.* Hillsdale, N.J.: Lawrence Erlbaum Associates.

Altmann, S. A. 1962. A field study of the sociobiology of Rhesus monkeys (*Macaca mulatta*). *Annals of the New York Academy of Sciences* 102:338–435.

Arendt, R., Gove, R., and Sroufe, L. A. 1979. Continuity of adaptation from infancy to kindergarten: A predictive study of ego-resiliency and curiosity in preschoolers. *Child Development* 50:950–959.

Argyle, M., and Cook, M. 1976. *Gaze and mutual gaze.* New York: Cambridge University Press.

Blanchard, M., and Main, M. 1979. Avoidance of the attachment figure and social-emotional adjustment in day-care infants. *Developmental Psychology* 15(4):445–446.

Bowlby, J. 1960. Separation anxiety. *International Journal of Child Psychoanalysis* 41:89–113.

———. 1969. *Attachment and loss. Vol. 1: Attachment.* New York: Basic Books.

———. 1973. *Attachment and loss. Vol. 2. Separation: Anxiety and anger.* New York: Basic Books.

———. 1980. *Attachment and loss. Vol. 3: Loss: Sadness and depression.* New York: Basic Books.

Burlingham, D., and Freud, A. 1944. *Infants without families.* London: Allen & Unwin.

Chance, M. R. A. 1962. An interpretation of some agonistic postures: The role of "cutoff" acts and postures. *Symposium of the Zoological Society of London* 8:71–89.

Connell, D. 1976. Individual differences in attachment related to habituation to a redundant stimulus. Ph. D. dissertation, Syracuse University.

Cullen, E. 1957. Adaptations in the Kittiwake to cliffnesting. *Ibis* 90:71–87.

Darwin, C. 1877. A biographical sketch of an infant. *Mind* 2:285–294.

Gaensbauer, T. J., Harmon, R. J., and Mrazek, D. 1979. Affective behavior patterns in abused and/or neglected infants. In *The understanding and prevention of child abuse: Psychological approaches*, ed. N. Frude. London: Concord.

George, C., and Main, M. 1979. Social interactions of young abused children: Approach, avoidance, and aggression. *Child Development* 50:306–318.

Grant, E. C. and MacKintosh, J. H. 1963. A comparison of the social postures of some common laboratory rodents. *Behaviour* 21:246–259.

Hansen, J. Unpublished manuscript. Multiple attachment figures: Monotropy and the function of subsidiary attachments.

Heinicke, C., and Westheimer, J. 1965. *Brief separations.* New York: International Universities Press.

Lewis, M., and Schaeffer, S. 1979. Peer behavior and mother-infant interaction in maltreated children. In *The uncommon child: The genesis of behavior,* ed. M. Lewis and L. Rosenblum, vol. 3. New York: Plenum Press.

Main, M. 1973. Exploration, play and level of cognitive functioning as related to child-mother attachment. Ph.D. dissertation, Johns Hopkins University.

_____. 1977. Analysis of a peculiar form of reunion behavior seen in some day-care children: Its history and sequelae in children who are home-reared. In *Social development in childhood: Daycare programs and research,* ed. R. Webb. Baltimore, Md.: Johns Hopkins University Press.

_____. 1981. Avoidance in the service of attachment: A working paper. In *Behavioral development: The Bielefeld interdisciplinary project,* ed. K. Immelmann, G. Barlow, M. Main, and L. Petrinovitch. New York: Cambridge University Press.

_____ and Stadtman, J. 1981. Infant response to rejection of physical contact by the mother: Aggression, avoidance and conflict. *Journal of the American Academy of Child Psychiatry* 20:292–307.

Main, M, Tomasini, L. and Tolan, W. 1979. Differences among mothers of infants judged to differ in security. *Developmental Psychology* 15(4):472–473.

Main, M., and Townsend, L. 1982. Exploration, play and cognitive functioning related to infant-mother attachment. *Infant Behavior and Development.* (In press.)

Main, M., and Weston, D. R. 1980. Security of attachment to mother and to father: Related to conflict behavior and the readiness to establish new relationships. *Child Development.* (In press.)

Matas, L., Arendt, R., and Sroufe, L. A. 1978. Continuity of adaptation in the second year: The relationship between quality of attachment and later competence. *Child Development* 49:457–556.

Medawar, P. B. 1967. *The art of the soluble.* London: Methuen.

Moynihan, J. 1955. Some aspects of reproductive behavior in the Black-headed gull and related species. *Behavior* (supplement), 4:1–201.

Robertson, J., and Bowlby, J. 1952. Responses of young children to separation from their mothers. *Courrier du Centre International de l'Enfance* 2:131–142.

Robertson, J., and Robertson, J. 1971. Young children in brief separations. In *The psychoanalytic study of the child,* ed. R. K. Eissler et al., vol. 26. New Haven, Conn.: Yale University Press.

Sroufe, L. A., and Waters, E. 1977. Heartrate as a convergent measure in clinical and developmental research. *Merrill-Palmer Quarterly* 23:3–28.

Tinbergen, N. 1959. Einige Gedanken uber Beschwichtigungs-Gebaerden. *Zeitschrift für Tierosychol* 16:651–655. (Translated in N. Tinbergen, *The animal in its world,* vol. 2. Cambridge, Mass.: Harvard University Press, 1973.).

_____, and Moynihan, M. 1952. Head flagging in the Black-headed gull: Its function and origin. *British Birds* 45:19–22.

Tinbergen, N., and Tinbergen, E. A. 1973. Early childhood autism: A hypothesis. In *The animal in its world,* by N. Tinbergen, vol. 2. Cambridge, Mass.: Harvard University Press.

Trivers, R. L. 1974. Parent-offspring conflict. *American Zoologist* 14:249–264.

Tronick, E.; Als, H.; Adamson, L.; Wise, S.; and Brazelton, T. B. 1978. The infant's response to entrapment between contradictory messages in face-to-face interaction. *Journal of the Amerian Academy of Child Psychiatry* 17:1–13.

Vine, I. 1970. Communication by facial-visual signals. In *Social behavior in birds and mammals: Essays in the social ethology of animal and man,* ed. J. Crook. London: Academic Press.

_____. 1973. The role of facial-visual signaling in early social development. In *Social communication and movement,* ed. M. von Cranach and I. Vine. New York: Academic Press.

Waters, E. 1978. The reliability and stability of individual differences in infant-mother attachment. *Child Development* 49:483–494.

_____, Matas, L. and Sroufe, L. A. 1975. Infants' reactions to an approaching stranger:

Description, validation and functional significance of wariness. *Child Development* 46:348–356.

Waters, E., Vaughn, B. and Egeland, B. 1980. Individual differences in infant-mother attachment: Antecedents in neonatal behavior in an economically disadvantaged sample. *Child Development* 51:208–216.

Williams, L. 1968. *Man and monkey*. New York: Lippincott.

3

Robert A. Hinde

ATTACHMENT: SOME CONCEPTUAL AND BIOLOGICAL ISSUES

Introduction

Talking about one of his first hospital appointments, child psychiatrist Professor F. Stone described the rain-soaked line of parents stretching down the gray street, waiting for the doors of the children's wards to open for the half-hour's visit they were permitted each week. James and Joyce Robertson had shown their first film on mother-child separation in the hospital just previously, and Stone was offered research money to "prove this Bowlby stuff to be nonsense." His efforts to increase parental visiting hours at first led to a near walkout of the nurses and were successful only after much patience and hard work. This, and the knowledge that restricted visiting hours are still normal in some countries, recently brought home to me anew how much we all, especially children, owe to John Bowlby.

On a more academic level, I think it is fair to say that the central concepts and attitudes of mind that Bowlby engendered marked a new era in the understanding of child development, from which we are just starting to reap the benefits. Here I would like to stress especially the value of his eclecticism. The seminars he ran at the Tavistock Centre in the fifties regularly included representatives of two schools of

I am grateful to Mary Ainsworth, John Bowlby, and Joan Stevenson-Hinde for their comments on the manuscript. The work was supported by the Royal Society, the Medical Research Council, and the Grant Foundation.

psychoanalysis and two varieties of learning theory, a Piagetian, often an antipsychiatrist, an ethologist, psychiatric social workers, and so on. They were bound together not by a particular theoretical outlook but by interest in a common problem. Attendance at those meetings was for me a very important scientific experience.

Such eclecticism is still necessary. While recognizing that theoretical approaches must be distinguished by labels, we must beware of treating "attachment theory" as though it were a self-contained system, a structure that is fully built instead of one that is still growing. "Attachment theory" must not lead to isolationism or carry the implication that we should be busy pitting this theory against others; rather we must carry on the eclectic approach that Bowlby initiated, and see where the insights that he and those who followed him (e.g., Ainsworth et al., 1978) can help us, where they are adequate and where they need to be supplemented from elsewhere.

In this chapter we are concerned with two issues: the conceptual background to work on attachment and its biological bases.

Conceptual Issues

Ainsworth (1979, Ainsworth et al., 1978) has recently discussed in some detail the three basic concepts used by those who work on attachment (see table 3-1). These are: attachment behavior, attachment behavior system, and attachment.

TABLE 3-1
Some Characteristics of Terms Used in Attachment Theory

	Data	Theory
elationship	ATTACHMENT An aspect of a relationship with someone perceived as stronger/wiser. Persistent over time and situations. Categorically assessed.	
interactions	ATTACHMENT BEHAVIOR Diverse items. Situation-dependent. Each item measurable along some dimension.	ATTACHMENT BEHAVIOR SYSTEM A postulated control system (see figure 3-1)

1: *Attachment behavior.* This refers to items of behavior "that share the usual or predictable outcome of maintaining a desired degree of proximity to the mother figure—behaviour through which the attachment bond is first formed and then later mediated, maintained and further developed" (Ainsworth et al., 1978, p. 302). Bowlby casts the net somewhat wider, referring to "proximity to some other differentiated and preferred individual, who is usually conceived as stronger and/or wiser" (1977, p. 203). In any case this term is clearly part of the data language (Estes et al., 1954) of the Bowlby/Ainsworth approach.

Attachment behavior is diverse. In principle it is possible to measure the strength of each type of attachment behavior. Insofar as the strengths of the several types of attachment behavior are correlated with each other, it might be possible to categorize the overall strength of attachment behavior. But overall measurement would be difficult because the units by which the several types of behavior (e.g., crying, approach) were assessed would not be compatible, and any attempt to measure attachment behavior in terms of its consequences (e.g., proximity) would be confounded by the behavior of the attachment figure. In any case, different types of attachment behavior may be alternative to each other, and thus not highly correlated.

2: *Attachment behavior system.* "Behavior system" is a term borrowed by Bowlby (e.g., 1969) from ethology, where it in effect took over some connotations of "instinct" when the latter was seen to be a nonexplanation which led to simplistic theorizing. Such a concept has been used, for instance, with reference to the nest-provisioning behavior of the wasp *Ammophila campestris* (Baerends, 1941) and to the reproductive behavior of the stickleback *Gasterosteus aculeatus* (Tinbergen, 1951) and of various birds (e.g., great tit *Parus major* [Hinde, 1953]; herring gull *Larus argentatus* [Baerends, 1976]).

As an example of a behavior system, figure 3-1 shows Baerends's scheme of the systems that must be postulated to explain the patterning of incubation behavior in the herring gull. The lower-level systems controlling behavioral acts are shown on the right, and the control systems postulated to explain the interrelations between the several types of behavior are shown on the left. The higher-order control systems are labeled N (nest activities, including incubation), E (escape activities), and P (preening). Thus while the scheme is based on behavioral observations, it is used in an explanatory sense to refer to systems postulated as controlling the behavior. However, there is no necessary implication that there are mechanisms in the brain isomorphous with the systems postulated: The explanation is a "software"

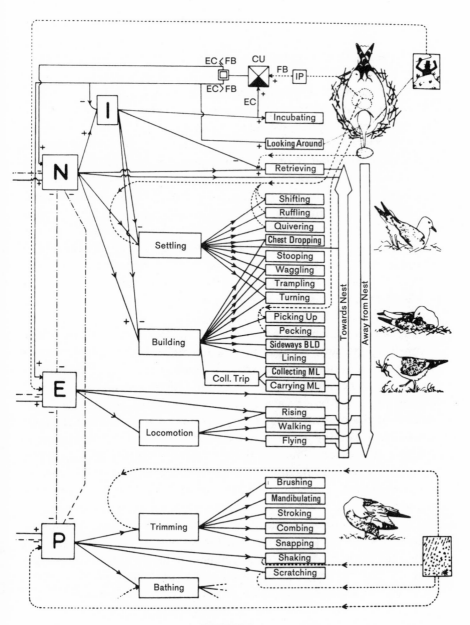

FIGURE 3-1

Three Behavior Systems Postulated to Describe the Occurrence of Interruptive Behavior during the Incubation Behavior of a Herring Gull

NOTE: The fixed action patterns are in the right column and superimposed control systems of first and second order are represented left of them (N = incubation system, E = escape system, P = preening system). The large vertical arrows represent orientation components with regard to the nest. Incubating is the consummatory act. Feedback stimulation from the clutch, after being processed in IP, flows to a unit (CU) where it is compared with expectancy, an efference copy or corollary on the input for incubation. This input is fed through a unit (I), necessary to explain the inhibition of settling and building when feedback matches expectancy. The effect of feedback discrepancy on N (and I), E, and P can be read from the arrows. The main systems mutually suppress one another; P is thought to occur as interruptive behavior through disinhibition of N and E. P can be activated directly by external stimuli like dust, rain, or parasites; E can also be stimulated by disturbances other than deficient feedback from the clutch. From Baerends, G. P., and Drent, R. H. (1970). The herring gull and its egg. *Behavior Supplement, No. 17*: 267. By permission of E. J. Brill, Leiden.

one, comparable to a computer program that performs a particular job irrespective of whether the computer into which it is fed employs valves, transistors, or integrated circuits (Baerends, 1976; Dawkins, 1976). The figure is largely self-explanatory, but the details do not matter for present purposes: The important points are that behavioral systems interact with each other and that each involves a number of different types of behavior which may be related to each other, directly or indirectly, in a variety of ways. Some patterns may be appetitive to others, some alternative to others; some might share positive causal factors, others might share negative (consummatory) factors; some might be mutually facilitatory, others mutually inhibitory. In some cases the precise nature or relative frequency of the responses may change with time—that is, with ontogenetic or reproductive development. In a similar vein, Bischof (1975) has developed a model which accounts for many aspects of seeking proximity with or avoidance of familiar versus strange individuals.

The "attachment behavior system" refers to a system postulated as controlling the several types of attachment behavior. Insofar as that attachment behavior serves a particular interpersonal relationship, the attachment behavior system must incorporate sensitivity to and expectations about the other participant—what Bowlby called a "working model" of the other. We can further picture the attachment behavior system as becoming differentiated to some degree with each such model incorporated. This is a theory-language way of saying that, as we accumulate more relationships, our expectations about and behavior in subsequent ones are conditioned by those we have (had) already. In practice there are some differences about the precise way in which the concept of an attachment behavior system is used—for instance, Bowlby takes the view that the system is either switched on, with the resultant display of attachment behavior or, when a "set-goal" is reached, switched off. Bretherton (1980), however, prefers to ascribe a continuous monitoring function to the system. Such issues need not detain us here.

Two points must be stressed. First, a behavior system is seen as existing *in an individual.* We shall return to this point later. Second, the concept of behavior system is explanatory in nature—it belongs in the theory language of the system.

3: *Attachment.* This has been used to refer to "the affectional bond or tie that an infant forms between himself and his mother figure" (Ainsworth et al., 1978, p. 302). Attachment is inferred "from a stable propensity over time to seek proximity and contact with a specific figure" (p. 303). "Attachment" is thus a label for a relationship or for aspects of a relationship, assessed over a span of time. The aspects of behavior by which attachment is assessed are assumed to depend in large measure on changing patterns of activity in the attachment behavior system.

Though attachment can be categorized on the basis of constellations of attachment behavior, its strength cannot be assessed along a single dimension. Nor is it to be seen as an intervening variable whose value depends on the extent of the correlations between dependent variables. Rather it depends upon a variety of different but interrelated types of behavior. This last point has been emphasized previously by Sroufe and Waters (1977) and by Ainsworth and associates (1978).

Five other points must be made here.

1. "Attachment" refers to an aspect of interpersonal relationships. However, it will be apparent that the term is used in a narrower sense than in colloquial speech: Even given Bowlby's extension, attachment is limited to ties with an individual perceived as stronger and/or wiser. However, since adult-adult relationships are multifaceted and may serve diverse needs, the term may properly be applied to particular aspects of or contexts within a relationship—namely, to those in which one is behaving to the other as if he or she were stronger and/or wiser. Such an extension is made the more necessary by the evidence that grief, mourning, and its resolution in later life are related to the security of early attachments to parental figures (Bowlby, 1980; see Ainsworth, chapter 1 herein). It is, of course, possible for two adult participants in a relationship to be attached each to the other in this sense (e.g. Weiss, 1974, and chapter 9 herein).

2. Does "attachment" refer to an individual or a dyad? In studies of dyadic relationships, developmental psychologists have often been happy to label measures as either "baby measures" (e.g., frequency of crying) or "mother measures" (e.g., latency with which mother picks up baby after it starts crying). Ethologists (e.g., Hinde, 1974) and some child developmentalists (e.g., Dunn, 1977), on the other hand, have emphasized that measures of behavior within an ongoing relationship are likely to reflect the characteristics of *both* partners: Frequency of crying depends on the mother as well as the baby, and latency to pick up depends on the baby's past behavior as well as on the mother.

However, the emphasis in the concept of attachment is clearly on the infant. Reference is made to the tie that *the infant* forms and to a

65

stable propensity on behalf of *the infant*. It thus refers not to the mother-infant relationship as a whole but to the child's side of that relationship.

Now in general the properties of an interpersonal relationship are influenced by the personalities of the participants, and the personalities of the participants are determined in part by the relationships in which they are and have been involved. The influence of relationships on personality is presumably greater early on, but persists throughout life. We can picture this as an ongoing dialectic between personality and relationships (Hinde, 1979). The behavior shown within a relationship at any point in time is determined in part by the current characteristics of the individuals and in part by the nature of the relationship.

This is highly pertinent to assessments of attachment. Ainsworth's strange-situation technique for assessing attachment has led to important new findings. However, those who have used the technique have experienced a certain difficulty in specifying precisely what it is that is being measured. For example, Sroufe and Waters (1977, p. 1,191) regard the strange-situation test as giving a classification of "patterns of organization in the attachment behaviour of one year olds," and discuss the categories as categories of *infants*. Waters (1978) writes predominantly about assigning *infants* to categories, though he also refers to the procedure as assessing the quality of infant-mother *relationships* (p. 486). Ainsworth and associates (1978) refer to the strange situation as "a controlled laboratory procedure in which individual differences among infants could be highlighted" (p. xi); nevertheless, they also sometimes write of the procedure as assessing the infant-mother *relationship*. Which is the more correct interpretation?

Because in the strange-situation test parental behavior is controlled while the infant's behavior is free to vary and forms the basis for later categorizing, it would be easy to suppose that characteristics of the infant are being measured. But given the dialectic between personality and relationship, it seems more accurate to regard the test as intruding on the relationship at a particular point in time and assessing an aspect of that relationship from the infants' point of view. Indeed such a view is necessary to accommodate the finding that an infant may be categorized in one way with his mother but in another quite different way with his father (Main and Weston, 1981; Grossmann and Grossmann, 1981). Thus whether or not the particulars of parental behavior in the situation matter, the affective/cognitive consequences of parental presence do. This view is also in keeping with the finding that, while categorization in middle-class samples is stable over the twelve-to eighteen-month period, categorization in less privileged families can change with changes in maternal security (Vaughn et al., 1979).

This point has been labored only because the strange-situation technique appears to be such a potentially useful one. The difficulty in specifying precisely what is being measured lies not in the test itself but in the nature of things—relationships exist over time and continuously influence and are influenced by the characteristics of the participants. Two things follow. The first is that the attachment approach has exceptional potential for studying both the effects of individual characteristics on relationships and the effects of relationships on individual characteristics—a potential less obvious in the other sources of principles available for discussing the dynamics of relationships. For example, exchange and interdependence theories (e.g., Thibaut and Kelley, 1959; Kelley, 1979) can contribute greatly to the understanding of limited sequences of interactions but, unless coupled with a knowledge of the structure of behavior, they are unable to predict the influence of one action on the probability of other related actions, let alone on that of apparently unrelated ones. For instance how far can contact comfort compensate for stomach cramps? How far can status in the peer group substitute for love in a dyadic relationship? (cf. Foa and Foa, 1974). An attachment-type theory has the capacity for coming to terms with these issues of the relations between different types of behavior and of behavioral outcomes.

The second corollary is that the maternal side of the picture also demands urgent investigation. It is not adequate to accept the mother as a given, able to be influenced perhaps by pediatricians but virtually uninfluenced by the child. The mother influences, and is influenced by, the child's behavior. Interaction affects and modifies both the child's attachment system and maternal propensities.

3. Affective/cognitive aspects. While attachment is inferred from behavior, it carries implications about the affective states of the infant. Furthermore, as the infant becomes more sophisticated, the attachment behavior must be guided by cognitive structures in the form of "working models" of his attachment figures.

4. Description or explanation? As used in many contexts, "attachment" is a shorthand for certain behavioral observations. We observe that a child moves towards his mother, is distressed when she leaves the room, and so on, and describe all this by saying that he is attached. However, it is easy to go further and to regard the affective/cognitive concomitants of attachment as in some sense explanatory of the behav-

ior. Indeed Ainsworth and associates (1978) unreservedly give the concept an explanatory status: "It is further suggested that it is useful to view attachment—as a construct—as an inner organization of behavioural systems. . . ." (p. 303). These systems are seen as hierarchically organized. This usage would create difficulties, for an initially descriptive concept now is becoming part of the language of explanation, and dangers of confusion arise when concepts are allowed to straddle awkwardly between the domains of description and explanation. Instinct theorists learned this the hard way, and it would be wise to profit from their experience. Functional categories of behavior are not necessarily coextensive with causal ones (Beer, 1963 *a, b*; Beach, 1965), and the mechanisms underlying behavior are unlikely to be coextensive with the behavior as we describe it. Furthermore such a usage seems unnecessary, as we already have the theory-language concept of attachment behavior system.

5. Attachment is not all. While attachment in the sense used here is the crucial aspect of a young child's bond with his parents, as time goes on other aspects become important. While the mother's sensitivity and role in providing security is paramount, she also teaches the child, plays with him, becomes irritated with him, and interacts in many other ways. In studying attachment we must not neglect other aspects of the parent-child relationship that affect the child's developing personality—or indeed other relationships. As yet it is an open issue just what types of interaction contribute to "security" (Bretherton, 1980); these may change with a child's age.

Biological Considerations

Ainsworth (1979; Ainsworth et al., 1978) has provided considerable evidence that it is more desirable for an infant for his attachment with his mother to be classed as "secure" rather than "insecure" (i.e., Group B rather than Group A or C; see chapters 1 and 2). Such dyads have a more harmonious mother-infant relationship; the infants are more cooperative, cry less, spend more time in exploratory play, are more outgoing toward and cooperative with a moderately familiar adult, and subsequently show higher scores on a variety of problem-solving and socioaffective measures than infants in "insecure" dyads. Furthermore, in several independent studies in the United States of America and in

Italy, the securely attached category has been found to be more common than either of the others. Although these findings have not been replicated in all samples (e.g., Matas, Arendt, and Sroufe, 1978; Waters, Wippman, and Sroufe, 1979), the bulk of the evidence is compelling.

Ainsworth (1979) also argues that "securely attached" babies have "developed normally, i.e., along species-characteristic lines" (p. 45). Because all seems to go well with such babies, she takes them to represent the norm, and to be what nature intended. And because inter-mother differences are primary in determining the nature of the relationship, she regards infants as "pre-adapted" to mothers who are responsive, intervene promptly when the baby cries, and so on. It is *only* the biological aspects of this argument, with the implication of adaptation, that I wish to discuss: the evidence that it is preferable in the United States of America to be securely attached is overwhelming.

The matter is made the more urgent since Grossmann and Grossmann (1981) found that the securely attached category is relatively much less common in a sample from Bielefeldt, West Germany, than in samples from the United States of America. Although this finding is yet to be replicated, the possibility that "securely attached" is the modal category in one culture and "avoidant" in another raises a number of questions. Grossmann and Grossmann ask which pattern should be considered "species adaptive" and raise the possibility that a German child-rearing strategy somewhat different from that common in the United States could have led to a disturbance of mother-infant relationships. I emphasize the word "disturbance," because their discussion implies that the pattern in the United States of America is the norm.

Now an important aspect of Bowlby's (1969) theorizing concerned the concept of man's environment of evolutionary adaptedness—an environment where danger lurked, security lay in proximity to the mother, and anxiety over actual or threatened separation from her was adaptive. Accordingly he postulated an adaptive value for an attachment behavior system in the infant and for a complementary one in the mother.

That is absolutely fair enough if one is concerned, as Bowlby was, with the broad principles of mother-infant interaction. But that battle is now won: We are no longer concerned with broad principles but with the nature of individual differences between mother-infant relationships. And at this point it behooves us to be increasingly sophisticated in our biological theorizing. Here I shall make three basic assumptions, each a commonplace to biologists.

1. Natural selection operates primarily on individuals, favoring those who survive and reproduce. More strictly, it operates through gene survival, so that what is important is "inclusive fitness," assessed not just in terms of individual reproductive success but in terms of the success of all related individuals, appropriately devalued according to their degree of relatedness. Thus one would expect individuals to have some interest in the successful reproduction not only of their own offspring, but also, for example, of their siblings, to whom they are also more genetically similar than they are to individuals taken from the population at random (Hamilton, 1964).

2. A given character may be advantageous in some circumstances and disadvantageous in others. A gorgeous tail or large antlers may be useful socially but a handicap in encounters with predators.

3. All societies are complex and diverse. For example, in groups of monkeys the mother-infant relationship is affected by the presence of other individuals, the mother's dominance status, the mother's relationship with the male, and so on. Conversely, the presence of an infant affects the mother's relationship with other adults (Hinde and Spencer Booth, 1967; White and Hinde, 1975; Berman, 1978; Seyfarth, 1976). That even greater complexities occur within human families and other groups hardly needs saying.

Thus in considering primate social behavior, we must think not in terms of the adaptedness of particular responses or response systems given an ideal partner, but of the adaptedness of alternative complexes of behavioral responses in alternative social situations. Consider the familiar dominance hierarchy. It may be best to be at the top, because this brings better access to food and mates and thus ultimately better gene survival. But animals that find themselves to be subordinate do not spend all their time striving to be at the top. In general it is better for them to bide their time; it is possible that better circumstances will arise later. One must conclude that individuals are constructed so that given one set of circumstances, they will strive to be or remain dominant while, given another, they will behave as subordinates (Lack, 1954, 1966). Such issues are discussed in tems of "conditional strategies" (Maynard Smith, 1979).

Similar issues arise over maternal styles. Altmann (1980), contrasting "restrictive" with "laissez-faire" baboon mothers, points out that the former are likely to have infants which survive better in the early months, because they are less exposed to kidnapping, predation, and so on. However, such mishaps are less apt to happen to infants of high-status females than to those of low status. Furthermore, "restrictive" mothering leads to independence being achieved more slowly: A "laissez-faire" style could thus produce infants better able to survive if orphaned. It could be, therefore, that the balance would swing toward a laissez-faire style for higher-ranking mothers. On this view there is no best mothering style, for different styles are better in different circumstances, and natural selection would act to favor individuals with a range of potential styles from which they select appropriately.

Thus the picture of an environment of evolutionary adaptedness serves well enough as a first stage in our thinking. But as we go beyond that, we must accept that individuals differ and society is complex, and that mothers and babies will be programmed not simply to form one sort of relationship but a range of possible relationships according to circumstances. So we must be concerned not with normal mothers and deviant mothers but with a *range* of styles and a capacity to select appropriately between them.

At one level of approximation there are general properties of mothering necessary whatever the circumstances. At a more precise level, the optimal mothering behavior will differ according to the sex of the infant, its ordinal position in the family, the mother's social status, caregiving contributions from other family members, the state of physical resources, and so on. *Natural selection must surely have operated to produce conditional maternal strategies, not stereotypy.* The maternal sensitivity which Ainsworth so rightly emphasizes must take account of the child's (and the mother's own) needs in the context of the total social situation. (The argument so far, it may be repeated, is concerned with the mother's biological inclusive fitness, not with psychological well-being in mother or child. Yet the reader will note that in chapter 2 Main and Weston likewise imply that infants must employ alternative strategies to cope with those of their mothers.)

In the human case the issues are further complicated by the importance of norms. Parents try to create parent-child relationships of a type regarded as desirable in their culture, and also have expectations with regard to their relationships with each other and with outsiders. Often obligations and expectations conflict, so that none are fully realized. This is familiar enough to family therapists, but it does raise problems if we try to specify the characteristics of parents, or of parent-infant relationships, that are to be considered either biologically or psychologically optimal, because what is best must be assessed against the whole fabric of family, social group, and cultural beliefs in which mother and child are embedded. Thus it is not enough, as in the preceding paragraphs, to talk in terms of natural selection for conditional strategies, with mother and baby preprogrammed to switch in different styles in different circumstances. In practice learning intervenes—though the course of that learning may be predisposed to follow some directions and constrained from following others. These

71

constraints and predispositions may be species characteristic, or they may be acquired through previous learning—in the human case this is one of the crucial consequences of socialization in a particular culture.

In a hypothetical environment of evolutionary adaptedness those constraints and predispositions in the child would be such as to produce subsequently an adult who would create a mother-child relationship which would, through the dialectic with the (next generation) child's developing personality, produce an adult with maximal inclusive fitness (i.e., gene survival). But given the complexity and diversity of societies in the real world, the outcome of that dialectic will vary with the social situation, so that a mother-child relationship which produces successful adults in one situation may not do so in another. In any case, in human societies gene survival is not all, and the course of learning may be affected by cultural norms in such a way that individuals seek to become celibate priests or barren heroes. I would stress that I am not here entering the lists over the argument as to whether the propensities that create nonreproductive and/or altruistic individuals are in fact adaptive, or whether such individuals are the consequence of propensities adaptive in other contexts. Nor am I taking a position of cultural relativism, though it seems to be a fact that differences in mothering styles between cultures are related to cultural desiderata (e.g., Mead, 1934; Whiting and Whiting, 1975; Leiderman, Tulkin, and Rosenfeld, 1977), and this is a fact that must be acknowledged by child developmentalists. Nor, yet again, am I for a moment arguing against the view that babies securely attached to one or both parents are likely to grow up into happy, mentally healthy adults in our society. My only worry concerns the use of an argument *from natural selection theory* that any one mothering style is necessarily best (cf. Blurton Jones, 1976).

Let us return to the provisional finding that mother-infant dyads falling into the "anxiously attached" and "avoidant" categories, while relatively infrequent in the United States of America, are the most frequent in a German sample. A variety of differences in cultural values could be operating to produce this result. For instance, German mothers may value independence more than do mothers in the United States of America and, as Grossmann and Grossmann point out, they may be more controlling, seeking for "obedience" rather than "compliance." It may also be that, when mothers in the United States of America use disciplinary tactics, they do so erratically, being somewhat ashamed of infringing on the cultural norms, whereas the German mothers might be more consistent. While this is mere speculation, insofar as German mothers reflect aspects of their culture, their maternal behavior may provide a proper preparation for life in that culture.

Babies from dyads classed as avoidant by the criteria developed for samples in the United States of America may not necessarily have a less favorable outlook in Germany than babies from dyads classed as secure have in the United States of America. Thus we must consider the possibility that not only may the best mothering style vary with the situation, as argued earlier, but also the significance of the strange-situation categories, in terms of predictions for other situations, may not be absolute and biologically based but may, in fact, differ among cultures. While this seems improbable, the possibility must be evaluated against cross-cultural data.

We may now turn to a second issue which arises from the concept of the environment of evolutionary adaptedness—namely, the assumption that infant behavior and maternal behavior are adapted to mesh with each other (e.g., Bowlby, 1969, Ainsworth, 1979). Now studies of rhesus monkeys (e.g., Hinde, 1974) and a wide variety of other species indicate that the rate at which infants achieve independence is determined primarily by changes in the mothers; maternal behavior forces independence on the infant before it would otherwise take it. Trivers (1974) has in fact argued that a degree of parent-infant conflict is to be expected on the basis of the theory of natural selection. The mother-infant relationship benefits the mother (in terms of her inclusive fitness) through its effect on the survival of the current offspring, but brings costs by reducing her probability of rearing successfully future offspring and in reducing their potential reproductive success. Benefit to the infant lies in its own reproductive success, cost in the reduction in reproductive success of its unborn siblings (more remote relatives are ignored for present purposes). The costs to the mother of nursing increase with the age of the infant, and eventually come to exceed the benefit to that infant, so that the mother's long-term reproductive success will decrease if she continues to nurse. However, the cost to the mother will affect the infant's inclusive fitness only half as much as it affects the mother's, since only half their (rare) genes are shared. Thus until the cost to the mother is more than twice the benefit to the infant, the infant's overall fitness will continue to be higher if it nurses than if it does not. Thus there will be a period during which natural selection will favor the mother's halting maternal behavior and the infant's eliciting it.

Thus we must think not in terms of mother and infant being coadapted to an idyllic partnership, but in terms of each being adapted to further his or her own ends in the particular circumstances prevailing at the time. It is in the interest of the mother to reject the infant before it is in the interests of the infant to be independent. This means in turn that infants must be adapted to cope with mothers who wean them before they would otherwise prefer it, and to emerge from the relationship as individuals able to cope with the society into which they have been born. While Bowlby was correct in arguing that natural selection would favor protective mothers, it is equally necessary to emphasize that natural selection would favor mothers who promote their infant's independence, and that infants must be adapted to (and thus presumably flourish best with) such mothers. We must not use one side of the biological argument without paying attention also to the other.

Conclusion

The advances in the study of child development that have resulted from the study of attachment were made possible by Bowlby's ability to weld together different scientific approaches. It is argued here that this eclectic approach must be maintained. By using biological data, Bowlby was able successfully to argue that children have a natural propensity to maintain proximity with a mother figure. The biological approach can still be useful, but as studies of attachment become more sophisticated, so must the biological arguments to which they are related. Due attention must be paid to the view that natural selection is likely to favor an ability to select between alternative behavioral strategies and to the importance of parent-offspring conflict.

The biological bases of Bowlby's approach are apparent also in the concepts used to study attachment. Discussion of these has led to an emphasis on the importance of discriminating clearly between data- and theory-language. But it has also led to the view that the difficulty in specifying precisely what is measured by Ainsworth's strange-situation test is not a defect in the theory, but rather is inherent in the complex nature of the phenomena with which the technique was designed to cope. Indeed a focus on the reciprocal effects of personality on relationships and relationships on personality suggests that the study of attachment, with its emphasis on both structure and dynamics, has exceptional potential for unraveling some of the complex problems of personality development.

REFERENCES

Ainsworth, M. D. S. 1979. Attachment as related to mother-infant interaction. *Advances in the Study of Behaviour* 9:2–52.

————, Blehar, M. C.; Waters, E.; and Wall, S. 1978. *Patterns of attachment.* Hillsdale, N.J.: Lawrence Erlbaum Associates.

Altmann, J. 1980. *Baboon mothers and infants.* Cambridge, Mass: Harvard University Press.

Baerends, G. P. 1941. Fortpflanzungsverhalten und Orientierung der Grabwespe, *Ammophila campestris.* Jur Tijdschritr roor Entomologie 84:68–275.

————. 1976. The functional organisation of behaviour. *Animal Behaviour* 24:726–738.

Beach, F. A. 1965. *Sex and behavior.* New York: Wiley.

Beer, C. G. 1963a. Incubation and nestbuilding behaviour of black-headed gulls: III. The pre-laying period. *Behaviour* 21:13–77.

————. 1963b. Incubation and nestbuilding behaviour of black-headed gulls: IV. Nest-building in the laying and incubation periods. *Behaviour* 21:155–176.

Berman, C. M. 1978. Social relationships among free-ranging infant rhesus monkeys. Ph.D. dissertation, Cambridge University.

Bischof, N. 1975. A systems approach toward the functional connections of attachment and fear. *Child Development* 46(4):801–817.

Blurton Jones, N. G. 1976. Growing points in human ethology: Another link between ethology and the social sciences? In *Growing points in ethology,* ed. P. P. G. Bateson and R. A. Hinde. Cambridge: At the Cambridge University Press.

Bowlby, J. 1969. *Attachment and loss. Vol. 1: Attachment.* New York Basic Books.

————. 1977. The making and breaking of affectional bonds. *British Journal of Psychiatry* 130:201–210.

————. 1980. *Attachment and loss. Vol. 3: Loss.* New York: Basic Books.

Bretherton, I. 1980. Young children in stressful situations. In *Uprooting and development,* ed. G. V. Coelho and P. I. Ahmed. New York: Plenum Press.

Dawkins, R. 1976. Hierarchical organisation: A candidate principle for ethology. In *Growing points in ethology,* ed. P. P. G. Bateson and R. A. Hinde, Cambridge: At the University Press.

Dunn, J. 1977. Patterns of early interaction: Continuities and consequences. In *Studies in mother-infant interaction,* ed. H. R. Schaffer. London: Academic Press.

Estes, W. K.; Koch, S.; MacCorquodale, K.; Meehl, P. E.; Mueller, C. G., Jr.; Schoenfeld, W. N.; and Verplanck, W. S. 1954. *Modern learning theory.* New York: Appleton-Century-Crofts.

Foa, U. G., and Foa, E. B. 1974. *Societal structures of the mind.* Springfield, Ill.: Charles C Thomas.

Grossmann, K., and Grossmann, K. 1981. Parent-infant attachment relationships in Bielefeld. A research note. In *Behavioral development: The Bielefeld Interdisciplinary Project,* ed. K. Immelmann et al. New York: Cambridge University Press.

Hamilton, W. D. 1964. The genetical evolution of social behaviour. *Journal of Theoretical Biology.* 7:1–52.

Hinde, R. A. 1953. Appetitive behaviour, consummatory act, and the hierarchical organisation of behaviour—with special reference to the great tit (*Parus major*). *Behaviour* 5:189–224.

————. 1974. *Biological bases of human social behavior.* New York: McGraw-Hill.

————. 1979. *Towards understanding relationships.* London: Academic Press.

————, and Spencer Booth, Y. 1967. The effect of social companions on mother-infant relations in rhesus monkeys. In *Primate ethology*, ed. D. Morris. London: Weidenfeld and Nicolson.

Kelley, H. H. 1979. *Personal relationships: Their structures and processes*. Hillsdale, N.J.: Lawrence Erlbaum Associates.

Lack, D. 1954. *The natural regulation of animal numbers*. Oxford, Eng.: Clarendon Press.

_____. 1966. *Population studies of birds*. Oxford, Eng.: Clarendon Press.

Leiderman, P. H., Tulkin, S. R., and Rosenfeld, A. 1977. *Culture and infancy*. New York: Academic Press.

Main, M., and Weston, D. R. 1981. Security of attachment to mother and to father related to conflict behavior and the readiness to establish new relationships. *Child Development* (in press).

Matas, L., Arendt, R. A., and Sroufe, L. A. 1978. Continuity of adaptation in the second year: The relationship between quality of attachment and later competence. *Child Development* 49:547–556.

Maynard Smith, J. 1979. Games theory and the evolution of behaviour. *Proceedings of the Royal Society, Series B*. 205:475–488.

Mead, G. H. 1934. *Mind, self and society*. Chicago: University of Chicago Press.

Seyfarth, R. M. 1976. Social relationships among adult female baboons. *Animal Behaviour* 24:917–938.

Sroufe, L. A., and Waters, E. 1977. Attachment as an organizational construct. *Child Development* 48:1184–1199.

Thibaut, J. W., and Kelley, H. H. 1959. *The social psychology of groups*. New York: Wiley.

Tinbergen, N. 1951. *The study of instinct*. Oxford, Eng.: Clarendon Press.

Trivers, R. L. 1974. Parent-offspring conflict. *American Zoologist* 14:249–264.

Vaughn, B.; Egeland, B.; Sroufe, A.; and Waters, E. 1979. Individual differences in infant-mother attachment at twelve and eighteen months: Stability and change in families under stress. *Child Development* 50:971–975.

Waters, E. 1978. The reliability and stability of individual differences in infant-mother attachment. *Child Development* 49:483–494.

_____, Wippman, J., and Sroufe, L. A. 1979. Attachment, positive affect, and competence in the peer group: Two studies in construct validation. *Child Development* 50:601–914.

Weiss, R. S. 1974. The provisions of social relationships. In *Doing unto others*, ed. Z. Rubin. Englewood Cliffs, N.J.: Prentice-Hall.

White, L. E., and Hinde, R. A. 1975. Some factors affecting mother-infant relations in rhesus monkeys. *Animal Behaviour* 23:527–542.

Whiting, B. B., and Whiting, J. W. M. 1975. *Children of six cultures*. Cambridge, Mass.: Harvard University Press.

PART II

Problems in Parenting

4

Judith Trowell

EFFECTS OF OBSTETRIC
MANAGEMENT ON THE
MOTHER-CHILD RELATIONSHIP

THERE HAS BEEN widespread interest in the parent-child relationship, particularly its establishment and development in the child's early life. The importance of obstetric management and the early postnatal days has emerged as the mother-child relationship has been studied more intensively. This relationship is a two-way process. During this period the mother develops an affectional bond with her child, which can be seen in the quality and to a lesser extent quantity of her social interaction. Her practical caretaking is linked with her social interaction but can be relatively independent of it. The child meanwhile is developing an attachment to mother, and the development of both sides of the relationship alters and influences the child's progress.

In order to look at the mother-child relationship an expedient has to be adopted; for a study to be manageable, one can only look in depth at a limited area. Researchers such as Ainsworth and Main (chapters 1 and 2 herein) are studying the infant's attachment to either parent, while others such as Klaus and Kennell (1979) and Richards and Bernal (1972) are studying the parent's affectional bond to the infant. A cohesive theory needs to integrate all aspects of this work. From birth there is a "cascade of reciprocal interactions between mother and infant" (Klaus and Kennell, 1979, p. 75); we need to understand all parts of this process to be able to facilitate its healthy growth and development and to be able to intervene effectively when it has gone wrong.

Klaus and Kennell propose a "maternal sensitive period" very soon after birth as the optimal time for a mother to form an affectional bond with her baby. This is seen as distinct from the formation of an infant's attachment to the mother, which is thought to develop gradually over the first year. The term "sensitive period" has been used by different workers to mean different things, but in general it implies that "an individual's characteristics can be more strongly influenced by a given event at one stage of development than at other stages" (Bateson, 1979, p. 470). One aspect of a sensitive period is that it may be at a time of rapid reorganization, when a developing individual is more easily destablized by deprivation or environmental insult (Bateson, 1979). If a young woman having a baby, particularly her first child, is thought of as an individual undergoing developmental change from woman to mother, then the application of the term "sensitive period" becomes clearer.

Obstetric practice now uses a variety of highly technical procedures in an attempt to reduce perinatal morbidity and mortality and to maintain a low maternal mortality. Some of these procedures have been explored to see if they influence the developing mother-child relationship.

Effects of Maternal Medication on the Infant

Brackbill (1979) has reviewed the effects of medication given during obstetric procedures. Both meperidine (pethidine) and phenothiazines produce sedation in the mother, and the latter crosses the placental barrier and may sedate the infant as well. Studies on the effects of medication on the infant show that:

1. Drugs given to mothers during labor and delivery have subsequent effects on infant behavior as shown by behavioral degradation or disruption. No study has shown functional enhancement. Infant behavior studied has included motor coordination, habituation to auditory or visual stimuli, responsiveness to feeding, and autonomic responses.

80

2. The effects are closely related to dose, that is, the most substantial results are where mothers received high-potency drugs or a high total dose.

3. The behavioral effects are not transient. The ages stated range from one day to one year, and in this age range there is little evidence of a decrease of overall effect.

4. The effects are pronounced in certain functional areas, particularly cognitive function (such as visual fixation time between novel and familiar stimuli) and gross motor ability (such as sitting, standing, and walking).

There appears to be little doubt that medication given during labor and delivery does affect both mother and baby, at a time when they are establishing a relationship with each other.

Effects of Infant-Mother Separation on Mother and Child

Richards (1978) has reviewed the possible effects of early separation of mothers and babies in the first few days after birth, where the babies have been admitted to special care nurseries. In 1975 in England and Wales, 18.4 percent of all live births were admitted to a special care unit. De Chateau (1976) found that nonseparated mothers held newborns on their left arm, but if there was a separation of twenty-four hours or more than there was a right-sided preference and a decrease in body contact. One third of primiparas carry their babies in their hands rather than arms, but fifteen to twenty minutes of immediate postpartum naked contact between mother and baby eliminated hand carrying in favor of arm carrying. Whiten (1975) studied primiparous mothers at the John Radcliffe Maternity Hospital, Oxford, one group of whom had normal hospital contact from birth, the other had babies admitted to special care for two to fourteen days. There were differences between the groups until the child was two months of age. The normal, unseparated group showed more eye-to-eye contact between mother and baby, the mothers smiled more at the babies, and were more responsive to them. By three months there were no differences in social interaction, but at six months the separated mothers gave their child a toy (put it into the infant's hand) whereas the contact mothers presented a toy so that the infant had to reach and grasp it.

81

Problems in Parenting

Retrospective studies of conditions that may result from disturbed parent-child relationships show them to be more common after perinatal complications (mainly low birthweight) that have given rise to early separation. These include failure to thrive (Shaheen et al., 1968; Fanaroff, Kennell, and Klaus, 1972); nonaccidental injury;[1] and sudden infant death (Froggatt, Lynas, and Marshall, 1971; Fedrick, 1974). Until the etiology of sudden infant death is known, its relationship with early separation is difficult to interpret.

The physical and psychological environment affecting infants in special care units has also received attention. Powley (1976) has shown that when jaundiced newborns were kept lying on washable sheepskins while under a phototherapy lamp, overall movements did not change but vigorous movements and crying were reduced. She concluded that stress in the baby was reduced by using the sheepskins. Other studies have been carried out in which intervention was designed to increase the levels of patterned stimulation and environmental variation. In one study (Scarr-Salopatek and Williams, 1973) newborns were randomly assigned to a stimulation or a control group. All the babies were in special care for between four and thirty-seven days and weighed 1,300 to 1,800 grams. The staff had to provide what approximated to good home conditions for the sample group. Mobiles were placed in the incubator; the nurse rocked, talked to, fondled, and patted the babies; and the babies were taken out of the incubator to be fed. The control group was kept in the incubators with minimum disturbance. When they were more mature, the infants were placed in cots. The stimulation group continued to receive more attention from the staff while the control group continued to receive standard pediatric care.

In spite of random assignment the control group weighed slightly more, had less oxygen therapy, fewer perinatal infections, and at one week rated higher on the Brazelton scale (which measures the behavioral development of neonates). At four to six weeks babies in the stimulated group were gaining weight faster and had higher scores on the Brazelton scale. At one year the stimulated group scored ten points higher on the Cattell infant scale. However, this study was carried out in North America, where babies are generally handled much less in intensive care units than in other countries.

Other studies (Rice, 1977; Kramer and Pierpoint, 1976) look at stimu-

1. See Klein and Stern, 1971; Lynch 1975; Elmer and Gregg, 1967; Shaheen et al., 1968; Skinner and Castle, 1969; and Oliver et al., 1974.

lation groups where the babies were handled more or placed in incubators with a waterbed that mechanically rocked them while playing tapes of a woman's voice. In both studies the stimulated group gained more weight, and in Rice's study they had better scores on the Bayley developmental scale.

Effects of Early Infant-Mother Contact on Mother and Child

Realization of the effects of admission to special care on infants and mothers led to further studies of the possible effects of hospital practices for normal full-term infants and their mothers. Klaus and associates (1972) studied primiparous mothers and their normal full-term infants. The control group had the usual hospital contact with their babies, the experimental group had one hour's contact with their naked baby straight after birth, plus five extra hours of contact each day for three days (sixteen hours of extra contact). The significant differences were that at one month the extra-contact mothers stood near their infants and watched during physical examination of their baby and showed more soothing behavior. These same mothers had more eye contact and fondled their babies more during feeding and were more reluctant to leave their infants with someone else. At one year the extra-contact mothers spent more time helping the physician during physical examination and soothing their infants when they cried. At two years linguistic behavior was compared in five experimental versus five control mother-child dyads. The extra-contact mothers used twice as many questions, more words per proposition, fewer content words, more adjectives, and fewer commands than the control mothers (Ringler et al., 1975). At five years of age the extra-contact children had significantly higher IQ scores (Stanford-Binet) and better scores on a receptive language test and tests of comprehension.

Klaus and Kennell (1970) had previously followed up low-birthweight infants who received extra contact and compared them with low-birthweight infants who had not. The extra-contact mothers cuddled and held their babies more, but differences disappeared one month after discharge from hospital. However, at follow-up at forty-two months the extra-contact group had significantly higher IQs than the controls (Klaus and Kennell, 1976).

Hales and associates (1977) studied Guatemalan primiparous mothers and babies. The sample group received forty-five minutes of skin-to-skin contact immediately after birth, one control group received forty-five minutes of skin-to-skin contact twelve hours after birth, and the other control group had no skin-to-skin contact. The mothers and babies were observed at thirty-six hours, and the sample group showed significant differences from the others. The sample mothers showed more eye-to-eye contact (*en face*), more fondling, caressing, kissing, looking at, smiling at, and talking to their baby.

De Chateau and Wiberg (1977) studied early-contact mothers given thirty minutes of skin-to-skin contact with their babies as soon as possible after birth. At three months postpartum the early-contact mothers spent significantly more time *en face* with and kissing their babies. The control mothers spent more time cleaning their babies. The early-contact infants cried less, smiled and laughed more than the infants of control mothers.

O'Connor and associates (1977) carried out a double-blind study involving 301 low-income primiparous women randomly assigned to either rooming-in or control postpartum beds. The control mothers were with their babies for thirty minutes at each four-hourly feed for the first two postpartum days while the rooming-in mothers had an extra six hours per day with their babies. The children were followed up until twenty-one months. Significantly more control children were admitted to the hospital for parenting disorders such as nonorganic failure to thrive, abuse, neglect, or abandonment leading to foster care, although all the children had had similar acute illnesses and visits to doctors.

Finally, work has been done on the link between contact early postpartum and the initiation and length of breast feeding. In Guatemala Sosa and associates (1976) studied poor primiparous women randomly assigned to two groups receiving either skin-to-skin contact for forty-five minutes immediately after birth or routine care. The mothers and babies were visited at home up to a year postpartum. Three different hospitals were involved, each having a control and an early-contact group. In two of the three hospital samples the percentage of mothers who successfully breast fed their infants was greater in the group given early contact. De Chateau and Wiberg (1977) showed that 58 percent of early-contact mothers and 26 percent of control mothers were breast feeding at three months. The early-contact mothers breast fed to a mean of two months longer than the controls.

Effects of Cesarian Section on Mother and Child

My own study arose from an awareness of difficulties experienced by mothers admitted with their babies to a mother and baby unit. The difficulties seemed particularly intractable when the mother had been delivered by cesarian section. This is particularly relevant in view of the rising rate of cesarian sections. In the United States the national rate has risen from 5 percent of all deliveries in 1968 to 11.4 percent in 1976 (Marieskind, 1978).

A group of mothers and babies delivered by emergency cesarian section were compared with a control group of mothers and babies delivered by normal spontaneous vaginal delivery (Trowell, unpublished manuscript). The criteria for inclusion were that the mothers were all primigravida between twenty and thirty years of age with no known previous conceptions. Only those who lived with the child's father in their own home were included, hence there was a predominance of mothers from upper and middle social classes. There was a small number of unplanned pregnancies in both groups. The children were delivered between thirty-eight and forty-two weeks of gestation, were

TABLE 4-1
Reason for Admission to Hospital

	Cesarian Section $n = 16$	Control $n = 18$
In labor (contractions)	1	13
Membranes ruptured	3	5
For induction	12	—
Reason for Cesarian Section		
Fetal Distress (on monitor)	4	
Prolonged Labor Fetal Distress	5	
Prolonged Labor	5	
Prolonged Labor with Suspected Cephalopelvic Disproportion	2	

85

over 2,500 grams at birth, and were normal healthy babies. The total group consisted of thirty-four mother-child couples, matched for child's sex and social class. The mothers were seen briefly in the obstetric unit and then the mothers and children were seen in their homes at one month and again at one year after delivery. The mother was interviewed and mother and child observed, recording social interaction and caretaking behavior. The children are now three years old and the final follow-up is being carried out.

All the mothers received medication during labor. The normal group was given gas, air, meperidine (pethidine), and the cesarian group all had their operation under general anesthesia, had received oxytocin intravenously as well as meperidine (pethidine) or epidural anesthesia, or both. In addition 67 percent of the control group and 44 percent of the cesarian group received tranquilizers. While it is not possible to give the results in detail, some of the statistically significant results will be reported (in all of which $p < .05$ using two-tailed chi square tests).

The length of labor for the cesarian group was significantly longer than for the control group; the time when the cesarian mothers recollected first seeing their baby, as distinct from when the mothers were actually shown their babies, was highly significantly longer (mean nineteen hours compared with forty-seven minutes). However, there was no difference between the groups in their recollected feelings on initial contact with their baby. Indifference or disappointment was most commonly reported.

The cesarian babies were significantly heavier, longer, and with greater head circumference at birth than the controls. They remained heavier at one month and one year. Comparing the date of delivery with the expected date of delivery (EDD), the mean for the cesarian group was EDD plus three days whereas the mean for the control group was EDD minus three days. Most of the control group mothers were admitted in labor, while the cesarian mothers were most often admitted for induction. There was no intergroup difference in babies' Apgar scores and the Brazelton initial and predominant state, probably due to the medication all the mothers received (Rosenblatt et al., 1979). The Apgar score uses five signs that are noted one minute after birth and give an indication of the need for resuscitation, heart rate, respiratory effort, muscle tone, color, and response to stimuli. None of the babies needed admission to the special care unit.

In their interaction at one month the mothers and children in the cesarian group showed highly significantly less eye-to-eye contact than the control group. This is especially relevant in view of the work of Robson (1967) and others of the importance of eye-to-eye contact in the establishment and growth of a mother's relationship with her baby. Robson thinks that it is specifically the contact when *en face* between the eyes of the mother and the infant that releases strong positive feelings in the mother. Klaus and Kennell (1976) have confirmed the importance of eye-to-eye contact in the development of maternal affectional bonding. Fraiberg (1974) studied mothers with blind infants who felt detached and distant from their babies until they had learned other means of communication.

The cesarian mothers were more critical in their attitudes to the pregnancy and birth in the interview one month after the birth; they also expressed more anxiety and apprehension about parenthood and its responsibilities even though before giving birth they had had more experience of other mothers' newborns.

One month after the birth there was more depression, resentment of the fathers, and anxiety with somatic symptoms in the cesarian group of mothers although in both groups there was evidence of mild depression as indicated by mood only. The symptoms included lack of energy, loss of appetite, and sleep disturbances over and above the demands of the baby. The cesarian mothers had high expectations of parenthood but, almost inevitably, reality was a disappointment. In practical ways they were less competent caretakers.

One year after the birth the cesarian mothers generally complained more about their child than the control group, and they thought they had experienced more problems with the child and themselves during the year. Overall motherhood had been more work and less pleasurable than expected, and they reported that they often let their child cry up to five minutes or more before responding, whereas the control group reported usually responding in two minutes.

Each mother in the control group saw her baby as a person at birth or very soon afterward, whereas the cesarian mothers stated that their babies became people and could recognize them at a later time (this was in response to the questions "When did you think your baby developed into a human person?" and "When did you think your baby recognized you as its mother?"). If this is linked with the much later recollection of first contact and the much reduced eye-to-eye contact at one month, a picture begins to emerge of a group of women delivered by cesarian section who had difficulties from the start of their baby's life. These women had the distress, crisis, and sense of failure produced by an emergency cesarian section (they had been admitted to the hospital expecting a normal vaginal delivery), their labors were longer, and they had more medication before and after delivery and were unconscious at the time of delivery. As a group they appear to have suffered a period of amnesia after the birth and then to have had to start a relationship while they themselves were suffering from the effects of major abdominal surgery. As a total group the cesarian and control mothers shared initial indifference and mild depressed mood at one month; however, the cesarian mothers were less able to compensate and they had less positive affective contact with their babies, whom they saw as nonpersons for longer than did the controls.

At one year the cesarian mothers kissed their children more than the control group of mothers during the observation period. But in play the control group mothers initiated more activities with their children, produced toys, and encouraged their child.

At one year of age the children and their mothers came to the clinic for the Ainsworth strange-situation test. The Ainsworth classification showed no intergroup differences. The results were Group A (avoidant attachment) 21 percent, Group B (secure attachment) 65 percent, and Group C (ambivalent attachment) 14 percent. During the strange-situation test the cesarian group of mothers and children had more interactions in total than the control group, which when subdivided consisted of more distance interactions (e.g., looking) than contact interactions (e.g., touching). Also the cesarian mothers initiated more interactions with their one-year-olds than the control mothers despite the fact that mothers had been asked to sit quietly and respond appropriately to the child when he initiated interactions but not to initiate interaction themselves.

The development of a child depends on the establishment of synchrony between mother and baby. Studies (e.g., Brazelton et al., 1975) have shown that where the mother responds inappropriately, the child can become confused; or where the mother is insensitive and either bombards the child with initiations or ignores the child, failing to respond to his interactions, the rhythmic reciprocity of a good mother-child relationship is not established. Hyman and Parr (1978) have shown in their modified strange-situation test with abused and control infants that child-abusing mothers initiate more interactions than control mothers where the child is male, and their style involves a generally less reciprocal manner of interaction. It seems that the cesarian mothers needed to initiate interaction rather than it being a part of a sensitive reciprocal relationship, that the mothers responded to their own needs rather than remaining sensitive to their child.

It appears that my sample of women delivered by emergency cesarian section are a particular group; they probably are different from those delivered by elective cesarian and perhaps also from those delivered by emergency cesarian for an absolute medical criterion such as antepartum hemorrhage. But they all share an experience of being delivered while unconscious, by the abdominal route. If a mother is preoccupied with her own body and her own emotional state, she is less available to her baby, less responsive, less sensitive, less adaptable. Her affective energy is directed toward herself and she is not free to embark on a relationship with her baby. She may not perceive the baby as a person for some time and may not be able to engage with her child, as shown by the reduced eye-to-eye contact.

The early period of sedation with subsequent amnesia experienced by the cesarian mothers may be an important factor contributing to the difficulties they experienced in establishing a relationship with their child. Most of the normal control mothers perceived their babies shortly after delivery, and only one took some hours to become aware of her baby. Nearly all the cesarian mothers were unaware of their baby when the child was shown to them on regaining consciousness; for most it was many hours (average nineteen hours) before they perceived their child. The cause of the amnesia needs further investigation. It is likely to be due in part to the medication given, in part to the separation caused by the period of unconsciousness, and in part as a defense against anxiety.

General Conclusions

My cesarian group of mothers appear to have had difficulties in the initiation and development of relationships with their babies. Perhaps they missed the optimum period for this to happen, even though such relationships can and do develop later. A "sensitive period" (Bateson, 1979) is a time of rapid reorganization. It is the outcome of interactions between a number of different factors, such as developmental age and experience. It may result in the narrowing of preferences, and the end of sensitivity may arise not so much through lack of capacity to learn as through a lack of willingness.

The implications of this for young women having a baby is striking. During labor, delivery, and the early postnatal days, new mothers (and fathers) pass through a period of emotional upheaval. At this time they are at their most open, most available emotionally, ready to embark on the new relationship. If this time is lost the relationship may be established more slowly and with more difficulty.

But as well as trying to increase our understanding of individual items, we need to be aware of the changed background that now surrounds the whole area of childbirth. There have been massive social, psychological, cultural, and political changes as described by Cartwright (1979) and Oakley (1980). Who holds power and where control lies has become a central issue; who "manages" has become a key point of contention. Mothers' and to a lesser extent fathers' loss of control over the mother's body and the takeover by midwives and doctors who now manage childbirth rather than assist at it has had profound effects.

It needs to be constantly borne in mind that childbirth is a major life event. My data suggest that it is characteristic of childbirth today for women to feel they have lost something rather than simply gained a child. They have lost a job, a life style, an intact couple relationship, control over their own body, and/or a sense of self. Male attitudes and characteristics continue to be valued and the fragility of women's self-esteem, the doubt that women can control their own lives, heightens their vulnerability to the stress of life events. It is all too easy for childbirth to be yet another trauma.

It must also be understood that how women feel about their childbirths is not the same as how they feel about their babies, and neither of these is coterminous with their attitudes to the social role of mother (Oakley, 1980). Men and women are uncertain about their roles as partners and as parents; to their role they bring their own hopes, fears, and anxieties. Comments about individual procedures must be seen against the background of the individual and of society as it is at present. For example, a familiar midwife giving meperidine (pethidine) to a woman who has asked for it and is delivering in her own home is a different situation from one in which the same drug is being given routinely as part of a set procedure in hospital.

In my study I looked in depth at the development of the mother's affectional bond with her baby and her caretaking behavior. I did this by using the ethological tool of observing the interaction and then carrying out a semistructured interview with the mother. In addition to repeating this at one year, I also carried out the Ainsworth strange-situation test to look at the infant's attachment to mother.

The results of combining these two lines of investigation leads me to suggest that to study an infant's attachment to mother without also looking at mother's background and her obstetric history means that crucial factors influencing an infant's attachment will be missed. Similarly, to study a mother's affectional bonding with her infant without looking at individual differences in the babies and their attachment could also be misleading. In order to draw conclusions about ways of formulating the development and growth of the mother-child relationship and intervening effectively when it has gone wrong, one needs to be aware of the circular nature of the process.

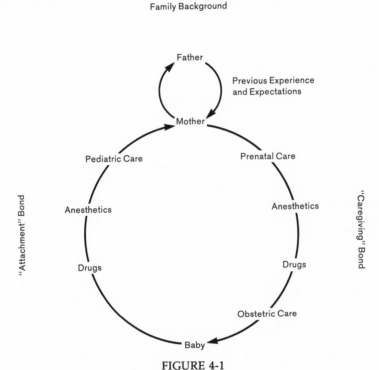

FIGURE 4-1

Immediate Influences on the Developing Relationship between Mother and First Child

Obstetric management should be concerned with facilitating the establishment of the mother-child relationship at all stages. The research reviewed here suggests a number of ways in which this could be done. During the pregnancy couples identified as likely to have emotional difficulties in coping with parenthood could be given help, for instance at prenatal groups. During labor drugs should be kept to a minimum and anxiety relieved by imparting knowledge of what is happening. Pain is likely to be less frightening and more bearable in the presence of a familiar staff member and an attachment figure.

All obstetric procedures tend to produce anxiety, but this can be reduced if the mothers participate as much as possible. If time is spent discussing the procedures and the mother's emotional reaction afterward, the mother can then be free to engage with her baby rather than remain preoccupied with herself. It is important that mothers and babies spend as much time together as possible after the birth. On the postnatal ward they should be together all the time; if the baby must be in a special care unit, then the mother should be there too, caring for her baby.

When new mothers go home they continue to need encouragement and support while they and their babies consolidate the relationship they have begun to establish. The emotional and psychological well-being of mother and baby are as important and need as much attention on the part of obstetric management as does their physical well-being.

REFERENCES

Ainsworth, M. D. S., and Bell, S. M. 1970. Attachment exploration and separation: Illustrated by the behaviour of one-year-olds in a strange situation. *Child Development* 41:49–67.

Apgar, V. 1953. A proposal for a new method of evaluation of the newborn infant. *Current Researches in Anaesthesia and Analgesia* 32:260.

Bateson, P. 1979. How do sensitive periods arise and what are they for? *Animal Behaviour* 27(2):470–486.

Brackbill, Y. 1979. Obstetrical medication and infant behavior. In *The handbook of infant development*, ed. J. Osofsky. New York: Wiley.

Brazelton, T. B. 1974. *Neonatal behavioural assessment scale*. London: S.I.M.P./Heinemann Medical Books.

————; Tronich, E.; Adamson, L.; Als, H.; and Wise, S. 1975. Early mother-infant reciprocity. In *Ciba Foundation Symposium 33, Parent-Infant Interaction*. Amsterdam, Holland: Amsterdam Associated Scientific Publishers.

Cartwright, A. 1979. *The dignity of labour?* London: Tavistock.

De Chateau, P. 1976. *Neonatal care routine: Influences on maternal and infant behaviour and on breast feeding*. Umea, Sweden: Umea University Medical Dissertations.

————, and Wiberg, B. 1977. Long-term effect on mother-infant behaviour of extra contact during the first hour post partum. First observations at 36 hours. *Acta Paediatrica Scandinavica* 66:145–151.

Elmer, E. and Gregg, G. S. 1967. Developmental characteristics of abused children. *Paediatrics* 40:596–602.

Fanaroff, A., Kennell, J. H., and Klaus, M. H. 1972. Follow-up of low birthweight infants—the predictive value of maternal visiting patterns. *Paediatrics* 49:287–290.

Fedrick, J. 1974. Sudden unexpected death in infants in the Oxford Record Linkage Area. *British Journal of Preventive and Social Medicine* 28:164–171.

Fraiberg, S. H. 1974. Blind infants and their mothers: An examination of the sign system. In *The effect of the infant on its caregiver*, ed. M. Lewis and L. A. Rosenblum. New York: Wiley.

Froggatt, P., Lynas, M. A., and Marshall, T. K. 1971. Sudden unexpected death in infants ("cot death"). Report of a collaborative study in Northern Ireland. *Ulster Medical Journal* 40:116–135.

Hales, D. J.; Lozoff, B.; Sosa, R.; and Kennell, J. H. 1977. Defining the limits of the maternal sensitive period. *Developmental Medicine and Child Neurology* 19:454–461.

Hyman, C. A., and Parr, R. 1978. A controlled video observational study of abused children. *Child Abuse and Neglect* 2:217–222.

Klaus, M. H.; Jerauld, R.; Kreger, N. C.; McAlpine, W.; Steffa, M.; and Kennell, J. H. 1972. Maternal attachment: Importance of the first post-partum days. *New England Journal of Medicine* 286:460–463.

Klaus, M. H., and Kennell, J. H. 1970. Mothers separated from their newborn infant. *Pediatric Clinics of North America* 17:1015–1037.

————. 1976. *Maternal infant bonding: The impact of early separation and loss on family development.* St. Louis: C. V. Mosby.

————. 1979. Early mother-infant contact. *Bulletin of the Menninger Clinic* 43:69–78.

Klein, M., and Stern, L. 1971. Low birthweight and the battered child syndrome. *American Journal of Diseases of Children* 122:15–18.

Kramer, L. I., and Pierpont, M. E. 1976. Rocking waterbeds and auditory stimuli to enhance growth of preterm infants. *Journal of Pediatrics* 88:297–299.

Lynch, M. A. 1975. Ill-health and child abuse. *Lancet* 2:317–319.

Marieskind, H. 1978. Evaluation of a cesarian section rate in the U.S.A. Summary of findings in a year's study for the U.S. Government. Paper presented to the American Public Health Association, 17 October 1978.

Oakley, A. 1980. *Women confined.* Oxford, Eng.: Martin Robertson.

O'Connor, S. W.; Vietze, P. M.; Hopkins, J. B.; and Altemeier, W. A. 1977. Post-partum extended maternal-infant contact: Subsequent mothering and child health. *Pediatric Research* 11:380.

Oliver, J. E.; Cox, J.; Taylor, A.; and Baldwin, J. A. 1974. *Severely ill treated young children in North East Wiltshire.* Oxford, Eng.: Oxford University Unit of Clinical Epidemiology.

Powley, M. 1976. Use of baby care lambskins with phototherapy babies. Student project. New Zealand: University of Otago.

Rice, R. D. 1977. Neurophysiological development in premature infants following stimulation. *Developmental Psychology* 13:69–76.

Richards, M. P. M. 1978. Possible effects of early separation in later development of children. Reviewed in *Separation and special care baby units*, ed. F. S. W. Brimblecombe, M. P. M. Richards, and N. R. C. Roberton. London: Heinemann Medical Books.

————, and Bernal, J. B. 1972. An observational study of mother-infant interaction. In *Ethological studies of child behaviour*, ed. Blurton-Jones. Cambridge, Eng.: Cambridge University Press.

Ringler, N. M., Kennell, J. H.; Jarvella, R.; Navojosky, B. J.; and Klaus, M. H. 1975. Mother-to-child speech at 2 years: Effects of early postnatal contact. *Journal of Pediatrics* 86:141–144.

Robson, K. S. 1967. The role of eye-to-eye contact in maternal-infant attachment. *Journal of Child Psychology and Child Psychiatry and Allied Disciplines* 8:13–25.

Rosenblatt, D.; Redshaw, M.; Packer, M.; and Lieberman, B. 1979. Drugs, birth and infant behaviour. *New Scientist*, 15 February 1979.

Scarr-Salopatek, S., and Williams, M. L. 1973. The effects of early stimulation program for low birth weight infants. *Child Development* 44:94–100.

Shaheen, E.; Alexander, D.; Truskowsky, M.; and Barbero, G. J. 1968. Failure to thrive—a retrospective profile. *Clinical Pediatrics* 7:255–261.

Skinner, A., and Castle, R. 1969. *Seventy-eight battered children: A retrospective study.* London: National Society for the Prevention of Cruelty to Children.

Sosa, R.; Klaus, M.; Kennell, J. H.; and Urrutia, J. J. 1976. The effect of early mother-infant contact on breast feeding, infection and growth. In *Breast feeding and the mother,* Ciba Foundation Symposium 45 (new series), Amsterdam, Holland: Elsevier.

Trowell, J. A. Unpublished manuscript. The effects of obstetric management on the mother/child relationship. A pilot study of emergency cesarian section.

Whiten, A. 1975. Assessing the defects of perinatal events on the success of the mother-infant relationship. In *Studies in mother-infant interaction. Proceedings of the Loch Lomond Symposium 1975,* ed. H. R. Schaffer. London: Academic Press.

5

Pauline P. DeLozier

ATTACHMENT THEORY AND CHILD ABUSE

ABUNDANT RESEARCH and clinical literature, particularly within the last decade, has revealed characteristics of abusing parents and abused children that fit the pattern of attachment disorders derived from attachment theory. Perhaps the most consistent finding is that child abuse follows a generational pattern. Fontana (1973) states: "the most constant fact is that the parents themselves were nearly always abused or battered or neglected as children" (p. 74). Steele and Pollack (1968; Steele, 1975a, b) found a pattern of three generations of abuse in some families and neglect and abuse in at least two generations of almost all families studied. The contention that abusing parents were generally abused themselves as children has been noted in numerous other studies and reviews of the literature.[1] Steele (1976) states: "We see an unbroken line of the repetition of parental abuse from childhood into adult years" (p. 15). In a review of the literature, at least one author (Jayaratne, 1977) raises questions regarding the nature of the generational phenomenon. He points to the confusion in the literature between actual physical abuse and emotional abuse in the parents'

The study reported in this chapter was conducted as doctoral dissertation research at the California School of Professional Psychology, Los Angeles. Acknowledgments go to committee members: the late Dr. Estelle Parness, Dr. Seymour Zelen, and Dr. Karl Pottharst.

1. See Ebeling and Hill, 1975; Gelles, 1973; Green, 1973; Helfer, 1973; Helfer and Kempe, 1974; Parke and Collmer, 1975; Paulson and Chaleff, 1973; Schneider, Helfer, and Pollack, 1972; Silver, 1968; Silver et al, 1969; Solomon, 1973; and Spinetta and Rigler, 1972.

background and, furthermore, to the dearth of findings that compare abusing parents with normal groups. Nevertheless, there seems to be convincing evidence for the probable transmission of disturbed patterns of parenting within child-abusing families.

In addition to the generational pattern, a specific constellation of characteristics of child-abusing parents has emerged in the literature. Research has shown abusive parents to be isolated and distrustful, viewing the environment as hostile, and unable or unwilling to form and maintain close relationships with others.[2] Generally, in the literature abusive parents have appeared to be isolated, impulsive, and "immature" (Fontana, 1971, 1973; Merrill, 1962; Paulson and Chaleff, 1973; Steele, 1975a, b). Depression or a depressive tendency, intense anger, and intense anxiety have been found consistently among this population. Steele (1970), reporting on a study of sixty families, found "an almost universal presence among abusing parents of some degree of depression, either overt or latent" (p. 450). Johnson and Morse (1968) reviewed 101 cases of physical abuse in Denver and described the abusers as hostile, depressive, impulsive, and anxious. Others have agreed with these findings (Ebeling and Hill, 1975; Galdston, 1965; Steele and Pollack, 1968). While the pattern of depression, anxiety, and anger may, to some extent, be in response to identification, it is at least possible that depressive and anxious features in these parents are longstanding.

Exceptionally strong "dependency needs" have been another frequently cited factor among child abusers.[3] Apparent helplessness, ambivalence, inability to make decisions, sensitivity to criticism, and low self-esteem have been noted, along with inappropriate demands for love and care. Yet these parents are, at the same time, unable to turn to others for genuine assistance because they have, according to some experts, learned early in childhood that their needs will not be met. Thus some parents appear as "pseudo-independent." At the same time, however, abusing parents are described as inverting the usual parent-child relationship and inappropriately seeking caretaking from their child (role reversal). This phenomenon has been held to arise from the parents' unsatisfied need for nurturance.

2. See Davoren, 1975; Fontana, 1973; Helfer, 1973, 1976; Paulson and Chaleff, 1973; Schneider, Helfer, and Pollack, 1972; Solomon, 1973; Steele, 1975a, b; Steele and Pollack, 1968.
3. See Ebeling and Hill, 1975; Green, 1973; Helfer, 1973; Holter and Friedman, 1968; Melnick and Hurley, 1969; Steele, 1970, 1975a, b; and Steele and Pollack, 1968.

Some authors[4] propose lack of adequate parenting (with or without actual abuse) as the crucial factor in the backgrounds of abusing parents. This view is closely related to the generational hypothesis. In 1968 Steele and Pollack, in their five-and-one-half-year study of sixty abusing families, found a "disruption of the maternal affectional system"—a "deprivation of basic mothering" leading to a lack of the sense of being cared for and about (p. 98). Since the parents, as children, never had had their own needs met, they were unable to meet the needs of their offspring. This reported breakdown occurred not in the mechanical sense, but in "motherliness," which involves sensitive, empathic interaction with the child. Numerous others have agreed with this finding (Green, 1973; Helfer, 1973, 1976; Justice and Justice, 1976; Paulson and Chaleff, 1973). Thus abusive parents appear not to have experienced adequate caretaking as children.

Various stress factors have been noted as important to the etiology of abuse. Environmental stress, such as unemployment or poverty, or circumstances related to individual parents, such as early marriages, or to individual children, such as prematurity or illness of the child, have been considered as relevant (see review of literature in DeLozier, 1979). However, not all or even the majority of families that fit any of these categories are abusive. Most premature babies are not abused, most teenage parents are not abusers, and so forth. While these variables may be relevant, they are not sufficient.

Last, the clinical and research information regarding abused children, although much less extensive than that regarding their parents, reflects many characteristics similar to those found in the adult abusive population. Abused children have been described throughout the literature as depressed, dependent, angry, anxious, and handicapped in their ability to form and maintain relationships with peers or with caretakers. Martin (1972, 1975, 1976; Martin et al., 1974) has provided the most comprehensive investigation of abused children. Martin (1972) reported on forty-two abused children seen for a period of three years. He noted that only a low percentage were difficult from birth (7 percent) and that, although 43 percent showed neurological damage after abuse, there was little evidence of damage or retardation before abuse. He described abused children as unusually empathic with adults, but superficial in these relationships, reluctant to trust, and excessively seeking of approval.

4. Most notable among these are Green, 1973; Helfer, 1976; Helfer and Kempe, 1976; Kempe and Helfer, 1972; Steele, 1975a, b; and Steele and Pollack, 1968.

Martin further discussed four characteristics related to adaptation to danger exhibited by abused children. These are (1) danger orientation, (2) visual and auditory hyperalertness, (3) use of avoidance and denial, and (4) hypertrophied ego functions (pp. 107–108). Furthermore, Martin reported on a study of fifty-nine abused children (at mean age of 4.5 years after abuse) and stated that on intelligence testing with the Wechsler Intelligence Scale for Children (WISC) and Wechsler Preschool and Primary Scale of Intelligence (WPPSI), these children had generally achieved their highest subtest scores on Picture Completion and Similarities subtests. Martin suggested that "perhaps the necessity for abused children to become sensitive to environmental cues in order to avoid punishment has helped them to develop skills of observation, categorization, and association of visual and verbal cues" (p. 58).

In addition to the role reversal seen in abused children—their extraordinary sensitivity to the needs of parents (Ebeling and Hill, 1975; Helfer, 1976)—these children have been noted to display a particular behavior called "frozen watchfulness" (Ounsted, Oppenheimer, and Lindsay, 1975). The behavior involves silence, extraordinary stillness, and a fixed gaze, even if in a painful situation. Ounsted interprets this behavior also as related to the need to avoid punishment. He states: "Frozen watchfulness we see as an adaptation to unpredictable behavior by the loving and loved parent who, without provocation, becomes transformed into an aggressor and then immediately reverts to good parental behavior" (p. 34).

According to attachment theory, the hyperalert behaviors noted in the state of frozen watchfulness are characteristically present when there is warning that the risk of danger is increased and when either (1) enough information has not been received to warrant action or (2) the individual is unable to increase proximity to an attachment figure and/or reduce proximity to the source of danger (Bowlby, 1973). In abusing families, when a parent becomes abusive, danger does increase, and the child is unable to take corrective action because of the conflicting tendencies to (1) approach the attachment figure and (2) avoid the source of danger. Furthermore, abused children frequently cling to abusive parents, despite pain and fear, and they seem fearful of changes (Ebeling and Hill, 1975). This behavior is also consistent with the increase in attachment behavior associated with an increase in danger.

Finally, the observational research by George and Main (1979 and chapter 2 herein) suggests that the social behavior of abused toddlers differs from that of normal children. In their study the abused one- to three-year-olds exhibited a higher frequency of aggressive behavior directed toward both peers and caregivers coupled with a tendency toward avoidant or overly cautious behavior with caregivers, especially in response to friendly signals.

Thus, there emerges a picture of the abused child as: (1) a "special" child who interacts differently with caretakers than do other children; (2) a child especially sensitive to the environment while simultaneously seeming not to interact with it; (3) a child who is frequently described as dependent and depressed; and (4) a child who shows difficulty in trusting people. The picture seems to have parallels with the constellation of behaviors seen in abusing parents, and behaviors of both parent and child appear understandable from an attachment theory framework.

Attachment and Child Abuse

It is proposed that the constellation of "dependent," fearful, anxious, hostile, and depressed behavior consistently found in abusing families, as well as parent-child role reversal and the generational pattern of abuse, reflects dysfunctional attachment and caretaking behavioral systems in these families. The descriptions in the literature can be seen as reflecting varying degrees of anxious attachment and detachment resulting from actual or persistently threatened disruption of attachments. The intense separation anxiety, dysfunctional anger, distrust of others and the environment, and restraints on the development of self-reliant behavior that are known to accompany attachment disorders are reflected in the consistent description of abusing parents and children as dependent, depressed, angry, anxious, isolated, hyperalert, and distrustful. Theoretically the development of such attachment pathology (anxious attachment and detachment) in a child's attachment system could later become incorporated into the adult attachment and caretaker systems and would thus affect both the development of parental behavior and the development of attachment in the next generation. Thus the transmission of abusive parent-child interaction could be seen as resulting, to a great extent, from patterns of attachment dysfunction that are perpetuated within the family.

To test out some of these hypotheses a research project was undertaken.

99

Research Project

It was proposed that patterns of abusive caretaker behavior reflect the inadequate earlier development of attachment in abusive mothers, as well as resulting current attachment disorders. These present disorders were expected to include dysfunctional levels of separation anxiety and anger. Physically abusive mothers were hypothesized to differ significantly from more typical mothers in having: (1) a greater incidence of early disruptions of attachments or threats of disruption; (2) expectations of significant others, including attachment figures, of a kind that would reflect inadequate attachment experience; (3) greater evidence of difficulties in attachment and caretaking at the time of the birth of the identified child; and (4) more frequent and severe indicators of current attachment disorder as manifested by present responses to stimuli associated with separation.

Parent subjects for the study were eighteen child-abusing mothers who were defined as having engaged in a known, clearly reportable act or acts of physical abuse against their preadolescent child within the previous two years. Neglecting and "passively abusing" mothers (mothers present when someone else abused the child) were not interviewed for this study. The degree of abuse varied among these subjects, ranging from a serious attempt to kill a child to relatively less severe attacks, such as prolonged periods of spanking and hitting a child when the mother was under great stress. Subjects in this group were predominantly married and from white, low-income ($12,000 a year), skilled labor, high-school educated families.

A control group of eighteen "typical" mothers was obtained. These were specified as mothers with a child in the comparable age range as the child-abusing mothers who were not known or suspected of having abused their child. In addition, these mothers had not, to the interviewer's knowledge, ever been referred for or received child-related psychiatric treatment. Typical mothers were recruited through elementary schools serving low-income families, as particular effort was made to obtain subjects in this group who were likely to be equated with the experimental group on socioeconomic and cultural factors. All subjects in both groups were unpaid volunteers.

A statistical analysis of the demographic data showed the two groups to be similar, with no significant differences in socioeconomic level, education, marital status, occupation, housing, age at first marriage, number of children, and age at which identified child was born.

The mothers did vary slightly in age (abusive: 31.17 years; typical: 35.56 years), as well as in age and sex of the identified child (more boys and somewhat younger children in the abusive group, though almost all children in both groups were elementary-school aged). More mothers in the experimental group are or were in a support group or therapy, as referrals were obtained from these sources.

Subjects in both groups were assessed by two measures: the Separation Anxiety Test and the Wallace-DeLozier Attachment Questionnaire. The Separation Anxiety Test (SAT) developed by Hansburg (1972, 1976, 1980) for use with adolescents and subsequently extended for use with adults (Hansburg, 1975, 1978) was used to assess the projective responses to separation from attachment figures for all mothers. The test consists of twelve pictures representing varying intensities of separation stimuli. Responses to the test are compiled into response patterns, which provide a profile of the individual's functioning when confronted with separation from significant others. Overall, the SAT assesses to what extent, given the separation stimulus, the person tends to think of moving toward an attachment figure and to what extent the person sees himself/herself as able to cope without the protection or comfort of others. The test is thus designed to assess the current attachment-separation complex in the individual, including what Hansburg calls "attachment need" (attachment response) and "individuation level" (self-reliance response); the affective responses to separation, such as separation hostility or fear; defensive functioning in response to the separation stimulus; and differential responses to mild versus strong projected separation stimuli.

The Wallace-DeLozier Attachment Questionnaire, a structured interview questionnaire designed for and utilized in this study, was an extensive revision of the questionnaire developed by Wallace (1977) for study of attachment issues in a postdivorce population. Both questionnaires are derived from attachment theory literature.[5] In the present research, the questionnaire was designed to assess the attachment history of (1) the mother with her own parents during childhood and (2) the mother and child at the time of the child's birth, including other significant figures available to the mother at that time, such as grandparents and other support figures. The questionnaire was also designed to assess other factors thought to be related to the mother's attachment behavior and possibly to her caretaking behavior: (1) mother's general expectations of significant others; (2) mother's per-

5. See Ainsworth, 1969, 1972, 1973; Ainsworth and Bell, 1970, 1974; Bowlby, 1969, 1973, 1975, 1976; Parkes, 1972, 1973; and Weiss, 1973.

ception of the availability of significant others at the time of the child's birth; and (3) mother's recalled perception of the presence or absence of cues held by Bowlby (1969, 1973) to be related to attachment behavior.

All data were collected in a scheduled two-hour structured interview, with measures administered in the order of the Separation Anxiety Test followed by the Wallace-DeLozier Attachment Questionnaire, and with all interviews audiotaped. The order of presentation was selected to obtain SAT responses that were uncontaminated by the attachment and separation questions on the questionnaire. Protocols were scored and interpreted blind, and all research data was analyzed by means of Chi-square, Mann-Whitney U, or t-test statistics.

The results strongly indicate a clear pattern of severe attachment disorders in the group of eighteen abusing mothers as compared with the group of eighteen typical mothers. The difficulties appear to originate from threatened disruption of attachments, as well as severe discipline, in early childhood; to have been influential in the childbirth experience of the mothers; and to be manifested currently both in their general expectations of significant others and in their pattern of response to projected separation from attachment figures.[6]

PRESENT MANIFESTATIONS OF ATTACHMENT DISORDER

In the clinical interpretation of the Separation Anxiety Test protocols, the abusing mothers exhibited a significantly higher number of factors thought to indicate anxious attachment (table 5-1). Twelve of the eighteen abusing mothers were found to be in the "severe" category, compared with only two controls. In contrast, only three abusing mothers were in the "mild" category, compared with ten controls. Furthermore, when protocols indicating severe levels of anxious attachment and those indicating detachment were combined, the abusing group was found to demonstrate evidence of severe attachment pathology at significantly higher levels (X^2, df=1, corrected for continuity = 7.31, $p < .005$, one-tailed) than the typical mother group. Fifteen of the eighteen abusing mothers' SAT protocols, as contrasted with only six of the eighteen typical mothers' protocols, showed strong evidence of attachment pathology in one or both of these categories. The abusing group's protocols were found to show response patterns to separation that were characterized by higher total levels of anger and

---

6. For more detailed presentation of method and results obtained from the reported study, see DeLozier (1979).

TABLE 5-1

Frequency of Factors Indicating Anxious Attachment in Abusive versus Typical
Mothers (Based on Clinical Interpretation[a] of SAT Protocols)

Group	n	None (0 factors)	Mild (1–2 factors)	Strong (3–4 factors)	Severe (5–6 factors)
Abusive mothers	18	0	3	3	12
Typical mothers	18	1	10	5	2

Corrected X^2 = 12.41
df = 3
p <.01, 2 tailed
[a] Protocols scored blind for presence of six factors indicating anxious attachment (Hansburg, 1976):
(a) High attachment with low self-reliance; (b) strong attachment in response to mild separations; (c) high levels of hostility and anxiety; (d) high avoidance response; (e) high self-love loss (rejection and self-blame); (f) high identity stress.

anxiety (high affective response), feelings of rejection and self-blame, high levels of attachment response to mild separation stimuli, and low self-reliance (table 5-2). The abusive mothers appeared to be more anxious in response to mild separation stimuli (e.g., child going to school) and more angry in response to strong separation stimuli (e.g., maternal hospitalization).

Thus the analysis of the Separation Anxiety Test protocols strongly supports the predicted hypothesis of attachment dysfunction, primarily anxious attachment, in the child-abusing group. The abusing mothers appear to be especially sensitive to separation stimuli and to respond with higher than usual levels of overall affective response (anxiety and anger), strong attachment response to mild separation, and feelings of rejection and self-blame, while simultaneously evidencing a significantly lowered capacity for self-reliance in response to separation.

EARLY ATTACHMENT EXPERIENCES

The results of the analysis of data collected on the Wallace-DeLozier Attachment Questionnaire—regarding early childhood attachment experience, general expectations of significant others, and the experience of the mother during the time surrounding the birth of the child she identified as the child that has given her the most difficulty (the abused child for the abusing group)—indicated a pattern of attachment difficulties that appears to coincide with the mothers' present manifestations of dysfunctional attachment (see table 5-3).

The frequent threat of attachment disruption during childhood appeared to be an etiological factor in the abusing mothers' current at-

103

TABLE 5-2
Mann-Whitney Analysis of Separation Anxiety Test Response Patterns of Abusive versus Typical Mothers

	mean rank	z-score	U-value	P(1) level	Glass Rank Biserial Correlation
1. Affective response (anger and anxiety)					
Total:					
Abusive	22.61	−2.341	88.0	<.01	20.85[a]
Typical	14.39				
A. Anger (hostility)					
Mild:					
Abusive	20.39	−1.091	128.0	.1875	N.S.
Typical	16.61				
Strong:					
Abusive	21.58	−1.757	106.5	<.05	11.71
Typical	15.42				
Total:					
Abusive	21.78	−1.867	103.0	<.05	13.28[a]
Typical	15.22				
B. Anxiety (tension)					
Mild:					
Abusive	22.19	−2.104	95.5	<.02	16.81
Typical	14.81				
Strong:					
Abusive	17.72	−0.443	148.0	.329	N.S.[b]
Typical	19.28				
Total:					
Abusive	19.56	−0.601	143.0	.274	N.S.[a,b]
Typical	17.44				
2. Self-Love Loss Response (rejection and self-blame)					
Mild:					
Abusive	22.64	−2.424	87.5	<.01	21.16
Typical	14.36				
Strong					
Abusive	22.11	−2.057	97.0	<.05	16.09
Typical	14.89				
Total:					
Abusive	24.50	−3.417	54.0	<.001	44.44[a]
Typical	12.50				
Self-Love Loss—Self-Esteem Preoccupation					
Total:					
Abusive	23.50	−2.849	72.0	<.0025	30.86[a]
Typical	13.50				
3. Attachment response					
Mild:					
Abusive	22.44	−2.247	91.0	<.02	19.6[a]
Typical	14.56				

TABLE 5-2 *(continued)*
Mann-Whitney Analysis of Separation Anxiety Test Response Patterns of Abusive versus Typical Mothers

	mean rank	z-score	U-value	P(1) level	Glass Rank Biserial Correlation
Strong:					
Abusive	15.33	−1.804	105.0	<.05	12.41[b]
Typical	21.67				
Total:					
Abusive	19.06	−0.316	152.0	.376	N.S.[b]
Typical	17.94				
4. Self-Reliance Response					
Mild:					
Abusive	14.33	−2.373	87.0	<.01	21.47
Typical	22.67				
Strong:					
Abusive	15.42	−1.757	106.5	<.05	11.71
Typical	21.58				
Total:					
Abusive	13.61	−2.784	74.0	<.003	29.52[a]
Typical	23.39				

Strong = strong separation stimuli (e.g., maternal hospitalization).
Mild = mild separation stimuli (e.g., child going to school).
Total = mild + strong separation stimuli.
[a] Predicted results.
[b] Unexpected lowering of attachment and anxiety responses in strong separation stimulus category (and therefore in total responses) due to detachment characteristics on a number of abusing-mother protocols, either instead of or, generally, in addition to anxious attachment features. Thus anxious attachment factors (including high anxiety) and detachment factors (including low anxiety) are combined in group comparisons, tending to cancel each other out.

tachment disorders. The reported childhood experience of the abusing mothers differed significantly from that of the typical mothers in the far greater incidence of threat of separation or termination of caretaking. Significant differences in item analysis were found for threats of divorce, especially with frequent threats, and threats to send the child to a foster home. Strong trends were found in threats to leave the child someplace, to send the child to live with relatives, or other harsh disciplinary threats. Thus the abusing parent, in her childhood, appears to have been or to perceive herself as having been constantly threatened with separation. Such threats are among those that Bowlby has cited as leading to anxiously attached individuals. In discussing "patterns of pathogenic parenting" that have been noted in individuals "described as overdependent or immature" Bowlby (1976) includes "threats by parents to abandon the family," "threats by one

105

TABLE 5-3
Summary Table for Corrected Chi-Square and t-test Values
for Reported Attachment Questionnaire Data

1. *Childhood Threats of Separation*

Overall Total: M_A = 2.500 SD_A = 2.256 $t_{(34)}$ = 2.90, p < .005
        M_T = 0.833 SD_T = 0.924

Types of Threats (Positive Response)	A	T	Corrected X^2	p, one-tailed
Divorce	12	5	4.012	<.05
Call police to get child	3	2	0.000	N.S.
Leave child someplace	4	2	2.531	p = .056
Send to foster home	6	1	2.837	<.05
Send to live with relatives	4	0	2.531	p = .06
Other harsh disciplinary threats (to beat, to kill, to maim)	7	1	5.786	<.02

2. *Actual Attachment Disruptions* (through death, divorce, illness, removal from home, other significant separations)

Overall Total:
Under age 18: M_A = 4.389 SD_A = 2.478 $t_{(34)}$ = 0.23   N.S.
         M_T = 4.222 SD_T = 1.833
Under age 6: M_A = 2.167 SD_A = 1.543 $t_{(34)}$ = 0.65   N.S.
        M_T = 1.889 SD_T = 0.963

Family Problem Causing Father to Leave Home	A	T	Corrected X^2	p, one-tailed
	9	3	3.125	<.05

3. *Childhood Anxious Concern for Parents*

Overall Total: M_A = 1.611 SD_A = .978 $t_{(34)}$ = 2.42   <.02
        M_T = 0.944 SD_T = .639

Types of Concern (Positive Response)	A	T	Corrected X^2	p, one-tailed
Thought that parents might be hurt or killed	11	9	0.1125	N.S.
Felt responsible for parents' safety and well-being	11	6	1.783	p = .09
Felt would be cause of parents' injury or death	7	2	2.737	p = .06

4. *Expectations of Significant Others*
  As Child

"Whom would you go to for help?" (Primary Figure Named):	A	T	Corrected X^2	p, one-tailed
	10	17	5.333	<.02

"Parents able to help in difficult situation?"
  (6-point scale: 1 = never; 6 = always)
    $M_A = 3.167$ $SD_A = 2.18$
    $M_T = 5.556$ $SD_T = 1.09$ $t_{(34)} = -4.16$ <.0005

"Felt could talk to about problems"
  (6-point scale: 1 = never, 6 = always, scored for each of 13 figures)

a. Primary attachment figures:
  Mean for all primary figures:
    $M_A = 2.972$ $SD_A = 1.875$
    $M_T = 4.333$ $SD_T = 1.465$ $t_{(34)} = -2.43$ <.02

  Highest single score for primary figure:
    $M_A = 3.611$ $SD_A = 2.279$
    $M_T = 5.222$ $SD_T = 1.263$ $t_{(34)} = -2.62$ <.01

b. Secondary figures (extended family):
  Mean for all secondary figures:
    $M_A = 2.042$ $SD_A = 1.099$
    $M_T = 3.028$ $SD_T = 1.018$ $t_{(34)} = -2.79$ <.005

  Highest single score for secondary figure:
    $M_A = 3.722$ $SD_A = 1.994$
    $M_T = 5.333$ $SD_T = 0.907$ $t_{(34)} = -3.12$ <.005

c. Nonfamily others:
  Mean for all nonfamily figures:
    $M_A = 2.144$ $SD_A = 0.994$
    $M_T = 2.222$ $SD_T = 1.031$ $t_{(34)} = -0.23$ N.S.

  Highest single score for nonfamily figure:
    $M_A = 4.111$ $SD_A = 1.967$
    $M_T = 4.056$ $SD_T = 1.798$ $t_{(34)} = 0.09$ N.S.

As Adult:
  "Could mother help if needed?"
    (6-point scale, 1 = never; 6 = always)
  $M_A = 2.765$ $SD_A = 2.02$
  $M_T = 4.765$ $SD_T = 1.44$ $t_{(34)} = -3.33$ <.002

  "Could father help if needed?"
    (6-point scale, 1 = never; 6 = always)
  $M_A = 2.118$ $SD_A = 1.58$
  $M_T = 4.278$ $SD_T = 1.90$ $t_{(34)} = -3.64$ <.001

  "Could extended family help?"
    (6-point scale, 1 = never; 6 = always)
  $M_A = 2.667$ $SD_A = 1.75$
  $M_T = 4.889$ $SD_T = 1.45$ $t_{(34)} = -4.15$ <.0005

TABLE 5-3 *(continued)*
Summary Table for Corrected Chi-Square and t-test Values
for Reported Attachment Questionnaire Data

5. *Childbirth Experience* (Attachment eliciting or terminating scales)
   Overall Total:

M_A = 30.566	SD_A = 4.162	$t_{(34)} = -3.58$	<.001
M_T = 35.111	SD_T = 3.428		

   Attachment-Eliciting Subscale:
   (Items scored: 1 = yes; 2 = no)

M_A = 18.556	SD_A = 3.014	$t_{(34)} = -3.76$	<.0005
M_T = 21.111	SD_T = 2.654		

   Attachment-Terminating Subscale:
   (Items scored: 1 = no; 2 = yes)

M_A = 12.000	SD_A = 2.169	$t_{(34)} = -1.70$	p = .0505
M_T = 13.000	SD_T = 1.237		

A = Abusive Group, N_A = 18.
T = Typical Group, N_T = 18.

parent to desert or even to kill the other or else to commit suicide," as well as "threats by parents not to love a child, used as a means of controlling him" (p. 18). Although threats of parental suicide appear minimal in both groups, the other types of threats noted by Bowlby were reported more frequently by the abusing mothers.

Specific analysis of the additional types of disciplinary threats used by parents of subjects showed that threats reported in the childhood of abusing mothers were much more severe than those reported by typical mothers. Only one typical parent reported severe threats in this category, but seven abusing mothers reported threats of severe beatings, threats to kill the child, or threats that the child's behavior would lead to death of the parent. Several abusing mothers reported more than one type of severe threat. The additional threats reported by typical parents were primarily those of spankings or being sent to their room. Thus the abusing mothers reported not only repeated threats of abandonment or separation, but threats to their physical well-being as well as to the physical safety of their caretaker. Data were not collected systematically regarding whether or not these threats were carried out, although spontaneous information from the abusing mothers indicates that this was often the case. In addition, abusing mothers indicated that these threats were not infrequent, but were an integral part of their recalled childhood.

It was predicated that the abusing parents would have experienced a greater number of actual separations from caretakers in childhood. While the abusing and typical mothers' histories did not differ signifi-

Margie —

cantly in this respect, it appears that the abusing mothers did experience a higher frequency of some types of parental absence, such as a parent leaving home temporarily due to family problems. In addition, father absences were reported for a much longer period of time (fourteen weeks) by the abusing group than the typical group (one week).

The threat of loss of caretaking, abandonment, or physical harm, especially if persistent or frequent, is one of the conditions that attachment theory has held to be related to the inadequate development of affectional bonds in children. Bowlby has proposed that constant anxiety regarding the continued availability of the attachment figure, with the accompanying low threshold for the eliciting of attachment behavior, results in the condition of anxious attachment. It appears that the abusing mothers in this study, who currently manifest severe attachment pathology, as children did not experience the certain accessibility of a dependable caretaker. The significantly greater incidence of threats to the maintenance of the attachment relationship appears, for these mothers, to have been a key variable in the formation of their present attachment difficulties.

While fear of separation from an attachment figure is considered natural, in a stable and predictable environment this fear is not constantly present and becomes less easily elicited as the child matures. But in an unpredictable environment, fear of separation from an attachment figure continues at an intensified level. This appears to have been the case in the childhood homes of the abusing mothers. In addition to exhibiting overall continued sensitivity to separation, the abusing mothers spontaneously described childhood fears of going to sleep at night or of going to school specifically associated with uncertainty about the continued availability of the attachment figure.

Furthermore, the significantly greater incidence of threat in the childhood of the abusing mothers would seem to be related to the inappropriate levels of affective response (anger and anxiety) expressed by these mothers in response to separation stimuli and in interaction with their children. Threats of loss or abandonment, according to attachment theory, can lead to violently angry responses in the individual. If the threats occur in childhood and especially if they are frequent, the child is unable to express the anger because of fear of precipitating the very event that is feared, that is, separation from the caretaker. The result is a *dysfunctional* response, in which anger and anxiety intensify and do not serve to restore proximity to the attachment figure. Such a development appears to have occurred in the abusing mothers in this study.

109

A significantly greater incidence of reported anxious concern for parents in childhood was predicted and obtained for the abusive versus the typical mothers, suggesting that these mothers may have experienced at least some perceived reversal of roles with their own parents in childhood. This was confirmed by the finding that the abusive group showed a trend toward a greater degree of perceived responsibility for their parents' safety and happiness than the controls. Almost two-thirds of the abusing group replied that they felt responsible for their parents; in contrast, two-thirds of the typical group reported that they had *not* felt any such responsibility. In addition, more than three times as many abusing parents (39 percent) indicated that they had felt their own actions or attitudes would be the cause of harm to their parent, often because they had been told so repeatedly by the parent.

Role reversal is a commonly found phenomenon in abusing families. Attachment theory places this type of parent-child interaction, as well as the resulting anger and anxiety, in a new, more understandable perspective. Bowlby suggests that when a caretaker exerts pressure on a child to act as an attachment figure for her, especially in conjunction with threats of the kinds that have been found in these mothers' histories, the children involved "are likely to become over-conscientious and guilt-ridden as well as anxiously attached" (1976, p. 19). Furthermore, both the threat of abandonment and the expectation that the child function as an attachment figure for the parent arouse anger in the child that he cannot express for fear of bringing about what he seeks to avoid—total loss of caretaking. Consequently, such parental behavior, which both arouses anger in the child and precludes its expression, results in "much partially unconscious resentment, which persists into adulthood life and is expressed usually in a direction away from the parents and towards someone weaker, e.g. a spouse or a child" (1976, p. 19). The inappropriate anger abusing parents express toward their children is thus intricately related to their own attachment experience. This possibility appears to be strongly upheld by the results of this study.

EXPECTATIONS OF SIGNIFICANT OTHERS

According to attachment theory, general expectations of significant others reflect internal representations that are derived from the early attachment experience of the individual. The results indicate that the abusing mothers' expectations of significant others have been adverse-

110

ly affected by their attachment experience. The abusing group reported primary attachment figures as significantly less accessible and helpful both in their childhoods and as adults.

Significant differences were obtained for whether or not a subject would, in childhood, turn to an attachment figure. For example, when asked whom they would go to for help as a child, seventeen of the typical mothers indicated that they would go to one or both of their parents, whereas only ten of the eighteen abusing mothers stated that they would do so. Perhaps even more important, fifteen of the typical group included their own mother specifically as someone they would go to as a child, compared with only seven of the abusing mothers.

Furthermore, in this series of questions, the typical mothers (with a single exception who named only a secondary figure) all included at least one primary figure that they would go to. In contrast, ten abusing subjects chose primary figures, four chose either secondary (extended family) or nonfamily figures, and four reported having had no one to go to in childhood. The same pattern noted in the responses concerning childhood was repeated in the responses regarding adulthood. The major difference between the adult-related responses and the childhood-related ones is that typical mothers reported clear accessibility to their primary caretaker in childhood and subsequently appear to have appropriately established adult affectional bonds (with spouse). Abusing parents, in contrast, report greater perceived inaccessibility and/or ineffectiveness of their childhood primary caretaker and far less expectation of available and helpful support figures in adulthood, even with their current husbands.

CHILDBIRTH EXPERIENCE

Last, the early attachment difficulties and resulting attachment disorders were predicted to have adversely influenced the abusive mother's childbirth experience with her own child. The birth of a child can be seen as a naturally occurring crisis that contains both hazardous risks and developmental opportunities. As such, it offers the opportunity for mastery and further development of confidence. Attachment theory, however, emphasizes that the ability of the individual to develop mastery is more likely to occur if he or she is confident of the availability of a secure base from which to operate. Therefore, mothers who have experienced attachment difficulties and who demonstrate attachment disorders should be less prepared to deal adequately with the experience of childbirth. Furthermore, as attachment behaviors are

111

expected to increase as a female member of a species prepares to give birth, both because she requires protection and because the event is relatively unfamiliar, it would seem that women with histories of attachment difficulties will experience greater difficulty in negotiating the natural crisis of childbirth than those with secure attachments.

In the reported study, the abusing group was expected to report perception of (1) significantly greater numbers of attachment-behavior-eliciting clues and (2) significantly fewer numbers of attachment-behavior–terminating clues surrounding the time of childbirth than would the typical group. Positive responses to items such as being alone, feeling unsafe, and feeling frightened were summed to produce an attachment-eliciting scale. Responses to other items such as feeling pleasure and being helped by others were summed to produce an attachment-terminating scale. Positive responses on the first subscale and negative responses on the second were summed to produce an overall total. Strongly significant differences in the predicted direction were obtained between the groups on the overall total score and on the attachment-eliciting subscale, and a strong trend was found on the attachment-terminating subscale alone.

Since no significant differences between groups were obtained for either stresses surrounding childbirth (such as family or financial difficulties, illness of self or baby, difficult labor or delivery) or the actual presence, type, or number of available support figures during this period, the abusing mothers' reported experience of this childbirth as involving feelings of being unsafe, alone, and frightened would appear to be attributable to some other cause. A tentative interpretation is that given the early childhood attachment experience of the abusing mothers, the representational models that appear to have been derived from their early experience, and their present manifestations of attachment disorder, these mothers have not developed an adequate "secure base" from which to explore.

At the time of childbirth, the development of caretaking behavior can be considered "exploratory" in the sense that it involves adaptation to the child, sensitive and appropriate response to the child's signals, and competent social interaction with the child. In turn, the accurate and prompt maternal response to infant signals leads to the development of competence in infants (Bell and Ainsworth, 1972). The abusing mothers in this study show evidence of severe attachment difficulties that would have resulted in their heightened attachment behavior at the time of childbirth and possibly in a lessened ability to engage in the initiation of adequate caretaking behavior.

CONVERGENCE OF FINDINGS

In summary, the analysis of the data collected in this study indicates that in childhood the abusing mothers experienced severe threats of abandonment and harm; self-expectations and possibly parental expectations that they care for their parents; and general uncertainty as to the availability of significant others. Their histories contain some indicators of childhood disruptive events such as family problems causing a parent to leave home, though not permanently. During childhood the abusing mothers appear to have had to watch constantly for indications of impending separation and other threats to caretaking. In adulthood there is evidence that they view significant others as being generally inaccessible. They appear not to have developed adequate internal representations of attachment figures and other significant individuals as reliable and accessible. Furthermore, the abusing mothers indicated that, at the time of the birth of the later-abused child, they were generally fearful, felt alone and unsafe, and were dissatisfied with the availability of significant others. Thus it appears likely that the abusing mothers were handicapped by their own attachment difficulties in their initial steps toward maternal caretaking.

All of these results were found to be consistent with the present manifestations of attachment difficulties as assessed by the Separation Anxiety Test. On this test the abusing mothers indicated a high current level of attachment disorder, primarily anxious attachment, but with some tendency toward detachment as well. Thus the abusing mothers in this study demonstrated their overall sensitivity to separation, especially mild separation, and their feelings of helplessness, anxiety, and anger in response to significant separation experiences.

These findings support, then, the prediction that the abusing mothers in the reported study have experienced difficulty in their childhood attachments and in the development of internal representations of significant others as accessible and reliable, resulting in consequent adult attachment difficulties as well as in possible difficulties in the development of appropriate caretaking behavior.

Implications

The pattern of attachment dysfunction found in the abusing mothers in this research suggests the attachment-related origin of at least some of the inappropriate parenting directed toward their children. The dysfunctional development of anger and anxiety are two components of anxious attachment, especially if the expression of anger has been prohibited by the child's fear of precipitating loss of caretaking. Once anxious attachment has developed, separation signals can trigger expression of intense anxiety and anger. It seems possible that abusing mothers, who exhibit a high degree of sensitivity to separation from significant others, interpret the normal behavior of their children as if it were actual or threatened rejection. If so, these mothers would be likely to respond to such a misperception with dysfunctional levels of anxiety and anger and with feelings of rejection, self-blame, and helplessness. Not only could the child's normal exploratory behavior elicit such a response, but even such behavior as normal crying could function as a danger signal to the anxiously attached mother. Thus the attachment-related response of the mother may result in the inappropriate direction of anxiety and anger toward the child who, due to the inverted parent-child relationship, may be viewed with the same expectations that the mother maintains regarding attachment figures—that they will be inaccessible and unreliable.

Furthermore, the development of competence in a child depends not only on the parent's appropriate response to his attachment behavior, but also on encouragement of the child's increasing self-reliance. If the parent, however, responds to normal parent-child separation with intense levels of anxiety or anger, increased attachment need, decreased self-reliance, and feelings of rejection, the parent will be more than likely to discourage the child's exploratory and self-reliant behavior, especially in inverted parent-child relationships, thereby even further hampering the child's development.

In conclusion, an attachment theory view of child abuse calls for the early detection of attachment disorders in both parent and child, assessment of the extent of attachment dysfunction in high-risk families, and intervention with abusive families to reduce separation anxiety and support the more adequate development of attachment bonds. In this regard, for example, the common practice of removal of the child from the home warrants careful inspection. Although sometimes mandatory for the child's protection, such an intervention further strains the poorly developed attachment relationships within the family and further adversely affects the development of attachment and self-reliance in the child. Moreover, if the child is to be returned home eventually, *separation in and of itself* will serve to activate attachment behaviors upon reunion that further stress parent-child relations, possibly eliciting further abuse.

From the attachment theory perspective, therefore, efforts should be made to: (1) direct child-abuse treatment to the family unit where possible, with the child either remaining in the home under close supervision or with frequent, prolonged contact between parent and child during separation; (2) provide interventions in abusive and potentially abusive families that support the development of attachment bonds in children and remedy attachment dysfunctions in both children and adults; and (3) direct attention toward the provision of support to all parents in their role as caregivers, thus enabling them to provide more reliable and accessible caregiving to their children.

REFERENCES

Ainsworth, M. D. S. 1969. Object relations, dependency and attachment: A theoretical review of the infant-mother relationship. *Child Development* 40:969–1025.

————. 1972. Attachment and dependency: A comparison. In *Attachment and dependency*, ed. J. L. Gewirtz. New York: Wiley.

————. 1973. The development of infant-mother attachment. In *Review of child development research*, vol. 3, ed. B. M. Caldwell and H. N. Ricciuti. Chicago: University of Chicago Press.

————, and Bell, S. 1970. Attachment, exploration and separation: Illustrated by the behavior of one-year-olds in a strange situation. *Child Development* 41:49–67.

————. 1974. Mother-infant interaction and the development of competence. In *The growth of conpetence*, ed. K. J. Connolly and J. Bruner. New York: Academic Press.

Bell, S. M., and Ainsworth, M. D. 1972. Infant crying and maternal responsiveness. *Child Development* 43:1171–1190.

Bowlby, J. 1969. *Attachment and loss. Vol. 1: Attachment.* New York: Basic Books.

————. 1973. *Attachment and loss. Vol. 2: Separation: Anxiety and anger.* New York: Basic Books.

————. 1975. Attachment theory, separation anxiety, and mourning. In *American handbook of psychiatry*, 2nd ed., vol. 6, ed. S. Arieti. New York: Basic Books.

————. 1976. The making and breaking of affectional bonds. Paper presented at the Maudsley Lecture, Institute of Psychiatry, London, November 1976. Published in *British Journal of Psychiatry*, 1977, 130:201–210, 421–431.

Davoren, E. 1975. Working with abusive parents: A social worker's view. *Children Today* 4:38–41.

DeLozier, P. 1979. An application of attachment theory to the study of child abuse. Ph.D. dissertation, California School of Professional Psychology.

Ebeling, N. B., and Hill, D. A., eds. 1975. *Child abuse: Intervention and treatment.* Acton, Mass.: Publishing Sciences Group.

Fontana, V. J. 1971. *The maltreated child: The maltreatment syndrome in children.* Springfield, Ill.: Charles C Thomas.

————. 1973. *Somewhere a child is crying: Maltreatment—causes and prevention.* New York: Macmillan.

Galdston, R. 1965. Observations on children who have been physically abused and their parents. *American Journal of Psychiatry* 122:440–443.

Gelles, R. J. 1973. Child abuse as psychopathology: A sociological critique and reformation. *American Journal of Orthopsychiatry* 43:611–621. Reprinted in S. Chess and A. Thomas, eds. *Annual progress in child psychiatry and child development*. New York: Brunner/Mazel, 1974.

George, C., and Main, M. 1979. Social interactions of young abused children: Approach, avoidance, and aggression. *Child Development* 50:306–318.

Green, A. 1973. The battered child syndrome: A special report to the 1973 Annual Meeting of the AMA. *Audio Digest Pediatrics* 19(9).

Hansburg, H. G. 1972. *Adolescent separation anxiety*. Springfield, Ill.: Charles C Thomas.

————. 1975. Some generalizations with regard to studies of families with the separation-anxiety test. Manuscript available from the author (Jewish Child Care Clinic, 345 Madison Avenue, New York).

————. 1976. The use of the separation-anxiety test in the detection of self-destructive tendencies in early adolescence. In *Mental health in children*, vol. 3, ed. D. V. S. Sankar. Westbury, N.Y.: PJD Publications.

————. 1978. Separation disorders of the elderly. Manuscript available from the author (Jewish Child Care Clinic, 345 Madison Avenue, New York).

————. 1980. *Adolescent separation anxiety. Vol. 2: Separation disorders*. Huntington, N.Y.: Robert E. Krieger.

Helfer, R. E. 1973. The etiology of child abuse. *Pediatrics* 51 (Suppl.):777–779.

————. 1976. *Child abuse: The diagnostic process and treatment programs*. Washington, D.C.: U.S. Government Printing Office. (U.S. Department of Health, Education, and Welfare Publication No. (OHD) 76-30069.)

————, and Kempe, C. H., eds. 1974. *The battered child*, 2nd ed. Chicago: University of Chicago Press.

————. 1976. *Child abuse and neglect: The family and the community*. Cambridge, Mass.: Ballinger Publishing Co.

Holter, J. C., and Friedman, S. B. 1968. Principles of management in child abuse cases. *American Journal of Orthopsychiatry* 38:127.

Jayaratne, S. 1977. Child abusers as parents and children: A review. *Social Work* 22:5–9.

Johnson, B., and Morse, H. A. 1968. Injured children and their parents. *Children* 15:147–152.

Justice, B., and Justice, R., 1976. *The abusing family*. New York: Human Sciences Press.

Kempe, C. H., and Helfer, R. E. 1972. *Helping the battered child and his family*. Philadelphia: Lippincott.

Martin, H. 1972. The child and his development. In *Helping the battered child and his family*, ed. C. H. Kempe and R. E. Helfer. Philadelphia: Lippincott.

Martin, H. P. 1975. Parent-child relations. In *Review of child development research*, ed. F. D. Horowitz. Chicago: University of Chicago Press.

————, ed. 1976. *The abused child: A multidisciplinary approach to developmental issues and treatment*. Cambridge, Mass.: Ballinger.

————; Breezley, P.; Conway, E. F.; and Kempe, C. H. 1974. The development of abused children. In *Advances in pediatrics*, vol. 21, ed. I. Schulman. Chicago: Yearbook Medical Publishers.

Melnick, B., and Hurley, J. R. 1969. Distinctive personality attributes of child-abusing mothers. *Journal of Consulting Clinical Psychology* 33:746–749.

Merrill, E. J. 1962. *Physical abuse of children—an agency study in protecting the battered child*. Denver, Colo.: Denver Children's Division, American Humane Association.

Ounsted, C., Oppenheimer, R., and Lindsay, J. 1975. The psychopathology and psychotherapy of the families: Aspects of bonding failure. In *Concerning child abuse*, ed. A. White. Edinburgh: Churchill Livingstone.

Parke, R. D. and Collmer, C. W. 1975. Child abuse: An interdisciplinary analysis. In *Review of child development research*, vol. 5, ed. E. M. Hetherington, Chicago: University of Chicago Press.

Parkes, C. M. 1972. *Bereavement: Studies of grief in adult life*. New York: International Universities Press.

————. 1973. Separation anxiety: An aspect of the search for a lost object. In *Loneliness: Social and emotional isolation*, ed. R. Weiss. Cambridge, Mass.: MIT Press.

Paulson, M. J., and Chaleff, A. 1973. Parent surrogate roles: A dynamic concept in understanding and treating abusive parents. *Journal of Clinical Child Psychology* 2:38–40.

Schneider, C., Helfer, R. E., and Pollack, C. 1972. The predictive questionnaire: A preliminary report. In *Helping the battered child and his family*, ed. H. C. Kempe and R. E. Helfer. Philadelphia: Lippincott.

Silver, L. B. 1968. Child abuse syndrome: A review. *Medical Times* 96:803–820.

————, Dublin, C. G., and Lourie, R. A. 1969. Does violence breed violence? Contributions from a study of the child abuse syndrome. *American Journal of Psychiatry* 126:404–407.

Solomon, T. 1973. History of demography of child abuse. *Pediatrics* 51:773–776.

Spinetta, J., and Rigler, D. 1972. The child-abusing parent: A psychological review. *Psychological Bulletin* 77:296–304.

Steele, B. F. 1970. Parental abuse of infants and small children. In *Parenthood: Its psychology and psychopathology*, ed. E. J. Anthony and T. Benedek. Boston: Little, Brown.

————. 1975a. Working with abusive parents: A psychiatrist's view. *Children Today* 4:3–5.

————. 1975b. *Working with abusive parents from a psychiatric point of view*. Washington, D.C.: U.S. Government Printing Office. (U.S. Department of Health, Education, and Welfare Publication No. (OHD) 75-70.)

————. 1976. Violence within the family. In *Child abuse and neglect: The family and the community*, ed. R. E. Helfer and C. H. Kempe. Cambridge, Mass.: Ballinger.

————, and Pollack, C. B., 1968. A psychiatric study of parents who abuse infants and small children. In *The battered child*, 2nd ed., ed. R. E. Helfer and C. H. Kempe. Chicago: University of Chicago Press.

Wallace, A. 1977. An application of attachment theory on the study of divorced people. Ph.D. dissertation, California School of Professional Psychology.

Weiss, R. S. 1973. *Loneliness: The experience of emotional and social isolation*. Cambridge, Mass.: MIT Press.

117

6

Andrea Pound

ATTACHMENT AND MATERNAL DEPRESSION

Introduction: Parental Psychiatric Disorder and Childhood Disturbance

There is now extensive evidence that the children of psychiatrically disturbed parents are themselves at high risk of developing emotional or behavioral disturbance. In one major study it was shown that almost three times as many children attending a child psychiatric department had parents with a history of psychiatric disorder than a matched group of pediatric and dental patients (Rutter, 1966). Disturbance in the mother was shown to be more significant for the child's emotional state than disturbance in the father, and affective disturbance was a common diagnosis in the parents of psychiatrically disturbed children. Psychiatric disturbance was particularly likely in the parents of the youngest group of children referred to the department. Involvement in the parent's symptomatology was also shown to be particularly pathogenic, which led the author to conclude that the children of depressed parents were at particularly high risk since the symptoms so often included hostility to the child and sometimes overt violence. When followed up after treatment it was also clear that a significant proportion of the children of psychiatrically ill parents made less satisfactory progress than other children.

Rutter considers the possibility of a genetic basis to the association but rejects it on the grounds that there is no connection between the type of parental disorder and childhood disorder. An environmental effect is more likely. A more extended discussion of the genetic question (Shields, 1976) concludes that there is considerable evidence of polygenic influences in the case of persistent criminality and psychopathy and in certain other disorders that come to psychiatric attention, such as dyslexia and enuresis. However, the inheritance of neurotic disturbance has been much less closely studied. The likelihood is that polygenic influences account for some part of the natural variance in temperament, and that what is inherited in neurosis is not the disorder as such but attributes such as poor adaptability or emotionality that are known to be associated with psychiatric disorder (Graham, Rutter, and George, 1973).

These findings have been confirmed and elaborated in more recent studies. The children of newly referred adult psychiatric patients have twice the rate of disorder of classroom controls, so that the association between child and parental disturbance holds in whatever direction it is studied (Rutter, Quinton, and Yule, in press). A similar study (Cooper et al., 1977) produced like results; the authors emphasize that it is not psychiatric disorder as such but the family turmoil it often produces that predisposes to disturbance in the child. They also point to the possibility that although some children in disturbed families may not show signs of overt disorder, they may grow up to repeat their parents' pattern of maladjustment, while the anxious children who show their distress may do better in later life: "The normal children who adjust well to the stress of parental illness may be more damaged through the defence mechanism of internalisation than others who react more vigorously and are judged to have psychiatric disorder in studies such as ours." In another study (Tonge, James, and Hillam, 1975, p. 521) a group of problem families was compared with control families living in the same housing estate. Not only was a high rate of psychiatric disorder found in the parents, particularly of neurosis in the mothers and personality disorder in the fathers, but a strong association between such disorder and disturbance in children was confirmed. In this and other studies marital conflict also emerges as a major variable associated with psychiatric disturbance in children. There is obviously a correlation between these two variables, but it is not clear from the reported data how much overlap there is between them.

Further evidence as to the importance of depression comes from the work of Brown and his colleagues, who have shown a high prevalence of depression in women with young children at home, especially if

119

they are working class and have little support from their husbands (Brown, Harris, and Copeland, 1977; Brown and Harris, 1978; and chapter 12 herein). The highest figure for depression was found in working-class women with a child under six (Brown, Bhrolchain, and Harris, 1975). Richman (1977) found a similarly high prevalence of depression in her community sample of mothers of preschool children (30 percent of the total sample) and confirmed the association with disturbance in the child. The reasons for the very high level of depression in this group are not yet clear. A small proportion may be ascribed to the persistence of postpartum depression (Pitt, 1968), but a large proportion seems to arise as a consequence of the isolation and demandingness of the maternal role, for which most women have had no realistic preparation or training (Ginsberg and Bolton, 1976). Economic problems and especially housing seem to be of major importance (Richman, 1974, 1976). However, it is not only the physical but also the psychological environment in which mothers carry out their task that affects their emotional well-being and especially the "esteem (or lack of it) ascribed to their child rearing activities" (Richman, Stevenson, and Graham, 1975 p. 285). In an increasingly mercantile society, unpaid work, no matter how skilled or necessary, can seem valueless. The loss of self-esteem involved in feeling undervalued may play an important part in the development of depression in such a large proportion of young mothers in the general population.

Maternal Depression and Child Psychiatric Disorder

There is thus considerable evidence that maternal depression is a serious hazard to a child's development during the early years. It is both alarmingly common among mothers of small children and also strongly associated with disturbance in the child. As yet there is little evidence as to the specific effects, although Cohler and associates (1977) showed deficits in cognitive development and in attention span in the children of psychotically depressed mothers compared not only with normal controls but also with the children of schizophrenic mothers. In their study of forty depressed women, Weissman and Paykel (1974) found that they were considerably impaired in their maternal role and most reported a high degree of friction between them and their children. In fact the children were more likely to be the recipients of the hostility and irritability that is so common in depression than were the husbands or other relatives or associates. The depressed women with preschool children were particularly impaired in their maternal function, and thirteen of the sixteen children of this group showed signs of disturbance. The mother tended to be either "over-concerned, helpless and guilty" or overtly hostile. The children tended to respond either by tyrannical behavior or by inability to separate from mother and "poor ego boundaries." In general, the depressed mothers found difficulty in being involved in their children's lives, in communicating with them, and in showing affection to them. They also reported strong guilt feelings about the family and resentment and ambivalence about their family duties.

Maternal Depression and Attachment Theory

The high prevalence rate for depression in mothers with young children has clear implications for the study of attachment behavior. The emphasis in most attachment research to date has been on the effects of the physical separation of the child from the mother in the early years, although Bowlby himself has always emphasized the importance of the quality as well as the continuity in time of the mother-child relationship: "What is believed to be essential for mental health is that the infant and young child should experience a warm, intimate and continuous relationship with his mother (or permanent mother substitute), in which both find satisfaction and enjoyment" (Bowlby, 1953 p. 11). The mother's responsiveness and sensitivity to the baby's signals have already been shown to be associated with the security of attachment (Schaffer and Emerson, 1964; Ainsworth and Bell, 1970). Threats of abandonment or of suicide may be even more damaging to the child's sense of secure attachment than physical separation or may compound the effects of actual separation when it occurs (Bowlby, 1974). High degrees of anxiety and "over-dependence" have also been found in children who have been subject to parents' irritability or disparaging remarks (McCord, McCord, and Verden, 1962). Unresponsiveness, irritability, and suicidal threats are all commonly found in depressed patients and can be assumed to be behaviors to which the young child of a depressed mother is frequently exposed, and to result in insecure attachment.

121

As we have seen in chapters 1 and 2, mothers of babies who showed avoidant or ambivalent behavior in the strange-situation test (Groups A and C respectively) tended to be less responsive to the baby's signals, less accepting and warm toward him, and less cooperative and accessible than mothers of securely attached (Group B) infants. Mothers of A babies were more rejecting, unexpressive, and compulsive than were mothers of C babies, and they revealed a particular dislike of close bodily contact with the baby. Their lack of expression was seen as a means of keeping suppressed anger under control, but it appears that the baby is sensitive to the hostility implicit in the mother's unnatural behavior and withdraws from it accordingly.

Securely attached infants who are distressed by separation can be easily calmed by close contact with the mother at reunion, but the A infant has unsatisfactory experiences of close contact and cannot assume that he will be similarly soothed into a calm state. He is likely, therefore, to avoid his mother's gaze and continue playing, in an effort to reduce the painfully high arousal level produced by activation of the attachment system when there is no likelihood of its assuagement.

Similar mechanisms may be expected to occur when a mother is depressed and either withdrawn from her child or irritable and intrusive toward him. The children of some depressed mothers are also likely to be confused by the mother's rapid changes of mood from one state to the other; either they have to perceive their mother's current affective state very clearly or protect themselves from possible rebuff by avoidant behaviors. The child who cannot sustain the intense watchfulness necessary to detect maternal changes in mood and who retreats into avoidant behavior then faces a further problem, namely that the depressed mother experiences the avoidance as rejection, leading to a deepening of her depression. It is possible that at least a proportion of A and C mothers are or have been depressed, and the child's response makes them more so hence they both become trapped in a vicious circle of mutual disappointment and distress. On the other hand, a child who does not withdraw may institute a fourth variant, that of "role reversal." This behavior will be considered later.

CLINICAL EXAMPLES

Recent developments in observational techniques have opened up the possibility of investigating the quality of mother-child interaction with a precision and subtlety that has not hitherto been possible (Lytton, 1973; Schaffer, 1977). The value of such advances in methodology for the study of attachment is unquestionable. One study in which the author is involved (supported by a grant from the Medical Research Council), is investigating the effects of maternal depression on preschool children. Some of the observations discussed here derive from the pilot stage of the study. The measures used should be sufficiently sensitive to demonstrate not merely an association between maternal and child disturbance but to illuminate some of the mechanisms by which disturbance is transmitted from generation to generation.

We anticipate finding at least two subgroups among the mothers: a withdrawn, anergic group and an agitated, intrusive group, with corresponding differences among the children (Weissman and Paykel, 1974). The children of the first group are likely to be more vociferous and demanding in order to obtain a response from the mother, while the children of the second group are more likely to be watchful, tense, and withdrawn. The depressed mothers in general are expected to be less warm and responsive to the child, and to have less effective control stategies and ways of calming the child's distress. They would also probably stimulate the child less and engage in less varied play. The effects of depression on the quality of attachment are less obvious, especially if one considers the attachment relationship to consist not only of certain classes of behavior toward the attachment figure but also of certain kinds of internal representations of that figure. Some predictions can be made on the basis of what is already known of the psychopathology of depression. The depressed woman withdraws her interest from the outside world and becomes increasingly preoccupied with an inner world in which loved figures are lost or unsatisfactory and the self is abandoned and unloved (Abraham, 1927). Her mood is therefore both sad and angry. She may give up engaging with the world or try desperately to control it in order not to risk any further loss or rebuff. In either event she is less aware of the realities of her environment and less responsive to the needs of the people in it. Those most vulnerable to her negative mood and impaired capacity for relating are likely to be her young children, who depend on her for their survival and who cannot escape the field however distressing the situation becomes.

With these considerations in mind we may now proceed to consider some observations of children and their mothers, some of whom are currently depressed while some are known to have been severely depressed in the recent past.

123

PETER

Peter is now aged five and has just started school. Almost immediately he began to get into trouble because of fighting with other children. He is so provocative in the classroom that the staff considered the possibility of excluding him from school, but when interviewed the parents had no complaint about him and said he was a model child at home. It soon emerged that both parents were deprived people who had had unhappy and difficult childhoods. They tend to distrust the world at large, while clinging to each other for support. The father is a loyal husband but a stormy neighbor and workmate, and the mother has many neurotic symptoms. She was depressed for several years after Peter's birth, but, although she has many anxieties and psychosomatic complaints, she is not currently depressed. In the clinic Peter remains quiet and subdued but when seen at home a different picture of him emerges. Every time the parents' conversation turns toward topics that anger or distress them, Peter interrupts with a joke or comical routine, a funny drawing, or an amusing imitation. During a particularly difficult time in the family when they were beset by financial problems, both parents commented on how they would have "gone mad" if it had not been for Peter's liveliness and good humor.

LUKE[1]

Luke is a two-and-a-half-year-old boy with a deeply depressed, withdrawn mother, and he is sitting at her feet playing. Maternal grandmother is around in the background helping with some kitchen chores. Mother is sunk in her thoughts, her only activity a feverish chain smoking. Luke plays quietly but checks her face from time to time, and throughout his bare feet are pressed gently against hers. She asks for an ashtray, and he brings one with alacrity. She kisses and fondles him, pressing him against her. He goes to get another ashtray and another and another until she has five and suddenly lashes out in irritation at him. He returns to his quiet watchful play. Later Granny goes out to buy some sweets for him. He asks his mother why she is leaving and is told, "She's had enough of you, that's why."

ROWAN

Rowan is a girl of four, and she is playing with her mother. The mother was very deeply depressed for a year or so when Rowan was between two and three years old. They lived on the tenth floor of a high-rise block and the child became hyperactive and uncontrollable. The relationship deteriorated, and the mother sometimes had to lock Rowan in her room to prevent herself from harming the child. During this time the child developed a pattern of running away whenever they went out and would sometimes be found by the police several miles away. Rowan no longer runs away and the mother is no longer depressed, but has now become agoraphobic and

1. I am indebted to Christine Puckering of the Institute of Psychiatry, University of London, for this observation.

highly anxious. They kneel on either side of a small table in almost total silence. The child directs the play, which consists mainly of formal games with strict rules, like noughts and crosses or snakes and ladders.

It is still and tense; there is no laughter and no touching. We are filming them, but they are enacting a ritual that is played out every afternoon when the child returns from her special school. The mother usually talks nonstop to any willing listener, but the child has told her not to speak and she obeys. Later on Granny arrives. The child embraces her and kisses her hands and then slowly stomps over to the mother with a grannylike walk and kisses her. The mother asks, "What's that for?" and the child replies, "Because I love you."

MICHELLE

Michelle is a three-year-old girl, and she is playing with Lego blocks on the floor. Her mother sits nearby drinking coffee. She has recently recovered from a depressive illness. A year ago the child had seemed grossly retarded with no speech and little play, but when recently tested on the Merrill-Palmer she received an IQ score of 130. She is trying to build an hotel, but it is too tall and complicated in design and continually collapses. The child is clumsy; twice she falls down crying bitterly, once going to her mother for support but returning with extraordinary persistence to the task. There is a frantic, desperate quality to the activity—it seems like a life-and-death struggle rather than play. At one point the mother says, "I won't help you because I might destroy it." The child in any case expects no help and finally succeeds in her task, filling the hotel with little people and capping it with a roof.

DISCUSSION

There is indubitably a definite attachment between each of these children and their mothers, but it is of a very unusual kind. It is intimate, even intense, but not warm; continuous but also continuously threatened; and the only satisfaction seems to be that somehow the relationship is preserved intact. Some of the unusual features of the relationship can be seen as arising from reversals of the balance of power and resource that normally prevails between mother and child. Instead of the mother holding the child in her concerned attention, the child watches her, ready to respond to her need as it arises, though in his naïveté he is likely to get it wrong and imagine, for instance, that five ashtrays are better than one. While the healthy mother sees herself as responsible for the child's survival, in depression the child may feel responsible for the mother's. In some cases he may indeed keep his mother alive by his expressions of love when there seems nothing else for her to live for. Some children like Peter become clowns to cheer the mother up and make her laugh—a different tactic with a similar aim.

The mother is usually the dominant partner of the mother-child pair. She may leave the child freedom to choose but within the boundaries of mealtimes, bedtimes, and other routines that she defines. Because of a depressed mother's helplessness and lack of contact with reality, her child may take control. Taking control serves several functions both for him and his mother, but it also creates further and sometimes intractable problems. It helps partly because by mastering the situation the child frees himself from identification with her hopeless state. A further reason is that both partners feel it is safer for the child to be in control. In the early relationship between Rowan and her mother, there had been a serious danger of the child being injured. The mother looks back on that time with intense guilt and pain and is terrified of ever harming her again. She is relieved that the responsibility has been taken from her hands, but the cost to the child is that she has to look after herself and her mother with the internal resources she already has. She is not able to listen and learn from adults, and she makes very slow progress at school. Her mother is also constantly reminded of her failure as a mother and cannot regain appropriate control, so that her depression is augmented by daily contact with her overpowerful child.

On the other hand, some children in this situation develop surprising capacities for constructive activity. They have survived by stretching all their capacities to the limit, by observing closely, inferring accurately, and creating their own sources of satisfaction and enjoyment. They do not look to the mother for instruction or advice; she may in fact depend more on them than they on her. However, they are likely, like Michelle, to be tense, anxious, and driven; the whole enterprise seems at any time likely to collapse, leaving them as helpless as their depressed mothers. In short, the child of a depressed mother is forced into a precocious maturity and has to become an attachment figure before he has had sufficient experience of being attached. Some children do not even attempt the task, of course, or if they do they fail to develop an adequate strategy for coping with such demands. The relationship often then deteriorates to the point of breakdown and the child is taken into residential or day care or the mother into a hospital.

In the children previously described, strategies for survival have been found and a relatively stable attachment system has been established, but at a high cost to the child's development. He is precipitated into what Winnicott (1958, p. 206) calls the "stage of concern" before he has fully completed the earlier stage of using and sometimes misusing the attachment figure to establish his own sense of identity. In many adult patients in psychotherapy, the therapist can reconstruct just such a course of events in early life and also observe the long-term consequences in terms of chronic anxiety, guilt, and feelings of inadequacy. These patients' close relationships tend to resemble the first relationship or sometimes to reverse it, so that the partner is either indulgently mothered or clung to helplessly as the mother clung to him. The direct expression of need may be almost impossible, not just because no one is expected to respond but because the actual perception of need states is so rudimentary. At the stage when he should have learned to identify and label them, attention was fixed on the need state of the mother rather than the self. One could say that some of these patients present with a "false self." They are unaware of most of their own impulses and emotions and have to construct their behavior on the basis of conventional expectations, with a resulting sense of emptiness, frustration, and dissatisfaction.

Not all the unusual features of the relationship between the depressed mother and child can be subsumed under the rubric of role reversal. The heavy gloomy atmosphere, for example, created by the mother's posture, sighing, or weepiness cannot be included although it does involve a reversal of the usual (or perhaps ideal) atmosphere in a family with young children. As Weissman and Paykel (1974) have made clear, the child is also likely to be the chief recipient of the mother's hostility and invective (e.g., Luke's mother's explanation of Granny's leaving). There is also frequently an extreme discrepancy between the mother's verbal and nonverbal cues; for example, some depressed mothers cuddle the child a lot to comfort themselves while keeping up a stream of criticism of the child. The combined effect of these behaviors is likely to be a pessimistic outlook, poor self-esteem, and confusion about the meaning of interpersonal behaviors. The lack of basic security that they produce is likely to result in a state of "anxious attachment" in some individuals or a precocious "pseudo-independence" in others, depending on their temperament and on other factors in the environment, such as the availability of alternative attachment figures or the ordinal position in the family that the child occupies.

The discussion so far has concentrated for simplicity on the effect of the mother's behavior on the child as if the child were a *tabula rasa* who contributes nothing of himself to the interaction. A fuller description would take into account the dyadic system that they mutual-

127

ly create, as well as the larger family system of which the dyad is a part. The advent of children to a family introduces new sources of stress to which a childless couple is not exposed, and there is some evidence that childless couples are likely to have happier marriages (Slater and Woodside, 1951; Humphrey, 1975). Malmquist and Kaj (1971) also found more physical and psychiatric illness in a group of women who had borne children than in their childless twin sisters. If childbearing and child rearing are themselves sources of stress, some children are also more stressful than others. It is now clear there are marked temperamental differences between children that affect the ease with which they adapt to caretaking routines, their emotional lability, and predominant affective state (Thomas and Chess, 1977). Some children are simply harder to rear than others and require a higher degree of skill and tolerance on the part of the mother. A child who sleeps or eats poorly or who is excessively sensitive to change can undermine the confidence of a vulnerable mother and make her feel she is a "bad mother" who cannot make her child happy. The stage is then set for a downward spiral into increasing depression on her part and increasingly disturbed behavior on the part of the child. Much will also depend on the response of the father and other family members to the situation. As Hinde (1979, p. 51) has recently pointed out, "The complexity of the family system ensures that simple relations between particular influences in infancy and childhood and subsequent behaviour will be the exception rather than the rule."

Hinde considers the possibility that the demonstration of no effect from a particular variable (e.g., separation or parental death) may reflect a genuine negative finding, the insensitivity of the measures used, or the short time scale of the study. There may be long-term or "sleeper" effects of certain experiences that are not apparent until much later, perhaps when the subject is an adult and exposed to demands for mature and responsible behavior. Women who have suffered early loss, for example, are more likely to have problems during pregnancy and more likely to have difficulties in the early child-rearing period (Frommer and O'Shea, 1973; Wolkind, Kruk, and Chaves, 1976). There are many children in disturbed families who show no symptoms of severe disturbance, although the clinician may be concerned about their excessively serious or overresponsible behavior that is obviously inappropriate for their age. It is possible that a sleeper effect operates here too since we know that children with behavior disturbances are at high risk of becoming antisocial adults whereas neurotic children are no more than averagely likely to become neurotic adults. The question arises as to which children do become neurotic in later life. It seems likely, as Cooper has suggested, that it is the children who make an apparently good adjustment to a bad situation, like some of those described here, who are at high risk of later disturbance and we should be as concerned about them as for their more overtly disturbed siblings.

Conclusion

Depression in the mothers of young children has been shown to be a common disturbance and one that is highly associated with psychiatric disorder in the children. The effects on them are likely to be severe, but will vary according to the type of depression, the child's temperament, and the alternative sources of nurture in the family environment. Reversal of the normal mother-child roles is frequently observed, as is ambiguity in communication and maternal irritability and lack of responsiveness. Even in children who appear to make a good adaptation to the stress to which they are exposed, the long-term effects are likely to reflect lack of inner security and disturbed personal relationships. The implications for preventive psychiatry of such a widespread hazard to healthy child development cannot be underestimated. They are comparable to those of early loss or separation to which attachment theorists have long paid deserved attention.

REFERENCES

Abraham, K. 1927. *Selected papers*. London: Hogarth.

Ainsworth, M. D. S., and Bell, S. M. 1970. Attachment, exploration and separation: Illustrated by the behavior of one-year-olds in a strange situation. *Child Development* 41:49–67.

Ainsworth, M. D. S.; Blehar, M. C.; Waters, E.; and Wall, S. 1978. *Patterns of Attachment*. Hillsdale, N.J.: Lawrence Erlbaum Associates.

Bowlby, J. 1953. *Child care and the growth of love*. London: Penguin Books.

———— 1974. Attachment theory, separation anxiety and mourning. In *American handbook of psychiatry. Vol. 6: New psychiatric frontiers*, ed. D. A. Hamberg and K. H. Brodie. New York: Basic Books.

Brown, G. W., Bhrolcháin, M. N., and Harris, T. 1975. Social class and psychiatric disturbance among women in an urban population. *Sociology* 9: 225–254.

Brown, G. W., Harris, T., and Copeland, J. R. 1977. Depression and loss. *British Journal of Psychiatry* 130:1–18.

Brown, G. W. and Harris, T. 1978. *Social origins of depression.* London: Tavistock.

Cohler, B. J.: Grunebaum, H. U.; Weiss, J. L.; Gamer, E.; and Gallant, D. H. 1977. Disturbance of attention among schizophrenic, depressed and well mothers and their young children. *Journal of Child Psychology and Psychiatry* 18:115–135.

Cooper, S. F.; Leach, C.; Storer, D.; and Tonge, W. L. 1977. The children of psychiatric patients. *British Journal of Psychiatry* 131:514–522.

Frommer, E. A. and O'Shea, G. 1973. Antenatal identification of women liable to have problems in managing their infants. *British Journal of Psychiatry* 123:149–156.

Ginsberg, S. and Bolton, N. G. 1976. The dilemma of the unsatisfied mother. Paper presented to the Annual Conference of the Association for Child Psychology and Psychiatry.

Graham, P., Rutter, M., and George, S. 1973. Temperamental characteristics as predictors of behavior disorders in children. *American Journal of Orthopsychiatry* 43:328–339.

Hinde, R. 1979. Family influences. In *Scientific foundations of developmental psychiatry*, ed. M. Rutter. London: Heinemann.

Humphrey, M. 1975. The effects of children upon the marriage relationship. *British Journal of Medical Psychology* 48:274–279.

Lytton, H. 1973. Three approaches to the study of parent-child interaction. *Journal of Child Psychology and Psychiatry* 14:1–15.

Malmquist, A., and Kaj, L. 1971. Motherhood and childlessness in monozygous twins II. The influence of motherhood on health. *British Journal of Psychiatry* 118:22–28.

McCord, W., McCord, J., and Verden, P. 1962. Familial and behavioral correlates of dependency in male children. *Child Development* 33:313–326.

Pitt, B. B. 1968. Atypical depression following childbirth. *British Journal of Psychiatry* 114:13–25.

Richman, N. 1974. The effects of housing on pre-school children and their mothers. *Developmental Medicine and Child Neurology* 16:53–58.

————, 1976. Depression in mothers of pre-school children. *Journal of Child Psychology and Psychiatry* 17:75–78.

————, 1977. Behaviour problems in pre-school children. *British Journal of Psychiatry* 131:523–527.

————, Stevenson, J. E., and Graham, P. J. 1975. Prevalence of behaviour problems in three-year-old children. *Journal of Child Psychology and Psychiatry* 16:271–287.

Rutter, M. 1966. *Children of sick parents.* Maudsley Monograph no. 16. London: Oxford University Press.

————, Quinton, D., and Yule, W. In press. *Family pathology and disorder in children.* London: Wiley.

Schaffer, H. R. 1977. *Studies in mother-infant interaction.* London: Academic Press.

————, and Emerson, P. E. 1964. Patterns of response to physical contact in early human development. *Journal of Child Psychology and Psychiatry* 5:1–13.

Shields, J. 1976. Polygenic influences. In *Child psychiatry—modern approaches*, ed. M. Rutter and L. Hersov. London: Blackwell.

Slater, E. and Woodside, M. 1951. *Patterns of marriage.* London: Cassell.

Thomas, A. and Chess, S. 1977. *Temperament and development.* New York: Brunner/Mazel.

Tonge, W. L., James, D. S., and Hillam, S. M. 1975. Families without hope: A controlled study of 33 problem families. *British Journal of Psychiatry* Special Publications no. 11.

Weissman, M. M., and Paykel, E. S. 1974. *The depressed woman.* Chicago: University of Chicago Press.

Winnicott, D. 1958. Aggression in relation to emotional development. In *Collected Papers—Through paediatrics to psychoanalysis.* London: Tavistock.

Wolkind, S. N., Kruk, S., and Chaves, L. P. 1976. Childhood separation experiences and psycho-social status in primiparous women, preliminary findings. *British Journal of Psychiatry* 128:391–396.

7

Beverley Raphael

THE YOUNG CHILD AND
THE DEATH OF A PARENT

THE POWERFUL NATURE of the young child's ties to his parents and his dependence upon them for much of his nurturance and survival has led to many concerns about the effect upon him of the loss of these bonds. A childhood history of the death or loss of a parent is common in the fields of adult psychiatric and social morbidity. However, more specific and scientific assessments of the effects of the death of a parent upon a young child, both at the time of the loss and subsequently, have been difficult. The multiple variables operating, the many disruptions associated with the death of a parent, and the different time spans that may operate before effects are evident all make it difficult to draw definite conclusions as to the pathogenic potential of parental loss.

This complexity is reflected in the broad literature on childhood bereavement. Thus there are, for instance, a great many retrospective studies of psychiatrically disturbed populations (e.g., Gregory, 1966) suggesting that those who have suffered a childhood bereavement may be more likely to develop psychiatric disorders in adult life. Proneness to depression and suicidal tendencies have been the main areas of morbidity (Birtchnell, 1972), but even schizophrenia has been

Grateful acknowledgment is made to Joystna Field, Helen Kvelde, Joanna Barnes, MeeMee Lee, and Robert Watton whose generous work with this project assisted in the preparation of this paper; to the bereaved families who so willingly involved themselves; and to the National Health and Medical Research Council of Australia, which supported the project with funding.

131

related to childhood bereavement (Watt and Nicholi, unpublished ms.). So has antisocial behavior in adult life, particularly alcohol problems and delinquency (Markusen and Fulton, 1971). As critical reviewers have pointed out, the methodological problems of these studies make it difficult to draw conclusions valid for current populations or for young children now experiencing such losses.

Studies of the actual responses of bereaved children are few. Many have been drawn from clinic populations of children already psychiatrically disturbed who have experienced a bereavement. Thus there is the classic paper of Arthur and Kemme (1964), which discusses many of the patterns found in eighty-three such children from age four and one-half to seventeen. These workers describe a range of behaviors from absence of any overt response, initial denial, sadness, and crying to numerous behavioral symptoms such as regressive soiling, clinging, aggressive behaviors, and sleep disturbance. Others have described the patterns of response seen in children who have already been in analytic treatment, but as these have been isolated case studies and the children were already disturbed enough to require analysis, it is difficult to draw many conclusions. Furman (1974) has made a useful contribution in her book *A Child's Parent Dies*, where she describes the experience of childhood bereavement reconstructed from extensive analytic data.

Only in more recent years has there been a number of research projects that attempt to look prospectively at childhood responses to the death of a parent. Black (1976a, b) describes her work with bereaved families where family intervention is aimed at helping the children's response to the death of a parent. Becker and Margolin (1967) describe a small study of the many difficulties faced by surviving parents as they attempted to help their children adapt to loss. Bedell (1973) notes how fathers often perceived their children as little affected by their mother's death and did not appear to recognize that some of their behavior reflected their grief. Lifschitz and associates (1977) studied responses and adaptation in different groups of Israeli children (a total of forty-eight children from thirty-one families) following the October War. She found that boys were more affected than girls, and kibbutz children less than other children, by their fathers' deaths. Where the mother's approach was "concretistic and affectionate" the adjustment was more positive than when this was not the case, especially so where the child was perceived as similar to one of the parent figures (especially the idealized father).

Findings in these studies of bereaved children are further complicated by the effects of parental deprivation. As Rutter (1972) has pointed out, these effects are certainly not simple, and the powerful influences of parental discord, disharmony, and dysfunction may be more clearly correlated with childhood pathology than with deprivation effects. A relevant question is whether or not the pathological effects observed in some but certainly not all children are related to the bereavement or to the prolonged absence of a parent from certain critical roles.

None of this work has provided an adequate theoretical or conceptual model with which to view the child's response to the death of a parent. Controversy exists regarding the child's capacity or incapacity to conceptualize the death and what has happened (Koocher, 1974; Nagy, 1948; Furman, 1964) and the child's affective response and the degree to which it reflects or differs from the grief of adults.[1]

There is much discussion as to whether or not mourning is possible for children and how similar it is to adult mourning. Some researchers, such as Wolfenstein (1966), suggest that mourning is not possible for young children until the resolution of adolescence when detachment from parent figures takes place. Kliman and associates (1973) and Bowlby (1963, 1980) suggest, however, that mourning similar to that of adults does take place in children.

Bowlby's current view is that the course of mourning in children is, in most respects, similar to its course in adults, and also that the conditions affecting its course are similar at all ages. Among conditions necessary for a favorable outcome are the child continuing to have a secure attachment, either to the surviving parent or to a substitute, and being fully informed about the death and given ample and repeated opportunities to discuss its implications. Unfortunately, as the following study shows, all too often these conditions are not met.

The Study Format

Contact was made with bereaved families who had been brought to our attention by doctors and other professional caregivers in the first few weeks following the death of a parent. Families were selected to include only those with children eight years of age and under. People who fit the criteria of our study were then contacted first by letter.

---

1. See Bowlby, 1960; Nagera, 1970; Mahler, 1961; Furman, 1964; and Kliman et al., 1973.

This letter explained that we were trying to understand the needs of parents and children when one parent died. It went on to state that people who were experienced in understanding the needs of bereaved families would like to call to discuss this with the parent and the surviving child or children. The families would then be contacted by phone or in person within one to two weeks of the letter's arrival. By this method, all the families (except one) that we had names and addresses for and that fit the study criteria agreed to be involved in the study.

The two psychologists carried out interviews and assessments with the families in their own homes. One member of the team worked with the surviving parent to assess his or her grief and perception of the child's or children's responses. The other worked directly with the child or children. Previous experience with bereaved families (Raphael, 1977) had suggested that both the bereaved spouse and child or children had intense needs, so assessment would need to be carried out in a sensitive and skilled manner. Further ethical issues involved the problem of gaining informed consent from such young children, as has been pointed out by Katz (1975). The project was carefully explained in simple terms to children and surviving parents, and they all readily agreed to participate. Many of these difficulties were dealt with in the pilot study, including definitions of the age group to be studied. The decision to concentrate on the younger age range was made because of the conceptual changes (in understanding death) described as occurring at or after this time and the vulnerabilities linked to bereavement at a younger age (e.g., Brown and Harris, 1978; Brown, chapter 12 herein).

ASSESSMENT WITH THE CHILD

The children of the study, aged two to eight years, were assessed as follows:

1. The interviewer introduced herself and gently queried the child about his willingness to talk and play with the interviewer.

2. The interviewer acknowledged the parent's death and that many children had feelings about such a thing happening and that the interviewer would try to learn of the child's own feelings.

3. The interviewer accompanied the child to a place in the house of the child's selection (almost invariably the children chose their own bedrooms) where they could play together.

4. The interviewer gently questioned the child about what had happened, what the child understood about it, and why and what had

happened in the family since with the surviving parent, siblings, and relevant others (e.g., grandparents, etc.) and at school, if the child attended school. As will be discussed, many children were able to respond directly and utilize the situation to discuss directly their perception of what had happened, to express their current feelings, and to reveal their fears.

5. *Doll play.* A portable dollhouse that opened up like a suitcase was utilized. Children were asked to select a family, initially allowed to play freely, and then asked to play through a number of regular sequences of family life, with gentle querying and exploration as they did so. If children were unable or unwilling to play through these sequences, then free play was allowed and noted. The family selected, themes, affect, and type of play and caregiving rituals were noted.

6. *Drawings.* Children were given papers and colored felt pens and asked to draw. After free drawings, which were noted, they were asked to draw a person, their family, and how they felt inside, as well as any other particular drawings they wished to do. Again, content, themes, affect, and children's descriptions of what the drawings represented were noted, as well as areas of difficulty.

7. *Picture cards.* Because of the apparent unsuitability of existing projective card tests, four other picture cards were devised in an attempt to further explore projective material. These were a scene of a woman sick in bed with family around; a mother sitting at the table with children; a father at the table with a child; and a child sitting alone with a dog outside the house. Children were shown the cards in this order and asked to tell a story about each card. The child's general response, content of story, themes, and affect were noted.

8. The assessment ended by the interviewer asking if there was anything the child wished to bring up. Attempts were made to deal with such issues if they were discussed. A brief family interview closed the session.

ASSESSMENT WITH THE SURVIVING PARENT

The data collected on the children was further augmented by descriptive data from the surviving parent, who was interviewed by the second interviewer. In a nondirective semistructured interview the following areas were explored with the surviving parent:

1. Demographic variables including social class, religion, and family structure.

2. Surviving parent's own background (e.g., previous bereavements, past health, etc.) and nature of relationship to spouse who died.

3. Description of the death and circumstances surrounding it, as well as surviving parent's response, current state and coping, and other crises and perceived unsupportiveness of social network. (These variables as well as the quality of the preexisting relationship have been shown to be relevant to the outcome of adult bereavement for widows surviving the death of a husband—Raphael, 1977.)

4. Surviving parent's description of each child's background, including: the parent's perception of the child's relationship to the dead parent; health, behavioral, and developmental history; schooling; patterns of family and interpersonal relationships; previous losses and separations; and perception of child's relationship to the surviving parent.

5. Surviving parent's description of each child's knowledge of, involvement in, and response to the death and to the absence of the dead parent, including: details such as what the child has been told; whether or not child saw the body or attended the funeral, showed any behavioral alteration, symptoms or health change, or any alteration of social or interpersonal functioning.

GENERAL OBSERVATIONS

General observational assessment was made of the interaction between the surviving parent and each child, between the children themselves, and of the whole family unit and their response to and interaction with the interviewers. In particular, note was taken of the ability to discuss the death and dead parent; the capacity to show affect relevant to the loss; awareness by the parent of the child's communications relevant to grief and the need for care; and the parent's capacity to respond to it.

The most appropriate time for contacting such recently bereaved families was determined from earlier experience and pilot studies. All of my earlier work suggests that during the first two to three weeks the families are still in a state of shock and denial, overwhelmed by practical matters, visiting relations, and so on. From that time onward increasing awareness of the loss and its reality usually leads the bereaved to wish to communicate intensely with others about what has happened. This desire diminishes after six to eight weeks as some form of adjustment, satisfactory or pathological, starts to consolidate. It was decided that contact with families would be, as far as possible, initiated during this period of two weeks to two months after the loss.

It was decided that assessments would be carried out over four sessions in the family's own home. This proved, for the most part, to be satisfactory in that rapport was established yet the relationship did not promise or provide more than the opportunity for limited exploration of difficulties.

This Sample

The following results are based on twenty families seen during one segment of the study that is still ongoing. This report covers thirty-five children between the ages of two and eight, twenty-one girls and fourteen boys. There was one family with three children, fourteen with two children, and four with one child. Families came from all socioeconomic classes from professional wealth to poverty. The homes in which they were interviewed varied from comfortable and spacious establishments in which each child had a private area of his or her own, to caravans with no heat or electricity (in which it was not possible to see the children by themselves). Parents had died from a variety of causes including the sudden deaths of young fathers in motor vehicle accidents or from heart attacks, to the prolonged and painful deaths of some of the mothers and fathers from malignancy. Family relationships as described prior to the death varied also, from warm and loving intimacy to antagonistic with chaotic and painful family situations in which separation would have occurred had the partner not become ill. However, in only one of these families did the surviving adults see the family as sick or themselves or the children as being in need of professional help.

PATTERNS OF PARENTAL LOSS

There were ten children who lost a *mother*, six girls and four boys, representing six families. Causes of deaths were malignancies in three instances, and in these families there had been a prolonged period of warning and some degree of family reorientation in preparation for the death. In the other families deaths had been sudden: for instance, accident, cerebral hemorrhage, and operative complications, with virtually no warning in any case.

There were twenty-five children who had lost a *father*, fifteen girls and ten boys, representing fourteen families. The causes of death ranged through murder, motor vehicle accident, and heart attack in the case of sudden unanticipated deaths in nine families, representing eighteen children. In five families, representing seven children, the more prolonged deaths all resulted from some form of malignancy.

BEHAVIORAL OR SYMPTOMATIC DISTURBANCE

One of the most dramatic and disturbing findings in this small study is the number of behavioral symptoms found in the children in these early weeks and months following the parent's death. A checklist of behavioral symptoms included the following: evidence of high anxiety, exaggerated separation responses, clinging behavior, excessive crying, marked aggressive behavior, sleep disturbance, disorders of eating or toileting, or other miscellaneous habit disorders and physical symptoms. All of these behavioral responses may well appear as manifestations of normal grief, and if they did appear because of the child's grief and mourning, they would be very similar to many of the behavioral responses and experiences of the recently bereaved adults who have been described, for instance, by workers such as Lindemann (1944) and Parkes (1972) (e.g., marked anxiety, withdrawal, clinging, crying, aggressive behavior, sleep disturbance, and physical symptoms).

Only seven of the thirty-five children were reported to show such symptoms prior to the bereavement: five girls and two boys whose fathers had died. According to their fathers' report, none of the children whose mothers had died were believed to have had any such symptoms before the mother's death, although this report may have been biased by the fathers' lack of perception of such behavior as opposed to the mothers'. It is also possible, of course, that the surviving parent in each instance was so distressed and preoccupied with his or her loss and their children's that everything before that time was viewed as positive and all difficulties since were overemphasized. However, the one in five (7/35) incidence of symptomatology prior to bereavement would fit with many studies of morbidity in unselected children (and be higher than some) and so does not seem unduly lowered.

Following the bereavement, however, parents reported extensive symptomatology. Thirty out of thirty-five children were reported by their surviving parents as having two or more behavioral symptoms from the list previously mentioned, twenty-four of the twenty-five whose fathers died and six of the ten whose mothers died. (This figure may be low as data was uncertain on two of the four children not reported as symptomatic.) Of those twenty-one children whose parents had died suddenly, all but one girl were symptomatic, and even nine of the fourteen children for whom there had been more warning regarding a parent's imminent death and thus opportunity for gradual adjustment showed behavioral symptoms.

It might well be suggested that distressed, bereaved parents could overestimate their children's disturbance, overreact to minimal behavioral changes, or even project some of their own behavioral responses and symptoms onto the child. This was not substantiated by the research workers' observations for they themselves found almost exactly the same incidence of behavioral symptomatology. They reported twenty-three of twenty-five children whose fathers had died and six of ten whose mothers had died to be symptomatic to at least a level equivalent to that suggested by the parents. Furthermore, this assessment was carried out by a separate research worker at a time when she did not know of the parent's perception of the child's level of behavioral disturbance.

The range of behavioral disturbance shown by the children ranged from wooden and frozen withdrawal, to bouts of uncontrollable aggression, to crying, clinging, and highly anxious excitement and severe separation responses.

CHILDREN'S COMPREHENSION OF WHAT HAD HAPPENED

It has been pointed out by many workers that children may have great difficulty conceptualizing the nature of death and thus in comprehending what has happened when a parent dies. Anthony's work (1940), Nagy's work (1948), and many more recent studies mentioned previously comment on the difficulty that the young child has in understanding the finality of death, especially prior to the age of four to five or perhaps even later. Others have pointed out how much the child's understanding may be interfered with by inaccurate information he is given and the taboos regarding discussion of death.

In this study it was impossible to assess children's perception or understanding of death before this bereavement occurred. Most of the surviving parents had not considered their children's understanding of death to be important previously, and most had not given thought to it beforehand, even in those cases in which there had been warning of the death.

In thirteen of the twenty-five children whose father had died and in five of the ten children whose mother had died, the children were specifically told the dead parent had gone to heaven. This was often related to strong religious affiliation in the family, Catholic or otherwise. But in several instances it was not. Surviving parents who themselves had no apparent religious faith or commitment stated they had told their children that their father or mother had gone to heaven because "what else could you tell them?" Parents seemed incapable of explaining the nature of death to their children when they themselves were struggling to avoid facing its reality. Frequently they conveyed to the children that they would meet their parents again some day, in heaven, where he or she had gone to be with God or Jesus. None of the parents seemed aware of their children's difficulties in comprehending an abstract concept such as heaven and their inevitably concrete interpretation of it. Even older children within the age group studied—for example, a girl of six—interpreted this so concretely as to go out to say "good night" to the father who was seen as a star in the night sky. Several children presented this idea of the dead parent now being a star in heaven.

At the time of assessment, two parents of girls of age three were unable to tell these children at all that the parent had died. In both instances these were sudden deaths, one of a mother and one of a father, in particularly tragic circumstances. In another instance the surviving mother of a three-year-old girl seemed almost unaware of the death (because of her own drug dependency problems) and had communicated nothing about it to her child. These were the most clear-cut instances of a total denial of reality by parents in their communications with the bereaved children, and it may be that their own identifications with the young child, their own sense of helplessness, or the particularly complex circumstances reinforced this solution.

It has been suggested by workers in the field of adult bereavement that seeing the body of the dead person and participating in the funeral are important aspects of recognizing the reality of death, which plays a significant role in subsequent adjustment. In fourteen instances when the father had died, and in six instances when the mother had died, the children were not taken to the funeral or included in any formal ritual. Of these twenty children, twelve had been told that the dead parent had gone to heaven. In eleven out of these twelve instances the death had been sudden with no warning. Thus the dead parent disappeared to a strange place called heaven from where he or she could not or would not come back. Even when an explanation such as heaven had not been given, those bereavements by sudden death where the children were not involved in the funeral and never saw the dead parent again were bound to be a source of confusion.

Assessment of the children themselves by the separate interviewer confirmed these findings. Ten of the seventeen children who had experienced a sudden death and not gone to the funeral gave evidence on more detailed assessment that they did not understand the nature of their parent's death or understand the parent's whereabouts, state, or the finality of their loss. This figure may have been higher, for in three children assessment of this particular aspect was difficult.

With respect to understanding the finality of the loss/death and some perception of its reality, age appeared to exert some influence. Lack of awareness of the finality and reality of the death was more pronounced among younger children and was rare in six- seven- and eight-year-olds, apart from one girl of eight.

Thus it is obvious that there is a considerable degree of misunderstanding in the child's mind surrounding the death and the place where the dead parent has gone. The child may be given many beliefs or may develop fantasies that will be his way of understanding what has happened. The findings documented above indicate many areas of misconception, but there is no evidence to link these directly to the child's subsequent adjustment or response to the death. Although these issues have been highlighted in the studies of adult bereavement as linked to problems and, in some instances, to poor outcome, the relationship between these variables and outcome of childhood bereavement remains to be established.

CHILDREN'S RESPONSES TO THE LOSS: GRIEF AND MOURNING

The children's responses to the loss were gleaned from a number of sources—the surviving parent's description of the child's response; the child's response as revealed directly and to the interviewer; and relevant material appearing more projectively in paintings, doll play, and stories.

Parent's Perception. By their very involvement in the research project it would appear likely that the parents of these children perceived some grief, some response to loss in their children. Many appeared anxious during the interviews as to whether or not their children's responses were normal and what they might expect. However, despite this overall background awareness of possible effects of the loss, a significant number of parents still did not see their children as being affected by the death. They appeared unable to perceive and respond to clear indications of their children's loss-related distress during the interview. In a total of fourteen cases (from nine different families), the surviving parent was unable to perceive the children's communications related to the loss. These parents, on interview, denied any evidence of the child's grief or mourning, or any effect on the chil-

141

dren of the loss of the dead parent. Yet all but one child in this group had significant symptoms that appeared since the loss, both according to the parent and on observation. Three of these nine parents were fathers surviving the death of their wife from cancer and cerebral hemorrhage. Six were mothers surviving their husband's deaths from malignancy, accident, and heart attack. Independent rating of these parent's own grief showed that all but one had pathological grief reactions themselves. It is possible that their own denied or distorted bereavement responses were at least one powerful factor interfering with their capacity to perceive their children's grief and mourning. And it is hardly surprising then that these parents were not only unable to perceive the children's grief-related responses, but also had great difficulty responding to them.

Thus it would seem that in 40 percent of the children (or 45 percent of families) there was a denial by the surviving parent that the child or children showed any response to the loss or that the child or children were affected by it. The pathological grief shown by these parents ranged from total denial of any affect of the loss with the parent carrying on as though nothing had happened, to a bitter, resentful, and continuing rage at the dead spouse's desertion and from a rapid replacement of the dead parent to a continuing guilty self-recrimination. Some vignettes of these families serve to exemplify the issues.

SUDDEN DEATH

Mrs. O had married a much older husband, a very wealthy grazier, who died suddenly and unexpectedly from a heart attack. In her fantasy she had believed he would always be there to support her and care for her, and her inner feelings were of infantile and helpless rage. The children had been seen by her as a source of security in the marriage, especially as her husband had been so closely involved with them. Although during assessments both girls were alternately distressed and clinging or withdrawn, she did not perceive them as having needs for care but said bitterly: "They're all right, they're young," "They'll get over it in no time." She raged at the world for letting a "good man, none better" like her husband die so unfairly. During the assessment interviews the younger daughter approached her to comfort and be comforted but was pushed away. This child had been the father's favorite and had been present at the time of his death, while Mrs. O had been away. Mrs. O's bitter resentments continued unabated with no other aspects of grief or mourning appearing during these months of assessment and follow-up.

LENGTHY ILLNESS

Mr. L had nursed and comforted his wife during her prolonged terminal illness from carcinoma. When she died in the hospital he showed little upset, telling the interviewer that he kept going by believing she was "still there" and would be home again one day. He had avoided going to the burial because he felt his place was with the children and they would have become too disturbed by it. Even two months after the death he had not cried or "broken down" and felt that this was what his wife would have wanted and what was best for the children. His four-year-old son's sleepless nights and bouts of restless aggressive and destructive behavior were seen by him as naughtiness, and he called for strict and rigid control. Whenever his son cried for his mother he told him that he should not, they should all be happy as Mummy was in a good and beautiful place and in no pain, and that one day they would all see her again. His seven-year-old daughter appeared deeply depressed and was described by her teacher as withdrawn and failing at school. Even though the teacher had approached Mr. L about this, he stated that his daughter was being "good," that there was nothing wrong, that she was just being the little mother that his wife would have wished her to be. Mr. L had been intensely dependent on his wife, and he had seen his prolonged care for her as in some ways reflecting the love he had been deprived of by his own mother's early death.

VIOLENT DEATH

Mrs. B had been shocked by her husband's tragic death in a motor vehicle accident. Her son John, aged three, was "all that was left of him" and she clung possessively to the little boy, never letting him out of her sight. She and her husband had had an intensely ambivalent relationship, heightened in her memory by the violent yet typical quarrel they had had the night before his death. Mrs. B had shouted at him during this quarrel that she wished he were dead, that that was the only way she would ever be free of him. She took the news of his death calmly and showed no overt grief. Despite this she idealized the memory of her husband, saying repeatedly what a really good man he was underneath his bad temper. She felt John's nightmares and regression to be of little significance. She constantly stated that they were adjusting well, but on closer inquiry she revealed that she was visiting her husband's grave daily. Her marital relationship had reflected her own poor self-esteem in that she had felt rejected by both parents with their constant quarreling and favoritism toward her younger brother (also called John).

It would seem that in these and the other instances the surviving parent's own deprivation in the face of the loss was particularly great and the sense of helplessness and rage not only reawakened painful earlier deprivations and losses but also perhaps blocked the parent's capacity to perceive the helplessness and distress of the child or children.

Children's Responses. Many of the children were able to utilize the researcher's interview to express their sadness and pining for the lost parent. All of the children whose mothers had died, except one three-

143

year-old, could show this sadness and longing for the mother's return and talk of her directly and how they missed her. Seventeen of the twenty-five children whose father had died could talk of him directly and of the fact that he had died. Eight could not mention or discuss the dead father, and a further three could not express their sadness or pining, to make a total of eleven (six out of ten boys and five out of fifteen girls) who, following the father's death, did not show any sadness or pining for their dead father during assessment. The boys tended to fall into the older age group, from five to eight years, and the girls into the younger age range, from three to four years. However, with such small numbers it is difficult to draw any firm conclusions. Many of the children showed some angry responses in relation to the loss except for seven of the girls and one of the boys whose fathers had died, and two of the older boys whose mothers had died. This group of ten included seven of those who did not show sadness or pining for the lost parent, as well as three others. These three did show pining and sadness but no anger at all appeared during assessments in relation to the loss.

When more projective assessments were made, these eleven children who showed no sadness or pining still had difficulty in showing the nature or effects of their loss in free play, doll-play situation, or drawings. But this block was by no means total, and some who had initially not shown much response gradually brought forth their feelings. For instance, one three-and-one-half-year-old from very disturbed family situation responded with doll play about a distressed little girl crying for a father who had "gone away." Another boy whose mother had died showed his longing for her in sad drawings. One little girl whose mother had died came from a situation in which her father wished to deny any effects of his wife's death. She did not communicate her longing for her mother directly but while the interviewer was temporarily out of the room she picked up the tape recorder, which was still recording, and said into it: "Mummy's gone . . . where's mummy . . . your mummy's not here . . . bye-bye mummy."

Some trends are to be seen in these findings. Older boys, as a group, appeared to have difficulty in expressing their sadness and longing for the dead parent. It was not easy for them to involve themselves in the doll-play situations, and the drawings of those who took part in this assessment were often more mechanical, avoiding sensitive emotional areas. Aggressive feelings and anger appeared more readily, both directly at interview and in the themes of play and projective material. Angry play was often very uncontrolled, with toy cars crashing down stairwells, tanks and trucks killing off wild animals, warlike and fero-cious happenings. One eight-year-old boy expressed to the interview-er the conflict he faced: "I like to play soldiers and wars and kill peo-ple. But I don't like it if they *really* die."

It is of course difficult to definitely relate these aggressive themes to the bereavement. Control studies suggest they are generally common in much of the spontaneous play of children of this age range. How-ever, anger and aggression were often expressed in direct relationship to the loss, suggesting that it was possible for these children to venti-late such feelings, as might a bereaved adult responding to a loss.

Sometimes the children's lack of pining, yearning, and sadness was clearly related to parental response and behavior. One three-year-old girl had not been told her mother had died, but that she was still in the hospital. The father had kept putting off her queries as to where her mother was. Often the surviving parent's own grief was pathologi-cal, avoiding the realities of the loss or the emotions involved. Conse-quently it was little wonder that the children were unable to acknowl-edge or bring forth their own feelings. The role models or sources of identification offered by the surviving parent might be a significant factor.

The ways in which children were able to bring up their fears and concerns directly and indirectly were of interest. Within the younger group (four years and younger) there were four children whose moth-er had died and nine whose father had died. They were, on the whole, just as likely as the older children to be able to talk of the dead parent longingly and with tears.

Anxieties related to the loss or absence of the dead parent appeared in many ways. A common theme of insecurity reflecting concerns at an oral level was shown in the children's concern with eating and food. When the mother had died the children were worried about who would feed them or cook and prepare the food. They talked, for instance, about whether or not older children could cook and what they would eat. When the father had died there were worries about where the money would come from to buy the food and who would provide it now that the father had gone. Some of the school-age chil-dren appeared anxious about the responses of others to them, now that they were "different" and without a father or mother. On the whole, however, families reported that schools seemed very supportive in their handling of the children after the death.

There were not many concerns among these children about the possi-bilities of their own death, such as might have occurred if death anxi-

145

eties had been triggered by the parent's death. This is probably related to the age range, supporting work that suggests that children's conceptualization of death as something that could happen to themselves is more likely to appear about the age of eight to nine (Anthony, 1940).

The Family Unit

The surviving parent's grief and response to the child's or children's needs following the death are almost certainly powerful factors in the child's or children's adjustment to loss, although obviously not the only influencing variables. The status and adjustment of the family unit as a whole is likely to be important, especially in children of this age range (two to eight years). There were some general observations of interest in the early assessments of these bereaved families.

First, there was an enormous range of prebereavement family functioning, though it must be recognized that these evaluations were carried out from parents' reports after the death. In at least four families breakup of the marriage had occurred temporarily and would have continued but for the diagnosis of malignant disease. These parents stayed together, some with a renewed and rich relationship, others with resentment and ambivalence. In one family the lover of both the husband and the wife stayed with the family during the terminal phase, and the children's distress about the death of their mother was complicated by their insecurity and confusion and the father's total rejection of one of them. In other families a clear schism had existed, with the children divided between the parents, one child "belonging" to one parent and one to another. The child whose parent had died seemed to feel overwhelming loneliness as these family systems struggled to adjust to the bereavement.

The role of extended families, grandparents, and surrogate parent figures in buffering the children and the family against the deprivation that followed the loss varied a great deal. In some instances, especially when the mother had died and there had been adequate warning of the death, the grandparents had already established new patterns of family ritual involving care for the children that appeared to greatly enhance the children's sense of security. This was most likely to occur when there had been considerable forewarning of the death, but it also happened when extended families responded to the emergency of sudden death of a young parent and established some sort of supports for continuity of family life in the everyday sense. Whether families could maintain this satisfactorily over the long term was often a source of anxiety, especially for the surviving parent who was torn between maintaining life "as normal as possible" and attempts to avoid dependence on parent figures. Sometimes further emergencies supervened, perhaps related to the stress of the bereavement. For instance, in two cases supportive members of the extended family became seriously ill themselves.

Extended families were not helpful in all instances. As has been noted in earlier research with widows, the parents-in-law (i.e., the parents of the dead person) sometimes became embroiled in bitter conflict with the surviving parent (Raphael, 1977). Sometimes it appeared that they wanted to take over the children for themselves, perhaps as a last remnant of or to make up for the loss of their own child. This type of behavior was often very distressing to the family unit as a whole, placing further strain on it during the period of crisis.

Difficulties of the Research

There are obviously multiple variables involved in the young child's response to the death of a parent. The data from the small group of children reported on to date in this study do not do justice to the complex effects and interrelationship of these many factors. It is hoped that as additional families are seen and followed up over a period of years the picture will clarify and the significance of the influences previously described will be verified.

It would be remiss, however, to put aside what has been reported by these families and to ignore what it may reveal. Many obstacles stood in the way of contact with them. These ranged from expressions of overt enthusiasm by some professionals who subsequently referred nobody to the researchers, to outright rejection by others on the ground that the whole project was "ghoulish." Few denied that bereaved children might have needs, but many showed a reluctance toward any method of finding out what these needs might be.

Once the families were contacted, they were, for the most part, willing to be involved. Their motivation appeared to include a curiosity about the normality or otherwise of their own responses, a wish for

147

care or for someone to talk to, and a desire to make something positive out of their pain and distress, in giving so that others could be helped. At another level some parents seemed to be attempting to deal with feelings of guilt about the children. They wished to make sure that they had "done the right thing" for the children. Yet often this amounted to asking the researchers to call, but being hesitant beyond this, rationalizing that they had had the children "checked out" and that was sufficient. Most parents, however, were deeply concerned for their children, aware of their own helplessness and lack of knowledge. They were preoccupied with their own grief and saw the project as helpful in providing at least some objective opportunity to discuss their concerns. The children themselves seemed to value their involvement; often they looked forward to sessions and were reluctant to see them end.

The fact that the sessions were valued by both parents and children, and that there was a wide discussion of the loss, with emotional release, suggests that a significant level of intervention was taking place in these research assessment sessions. All sessions were tape-recorded. Specific interpretations or direct interventions of a psychotherapeutic kind were avoided except where they were essential to clarify information or obtain data. Notes were made of all "interventions" as well as ordinary interchanges so effects could be taken into account at follow-up. Bereaved groups who have not been assessed in this way but simply evaluated at follow-up will be utilized for comparison so that the intervention effect can be measured.

The research assistants themselves were skilled and qualified psychologists, trained to work in situations of personal distress. Yet this work proved immensely stressful for them. Independent sessions were arranged for them to talk over their experience of the children and parents with a consultant not connected with the project. It was hoped that this would provide support while lessening any potential bias. Their feelings at one level revolved around concern for the children's loss, the circumstances and poor resources that added to the burden for some families, the enormity of conflicts awakened by the loss in some instances, and the long-term difficulties to be expected among children growing up in a single-parent family.

However, at other levels deeper and more significant conflicts within the research team were touched upon by this research. These underlie many of the difficulties of research and work in this field, leading to conflict and resistance in those who would be involved. Some of the conflict themes included identification with the bereaved child, surrogate-parent responses with a wish to make up for the child's losses, intense feelings of helplessness as there was no "cure" for this painful situation, anxieties about death and vulnerability to it of themselves and their families. There was also often a sense of depletion and a feeling of need for special succor and support.

Conclusions

The child's experience of the death of a parent is obviously painful. There is much to suggest that a parent's death brings about in the child a level of "symptomatic" disturbance not dissimilar from that of acute grief in adults. Whether or not children's grief is "pathological" with this level of symptomatic disturbance is difficult to say. The only convincing evidence of pathological effects must come from long-term follow-up with careful control, so judgment in this aspect must be reserved until this has been carried out. The loss may come with forewarning or suddenly and unexpectedly, as an unbelievable nightmare, disrupting the warmth and continuity of family life. For some children this bewilderment, pain, and chaos is superimposed on family situations already filled with rejection, loss, and pain. In others it may cut across a warm and loving intimacy. The children may be told many things about the death, often adding further to their confusion—or they may not be told anything at all. Many are able to show their pining, sadness, and loss directly, but others cannot. The surviving parents, torn by their own grief, may be unable to perceive or respond to their children's needs at this time. That some young children, with support, do grieve and mourn for the dead parent seems likely, but certainly for many others mourning takes on a pathological form. The painful crisis of the death is just the beginning of a long period of readjustment for the child and the surviving parent. It is likely that many more important variables influencing outcome will become obvious as resistance to work in this area is lessened. It is hoped that ultimately such data will provide a sound basis for services to support these children and their families and prevent unfavorable outcome.

149

REFERENCES

Anthony, S. 1940. *The child's discovery of death.* London: Kegan Paul Trench Trubnor.

Arthur, B., and Kemme, M. 1964. Bereavement in childhood. *Journal of Child Psychology and Psychiatry* 5:37–49.

Becker, D., and Margolin, F. 1967. How surviving parents handled their young children's adaptation to the crisis of loss. *American Journal of Orthopsychiatry* 37:753–757.

Bedell, J. 1973. The maternal orphan: Paternal perceptions of mother loss. Paper presented at Symposium on Bereavement, Foundation of Thanatology, New York, November 1973.

Birtchnell, J. 1972. Early parent death and psychiatric diagnosis. *Social Psychiatry* 7:202–210.

Black, D. 1976a. Working with widowed mothers. *Social Work Today* 6(22):684–687.

————. 1976b. What happens to bereaved children. *Proceedings of the Royal Society of Medicine* 69:38–40.

Bowlby, J. 1960. Grief and mourning in infancy and early childhood. In *The psychoanalytic study of the child,* ed. R. S. Eissler et al., vol. 15. New York: International Universities Press.

————. 1963. Pathological mourning and childhood mourning. *Journal of the American Psychoanalytic Association* 11:500–541.

————. 1980. *Attachment and loss. Vol. 3: Loss: Sadness and depression.* New York: Basic Books.

Brown, G., and Harris, T. 1978. *Social origins of depression.* London: Tavistock.

Furman, E. 1974. *A child's parent dies.* New Haven, Conn.: Yale University Press.

Furman, R. 1964. Death and the young child. In *The psychoanalytic study of the child,* ed. R. S. Eissler et al., vol. 19. New York: International Universities Press.

Gregory, I. 1966. Anterospective data concerning childhood loss of an adult. *Archives of General Psychiatry* 15:362–367.

Katz, B. F. 1975. Children, privacy, and nontherapeutic experimentation. *American Journal of Orthopsychiatry* 45(5):802–812.

Kliman, G.; Feinberg, D.; Buchsbaum, B.; Kliman, A.; Lubin, H.; Ronald, D.; and Stein, M. 1973. Facilitation of mourning during childhood. Paper presented at Symposium on Bereavement, Foundation of Thanatology, New York, November 1973.

Koocher, G. 1974. Talking with children about death. *American Journal of Orthopsychiatry* 44:404–411.

Lifschitz, M.; Berman, D.; Galila, A.; and Gilad, D. 1977. The effects of mothers' perception and social system organization on their short-term adjustment. *Journal of the American Academy of Child Psychiatry* 16 (2):272–284.

Lindemann, E. 1944. Symptomatology and management of acute grief. *American Journal of Psychiatry* 101:141–148.

Mahler, M. 1961. On sadness and grief in infancy and childhood. In *The psychoanalytic study of the child,* ed. R. S. Eissler et al., vol. 16. New York: International Universities Press.

Markusen, E., and Fulton, R. 1971. Childhood bereavement and behaviour disorders: A critical review. *Omega* 2:107–117.

Nagera, H. 1970. Children's reactions to the death of important objects—developmental approach. In *The psychoanalytic study of the child,* ed. R. S. Eissler et al., vol. 25. New Haven, Conn.: Yale University Press.

Nagy, M. 1948. The child's theories concerning death. *Journal of Genetic Psychology* 73:3–27.

Parkes, C. M. 1972. *Bereavement: Studies of grief in adult life.* London: Tavistock.

Raphael, B. 1977. Preventive intervention with the recently bereaved. *Archives of General Psychiatry* 34:1450–1454.

Rutter, M. 1972. *Maternal deprivation reassessed.* London: C. Nicholls.

Watt, N. F., and Nicholi, A. Unpublished manuscript. Death of a parent as an etiological factor in schizophrenia.

Wolfenstein, M. 1966. How is mourning possible? In *The Psychoanalytic study of the child,* ed. R. S. Eissler, et al., vol. 21. New York: International Universities Press.

8

Dorothy H. Heard and Muriel Barrett

ATTACHMENT AND THE FAMILY RELATIONSHIPS OF CHILDREN WITH SPECIFIC READING DISABILITY

Introduction

Rutter and Yule (1975) have shown that a strong case can be made for distinguishing from all children backward in reading a special group who have severe reading retardation (S.R.R.) and in whom the outstanding feature is the intractability of the condition. Though the children are shown to be of normal intelligence by standard tests and no demonstrable neurological deficit is evident, they find it extremely difficult to learn to read, and it follows that teachers find it difficult to teach them.

Our views on S.R.R. are based on clinical work with thirty-five families, each with a child suffering from S.R.R. Twenty-three of these children lived with both of their biological parents. We used an approach to the teaching of reading first developed by Caspari (1974). Caspari's approach employs many of the principles and methods commonly employed by remedial teachers, but, in addition, it links teaching skills with an understanding of family dynamics. Those who worked with the children referred to in this chapter had undertaken postgraduate or in-service training to this end.

Our current working hypothesis is that the difficulties most children with S.R.R. have in learning to read come from a combination of potentially surmountable constitutional factors along with lasting exposure to a particular pattern and intensity of interindividual behavior that affects the child in two distinct ways: first, by contributing to the building up of a negative attitude toward learning to read and to a sense of low self-esteem; and second, by continually evoking feelings and behavior that in themselves interfere with learning and strongly reinforce the sense of low self-esteem and the negative attitude toward learning to read.

Despite our clinical experience, we have been unable to test any specific hypothesis concerning the role played by family dynamics in S.R.R. until we defined in operational terms (1) those qualities in the relationships within families and between family and potential helpers that seem to contribute to the child's difficulties in learning and (2) those qualities in the relationship between teacher and child and between teacher and family that appear to facilitate learning.

Our aim herein is to identify a number of characteristics of interindividual behavior seen in S.R.R. families in which the child lived with both biological parents. We have compared the behavior of family members with the behavior of the person who eventually taught the child to read. The characteristics are described together with a rationale for making this selection. The characteristics are presented in a form in which they can be observed, recorded and quantified, and used to test specific hypotheses about the effects of family dynamics on the ability of children with S.R.R. to learn to read. Moreover, because items in our selection are seen in both S.R.R. families and other families in which the children have learning difficulties, they can be used to investigate whether certain kinds of family dynamics may hinder, while others may facilitiate, the ability of particular kinds of children to learn specific skills.

Rationale for Selection of Interindividual Behavior

We have chosen to depict the quality of relationships by describing certain aspects of the interactions that take place between child, parents, and teacher when the interaction is focused on learning a new skill—in this instance reading. The term "interaction" is used in the sense described by Hinde (1976) as a sequence in which A shows or does something to B and B responds with Y; but in addition we add that the showing and doing include the verbal expression of what people think and feel about, and expect from, each other.

In his paper Hinde discusses the problems in studying human relationships. He begins with the observation that anyone examining the literature on interindividual relationships cannot fail to be struck by the diversity of theoretical and methodological approaches used and by the dearth of attempts to integrate them. He argues that description and classification are essential first steps in order to discuss and compare relationships and the conditions under which they occur. Description, however, involves selection from among the phenomena available for description; and selection must be guided by the uses to which the description is to be put. Hinde raises the question of the basis on which one can make a meaningful prognostic selection when we are still far from having enunciated a comprehensive theory of interindividual relationships. He suggests, with an eye on the dangers of so doing, that the quickest, and possibly sometimes the only, way to meaning may be through *introspective* evidence. With this preamble he goes on to review and discuss eight dimensions in which characteristics of relationships have been described.

Hinde makes the point that this list of dimensions is not exhaustive, nor are the dimensions independent of one another. They are presented as a temporary framework. We found that some of the dimensions fit our material, particularly those that covered content of interaction, diversity of interaction, complementarity versus reciprocity, and "meshing." Nevertheless, we found that the list does not cover certain aspects of relationships that seem to be of particular importance when the context of the interaction is a child learning a new skill. We have therefore turned to attachment theory (Bowlby, 1969, 1973, 1980) as the general theory of human interindividual behavior that best fits the data gleaned from our clinical experience and provides us with a working model that covers an interrelationship between parenting and learning.

Two well-known concepts to do with general psychological organization provide a background for Bowlby's own concepts regarding attachment behavior. They are both discussed fully by Bowlby; here we will present a brief outline in order to explain the view taken in attachment theory about the way the actions of others and expectations about such actions affect an individual's actions and self-image. These are points we illustrate in some detail later.

The first concept is that much behavior, including interactional behavior, can be seen as efforts, often planned in sophisticated ways, to reach definable aims or goals. It carries the assumption that the environment is constantly monitored to ensure that behavior is oriented to move toward the desired aims; and therefore it postulates that goal seeking is governed by a control-systems type of mechanism.

The second concept states that, in order to plan to reach a goal, it is necessary to have internal working models of the world—and of the people in it—in which the plan is to be enacted; and at the same time to have models of oneself in action in the world. Such internal representations are expressed as beliefs and revealed in attitudes. In the ordinary course of events these representations of the world and self are constantly updated and modified in the light of experience. In some instances, however, they appear to remain remarkably fixed.

These assumptions about goal-directed behavior and internal representations imply that we carry in our heads collections of working models, built up over time, of the relationships we have with every person we know in each of many different situations. It also implies that in every interaction we engage in, we plan actions and anticipate the outcome according to our current working model of the other person (or people) and of ourselves, in whatever context the interaction takes place. And here the arousal of feelings has to be taken into account.

Reaching or not reaching goals arouses feelings; feelings, for example, of satisfaction—and often of well-being—are usually aroused when goals are reached. In contrast, feelings of disappointment and frustration are frequently evoked when goals are not reached. Similarly, while plans are being contemplated and put into effect, feelings such as excitement, uncertainty, apprehension, or dread are aroused about the possible outcomes of such plans. Individuals, by and large, tend to seek satisfactions, to dislike failure, and to avoid feelings of loneliness, worthlessness, and rejection especially if these involve people important to them. In many instances we have found that an individual's plans to avoid feelings such as rejection and worthlessness interfere with and may take precedence over plans to reach other goals. For example, a child may show clearly that he wishes to achieve the satisfaction of learning to read but at the same time to avoid the process of learning to read because he considers that in that context he is, and also will be made to feel, "stupid" and "no good." Thus it is not surprising that children with S.R.R. have a similar view of themselves, certainly in the context of reading if not also in relation to other skills. This point is taken further later in the discussion of defense mecha-

154

nisms and the problems to be met in the recognition of attachment behavior in adults and older children.

For clinicians looking for working models that will make the job of understanding intrafamilial behavior and of planning effective intervention easier, Bowlby's concept of attachment behavior and caregiving behavior and his use of the concept of goal-directedness fits clinical experience the better after adding two observations by Ainsworth and associates (1978); first, that in circumstances in which attachment behavior is likely to be aroused exploratory behavior is diminished; and second, that the infant uses his mother as a safe base from which to explore the world. When seen in the light of Winnicott's (1971) concept of creative play and its vital importance in child and adult life, Ainsworth's work led to the idea that exploratory, attachment, and caregiving behavior might be geared together and function as a single dynamic—the attachment dynamic (Heard 1978, 1981).

The working model provided by the attachment dynamic can be outlined briefly, in clinical language, as follows. The term "exploratory behavior" is used to cover natural curiosity and the urge to find meaning in whatever happens; hence it includes the desire to learn. This definition of exploratory behavior is exemplified in psychotherapy with people who are angry about—and in fact are mourning—the lack of opportunity to do things that might satisfy their curiosity or lead to a sense of understanding and mastering something so far unknown or incomprehensible to them. This is a frequent experience in our psychotherapeutic work.

The tendency to explore is balanced, however, throughout life by a more cautious attitude. Whenever one meets with unknown or fearful situations, one explores them while lines of retreat to an accessible safe "base" are kept open (minimally aroused attachment behavior). This "base" may on occasion be a symbolic reminder of an internal representation of a "good enough" attachment figure; or alternatively, if the going gets too hard, it may be familiar approachable people (attachment figures) who are trusted and with whom interaction that will assuage fear are sought, leaving one better able to cope with the unknown or fearful situation than before. Once this kind of interaction has taken place one is ready to explore again and is better equipped psychologically by having acquired new meaning and knowledge. So long as the safe base remains available and functional, one remains able to enjoy life and satisfy curiosity.

From this outline of the attachment dynamic it can be seen that the

155

function of attachment and caregiving behavior is to promote security, well-being, and maturation by the assuagement of fear and uncertainty and by the awakening of exploratory behavior. When the dynamic fulfills its function, the result is adaptive social behavior by family members within and outside of the family. Nevertheless, when parents are anxious and fearful with no one to turn to for their own assuagement, they are unable to assuage the fears of their children, who then suffer from some degree of continuous attachment behavior. In consequence such family members live in a state in which they suffer (and defend against) fears and anxieties in various ways, and their exploratory behavior is inhibited or undertaken with anxiety.

Interindividual Behavior Selected from Clinical Data

In this section we describe the behavior of S.R.R. children, their parents, and clinic staff, as it was seen during clinical interviews and teaching sessions, in order to illustrate the four patterns of behavior introduced in the preceding section. Caregiving that assuages attachment behavior is illustrated by (1) the behavior of the teacher that was followed by the child taking an interest in reading and (2) the behavior of the teacher (and other members of the clinic staff) that seemed to allay fears that parents had about the way they were thought of by clinic staff. We consider some degree of assuagement had taken place for the parents because their behavior toward the clinic team became more "open" and trusting, and, coincidentally, they began to behave in a more supportive way toward the S.R.R. child. Furthermore, although the teacher was putting emphasis on reawakening an interest in learning, there are nevertheless sufficient similarities between the behavior used toward the child and toward the parents to consider that assuagement is a process distinct from, although an essential concomitant to, awakening an interest in learning.

Unassuaging caregiving behavior is exemplified by the behavior the parents showed toward the S.R.R. child when they first attended the clinic, together with reports of how they behaved at home. Exploratory behavior was observed in the behavior of the child when he had begun to make some progress in reading.

Last, we describe behavior of the parents and the S.R.R. child that may reflect aspects of attachment behavior as it is shown by adults and older children.

The recognition of attachment behavior at all ages beyond infancy, and its definition in operational terms, presents major difficulties because, as children get older, the maintenance of proximity to attachment figures becomes increasingly, an internalized and symbolic process (Cohen 1974). Cohen considers that the clinical observations of Fairbairn (1952) and others suggest that internal representations of attachment figures become intertwined with representations of the self and have a pervasive effect on everyday thinking and behavior. The experience of one of us[1] using attachment theory in analytic psychotherapy supports Cohen's suggestions and Bowlby's (1980) theoretical views that defensive exclusion of information is the basis of psychological defense mechanisms. Bowlby holds that a process of "deactivation" of systems mediating attachment behavior, thought, and feeling is put into effect when attachment is not terminated by a parent. This happens more especially when the lack of termination is accompanied by active rejection or punishment for showing a desire for proximity or for interaction (as we have seen in chapters 2 and 4). Such "deactivation" can proceed to a stage of more or less complete defensive exclusion of any kind of sensory flow that might activate attachment behavior and feeling; the result is a state of emotional detachment that can be either partial or complete. In this context Bowlby also draws attention to the phenomenon of parental insistence and pressure for the child to see the parent in a favorable light. To do so a child often appears to have to construe himself in an unfavorable light and to redirect toward himself anger he had originally directed toward an unassuaging parent.

It is therefore to be expected that if a child—or an adult—has a history of frequent lack of termination of attachment behavior, accompanied by anger, rejection, or insistent pressure on the part of parents or significant attachment figures, he will substitute defensive ways of behaving toward such figures in situations in which anger or rejection is expected as well as in situations likely to arouse attachment behavior. Psychotherapeutic experience suggests that there is a wide range of defensive modes of behavior; and the particular mode demonstrated in a particular context will depend partly on the mood attributed to significant attachment figures. Therefore under the heading "defensive

1. Dorothy H. Heard.

attachment behavior" we have described patterns of behavior seen in early interviews when children with severe reading retardation were relating to clinic staff who were both strangers and seen as authority figures.

ASSUAGING CAREGIVING

Caregiving is a highly complex form of behavior. To give some reference points and structure to the list of items we have selected, we have identified five aims the teacher has in mind when working with a child (or an adult). However, any teacher is held back to a greater or lesser extent in fulfilling these aims, partly because of difficulty in assessing cues from the child accurately enough to act in an empathic way and partly because of habitual patterns in the teacher's behavior that she[2] has not yet discovered how to modify. Until they are pointed out the teacher may not even be aware they exist and run counter to declared aims. It is our experience, however, that the more consistently the teacher adopts the behavior to be described, the more effective will be her work with the child, given that the parents are in agreement with the approach taken.

The aims of the teacher are:

1. To show interest in, and acceptance of, the behavior shown and the opinions expressed by the child. It may be noted that "acceptance" is seen as an activity distinct from "agreeing with" or "going along with" another person over some particular issue.

2. To avoid arousing a degree of fear or anger that leads a child to withdraw from interaction, especially over the issue of reading; and to reduce the commonly found high level of fear over making relationships with authority figures.

3. To introduce the child to alternative ways of coping with new, strange, or perhaps frightening experiences.

4. To help the child build an image of himself as: (a) capable of developing a higher level of skill in a range of activities and (b) able to exercise certain skills (at present associated with pain) in a way that will bring him satisfactions.

Signals and messages that will fulfill the aims are given through recognized modes of communication; one signal may serve several aims. The modes of communication distinguished are: (1) bodily posture, gesture, and facial expression; (2) tone of voice; (3) the way syn-

2. As most teachers in our study were women, the feminine pronoun will be used when discussing them.

tax is used in utterances; and (4) the overt information in utterances. The act of distinguishing these four modes of communication serves to introduce the fifth goal for assuagement:

5. To insure a high level of congruence and consistency between the messages and signals conveyed in each of the four modes.

Because many of our examples come from teacher-child interaction or teacher- or staff member-parent interaction, in what follows, the word "teacher" is used to denote any professional caregiver.

We have chosen the giving of attention as one way in which acceptance and interest is signaled. In a one-to-one situation the teacher frequently orients toward the child, modulating the way she does so according to the mood she judges the child to be in. In a group of children (or in a family interview) the teacher shares her attention among the members so that no one is left out and interacts with the group as a whole as well as with individuals.

Because interaction is, on many occasions, an essential part of assuagement, the second characteristic we have selected is behavior associated with inviting, initiating, maintaining, and terminating interactions between pairs, trios, and other combinations of a small group (six to eight people).

"Seeking interaction" is the term given to a gesture or verbal communication that invites interaction with a person or people but that, because it is not responded to, does not result in interaction. "Initiating interaction" refers to a signal that results in at least one exchange of signals between two persons. An interaction is "established" when there have been several exchanges between at least two persons. People can "join" or "leave" an established interaction, but interaction is "terminated" when signals are no longer exchanged. Interactions are further distinguished according to duration and the activities engaged in by the participants.

The activities most commonly seen in the situations in which we observed the child and his family were (1) exercising a particular skill, (2) constructing an artifact, (3) playing imaginatively, (4) playing a game with rules, (5) talking about a particular topic, (6) arguing, (7) "daydreaming," (8) "fiddling about," and (9) watching people. We noted how active particular people are as (1) invitors, initiators, and terminators of interaction; (2) initiators of particular activities during interaction and how often an individual changes his activity during a period when he is not interacting. The frequency and duration of activities and on whose initiative they are taken up or terminated are measures used to assess the mood of a particular person to: (1) engage in specified activities, (2) withdraw from specified activities, (3) engage in activities in cooperation with particular others or "by myself."

Because we have worked with families in a small interviewing room, we have assessed proximity keeping only by noting (1) eye-to-eye contact, (2) easily identifiable movements toward or away from specific people, and (3) physical contact.

In addition to the giving of attention, "acceptance" and "interest" in a person are assessed by the number of invitations given, the number of established interactions initiated, and by certain nonverbal signals. The teacher's stance is calm, relaxed, and alert. Her facial expressions are friendly, she listens attentively, and she responds promptly although her actions are unhurried. She will show pleasure in a child's various achievements and share in the child's expression of pleasure or sadness while avoiding the expression of either emotion to a degree that interferes with her aims. She avoids any demonstration of alarm, disapproval, or anger and the use of dismissive gestures. She speaks clearly and quietly, but uses a range of tone and pitch that is lively and attuned to the mood she judges the child to be in. Nevertheless, whenever the child is excessively active or excited, she speaks with firmness but avoids a rising pitch and strident or threatening tone.

The teacher's invitations to interaction are based on her empathic understanding of the current state of the child or adult; consequently they are impossible to predict. She will, however, always try a different form of invitation should the child or adult fail to respond. Once an interaction is established in a one-to-one situation, she will (1) continue with an activity, (2) change it, or (3) follow the child's lead according to her empathic reading of the child's responses. In a group interaction, the teacher tries to avoid having her attention "captured" by any one member. Should one person demand more prolonged attention, an intimation is given to the others of what is going to happen, while the sense of still being in "interaction" with them is maintained by occasional eye contact or more rarely—and usually only with children—through a touch. The termination of an interaction in an abrupt manner is avoided as far as possible.

In the activities in which she engages with a child and in what she says, the teacher first sets about finding an activity—whether it be a game or using plasticine—in which the child takes an interest and can achieve some success. Around such activities they begin to establish a relationship in which the child discovers that the teacher is friendly, patient, and shows satisfaction with his current achievements. As the relationship becomes established, activities the child associates with failure are gradually introduced, carefully graded so that failure is minimal. If the child makes many mistakes or seems unable to continue, the teacher makes a move to change the activity by a remark such as "This seems to be rather difficult today. Shall we do such and such?" Confrontations are avoided as are exhortations for the child to reach a goal beyond his grasp. The teacher comments on any achievement that the child attains in an unexaggerated way, thus indicating that the achievement is within the child's competence. The following example helps to explain why behaving in this manner might be important.

A boy always became excitedly anxious when told by his father that any achievement was "not good enough, it should be better." In learning to read, it became explicit that the boy expected the same behavior from his teacher that he received from his father. When the boy finally discovered that the teacher reacted differently and was accepting of what he was able to do, the excited, anxious behavior diminished and he began to make progress. It would seem that the view of the self held by parental figures is always accepted by a child as 'correct.' The father here had always expected a higher standard and could not accept the current achievement demonstrated by his son. Consequently the boy was unable to build into his self-image the fact that he had made progress in reading; instead he considered himself to have failed and reacted accordingly.

The next vignette illustrates the relationship with the teacher at a time when Jane, aged eight, was beginning to handle her own fears.

For a long time Jane had had great difficulty in handling fear in a learning situation. She was beginning to do so and to read better when the room next door began to be used by children who made a great deal of noise. One day the noise was particularly loud. Jane was unable to go on with her reading so she went into a playhouse. While doing this she appeared frightened. As part of the play within the playhouse the teacher said that "the neighbors seem to be very noisy today." They had a brief conversation on this subject but Jane could still not settle down and left the playhouse. After trying out a game with boxes, of which she was very fond, she finally turned to the teacher and said, "Let's play Beat Your Neighbor." The two of them exchanged a laugh, played the card game for a short while, and then went back to her reading while the noise next door continued unabated. Earlier in the relationship between Jane and the teacher all changes in activity had been made on the teacher's initiative, especially moves toward reading. Now the teacher initiated only one interaction, albeit at a time when she judged Jane could respond, and Jane finally returned to reading on her own initiative.

UNASSUAGING CAREGIVING

In the previous section the behavior of the teacher was described by including statements of what she avoids doing. By and large, parents of S.R.R. children behave toward their children in ways that the teacher tries to avoid. Here examples are given of the behavior we have seen most frequently. Parents regularly regard our approach as mad or a waste of time. For example, Mr. A constantly told us we were wasting our time: "You must hammer words into Keith. This is the only way he can learn." The A family did in fact change their view—and we were thanked for helping—after the parents had joined in a game (a variant of Scrabble) which Keith won. During the game Mr. A had realized that Keith was working and no longer "sciving."[3]

In our study group, with one apparent exception, parents were at heart angry, anxious, and despairing over the failure of the child to read. The exceptional family "was not bothered." In this case the father "had been the same and had picked it up later." In the other families, children were told regularly they were stupid, lazy, good-for-nothing, or a worry to their parents. Gloomy predictions were made that the child would never read and would never get anywhere. Parents at first showed little empathy for the child. Discussion of the child's achievements in other spheres evoked angry comments such as "Why can he do so and so (which is usually not considered important) and yet not be able to read?"

The majority of fathers were background figures: To quote one son speaking to his overbusy shopkeeper father "You care more for the light bulbs than you do for me." A few fathers were overinvolved in helping their child, constantly exhorting him ("You can do it if you try harder"), using persuasion and threats. Mothers on the whole treated the child as younger than he was and seemed to enjoy his company so long as he fell in with her wishes. Some openly preferred another child.

We will not discuss the marital relationship in this chapter. It was difficult to assess because it was usually effectively concealed, but communication between the parents always appeared to be poor and conflict ridden, although we have seen a few parental alliances with both parents angry with the child for his failure.

---

3. Army slang for lazily avoiding duties.

EXPLORATORY BEHAVIOR

We regard exploration as a form of behavior that can be undertaken during interaction with another or "by myself." It is recognized by:

1. The degree of initiative taken to engage in and contribute, in a resourceful way, to an activity that has a recognizable end product. The end product may be any kind of artifact or the making of a recognizable degree of progress in learning a skill.

2. The length of time attention is held by such an activity and how much it is interrupted by turning to other behavior.

3. Statements that show (a) that consideration has been given to a subject and that someone's view has been extended as a result or (b) questions asked that indicate reflection on a subject and the making of a deduction.

DEFENSIVE ATTACHMENT BEHAVIOR

There were always marked differences in the behavior of the parents directed toward the staff and toward the S.R.R. children; children behaved largely in the same way toward parents and staff. To a greater or lesser extent, all the families were difficult to engage. Appointment arrangements were often misunderstood and late arrivals were commonplace; not infrequently one parent, often but not always the mother, would attend with the child when both parents and child had been invited.

When first seen the parents were all very reluctant to talk about themselves or life at home although this was not always immediately apparent. Some would appear friendly and anxious to be told what to do; they talked volubly but were adept at avoiding direct responses to inquiries. An example is the response of Mrs. C to an inquiry about her son Paul's reading. She spoke at length (turning occasionally to her son for affirmation of her opinion) about Paul's three siblings, his father, two other adopted children, and various friends. Other families left all the initiative for interaction to the clinic staff, giving laconic replies that were largely uninformative. The message the majority of these families put across at the first meeting was that they were a very normal family (an adjective frequently used) that functioned well and happily and whose only problem was a child who was unable to learn to read.

In listening to what the parents said and the way in which they spoke, it seemed that many parents expected to be blamed for their child's failure to read and were determined not to be considered blameworthy. Another group appeared to be forestalling the adverse criticism they seemed to detect in any behavior of the clinic staff that did not come well within the range of behavior described above as "accepting." A few families were despairing in that they presented themselves as unable to do anything about their situation and were overwhelmed by many problems. Such families tended not to be able to attend a clinic at all and were seen in domiciliary visits.

A common feature of all families was an intense interest in the causation of the condition. The implication that was made overt was "if we knew the cause we would know what to do." Efforts would be made to draw clinic staff into such discussion; and private theories—which included many attributions about the child delivered in his presence—were presented in a way that invited affirmation. Little interest was taken in the topic of possible forms of intervention. Common attitudes were: (1) nothing can be done, we have tried everything; (2) we cannot do anything, but you are experts, please take over, yet we doubt whether what you do will be effective.

Parents tended to address their attention and remarks to the clinic team. Often one or both parents would interact with one member of the team only, the other being disregarded. Occasionally parents would try to establish a one-to-one conversation, each with a different staff member, so that conversations could easily develop. Parents seldom interacted with each other or looked at each other and they often ignored the child and discussed him as if he were not there.

Parents would often interrupt a comment addressed to a child and respond for him. However, when a child found it difficult to respond to a staff member's comment, the parents seldom gave encouragement or help. Often there would be a silence, broken by the staff member, with both parents looking ill at ease; alternatively the child would be exhorted to "say something" or "talk to the nice lady." Parents would frequently send different messages to the child. For example, one of them (parent A) would be angry with the child, and parent B would become angry with parent A for the way the child had been treated but would meanwhile—and afterward—leave the child unsupported. The following vignette gives a typical example of parental behavior toward a child in a first interview.

Mr. and Mrs. W, middle-aged parents of ten-year-old Mark, agreed that Mark had a reading problem. They appeared interested in the idea put forward by us that, as Mark's parents knew him better than we, we should all work together to try to discover ways in which Mark could learn. Mrs. W, who sat stiffly (inside a thick, firmly buttoned winter coat), began by attacking her husband for never being available to play football with Mark as he was on night shift and asleep during the day. Mr. W countered by asking our opinion as to how much television Mark should be allowed to watch. Mark appeared to switch off and was unable to answer his father when he was asked why he found reading so difficult. Mr. and Mrs. W seemed angry that he wouldn't respond. It was suggested that perhaps Mark was rather confused and had given up trying to understand why adults were discussing television and spare-time activities when we had said we were here to help him with his reading. Mark was then able to respond to a question about ways in which reading was a problem in school. He answered that teachers didn't always give him enough time to look and think about words. Mr. W became angry about teachers, and Mrs. W took up this theme by relating her useless visits to the school to complain and that nothing had been done. At this point Mr. W reprimanded Mark for not asking the class teacher 'to go more slowly and help him.'

Unassuaging attempts at caregiving by parents were in fact often observed in situations in which defensive attachment behavior would, in our experience, be seen. Because the more extreme forms of unassuaging caregiving were observed in early interviews, and because the behavior of the parents changed to being more assuaging after they had been treated in an assuaging manner, we consider that much unassuaging caregiving can be seen as attempted caregiving that has been overridden, to a greater or lesser extent, by the parents' own defensive attachment behavior.

Three patterns of attachment behavior were commonly shown by children:

1. *Withdrawal with "switching off"* is a state in which the child looks expressionless, tends to slouch, and his movements are careless; he is liable to sit and stare—often into space. He responds only to invitations to interaction that fall well within the range of behavior defined earlier as "accepting." When approached he usually averts his gaze and looks to the floor. When present to a modest degree, a child with this behavior can be described as being shy and awkward. It becomes more marked over a brief period of time following (a) the introduction of certain topics, (b) brisk approaches from an adult, or (c) being told to take an action that the child associates with failure to reach a required standard.

2. *Withdrawal with arguing* was seen less commonly. The child frequently looks sulky, sullen, or defiant; his movements are deliberate and he looks around feigning disinterest. He tends not to respond to

invitations to interact but may follow such invitations by fiddling with objects, such as telephones or desk drawers. He will frequently ignore requests to stop an activity and on occasion will get into an argument with either parent or sometimes both. He tends to be off-hand with staff, which sometimes, although by no means always, is followed by a reprimand from a parent that he often appears to ignore.

3. *Entertaining* describes a third form of defensive attachment behavior seen in children. These children are bright and attractive and appear interested in their surroundings. They respond in an entertaining and often amusing way to invitations to interact from staff and from parents, who interact more with these children than with those in the first two categories. Through their nonverbal behavior entertaining children appear to elicit more responses than they invite verbally. They come across as rather polite, bright children eager to respond and to get it right. Nevertheless, one finds that activities are changed frequently especially if things do not go as the child seems to hope. Reading and associated activities are avoided, if not carefully introduced so that failure is avoided. If pressed these children begin to withdraw in a "switching off" manner. Children in each of these categories are all careful to avoid making mistakes.

Conclusions

Caspari's approach proves to be effective with many underachieving readers; nevertheless it succeeded with children with severe reading retardation only when three conditions were met. First, the person who taught the child had to have succeeded in building up an assuaging caregiving relationship with him as previously described. The child then appeared to show some improvement but overall he had remained stuck, unable to remember and use what he appeared to have learned until two other conditions were established. Second, both parents had to have shown that they were in agreement with the approach to the reading task taken by the teacher. And third, certain changes had to have taken place in the way the parents related to the child so that his attempts at reading were no longer associated with increasing anxiety that had not been assuaged. On the other hand, unresolved and continuing arguments between the parents appeared to play a part in maintaining the severe reading retardation. We found that when the parents had a quarrelsome relationship with each other when they were seen in the clinic, the level of the child's reading remained, for practical purposes, unchanged. Our experience with such parents has been that they ultimately withdrew from the program without a change taking place in the family dynamics.

Thus our work has led us to the view that, whatever constitutional genetic factors underlie the difficulties these children have in learning to read, the quality of their family relationships constitutes an important environmental factor in maintaining the disorder. Attachment theory has provided a framework for both understanding and treating such families.

REFERENCES

Ainsworth, M. D. S.; Blehar, M. C.; Waters, E.; and Wall, S. 1978. *Patterns of attachment: A psychological study of the strange situation.* Hillsdale, N.J.: Lawrence Erlbaum Associates.

Bowlby, J. 1969. *Attachment and loss Vol. 1: Attachment.* New York: Basic Books.

_____. 1973. *Attachment and loss. Vol. 2: Separation: Anxiety and anger.* New York: Basic Books.

_____. 1980. *Attachment and loss. Vol. 3: Sadness and depression.* New York: Basic Books.

Caspari, I. M. 1974. Educational therapy. In *Psychotherapy today,* ed. V. Varma. Edinburgh: P. Constable.

Cohen, L. J. 1974. The operational definition of human attachment. *Psychological Bulletin* 81:207–217.

Fairbairn, W. R. D. 1952. *Psychoanalytic studies of the personality: The object relation theory of personality.* London: Tavistock and Routledge & Kegan Paul.

Heard, D. H. 1978. From object relations to attachment theory: A basis for family therapy. *British Journal of Medical Psychology* 51:67–76.

_____. 1981. Family systems and the attachment dynamic. *Journal of Family Therapy.* (in press).

Hinde, R. A. 1976. On describing relationships. *Journal of Child Psychology and Psychiatry* 17:1–19.

Rutter, M., and Yule, W. 1975. The concept of specific reading retardation. *Journal of Child Psychology and Psychiatry* 16:181–197.

Winnicott, D. W. 1971. *Playing and reality.* London: Tavistock.

PART III

Bonding in Adult Life

9

Robert S. Weiss

ATTACHMENT IN ADULT LIFE

Infant Attachment

Bowlby (1969, 1973, 1980), Ainsworth (1969 and chapter 1 herein; Ainsworth et. al., 1978), and others have documented the critical importance to an infant's well-being of the infant's relationship to his primary caretaker. Within a set of generalizations regarding the functioning of attachment, Bowlby offers the following descriptions of attachment behavior:

> ... the behaviour may consist of little more than checking by eye or ear on the whereabouts of the [attachment] figure and exchanging occasional glances and greetings. In certain circumstances, however, following or clinging to the attachment figure may occur and also calling or crying, which are likely to elicit his or her caregiving.
> ... the systems mediating attachment behaviour are activated only by certain conditions, for example strangeness, fatigue, anything frightening, and unavailability or unresponsiveness of attachment figure, and are terminated only by certain other conditions, for example a familiar environment and the ready availability and responsiveness of an attachment figure. ...
> The unchallenged maintenance of a bond is experienced as a source of security and the renewal of a bond as a source of joy. (Bowlby, 1980, pp. 39–40)

Of particular importance in Bowlby's descriptions are: (1) the association of the attachment figure with feelings of security; (2) the greater

Work on this chapter was supported by a grant from the National Institute of Mental Health (1-R01-MH31716), "Single Parent Influences on Transitions to Adulthood." The author thanks, for criticism and suggestions, Carolyn Bruse, A. Scott Henderson, Joan Stevenson-Hinde, C. Murray Parkes, and Peter Marris.

171

likelihood of attachment behavior when the infant is in a situation of apparent threat; (3) the tendency of infants to attempt to ward off or to end separation from an attachment figure by calling or crying. What is understood as attachment should, therefore, express itself in these three ways:

1. The infant will attempt to remain within protective range of the attachment figure, a range that is reduced in strange or threatening situations. When a situation appears to the infant to have become less secure, he will attempt to reduce the distance between himself and an attachment figure either by moving to the attachment figure or by calling on the attachment figure to move toward him.

2. In the presence of an attachment figure, so long as there is no threat, an infant will give indication of comfort and security. Attachment behavior may not be evident; instead, other behavior systems, such as those involved in confident exploration, may be displayed.

3. Threat to continued accessibility of the attachment figure or actual separation from the attachment figure will be seen by the infant as a threat to his well-being and will give rise to protest and to attempts to ward off the attachment figure's loss or to regain the attachment figure's presence. (Should there be prolonged separation, however, initial protest may give way to despair and detachment.)

Infants seem, without exception, capable of forming bonds of attachment with one or more caretakers, and the great majority of infants seem not only to form such bonds but to maintain them for some time. The question this chapter addresses is whether such bonds are maintained into adulthood and, if they are, how they express themselves.

Adult Attachment

Do adults maintain bonds that display the three criteria for attachment just mentioned? Interview studies conducted at the Harvard Medical School Laboratory for Community Psychiatry suggest that they do. Bonds that meet the three criteria for attachment are to be found regularly within well-functioning marriages, and even within marriages that are not functioning well (Weiss, 1975); within committed nonmarital relationships (Weiss, 1978); on occasion within the relationship of an otherwise lonely single parent and the parent's elder child (Weiss, 1979); and, in situations of high stress, in the relationships of men who are buddies (Little, 1964). They may also, on occasion, be found in the relationships that unmarried women maintain with best friends, sisters, or parents (Weiss, 1979). In all these instances individuals display need for ready access to the attachment figure, desire for proximity to the attachment figure in situations of stress, heightened comfort and diminished anxiety when in the company of the attachment figure, and a marked increase in discomfort and anxiety on discovering the attachment figure to be inexplicably inaccessible.

Although attachment in adults meets the criteria for attachment set out previously, it differs from attachment in infants in three important ways. First, instead of appearing in relationships with caretakers, as is true among infants, attachment in adults usually appears in relationships with peers, although, to be sure, peers who are felt to be of unique importance. The peers may be perceived as sources of strength, but they need not be perceived in this way; they may instead be perceived as fostering the attached individual's own capacity for mastering challenge. Second, attachment in adults is not nearly so capable of overwhelming other behavioral systems as it is in infancy. Infants often seem unable to give energy or attention to other matters when attachment bonds are imperiled. Adults, in contrast, can attend to other relationships and other concerns despite threats to attachment. (They may, however, experience difficulties of concentration when such threats impinge on their attention.) Adults, too, are usually better able to tolerate temporary separation from attachment figures, because they have more confidence in the arrival of anticipated futures and more confidence in themselves. The third way in which attachment in adults is different from attachment in children arises from the fact that in adults it is often directed toward a figure with whom a sexual relationship also exists.

However, to establish that attachment is present in some adult relationships does not establish that it is as unique a relationship for adults as it is for infants. For might it not be present in all adult relationships? Or, at least, in all those in which there is affection, solicitude, and desire for continued contact? Might not attachment, perhaps at a low level, be present in most friendships, kin ties, relationships with children, relationships with physicians and other professionals, even nonreciprocated relationships with public figures for whom there is genuine regard?

Several years ago I conducted a small study whose aim was to decide between two alternative hypotheses: whether the bond of attachment is to be found in all close, face-to-face relationships, the kind of relationship that Cooley (1909) referred to as "primary"; or, alternatively, whether attachment is to be found only in some of the adult relationships that might be thought of as "primary," but not in others. The study consisted of interviews and informal discussions with individuals who were experiencing one of two complementary deficits in relationships. One group included individuals who had recently ended their marriages and, to obtain help in dealing with the emotional and practical problems they then encountered, had joined an organization of single parents. The other group included individuals whose marriages remained intact, but who were without other close face-to-face relationships because they had recently moved into their present neighborhoods from homes located over five hundred miles away.

I found that individuals who had recently ended marriages reported a feeling state they generally characterized as "loneliness." Their loneliness was not reduced by friendships. Friendships did make the loneliness easier for them to deal with by reassuring them that others, too, felt as they did and that they were neither isolated nor odd. However, the only relationships that seemed actually to allay their loneliness were those that by their sexual and emotional intimacy resembled the marital relationship. Such relationships appeared to meet the criteria for attachments previously listed.

On the other hand, friendships, too, proved to be of critical emotional importance. Individuals who were without access to a community of others—who, because they had moved from some distance away, currently had neither friends nor kin nor co-workers—also reported distress. Unlike loneliness, their distress could not be allayed by the availablity to them of an emotionally intense sexual relationship. What they lacked might be characterized as "affiliation"—associations in which shared interests and similarity of circumstances provided a basis for mutual loyalty and a sense of community. They felt isolated; there was no group within which they had a place (Weiss, 1973, 1974).

If we accept for the time being that loneliness indicates an absence of attachment, then the finding that friendships could not allay loneliness implies that only certain close, face-to-face relationships function as relationships of attachment. The finding that deficits can be experienced despite functioning attachments implies that attachment is neither the only basis for "primary" relationships among adults nor the only bond whose provisions are of emotional significance. Bonds of attachment are to be found in some, but not all, adult relationships of emotional significance. Indeed, they are to be found only in those relationships that are recognized as of central importance.

174

The Continuity of an Attachment-Establishing System

I have to this point argued that adults establish a bond to other adults that is, in essential respects, identical to the attachment that children make to their primary caretakers. I have also argued that this bond is *not* to be found in some degree in every emotionally significant relationship adults maintain but rather, just as is the case with attachment in children, it appears only in relationships of central emotional importance. I now want to argue that attachment in adults is an expression of the same emotional system, though one modified in the course of its development, as is attachment in children.

Until children become adolescent, at which point they begin actively to establish their independence from their parents, we can recognize the continuity of their attachment to their parents through their uninterrupted readiness to display attachment behavior under appropriate circumstances. When uneasy, they seek out their parents. In the presence of their parents, they are comparatively relaxed; almost always, it is easier for them to sleep when their parents are in the home. Notice of impending parental inaccessibility, as when parents plan to be away for a weekend, is apt to elicit their protest. Actual parental inaccessibility is likely to produce separation distress, a syndrome whose elements express clearly the children's desire for the reestablishing of contact. They include a focusing of attention on the parents' absence, so that it is difficult for the children to concentrate on other matters, a state of tension that discourages both sleep and appetite, and an impulse toward searching for the parents. This syndrome may also appear when the children are away from their homes and their parents, in which case we speak of "homesickness." It appears most sharply when children are removed from parents in situations that are stressful for the children, as when the children are hospitalized. With increasing maturity, children are better able to tolerate distance from their parents, yet they continue to demonstrate in many ways that their sense of security is dependent on their parents' continued accessibility.

As children move through adolescence, their relationships with their parents undergo change. Adolescents sometimes seem to want assurance that their parents' investment in them continues while insisting on intervals in which they are free of parental surveillance. Many adolescents, not at all estranged from their parents, seem to welcome intervals in which they and their parents will be apart. They

175

may say that only when their parents are away from their homes can they fully relax. There is bravado in such statements, to be sure, and sometimes adolescents' feelings are more mixed than they will admit, yet it does seem to be the case that they no longer need their parents' continued accessibility.

As adolescents move on in their development, there are intervals of increasing duration in which parental accessibility does not contribute to their feelings of security. The adolescents may still require confidence in their parents' commitment to them, but they no longer, for example, feel anxious on coming home to an empty house. During these intervals in which adolescents no longer experience their parents as attachment figures, their parents appear to them in a new light. No longer are the parents awesome, larger-than-life repositories of strength. Instead they are seen as ordinary people with the usual budget of frailties and problems.

These observations regarding the changing character of attachment in adolescence are in large part based on interviews with adolescents that my colleagues and I are conducting as part of an exploratory study of the role parents play in adolescents' adoption of mature roles and outlooks. This work suggests that there is more than one way in which parents support adolescents' feelings of security, and that even when parents no longer function as attachment figures in that their presence no longer allays anxiety, they may yet be felt by their adolescent children to be essential allies in coping with the challenges of maturation.

Late adolescents who have been away from home may harbor the hope that their parents may function for them as attachment-figures-in-reserve, that is, figures with whom attachment can be reinstated under appropriate circumstances. They may return home from their absence expecting to experience again the sense of comfort once provided by the presence of their parents. Sometimes they then discover that their home is a place they have left emotionally and their parents are now only fellow humans. Attachment to parents may be relinquished without the adolescents being entirely aware it has happened.

The process by which parents are relinquished as attachment figures appears not to be one of gradual withdrawal; rather, it appears to be one in which the adolescents experience interruptions of the ongoing attachment to the parents, ordinarily at first widely spaced, then gradually becoming more frequent and longer in duration, until it is the interruption that is the steady state that at intervals gives way to brief resurgences of attachment. Insofar as this description is correct, attachment does not fade in the sense of becoming progressively weaker, but rather is entirely absent for longer and longer intervals.

When parents lose their position as attachment figures, an adolescent may become attached to a new figure, ordinarily a peer of the same sex or the other sex. In the new relationship all the indicators of attachment can be observed: desire for the other's company, feelings of comfort and relaxation in the other's presence, and, should there be a rift, separation distress. Often, in speaking of relationships with peers that ended, adolescents indicate that they were more upset and distressed than they feel to have been justified, given that they always understood the relationship to have been transitory.

Adolescents as well as adults seem sometimes to display attachment to a small, cohesive, reliable, and accepting group of peers rather than to an individual. It is the group that seems to foster feelings of comfort and whose loss is protested, rather than any particular individual in the group. If only one member of the group is present, the adolescent is likely to feel the situation to be unsatisfactory; only when an adequate number of group members are present does the adolescent experience the comfort and at-homeness associated with proximity to attachment figures.

These observations are consistent with either of two hypotheses: In adolescence a single perceptual-emotional system, the attachment system, shifts in object while retaining its fundamental character; or, alternatively, in adolescence the attachment system of childhood gives way to a different perceptual-emotional system, which might be characterized as the attachment system of adulthood. The similarity of separation distress in response to loss, no matter whether it is an early attachment figure (a parent) or a later one, together with the absence of overlap of attachment to parents and attachment to peers makes it seem much more likely that a single perceptual-emotional system continues in force while undergoing a change in object.

The Relinquishing of Parents as Attachment Figures

Parents appear to be relinquished earlier as attachment figures when the parents are "deidealized" as a result of children's awareness of the parents' frailties or when the parents are inadequately accessible or impose emotional distance by being preoccupied with their work or

177

other matters. On the other hand, there appear to be a variety of ways in which parents may impede their children's relinquishing them as attachment figures. Parents whose own loneliness has led them to form attachments to their children (in addition to maintaining the usual parental investment in them) may encourage their children to remain closely bound to them and make them feel guilty should they draw away. Parents may also impede children's movements toward independence by undermining the children's confidence in their abilities to function autonomously. Apparently there is no biological clock that requires the suspension of attachment to parents in adolescence; rather, there appears to be a readiness for attachment to be redirected, but redirection can be fostered or frustrated by the nature of the relationship with the parents.

Relinquishing parents as attachment figures leaves young people vulnerable to loneliness. The symptoms of loneliness are in many ways identical to those of separation distress; they include anxiety, tension, and a restlessness similar in character to the compulsion to search associated with separation distress. But whereas in separation distress a definite figure has been lost and search is directed to rejoining that figure, in loneliness the individual experiences pervasive barrenness and emptiness. Loneliness is separation distress without an object.

Harry Stack Sullivan (1953) has commented that it is not until adolescence that individuals can experience loneliness. We have here an explanation for his observation. Until parents are relinquished as attachment figures we can experience separation distress, but only on relinquishing them as attachment figures does our distress become objectless. We might also note that just as separation distress indicates interrupted attachment, so loneliness indicates the absence from one's internal world of an attachment figure.

The Formation of Attachment to Specific Figures

Much in the development of attachment feelings and their direction toward specific figures is accessible to cultural shaping. Either parent may serve as primary caretaker, or the primary caretaker may be a sibling or someone else; the first attachment figure may foster continued attachment or, alternatively, early redirection of attachment; new attachments may be made easily or only with difficulty; the individual may experience greater or lesser stress, with attachment in consequence of more or less urgency; and new attachment figures may be of various kinds. In all these ways we might expect the development of attachment to vary from society to society and among individuals in a given society.

In our society, where individuals are free to choose those outside their families with whom they will most closely associate, we have the question of what leads to particular new figures becoming objects for attachment. It may be that the image of the figure chosen corresponds in some way to an image to which the individual's attachment behavior system is already prepared to respond. There is reason to suspect that resemblance to the parent to whom there were strong positive affective ties—not necessarily the parent of the other sex—plays some role in mate selection (Strauss, 1946).

Judging from reports and observation, the process by which attachment is formed is the same sort of process as its ending: Rather than attachment steadily becoming stronger, attachment appears to take hold all at once, in full strength. However, attachment can at first easily be interrupted. Only as a relationship is integrated into an individual's life does attachment become more nearly constant. A relationship of attachment develops, not by the attachment becoming stronger but by it becoming steadier.

The experience of individuals whose marriages have been arranged by their parents would suggest that most people, under appropriate circumstances, can establish feelings of attachment toward quite a wide range of others (Blood, 1967). Indeed, the institution of marriage fosters attachment, whatever the initial relationship of the couple. It makes the couple live in close proximity, so that each is reliably accessible to the other. At the same time it introduces barriers to the formation by either of a close relationship outside the marriage, and so makes individuals not attached to their marital partners vulnerable to painful loneliness. Thus marriage not only imposes intimacy and so facilitates attachment, it also may punish, with loneliness, those who, for whatever reason, fail to become attached to their spouses.

There is some evidence that the heightened emotional state of fear facilitates "falling in love" (Walster and Walster, 1978). So also, we might suppose, does the heightened emotional state of sexual transport. If this is so, it would be still another reason for marriage making likely the development of attachment.

Attachment, however, should not be considered to be a more technical term for "love." Attachment is very likely a component of most relationships characterized by those maintaining them as relationships of love, but it seems to be absent from some such relationships. In a study of a small number of courting couples conducted at the Laboratory of Community Psychiatry by Rhona Rapoport (see Rapoport and Rapoport, 1964), two couples insisted they were in love but gave evidence of absence of attachment. They tolerated with complacency intervals of days in which they were not in contact, and did not have any definite time for reestablishing contact. (One of the couples returned prematurely from the honeymoon they had taken after their marriage because both husband and wife were homesick.) Furthermore, attachment may be present even though love is denied. Many couples who have ended unhappy marriages discover that they are for a time still drawn to each other although they are entirely certain that their love for each other has ended.

With sexual maturity, attachment seems ordinarily directed toward a figure who is also an object for sexual feelings. It might be speculated that attachment, in a relationship in which sexual contact is both desired and justifiable, makes such contact seem an urgently required affirmation of the other's accessibility. Conversely, sexual contact, by producing a state of heightened emotion, may foster attachment. But there is no necessary connection, and attachments may well be unaccompanied by either manifest or latent sexual desire. Even when attachment and sexual desire have both been directed to the same figure, it should be possible for sexual desire, since object constancy is not one of its properties, to become fixed on new figures in addition to, or in place of, the attachment figure. The intermeshing of attachment and sexual desire need not be permanent.

Insofar as attachment and sexuality involve distinct behavioral systems, jealousy may come in two forms. The first form might be a response to a threatened loss of an attachment figure, the second a response to a threatened loss of a figure sexually desired. The first form would then be associated with feelings of abandonment, the second with feelings of frustration. It might be suspected that the first form would be the more intense.

Attachment *behavior* appears to be at its strongest in infancy and to decline in strength gradually but steadily thereafter, so far as one can judge both from the rapidity with which separation distress appears on discovery that an attachment figure is inaccessible and from the intensity of the separation distress. In adolescence attachment is for the first time directed to nonparental figures. This means that it may be in adolescence that attachment behavior in relationships other than those with parents is at its strongest and the loss associated with the endings of these relationships at its most painful.

The only indicator we have for the strength of an individual's readiness to form an attachment is the intensity and steadiness of the individual's experience of loneliness. It does, indeed, appear that the likelihood of the occurrence of loneliness, as well as the intensity of loneliness, should it occur, is much greater in the early postadolescent years than in the later years of life (Rubenstein and Shaver, forthcoming). It has been reported that older people often treat time alone as welcome solitude rather than lonely aloneness (Townsend, 1966). This seems unusual among adolescents. It may be that the attachment behavior system, so powerful in the early years of our lives, retains much of its power through our young adult years; then, as we enter the later years, it begins gradually to release its hold on our motivation and behavior.

Attachment in Adults as Contributing to "Inclusive Fitness"

The wide distribution in a population of a behavioral characteristic that could not have resulted from cultural shaping suggests that the characteristic in some way contributed to the "inclusive fitness" of those who, in earlier generations, displayed it; that is, it contributed to the survival of disproportionate numbers of progeny in successive generations. While the direction of attachment among adults does seem accessible to cultural shaping, adults' capacity to display attachment behavior does not. How might this characteristic of adults have contributed to "inclusive fitness"?

Attachment in children contributes to children's keeping close to protective adults, particularly in apparently risky circumstances. Attachment in adults contributes to the adults' keeping close to potentially helpful fellow adults, again particularly in apparently risky circumstances. Insofar as attachment is reciprocated, it provides a basis for pairing.

Attachment is clearly a better basis for a reliable pair bond than the obvious alternative of sexual desire. Attachment, once established, is highly persistent. It resists extinction even when there appears to be no positive gain from the relationship. Sexual desire, on the other hand, is sometimes persistent, sometimes not. Furthermore, attachment becomes the more reliable the more established a relationship is; sexual desire is often less urgent as a relationship is established. Attachment and sexual desire are affected differently by threat. Then attachment needs become powerful, whereas sexual desire is likely to be suppressed. Finally, attachment is strongly associated with particular figures and resists redirection. Sexual desire, on the other hand, seems more nearly accessible to new figures. Attachment, in sum, is persistent over time, more reliable as a relationship is more nearly established, and dominant over other behavior systems under conditions of threat. None of these characteristics is true of sexual desire.

But why should reliable pair bonding contribute to inclusive fitness? There is evidence from study of present-day families that children in single-parent families have available for their care less parental time and energy than is available to children in two-parent families and, also, that the time and energy available for the children's care is less than their parents believe to be adequate. In addition, there are grounds for speculation that the children's own parental behavior when they become parents themselves may be negatively affected by having experienced inadequate nurturance when they were growing up (Weiss, 1979; see also DeLozier, chapter 5 herein, for the extreme case of abusing parents). These observations from present-day families are only suggestive in regard to the possible values of pair bonding in families of an earlier era, but it seems likely that today's social organization would make it easier, rather than more difficult, for parents to raise children alone.

There is some evidence that any second adult within the household, so long as that adult is committed to the children, can be useful in supporting the children's development. Kellam, Ensminger, and Turner (1977) report that "mother-alone families" had fewer children adapting well to school than any other family type. They show that not father absence, but mother-aloneness predisposes children in mother-alone families to social maladaptation. Mother-grandmother families appeared to prevent social maladaptation about as well as did mother-father families. Second adults in the household who were not directly committed to the children's welfare, such as stepfathers, seemed less useful. Quite possibly the mother-father household is not the only one that can provide effectively for children's development. It would seem plausible that the attachment behavior system can be elicited in a variety of relationships, and so reliable bonds can be formed in relationships that are not sexual as well as in those that are.

182

I will not attempt to work out what might be the most desirable strategies, from the standpoint of "inclusive fitness," for men and for women in relation to their management of attachment. Issues that might require consideration if such an attempt were to be made would include the relative "advantages" of commitment to a single relationship compared with pursuit of a number of relationships, the importance of demanding indicators of attachment from a potential fellow caretaker of the children before becoming attached oneself, and the relative "advantages" of attachment to a sexual partner compared with attachment to a blood relative. For the purposes of this chapter it may be sufficient to recognize that the properties of attachment in children are just those required for effective pair bonding in adults, and that this may account for the very evident capacity of human adults to display attachment.

REFERENCES

Ainsworth, M. D. S. 1969. Object relations, dependency and attachment: A theoretical review of the infant-mother relationship. *Child Development* 40:969–1025.

———; Blehar, M. C.; Waters, E.; and Wall, S. 1978. *Patterns of attachment: A psychological study of the strange situation.* Hillsdale, N.J.: Lawrence Erlbaum Associates.

Blood, R. O. 1967. *Love match and arranged marriage.* New York: Free Press.

Bowlby, J. 1969. *Attachment and loss. Vol. 1: Attachment.* New York: Basic Books.

———. 1973. *Attachment and loss. Vol. 2: Separation: Anxiety and anger.* New York: Basic Books.

———. 1980. *Attachment and loss. Vol. 3: Loss: Sadness and depression.* New York: Basic Books.

Cooley, C. H. 1909. *Social organization: A study of the larger mind.* New York: Charles Scribner's Sons.

Kellam, S. G., Ensminger, M. E., and Turner, R. J. 1977. Family structure and the mental health of the children. *Archives of General Psychiatry* 34:1012–1022.

Little, R. 1964. Buddy relations and combat performance. In *The new military,* ed. M. Janowitz. New York: Russell Sage.

Rapoport, R. and Rapoport, R. 1964. New light on the honeymoon. *Human Relations* 17(1).

Rubenstein, C. M., and Shaver, P. 1982. The experience of loneliness. In *Loneliness: Theory and research,* ed. A. Peplau and D. Perlman. New York: Wiley

Strauss, A. 1946. Influence of parent-images upon marital choice. *American Sociological Review* 11(5):554–559.

Sullivan, H. S., 1953. *The interpersonal theory of psychiatry.* New York: W. W. Norton.

Townsend, P. 1966. *The aged within the welfare state.* London: G. Bell.

Walster, E., and Walster, G. 1978. *A new look at love.* Reading, Mass.: Addison Wesley.

Weiss, R. S. 1973. The contributions of an organization of single parents to the well-being of its members. *The Family Coordinator,* July, pp. 321–326.

———. 1974. The provisions of social relationships. In *Doing unto others,* ed. Z. Rubin. Englewood Cliffs, N.J.: Prentice-Hall.

———. 1975. *Marital separation.* New York: Basic Books.

———. 1978. Couples relationships. In *The couple,* ed. M. Corbin. New York: Penguin Books.

———. 1979. *Going it alone: The family life and social situation of the single parent.* New York: Basic Books.

10

Peter Marris

ATTACHMENT AND SOCIETY

THE RELATIONSHIPS that matter most to us are characteristically to particular people whom we love—husband or wife, parents, children, dearest friend—and sometimes to particular places—a home or personal territory—that we invest with the same loving qualities. These specific relationships, which we experience as unique and irreplaceable, seem to embody most crucially the meaning of our lives. We grow up to look for such relationships. If we do not find them, our lives seem empty; pleasures, ambitions, ideals, career tend to lose their interest or their purpose without this context of unique personal bonds. If we lose these bonds, we suffer grief; and in the depth of grieving, the bereaved cannot be consoled by any substitute relationship. Even the idea of such consolation is abhorrent, because it seems to deny the unique value and meaning of what has been lost.

This involvement in unique relationships begins early in life, as the work of John Bowlby and his colleagues has shown. A child's attachment to specific nurturing figures becomes crucial to its well-being; no amount or quality of care from others can altogether overcome the anxiety of separation from them. As we have seen in chapter 9, adult bonds of love seem to grow out of these earliest attachments.

I want to explore this quality of uniqueness in the relationships that matter most to us, because it is inherently difficult to understand and so, I believe, it is often ignored or disparaged in the organization of social relationships. We have, I think, created a society that is embar-

I would like to thank especially Robert S. Weiss and Colin Murray Parkes for their comments on an earlier draft of this chapter.

185

rassed and uncomprehending of grief and doubtful of bonds of love; neither grief nor love are compatible with the mechanism of its science or the utilitarianism of its policy. Yet at the same time this rationalism provokes in reaction an idealization of love and mothering that endows them with almost sacred qualities. No inquiry into attachment can avoid becoming implicated in these ideological impulses, however rigorously impartial it sets out to be. Too much is at stake—the legitimacy of economic exploitation, the patterning of sex roles, the ideal of community, are all bound up in the way we rationalize attachment. So before I try to explain why unique relationships are so crucial to us, let me turn first to the complex and ambivalent ideological context with which any such account must contend.

Ideologies of Attachment

Uniqueness is an inherently paradoxical subject for theoretical treatment, since theory presupposes generalizability. Unique relationships can only be thought about, as a class, in terms of what they share in common. And from this it is easy to fall into the fallacy of assuming that relationships that share common properties must be interchangeable—that a new love can replace a lost love—especially because they are then much more amenable to manipulation. There is therefore a constant temptation to reduce them to particular expressions of needs or satisfaction that are, in themselves, generalizable after all. So, for instance, Freud (1925, p. 154), in discussing in *Mourning and Melancholia* the intensity of grief and the reluctance to give up the lost object of love, adds this comment: "Why this process . . . should be so extraordinarily painful is not at all easy to explain in terms of mental economics." Why *should* grief and love be explicable in economic terms? The bias of Freud's inquiry, in search of generalizable elements of psychic behavior, prescribes a reductionist answer in the act of asking the question. It is hard not to fall into this trap, in one way or another. But as soon as we treat unique relationships as if they must be, somehow, the idiosyncratic expression of generalizable needs, we risk imposing a logic whereby it *ought* to be possible to supply an alternative satisfaction of that need. Since lovers and mourners repudiate any such substitution, their behavior looks puzzling, irrational, and so, by a short step, morbid.

This reductive logic reflects the ideology of a market economy, whose psychic equivalent Freud seems intent on composing. The rational distribution of social goods requires that wants be treated as aggregatable and interchangeable units of demand. The welfare of society appears as a calculation of costs and benefits traded off against each other in some utilitarian ideal of the collective good. Within that framework, unique relationships seem intractable and unadaptive. At worst they are sentimental, conservative inhibitions to the maximization of well-being; at best, natural foibles to be coaxed into conformity with reality.

But if the ideological structure of both science and capitalism seems to disparage unique relationships, there is a reactive tradition that seeks to enhance them, separating the spiritual from the material world, home from work, women's sphere from the inexorable logic of the masculine order. This tradition recognizes that productive activities, as capitalist society perceives them—earning a wage, making a profit, reducing everything to the exchange of commodities—cannot in themselves be meaningful, except as means to sustaining relationships that do have intrinsic meaning—the unique bonds of home and family. These truly valuable relationships, which validate all the rest, must therefore be protected against contamination, isolated from the sordid calculations that nonetheless establish the rational foundation of their prospering. The Victorian ideal of home is a refuge from a heartless world, where people find in faithful devotion to those they love the meaning and justification of the inhumanity of their working lives. Family relationships, therefore, must be everything that working relationships cannot be—spiritual, forgiving, warm, and above all uncalculating in their commitment. But since men must go out every day into that other coldly rational world to earn the family's living, only women can sustain uncorrupted these ultimately meaningful relationships. Women bear the responsibility for that uncalculating devotion that makes everything else worthwhile, and so they become enshrined and imprisoned in an ideal of domestic altruism.[1]

So industrial capitalist societies have evolved complementary ideologies of attachment, which have stereotyped—at least in Britain and the United States—relationships in remarkably polarized, gender-differentiated, and spatially segregated categories. On the one hand,

---

1. The most developed exposition of this ideology in the nineteenth century is probably Catharine Beecher and Harriet Beecher Stowe's very influential best seller, *The American Woman's Home* (1869). See Dolores Hayden (1977) and, for a modern restatement, Christopher Lasch (1977).

the provision of social needs required that all claims upon resources be reducible to measurable units—whether these were represented as purchasing power, votes, or rights to a given quality of subsistence. Only in this way could the deployment of capital (and so of taxable resources and social welfare) be submitted to rational calculation. And only by corresponding procedures could the understanding of social behaviors be submitted to the methods of those sciences that sustained the growth of industrial technology. But on the other hand, because this rationalism cannot comprehend our yearning for the unique ties of affection that alone seem to make life worthwhile, bourgeois industrial society idealized and romanticized the home as a world apart, where women gave unbounded love to their children and their men, redeeming the emptiness of making money. Women's love thus becomes sacred, in Durkheim's (1915) sense that whatever symbolizes the ultimate meanings binding a society together is sacred. Sacred things do not need explaining; they explain everything else. Above all mother love, because it represents most unambiguously the uncalculating commitment of oneself to another human being, becomes the paradigm of a truly meaningful relationship.

This conception of sex roles and social organization has been codified in the work of Talcott Parsons, whose influence pervaded Anglo-American sociology in the 1950s and 1960s. The stereotypical household of working father, housekeeping mother, and their dependent children, living together apart from other intimate ties, represents the normative "nuclear" family to which modern civilization has progressed. Within that family men are primarily responsible for instrumental and women for affective relationships; he deals with things and she with feelings. Between them they organize a meaning to their lives at once emotionally and practically competent—and remarkably self-contained. The nuclear family, because its significant relationships are all internal, could fit in anywhere. It is socially and geographically adaptable to an economy constantly reorganizing under the pressures of technological innovation.[2] This norm has survived in conventions

---

2. To quote Parsons:

Very broadly this [integration with an industrial occupational system] tends to be accomplished by confining the most stringent kinship obligations to the conjugal family of procreation, and isolating this in a relative sense from wider kinship units. Further, the involvement of the kinship unit with the occupational system tends to be primarily focused on the adult male. Especially with a system of formal education, which serves functions espe-

of social thought and policy, although half or more of married women with children now go out to work and the family's standard of living relies increasingly on their earnings. Though they have taken on the extra work, they are held as responsible as ever for upholding loving relationships. In these circumstances, any inquiry into child-mother attachment can seem to be putting working mothers on trial, on suspicion of betraying their fundamental duty.

These ideologies have come to be seen by more and more women and men as oppressive. The rationalism of scientific management denies the validity of personal affection and loyalties in most of the work men do, while the idealization of domesticity denies the validity of rational self-interest in a woman's management of her mothering. Men want the chance to be loving and women to be self-interested, so that both can find themselves in some meaningful structure of relationships. But each seems to threaten the other, as men fear that feminists want to drag the only relationships uncontaminated by buying and selling into the marketplace of professional child care, wages for housework, and take-home fast foods; and women that men, once again, are undermining sexual equality by their age-old romance with mothering.

Metaphors of Attachment

Any understanding of unique relationships has to take account of this complex ideological context. It cannot simply take refuge in the impar-

---

cially of technical training for occupational roles, and is, in one primary aspect, a kind of system of pre-occupational roles, the relative exclusion of minor children is relatively easy. The primary problems and strains center on the role of the wife and mother. The "easy" solution is for her to be completely excluded from the occupational system by confining herself to the role of housewife. In most industrial societies, however, there tends to be a good deal of adaptation and compromise relative to this solution. The second important feature is the accent on affectivity in the kinship system. This has partly the function of inhibiting the development of some of the kinds of kinship patterns which would be a threat to the operation of an individualistic type of occupational system. Partly, however, it serves as a counterbalance to the accent on neutrality in the occupational system in that it offers a field for diffuse affective attachments which must be inhibited in the occupational realm. (1951, pp. 186–187)

tiality of empirical science, because those claims of impartiality, and the intellectual operations they favor, are themselves inextricably bound up with this ideological context. However rigorously evidence is tested, however accurately we observe, we are bound to interpret what we see in terms of some predisposing conceptual organization— a guiding metaphor consciously or unconsciously assumed. The first step, then, in understanding unique relationships is to avoid thinking about them in terms of metaphors that are inherently reductionist, such as "mental economics"; or overdetermining, such as "imprinting"—not because these are, in themselves, bad or unenlightening metaphors, but because they have the particular ideological implications I wish to avoid.

Freud's "mental economics" is a version of a range of metaphors that have dominated psychology, and have in common an image of growth as the investment of generalized capacity in differentiated systems. "Until the mid-1950s only one view of the nature and origin of affectional bonds was prevalent, and on this matter, if on few others, psychoanalysts and learning theorists were at one," as John Bowlby writes.

> Bonds between individuals develop, it was held, because an individual discovers that, in order to reduce certain drives, e.g. for food in infancy and for sex in adult life, another human being is necessary. This type of theory postulates two kinds of drive, primary drives and secondary ones, and categorizes food and sex as primary. . . . As Anna Freud puts it, it is a cupboard love theory of human relations. (Bowlby, 1973a, pp. 40–41)

In place of drives, John Bowlby proposes a metaphor of control:

> Instead, the behaviour I have been describing [attachment behaviour] can be conceived best, I believe, in terms of a set of control systems—systems that are activated by certain conditions, for example, isolation or alarm, that when active mediate one or more of those forms of behaviour that I am classifying as attachment-behaviour, and that are inactivated again when the attachment figure is in sight or grasp. . . . the kind of apparatus I am proposing is conceived as analogous to the kinds of apparatus that physiologists believe responsible for maintaining body temperature at a certain point or blood sugar at a certain level. (Bowlby, 1973a, p. 50)

These systems for controlling attachment behavior, Bowlby suggests, have evolved because they are adaptive for the survival of the species.

But this reformulation substitutes another essentially mechanical metaphor, and still has the drawback of making grief appear to be unadaptive. Assuming that adult bonds of affection are associated with attachment, and provoke similar anxieties and searching when they are disrupted, then grieving seems to be an acute attack of anxiety accompanied by alternating fits of despair and futile search for the lost person. We are back with Freud's puzzlement: Why does not the control system, having realized that the attachment figure is irretrievably lost, switch itself off or convert as soon as a replacement can be found to a new figure capable of providing the same kinds of reassurance? The answer seems to lie in the metaphor of "imprinting." Once a page has been printed, that message may be overprinted, scratched out, annotated, blotched, but it can never be erased without destroying the page itself. This represents, vividly, the uniqueness of the bond, yet I think it still does not explain very well the nature of adult grieving.

ATTACHMENT AND LEARNING

Instead let me set out a way of looking at unique relationships that sees their development as analogous to learning; and though this has its own drawbacks, I believe it is a useful way to begin. Unique relationships, I suggest, are crucial to the structure of meaning that each of us develops to make sense of our experience and direct our lives. I use the phrase "structure of meaning" rather than Bowlby's "working models" or Colin Murray Parkes's "assumptive world" because I want to emphasize not only the interpretative structure that enables us to classify and predict, but the structure of purposes and feelings that inform the evolution of that interpretation and direct its attention. I want to imply the sense of meaning in a phrase such as "a falling barometer means rain" *and* in "music means a great deal to me."[3] Our use of the same word in both is not, I believe, either accidental or misleading. The ability to make sense of experience depends on connecting feeling to action by way of purpose; the acknowledgment and placing of emotion is therefore fundamental. Indeed, I do not think we can be said to experience emotion until we have made sense of it. A lump in the throat, a sinking feeling in the stomach, may be sorrow or indigestion, depending on the context. Emotions, like other interpretations, are open to revision: "I didn't realize, until afterward, how frightened I was," "I never really loved her," "I wasn't really angry with you, just overtired." These are comments, not only on what hap-

---

3. Meaning is of course a complex problem of epistemology. But in everyday life we talk about meaning as an aspect of our experience, and I think it is possible to talk about the structure of meaning in this sense, without becoming involved in philosophical questions of how, exactly, language comes to express meaning or what the criteria of validity are.

pened, but on what someone felt about it at the time. In describing attachments as learned, or grief as a response to the disintegration of meaning, therefore, I do not intend to deny their intensity as feelings. Rather I want to suggest that meaning is inherently emotional, even in its apparently most dispassionate expressions.

From their earliest years, children act upon their surroundings, discovering that there are objects that stand in regular relationship to their wants and movements. Babies soon find out that they can make things happen. As they grow up, they begin to identify, classify, group, and compare, evolving notions of space, of speed, time, cause and effect, of reversibility and conservation, in a developmental sequence most fully studied and described in the work of Piaget (1971) and his colleagues. Action and the coordination of actions evolve into a perception of the way reality is organized that becomes increasingly logical, abstract, and generalizable; until in maturity we begin to articulate them as ideologies or theories—systems of thought that define reality in terms of its desirable and possible transformations. Unless we were able to organize experience systematically, we could not grasp it at all. Our reality *is* what we are able to take hold of—in infancy literally, in maturity metaphorically: a set of actual or potential operations, organized by increasingly self-conscious principles of classification and lawful association. So, by our interaction with our surroundings, we give them form and meaning, creating the intelligible, generalizable regularities that enable us to predict, manipulate, and outwit the dangers that beset us (see also Brown, chapter 12 herein).

In part, these mature structures of meaning can be represented as the common knowledge into which the members of a society are inducted by the language they learn, the principles of classification and causality they are taught—its science, cosmology, ideology, and cultural assumptions. But they also interpret the unique experience of each personal history.

The structuring of meaning is as much an articulation and organization of purposes and emotional responses as the perception of a relevant order in the world about us. As from earliest childhood we act upon the world and discover how and when we can ward off frightening events and encourage satisfying ones; we learn to generalize this power of control in an increasingly elaborate hierarchy of purposes. At the same time our emotional responses are forming and being formed in the same structural evolution. How we grasp reality, what we feel about it, and what we want to do about it are constantly interacting in a more and more reflexive, self-conscious, and established ordering of life, which comes to represent our grownup competence to make enough sense to survive. This structure of meaning is self-confirming, because wherever we can, we will tend to impose it on events we can control, creating relationships that conform to it. And we will tend to ignore, deny, or misperceive events that do not fit.

I am suggesting, then, that the development of meaning can be looked at in much the same way as the development of conceptual understanding. Organizing principles of the structure become established at crucial stages in biological maturation. The structure of meaning is intentional and full of feeling, not merely conceptual, but as with the conceptual structure, the earliest principles of organization to be established will set the framework within which everything afterward is perceived, chosen, or rejected, and so have a fundamental guiding influence upon the way our sense of the meaning of life evolves. Attachment behavior shows that reliance on one or two specific nurturing figures becomes established very early. These figures mean comfort and safety. Just as the maturing child is predisposed to perceive, at the right stage in development, concepts of number, so he or she is predisposed to develop emotional and intentional organization around these specific nurturing figures. Purposes and feelings therefore become structured very early through vitally important relationships to specific individuals. As Bowlby writes:

> ...no variables...have more far-reaching effects on personality development than have a child's experiences within his family: for, starting during his first months in his relations with both parents, he builds up working models of how attachment figures are likely to behave towards him in any of a variety of situations; and on those models are based all his expectations, and therefore all his plans, for the rest of his life. (Bowlby, 1973b, p. 369)

As we grow up, we expect the meaning of life to be embodied in such relationships; and expecting it, we try to make it so. That is, the idea that a primary bond to one or two specific people is crucial to the whole organization of an environment in which we can survive is incorporated very early into our learning. So it has a powerful determining influence on the way our purposes, emotional responses, and conceptions of how to operate develop ever after. At the same time, the more we are able to control our circumstances, the more we will create patterns of relationship that embody this sense of life.

I do not mean to imply that ties of love and affection in adult life are simply projections or transformations of childhood attachment,

193

only that this experience of attachment provides a model that becomes deeply embedded in the way we are predisposed to structure the meaning of relationships. We expect to center our lives on some crucial bond, about which other ties of affection to specific people and places ramify and to which other relationships are instrumental. And conversely, I suggest, we find it hard to conceive of a meaningful life that is not so centered—where there is no hierarchical ordering in our commitments, or where all relationships are conceived as instrumental. The only way we can grasp the meaning of life in terms of unspecific, generalizable relationships is by representing them in the light of some superordinate commitment—to God or an ideal—that takes the place of and is treated emotionally like a primary bond of love.

The relationships of our lives cannot, therefore, be conceived as a particular set in which a preexisting, generalizable meaning has been invested. Someone may say, for instance, "I want to get married and have children" as an expression of how she expects to define the meaning of her life, but once involved in an actual relationship, the relationship itself very soon begins to evolve its own structure of meaning—not the meaning of an idealized, theoretical marriage but a set of understandings, purposes, feelings, problems, evolving in a constant process of learning. The conceptual structure, by which we interpret reality, and the structure of relationships through which we live constantly interact with each other, as we learn from experience and apply what we have learned to organize the future. What at one moment is given—the way people are, the nature of relationships, how the world works—is at another moment being created by some act of interpretation that reproduces or changes it. The organization of reality on which we depend to make sense of our situation and behave purposefully is inextricably embodied in and derived from the particular relationships of our lives.

BEREAVEMENT AS LOSS OF MEANING

I emphasize this because we commonly but mistakenly suppose that as mature adults we possess a generalized knowledge and understanding capable of making sense of reality independent of what happens to our personal lives. The evidence suggests that this is not so. When people are bereft of a crucial relationship, nothing seems to make sense any longer: The world has become meaningless. Instead of a generalizable structure of beliefs sustaining the bereaved through the particular loss, interpreting it and setting it in a larger context of meaning, the beliefs themselves are invalidated, compounding the

194

sense of loss. So, for instance, C. S. Lewis (1961) describes how, on his wife's death, he underwent a bitter crisis of faith; and widows I interviewed in a London study described the same rejection of religious consolations in which they had believed (Marris, 1958).

In these terms, the refusal to abandon a "love object," as Freud put it, which so puzzled him, becomes more readily intelligible. Losing someone you love is less like losing a very valuable and irreplaceable possession than like finding the law of gravity to be invalid. While it would seem only rational to give up a lost object "at the behest of reality," it is not at all so obviously rational to give up a relationship whose meaning has been crucial to one's sense of life. Grief is a reaction to the disintegration of the whole structure of meaning dependent on this relationship rather than to the absence of the person lost. There is no "behest of reality" to require the bereaved to accommodate to this collapse of meaning; the intense anxiety and hopelessness of the bereaved arise from their sense that no claims of reality can any longer mean anything to them.

Correspondingly, people work through grief by retrieving, consolidating, and transforming the meaning of their relationship to the person they have lost, not by abandoning it. Through the weeks and months of mourning, as they try to make sense of their new situation, the meaning of the relationship becomes almost obsessively important to them. If, even for a short while, they forget their bereavement, they feel they have betrayed this meaning; while in their anxiety to recapture and relive it, they reactivate the intensity of loss and confront once again the emptiness of the present. Through this ambivalence runs an insistent search for some reason to go on living that will not repudiate or invalidate the cherished and now-fragile meaning of the relationship they have lost. Gradually the sense of what it meant to them becomes abstracted, as a set of purposes, ideals, things to care about, whose continuing relevance does not depend upon the living person to uphold them. So, for instance, widows who in the first weeks of their bereavement may vividly sense their dead husband's presence, talk to him, treat him almost as a still living but invisible partner, come to think about what he would have wanted, advised, believed in, treating his memory more and more symbolically as an organizing principle, until finally these reformulations of meaning are no longer constantly referred back to him and the work of grieving is largely finished (Marris, 1974).

Although such idealization of the dead is characteristic, the way in which the continuity of meaning is resolved depends on the bereaved

195

person's whole pattern of organizing meanings. The resolution of grief is as idiosyncratic as the quality of each human life. But however it is achieved, the recovery from a severe loss seems to depend on restoring the continuity of meaning. Until then, the bereaved are vulnerable to recurring moods of futility and despair. In that sense, although we can discuss very generally the processes of grief, all those who have suffered a severe loss have to find their own terms in which to restate a meaning for their lives, and no one else can tell them how to do it.

Three other observations seem to confirm that loss of meaning, not loss of a loved person itself, provokes grief. First, the death of someone much loved does not cause intense grief if the relationship is no longer central to one's life. Married children, for instance, do not usually grieve deeply for the death of an elderly parent, though they may feel sorrow and miss him or her. (By contrast, the loss of an ambivalent relationship may cause exceptionally intense and painful grief if the bereaved was deeply involved in it, because its meaning, unresolved in the past, is all the more difficult to resolve for the future.) Second, the absence of someone you love, even for a very long time, does not cause grief, though it may be a source of great anxiety, so long as you expect them to return. Rather the meaning of life becomes reorganized around waiting and preparation. Third, by contrast, the loss of the meaning of a relationship can arouse intense grief even though the relationship itself continues apparently unchanged—as, for instance, when a lover is discovered to have been secretly unfaithful. Relationships have their meaning in an "assumptive world," as Parkes (1971) has called it. If assumptions about the future, as well as the past, have to be changed, the meaning of a relationship may be in jeopardy.

But if people may grieve for loss of meaning, even when the relationship is still ostensibly intact, do they not also sometimes grieve for a loss, even when it does not seem crucially to affect the purposive structure of their lives? Did not Victorian parents grieve for the loss of a child, though it might be one of six or eight and the death of children a common misfortune? I do not know of studies that have examined specifically the effect of losses of this kind, but I would suppose that their disruptiveness cannot be determined simply by whether they entail much change in the outward circumstances and purposes of the bereaved parents. A child's death could undermine someone's trust in the goodness of life, perhaps in him- or herself as a parent, in the worth of making plans, so as to change profoundly the meaning of all relationships. Or it could be accepted, as so many Victorian families must have accepted it, with sorrow and resignation rather than lasting grief. But the loss of any unique relationship is potentially disturbing, because it evokes the vulnerability of all of them—their inescapable fragility and our uncertain ability to protect what we love.

This way of looking at unique relationships, as analogous to the principles of organization that underlie a conceptual structure of understanding, might seem to impose too rational a construction on bonds of affection. I have discussed only that structure of meaning of which people are more or less conscious and that they can at least operationally interpret. Psychoanalysis is largely preoccupied with what is not conscious, just because this has so profound and unrecognized an influence on the structure of our behavior. But the interpretation I have presented does not deny this. The structure of meaning reflects an organization of experience and emotional response whose foundations in earliest childhood are inaccessible to us. But psychoanalytic theory still assumes, as I would, that the nature of this underlying structure can be seen in the conscious, accessible structuring of meaning and is, if only through a long and difficult process of relearning, capable of reconstruction in the light of conscious meanings. Although I have tried to explain the importance of unique relationships in terms of their crucial importance to the evident structure of our lives, the underlying layers of behavioral structure would, I think, tend only to reinforce this importance, because the less accessible to conscious manipulation these structures are, the less easily can their principles be abstracted from the experience of particular relationships.

Attachment Theory and Social Ideals

Let me now come back to the ideological issues I raised at the beginning of this argument: I suggested that in reaction against the abstract and impersonal rationalism of industrial society there arose a corresponding idealization of the family, and especially of a mother's love, as the paradigm of truly meaningful relationships. The theory of attachment behavior has been taken as support for this ideal, both by advocates and opponents of the conventional family, and this, I believe, has led to two great misunderstandings: first, that attachment

197

theory is a sociological theory about family structure; and second, that all unique bonding is the outcome of a particular family structure implied by attachment theory. So, from a feminist point of view, attachment theory becomes confused with the gender differentiation characteristic of the Victorian, bourgeois family; and from communitarian points of view, with the narrow, private, selfish loyalties that inhibit the formation of a true human community. Correspondingly, conservatives mistake it for proof of the biological inevitability of a pattern of sex roles. These ideological biases cannot, I think, simply be ignored, because they represent deeply held prejudices about the possibilities of social change and inhibit our understanding.

The view of unique relationships I have presented here can, I think, help to clarify both the connection between attachment behavior and family structure, and its connection to other unique relationships. If we assume that a baby, all being well, forms an attachment to a nurturing figure very early in life, then feelings, purposes, patterns of behavior will begin to become structured around that relationship. But as a principle of organization, this model of relationship can be applied to other figures who seem to behave in the same way and respond as lovingly. The earliest experiences of attachment to a mothering figure must, I think, in any society establish in a young child the predisposition to understand nurturing relationships as embodied in unique figures. Being mothered is from the first associated with a particular, identified, special person, and that quality of relationships, therefore, is extended only to other particular, identifiable, special people. The range of constant, reliable, nurturing figures a child finds varies from the great traditional family compounds of a West African Yoruba lineage to a single parent's anonymous apartment in a city block. Unless children learn early that there can be several unique nurturing figures in their lives who seem to have a particular, special love for them, they are not, I think, likely later on to create the conditions in which they can discover or understand it. I am suggesting, then, that children learn, first through their experience of attachment, that there is a class of relationships (which may, however, have only one or no constant examples in their lives) in which they can recognize a unique bond between themselves and each other person of this class. Perhaps the easiest way to see uniqueness as a generalizable quality is in intimate friendships. We evolve with each of our closest friends an idiosyncratic relationship of mutual loyalty. Each is irreplaceable, and its loss would grieve us. Yet we can sustain, if we are lucky, a good many intimate friendships. All these unique relationships share the same qualities: They are nurturing, can claim priority, and are more or less exclusive. They are not primarily instrumental but to be enjoyed for their own sake, and so embody the meanings around which we organize our lives.

I am suggesting, then, that while attachment behavior itself, as Bowlby describes it, arises from an innate predisposition, the way in which the experience of attachment comes to be interpreted and developed in a child's evolving structure of meaning is learned. Yet I do not believe that any pattern of child rearing could inculcate a structure of meaning in which unique relationships cease to be important. Communitarian idealists have sometimes argued that any selective, exclusive bonds—whether of marriage, parenting, or friendship—are narrow, selfish, and inhibit the growth of true community spirit. The Oneida community, for instance, which flourished in upstate New York between 1848 and 1879, practiced a form of "complex marriage" where exclusive sexual partnerships were forbidden and "philoprogenitiveness" (maternal love for one's own children) was constantly rebuked (Hayden, 1976; Kern, 1979). Yet, despite three decades of preaching and stern repression, the women of the community were convinced more than ever at the end of its long and, on the whole, happy career that they wanted husbands and children of their own.

Why should it not be possible to educate the earliest experiences of attachment into a diffused, undifferentiated, loving, caring relationship with all the members of one's society? The most obvious and perhaps most fundamental reason is that loving, caring relationships depend upon selective loyalties. I can try to behave in a loving way toward everyone, but I can only give the attention, care, and support that love requires to very few. The meaning of a relationship, in the structure of my life, depends on its degree of priority in a hierarchy of claims, on what I will willingly give up for its sake. In practice, I would argue, it is virtually impossible to structure the meaning of one's life—either conceptually or socially—without a hierarchy of priorities. Otherwise one would have no basis for choosing between the claims of relationships, always bewildered and unreliable. So those who try to live without exclusive ties of relationship, like the people of Oneida or the members of a monastic order, have to create a surrogate that will fulfill for them the same structural need for some ordering of priorities of concern. Characteristically, they find it in a symbolic relationship with the same emotional connotations as a personal bond; they are brides of Christ, children of a supernatural father. The young women of Oneida pledged to John Humphrey Noyes, the community's founder and leader, in 1869 that "we do not belong to ourselves in any respect, but that we first belong to *God*, and second to Mr. Noyes as God's true representative. . . . Above all, we offer ourselves 'living sacrifices' to God and true Communism" (Kern, 1979, pp. 184–185).

Such symbolic relationships define the crucial bond that gives life its meaning, but because they preempt any mundane human ties of affection, they do not provide principles of organization until they are interpreted. The emotional commitment to the symbol becomes a practical subordination to the symbol's interpreter, each implying the other, so that societies structured around such meanings will tend to be highly authoritarian. As time goes by and this subordination to the communitarian ideal becomes routinized in the traditions and principles of an established social order, the followers will find it harder and harder to identify this institutionalized authority structure with an unique symbolic bond, and they will begin to search again for someone of their own to love.

These communitarian experiments are not, though, merely bizarre aberrations. They represent a fundamental dilemma of social organization. We want all the relationships on which we depend to be nurturing and supportive, as if all the members of society were brothers and sisters, parents and children to each other. We idealize society as a family, membership in it as a fraternity, our loyalty to it as loyalty to mother- or fatherland. Yet the actual relationships that this ideal reflects are necessarily selective and exclusive. They serve to differentiate claims and obligations within society, contradicting the notion of a universal family. The communitarianism of the Oneidans and the opposite emphasis on the private family as the only legitimate refuge of loving relationships represent equally extreme refusals to acknowledge the dilemma. Both are inherently strained, uncompromising resolutions of an underlying ambivalence.

REFERENCES

Beecher, C., and Stowe, H. B. 1869. *The American woman's home.* New York: J. B. Ford.
Bowlby, J. 1973a. Affectional bonds: Their nature and origin. In *Loneliness: The experience of emotional and social isolation,* by R. S. Weiss. Cambridge, Mass.: M.I.T. Press.
———. 1973b. *Attachment and Loss. Vol. 2: Separation: Anxiety and anger.* New York: Basic Books.

Durkheim, E. 1915. *The elementary forms of religious life,* trans. J. W. Swain. New York: Macmillan.

Freud, S. 1925. Mourning and melancholia. In *Collected papers,* vol. 4. London: Hogarth Press.

Hayden, D. 1976. *Seven American utopias.* Cambridge, Mass.: M.I.T. Press.

————. 1977. Catharine Beecher and the politics of housework. In *Women in American architecture: A historic and contemporary perspective,* ed. S. Torre. New York: Whitney Library of Design.

Kern, L. J. 1979. Ideology and reality: Sexuality and women's status in the Oneida community. *Radical History Review* 20 (spring/summer): 180–205.

Lasch, C. 1977. *Haven in a heartless world.* New York: Basic Books.

Lewis, C. S. 1961. *A grief observed.* London: Faber & Faber.

Marris, P. 1958. *Widows and their families.* London: Routledge & Kegan Paul.

————. 1974. *Loss and change.* London: Routledge & Kegan Paul.

Parkes, C. M. 1971. Psycho-social transitions: A field of study. *Social Science and Medicine* 5:101–115.

Parsons, T. 1951. *The social system.* New York: Free Press.

Piaget, J. 1971. *Genetic epistemology,* trans. E. Duckworth. New York: Norton.

PART IV

Disorders in Adult Life

11

Scott Henderson

THE SIGNIFICANCE OF SOCIAL RELATIONSHIPS IN THE ETIOLOGY OF NEUROSIS

EPIDEMIOLOGICAL STUDIES of nonpsychotic mental disorders have so far yielded only sparse information about their causes. One reason for this may have been the lack, until recently, of methods for reliably identifying symptoms and thereby defining syndromes and cases, so that one could be sure of the type and severity of the disorder being investigated. These fundamental problems have now been largely overcome through the development of interview instruments such as the Present State Examination (PSE; Wing, Cooper, and Sartorius, 1974), which insures for the first time that different investigators, in different parts of the world, can be confident that the type and severity of the disorders they are studying are similar, provided they are competent in using the instrument. Consideration of etiology can now proceed apace, without the concern that investigators may be studying different phenomena.

But case definition is not the main reason for psychiatric epidemi-

The work on social relationships described in this chapter has been pursued with a number of colleagues over the last few years. What is reported here is an account of essentially collaborative work with Paul Duncan-Jones, D. G. Byrne, Ruth Scott, Sylvia Adcock, Richard Craft, and Mervyn Silvapulle, each of whom has brought particular skills to the empirical investigations we have undertaken in this intricate area. My warm appreciation is due to them as well as to other contributors to this volume for their criticism.

ology's low yield. A greater barrier has been its failure to examine social and personal variables that directly affect individuals in their daily lives. Consideration of coarse sociodemographic attributes such as age, marital status, or social class can give only a distant glimpse of people's actual living conditions. Such variables say little about personal experience and carry little clinical relevance in themselves. They are certainly quite legitimate as a starting point for research because they may provide etiological clues, such as those so usefully reviewed by Dohrenwend and Dohrenwend (1969). As Robins (1978) rightly asserts, we now need to be able to say what it is about being old, female, or unmarried that increases the risk for particular diagnoses. Workers who have used abstract constructs of a macrosocial kind, such as anomie or sociocultural disintegration (Leighton, Harding, Macklin, Macmillan, and Leighton, 1963; Leighton, Lambo, Hughes, Leighton, Murphy, and Macklin, 1963), face the problem first of measuring these in satisfactory ways, then of trying to explain what impact such factors may have on the individual to make him more likely to fall ill. An alternative to trying to identify abstract societal factors is for the epidemiologist to study the experiences of individuals. This has to be done in a coherent theoretical framework; and it has to have methods and instruments equal to the task.

Most of the theory about the causes of neurosis in adults is psychodynamic, placing much emphasis on experiences in the formative years of infancy and childhood. By contrast, pathogenic factors in the person's more recent past have not been given the same attention. Recently the individual's exposure to adverse life events or experiences has been studied extensively, with results that suggest that causal effects are probable, though there is dispute about how much of the variance in subsequent morbidity these explain (Rabkin and Struening, 1976). The interpretation of life-event data has to be extremely cautious because of the many methodological hazards in this field, hazards that equally beset studies of social ties, as we shall describe. It has seemed to us that adversity is unlikely to be the only current extrapersonal factor contributing to the onset of neurosis. Insofar as the sociodemographic variables offer clues to other causes, only two stand out as having a consistent association with higher prevalence rates for neurosis: sex and marital status. The findings for age and social class have proved very variable, with no clear pattern to be discerned (Dohrenwend and Dohrenwend, 1969), but the rates for neurosis were higher for women in seventeen out of twenty-one surveys reviewed

(Dohrenwend and Dohrenwend, 1969) and the married have usually been found to have lower rates of neurosis than the single or the no-longer-married (Malzberg, 1964; Pearlin and Johnson, 1977). At the epidemiological level, this observation seemed to be a pointer: Among the many possible interpretations of these patterns, one economical explanatory hypothesis is that there may be an inverse association between neurosis and the personal relationships available to individuals within their primary groups.[1] Women and the nonmarried may possibly have fewer personal relationships, or those that they do have may less often be satisfying. We concluded, at this early stage in our thinking, that what was needed was an etiological hypothesis relating the lack of social relationships to neurosis (Henderson, 1977; Henderson, Ritchie, McAuley, and Duncan-Jones, 1978).

The origins of such a hypothesis, its investigation, and the conclusions we have reached have been set out in some detail in our monograph (Henderson, Byrne, and Duncan-Jones, 1981).

CARE-ELICITING BEHAVIOR IN PSYCHIATRIC PATIENTS

The starting point for this hypothesis came from observations made in the course of treating nonpsychotic patients in the psychiatric clinic of a general hospital. If the type of symptom or behavior that led to their referral or admission was set aside, one could ask oneself if there were any recurrent features to be discerned in the current social environments of these individuals or in their reports of it. We were strongly impressed by how often nonpsychotic patients perceived themselves to be receiving insufficient care-taking behavior from others, and how their symptoms had at least a temporary effect on their primary group to correct this. The patients' symptoms and some of their behaviors could, we began to suspect, be seen as somewhat of the same character as the care-eliciting behavior described in the ethological studies of J. P. Scott (1969) on the emotional basis of social behavior. Care-eliciting behavior is most clearly seen in the context of the attachment of the young to their mothers. We recognized, though, that behaviors of the same class can be identified in the interpersonal transactions of adults. It was postulated that some nonpsychotic symptoms and behaviors could very comfortably be placed in a category to

---

1. The term "primary group" was used by Cooley (1909) to refer to those in an individual's social world with whom one has interaction and commitment. See also Broom and Selznick (1973), pp. 132–161.

be called abnormal care-eliciting behavior. These are legitimately called abnormal because they are disruptive, either to the self or to others. Examples of such states are parasuicide, neurotic depression, and, not least, that remarkable group of disorders that Pilowsky (1969, 1978) has called the abnormal illness behaviors. These include hypochondriasis, psychogenic overlay, conversion hysteria, psychogenic pain, accident neurosis, dermatitis artifacta, and the Munchausen syndrome. It was argued that the patient showing any of these nonpsychotic states, finding himself deficient in care-taking behavior from others, has usually worked up a hierarchical repertoire of socially less disruptive care-eliciting behaviors, only as a last resort having recourse to ones that lead to medical or psychiatric attention. The postulated phenomenon was described as follows:

> In abnormal care-eliciting, instead of crying, clinging, or using verbal appeals, the individual used other signals. These signals cause distress to himself and often to others, but their consequence is developmentally ancient: they bring important others closer. (Henderson, 1974)

It is implicit in the care-eliciting hypothesis that the individual is, or perceives himself to be, deficient in the receipt of caring behavior from others. These others may be present in his daily life but either unable or unwilling to meet his requirements; or there may be an absence of such persons, as in the case of the truly isolated. All such persons are in a state we might in clinical discourse conveniently call *anophelia*, a term derived from the Greek ὠφέλια (ophelia, as in the woman's name, which means care, succor, or support). This is the very commodity they lack. We noted that in Western and some other populations there is probably a strong sex difference in the prevalence of care-eliciting behavior, with women in general showing greater attachment requirements; and there certainly is a female excess of the care-eliciting syndromes themselves, as inspection of the list will confirm. Similar observations on neurosis in women are to be found in the epidemiological data of Carstairs and Kapur (1976) in Karnataka State, India, and of El-Islam (1975) in Qatar. This might be because adult females either have an increased requirement for caring behavior, which would increase genetic fitness through insuring protection, or they may tend to be deprived of it for cultural or subcultural reasons. For the present, these observations are invoked only as leads; it is premature to interpret them further.

Pointers to the Social Bond Hypothesis

The care-eliciting hypothesis was a starting point in formulating a social causation for the neuroses and other nonpsychotic disorders. The attraction was that it implicated the individual's current social milieu, a field that we felt had so far been too scantily considered. Before looking for other observations that might support a link between such morbidity and deficiences in social bonds, we next noted the biological advantages conferred in primate and human evolution by the capacity to form interindividual ties. In many primate species, and certainly in hunting and gathering humans, individuals actively prefer to be in the company of others most of the time. These others are not indiscriminately chosen but are members of the individual's band, commonly twenty to thirty in number. This is close to the size of the primary group referred to earlier. After an exhaustive review of the ethnographic and anthropological evidence, Goldschmidt (1959) concluded that man is, indisputably, by nature a social animal. The development of speech can itself be seen as a major advance in the biological apparatus for conducting social relationships. With the disappearance of estrus and a typically promiscuous pattern of mating came the psychological capacity to form an enduring pair bond with an adult of the opposite sex. The genetic fitness conferred by the ability to form and maintain these and other interindividual bonds has been discussed by Washburn and Jay (1968), Washburn and Harding (1976), and by Hamburg (1968a, b). It is reasonable to conclude from this evolutionary consideration that the continued absence of others is an atypical environment for humans; that it is likely they are biologically programmed to prefer to be a member of a group, to have the capacity to form relatively enduring pair bonds, and to display emotional distress when the presence of important others is lost or not available for any substantial period (see also Weiss, chapter 9 herein). It would therefore not be surprising if a link were to exist between affective state and social bonds. The same notion is expressed by Maslow (1968) in his hierarchy of human needs, in which relationships with others comes immediately after the biologically essential ones of food and shelter.

A second pointer is to be found in that particular class of social bond called attachment. Although attachment theory developed through observations of the young, Bowlby (1973, 1977) has proposed that adults also form, and indeed require, attachments. In most contemporary societies, it is through these attachments that the greater part of caretaking behavior is exchanged. The making and breaking of attachments have a marked influence on mood, effects that deserve much more attention in clinical research. In discussing the causes of anxiety, Bowlby (1973) notes that "insufficient recognition has been given to the enormous roles that an individual's personal and familiar environment, including his familiar companions, plays in determining his emotional state" (p. 148). His work on attachment, when translated to an adult context, seemed to us to be a very promising avenue for social psychiatry in its search for better causal variables. We believed it reasonable to abstract from attachment theory some support for the proposition that deficiencies in social bonds may contribute to nonpsychotic psychiatric morbidity (Henderson, 1977). It should be noted that this proposition contains a statement about a possible causal process. In clinical psychiatry itself, previous work offered only a few leads. In a study of the "social orbit" of psychiatric outpatients at the Maudsley Hospital, London, Post (1962) had noted that many of his patients were markedly deficient in social contacts. In the course of their studies of depression in women, Brown and his colleagues (Brown, Bhrolcháin, and Harris, 1975; Brown and Harris, 1978; and Brown, chapter 12 herein) found that in the presence of severe adversity, having a close confiding relationship with another—usually but not always male—was associated with markedly lower inception rates for clinical depression. They concluded that having an intimate relationship was likely to be protective against depressive illness.

Though largely narrative in quality, there are a number of natural observations from wartime and disasters that consistently point to the advantages conferred by the presence of trusted others when individuals are in extreme danger (Killian, 1952; Beach and Lucas, 1960). Their presence is thought to have a protective effect. In a group of merchant seamen adrift on a raft off Tasmania and later marooned for a total of thirteen days with no food and little water, Henderson and Bostock (1977) reported that preoccupation with attachment figures and a persistent drive to be reunited with them were effective coping behaviors in these men during their ordeal. There is reason to believe that close bonds sometimes develop between terrorists and their hostages, and this can at times be life saving. But a similar process seems to take place in brainwashing, where the captive sometimes becomes fond of his interrogators. It is likely that close confinement in a state of high arousal may promote the formation of affectional ties where none existed previously, and that this phylogenetically ancient mechanism can be exploited by either party.

In medical epidemiology, there have been some remarkable observations on the effect of social bonds on both morbidity and mortality. Cassel (1974) reported an increased prevalence of hypertension and stroke in groups deficient in social supports. In an important paper entitled "The Contribution of the Social Environment to Host Resistance," Cassel (1976) argues that social supports may protect against stressor situations by acting as a buffering or cushioning agent. More recently Berkman and Syme (1979) have reported an increased mortality, not just morbidity, among those deficient in social ties in their nine-year prospective study of 6,928 adults in Alameda County. The age-adjusted relative risks for those most isolated and those with most social ties were 2.3 for men and 2.8 for women. These findings seem not to be easily explained by contamination between dependent and independent variables, nor by deficiencies in social ties being an indirect expression of some other attribute known to be associated with increased mortality risk, such as social class or nutrition. The implications of this are considerable: It is a prospective study and it refers to physical pathology. If these findings are confirmed, it will be necessary to seek some explanation of how social relationships could influence the processes of physical pathology.

Last, we noted that in life-event research, which has so dominated social psychiatry in the last decade, a substantial proportion of the items on typical schedules could alternatively be interpreted as losses of social bonds. In the Schedule of Recent Experiences (Holmes and Rahe, 1967) and the life event scale by Paykel, Prusoff, and Uhlenhuth (1971), all of the more severe events *are* losses, or threatened losses, of important social relationships. Many other events have such exits coming as a secondary effect, as in the case of retirement. If life events do contribute to the onset of psychiatric or physical morbidity, as the work of Brown and his collaborators strongly suggest (Brown and Harris, 1978), this effect could be due at least in part to the consequent deficiencies in social bonds. The notion that a lack of social support may contribute to the onset of neurosis is a theme now being pursued in a number of centers, notably by Miller and Ingham (1976) in Edinburgh, and by Lin and her colleagues in Washington, D.C. (Dean and Lin, 1977; Lin et al., 1979).

The Hypotheses

From the leads provided by the studies just described, we set up two hypotheses for testing. These are that:

1. A lack of social relationships is a causal factor in the onset of neurosis.

2. A deficiency in either close affectional ties or in more diffuse ones (social integration) is a causal factor in the subsequent onset of neurosis, independent of the amount of adversity.

What Components of Social Relationships Should Be Selected as Independent Variables?

The concept of care-eliciting behavior directed our attention principally to affectional ties between adults rather than more diffuse relationships, because it was strongly our impression that the deficiencies patients described were in these closer reaches of their primary group and, in particular, in those to whom they were emotionally attached. Yet patients could accept fairly readily substitute sources of caring behavior. This was to be observed taking place between them and their doctors (sometimes), nurses, social workers, or other team members; and not uncommonly the caring behavior came from nonprofessionals such as ward maids or, of particular interest to us, other patients. This suggested that one might see social relationships as a vehicle for a range of commodities, which are usually fairly specific to the type of relationships. Intimacy and the opportunity to confide or express painful affect are usually found in close affectional ties, such as may felicitously occur in marriage or in special friendships. Friends and work associates may carry rather different functions, such as providing confirmation of appropriate behavior or endorsement of personal worth. We therefore saw some advantage in leaving aside a traditional categorization of social relationships in the form of intimates and immediate kin, friends, neighbors, work associates, and so forth. Instead, the individual's social environment can be construed as the source of certain psychological supplies that may be necessary for most people to maintain normal mood. The typology then becomes based not on persons but on the commodities they provide. If people do in fact need other people, we argued, it is appropriate for social psychiatry to ask what it

212

is these others supply. One is unlikely to be able to establish an exhaustive list of these commodities, precisely specified, but it seems feasible to identify constructs that come close to some of them.

Little progress can be made in this field until reliable and valid methods have been developed for describing an individual's personal network and what it provides for him. In this task, social psychiatry must start from scratch. Sartorius (1977), in his review of research priorities likely to be useful for psychiatric services, reports that no instrument was available to describe an individual's immediate social environment. Whether it be for testing etiological hypotheses or for studying the interpersonal consequences of illness, this has been a serious impediment.

A cardinal contribution to this field has been made by Weiss (1973, 1974). On the basis of his work with groups in Boston conspicuously deficient in social bonds, such as single parents and new arrivals in the suburbs, he proposed six "provisions of social relationships" that are supplied by the others in an individual's daily life. Clearly there is no reason for assuming that these six are exhaustive. Although a more complete account of the nature of these provisions is given by Weiss (1974), it is important to review them here. The six provisions he defines are: attachment, social integration, opportunity for nurturing others, reassurance of worth, a sense of reliable alliance, and the obtaining of help and guidance. As we have seen in chapter 9 and elsewhere in this volume, *attachment* is provided by relationships from which participants gain a sense of security and place. Relationships that provide attachment make the individual feel emotionally comfortable and at home. Without them he feels lonely and restless. Prolonged separation from those to whom an individual is attached, or their loss through death, invariably leads to acute distress. *Social integration* comes from relationships in which there are shared concerns. These provide a source of companionship and a base for social activity, without which life tends to become dull. Weiss suggests that being a member of a network with common concerns permits the development of pooled information and ideas and a shared interpretation of experience. *Opportunity for nurturing others* applies particularly to the satisfaction adults obtain from having responsibility for the well-being of a child or other person. For many this seems to provide a meaning to life and motivation to keep going, particularly in the face of serious adversity. This was certainly the case for some who survived the Nazi concentration camps, as many witnesses have told. *Reassurance of worth* is important as the provision that, above all others, promotes self-esteem. According to one's social role, it is obtained from colleagues or family. It is provided by relationships that give confirmation of an individual's competence in a particular role. *A sense of reliable alliance* comes primarily from kin. Weiss argues that it is only within kinship ties that continuing assistance can be expected, whether or not there is mutual affection. The decreased amount of contact with kin said to be common in modern urban living may lead to shortage of this provision. *The obtaining of guidance* is important when individuals are facing real adversity. The majority of people appreciate having access to someone who is trustworthy and authoritative, thereby furnishing them with emotional support and an opportunity to formulate plans of action. It is better still if that person has the quality the Romans called *gravitas*.

Development of the Interview Schedule for Social Interaction

Weiss's schema provided us with a basis for the construction of an interview to determine a person's field of social relationships and the provisions he obtains through them. This is the Interview Schedule for Social Interaction (ISSI; Henderson, Duncan-Jones, Byrne, and Scott, 1980). We placed particular emphasis on the examination of close affectional ties and the provision by them of what in this volume has been called attachment, because we believed that this would be particularly relevant in the etiology of psychiatric disorder. Bowlby (1973) noted that not only young children but adults of all ages were "found to be their happiest and to be able to deploy their talents to best advantage when they are confident that standing behind them are one or more trusted persons who will come to their aid should difficulties arise" (p. 359).

From early pilot interviews on psychiatric outpatients, we began to appreciate that it was not sufficient for our purposes to ask only what was available to an individual; it was equally important to obtain some expression of how adequate this was in the respondent's eyes. A person might have an apparently abundant supply of a particular provision but find this insufficient for his requirement, either by reason of personality or because of the context, such as adversity or physical or mental ill health. Accordingly, we constructed items on both the *availability* and the *reported adequacy* for each example of a provision. The wording and response categories of each item were improved over a period of a year by administering the instrument in its several pilot editions to persons of diverse age, state of health, social class, and marital status. We conducted over 130 pilot interviews in two health centers, a psychiatric outpatient and inpatient clinic, a physical rehabilitation unit, and a club for senior citizens. In this way we tried to insure that the instrument was widely applicable to the adults of a general population. Detailed guide notes were drawn up on the basis of this field experience. Finally, the ISSI was administered to a sample of 151 persons in the pilot study for the 1977–1978 population survey in Canberra (Henderson, Byrne, Duncan-Jones, Adcock, Scott, and Steele, 1978).

In its final form, the ISSI has fifty-two items and takes about one hour to administer. It is conversational in style. The availability and reported adequacy of each of the Weiss provisions is systematically explored. An attempt is made to identify all those persons to whom the respondent feels affectionally close. For each aspect of attachment, the principal individual who supplies this is recorded. For all provisions, any increase or decrease of availability or of adequacy between the present and one year ago is recorded. Finally, there are three items that inquire about arguments with close others and with persons outside the home. Although the principal aim of the instrument is to describe positive aspects of social relationships, we recognized that these are invariably accompanied by affectively unpleasant elements, which must be taken into account. In an earlier study of psychiatric outpatients, striking differences were found between them and a normal comparison group in the amount of affectively unpleasant interaction recently experienced within their primary groups (Henderson, Ritchie, McAuley, and Duncan-Jones, 1978).

SCORING

The methods for scoring the ISSI were initially conceived during its development. They were worked out in full using the data from the population study (Duncan-Jones, 1981a, b). We divided Weiss's concept of social integration into relationships with friends and with acquaintances but discarded the concept of obtaining help and guidance because it did not add much information to what was already being supplied. This left six provisions for which expressions could be derived for availability and for reported adequacy. Duncan-Jones explored the structure of the ISSI data obtained from our population sample of 756 persons in order to determine how well the data could be expressed in

215

terms of these six pairs of variables. His conclusion was that little information is lost by summarizing all the provisions, save attachment, under a single heading, which we called social integration. This leads to seven summary indices:

AVAT: The *av*ailability of *at*tachment.

ADAT: The perceived *ad*equacy of *at*tachment.

ADAT%: The ADAT score, expressed as a percentage of the number of ADAT questions it was appropriate to ask the particular respondent. (Not all respondents have the same availability of attachment on which to express their perceived adequacy. It is therefore more logical than ADAT itself.)

NONAT: The number of facets of attachment relationships the respondent says he does not have, but that he feels nevertheless he can do without. (This index is an expression of ability to tolerate not having attachments.)

AVSI: The *av*ailability of more diffuse relationships, as with friends, work associates, or acquaintances, here called social integration.

ADSI: The *ad*equacy of these more diffuse relationships.

ATTROWN: The number of attachment persons with whom the respondent has recently been having arguments.

The reliability and validity of the instrument was investigated in the course of the population study, as is described in the following sections.

Neurosis and Social Relationships in a General Population

THE MEASUREMENT OF MORBIDITY

Having developed an instrument for measuring these seven aspects of social relationships, we were closer to being able to examine the association between them and neurosis. However, we knew the direction of causality would prove to be particularly difficult to investigate. Here we consider only the association, because this is itself an essential step in pursuing clues in epidemiological research.

A sample of those presenting for treatment in general practice or hospital clinics would have been unsuitable for our purpose, because a deficiency in social relationships might have led people to seek help for neurotic symptoms, rather than have brought about the emergence of the symptoms themselves. That is, it might have been mainly those neurotics with deficient social bonds who came for professional help. Only a general population sample, we felt, could provide the necessary data that would be free of such a bias. This principal holds quite commonly in etiological research, but it is by no means sufficiently recognized.

An immediate difficulty with general population studies is that one has to examine quite large numbers to accrue sufficient cases for worthwhile analysis. We tried to overcome this problem by using a two-phase design, as described elsewhere in relation to our work on the measurement of psychiatric morbidity as the dependent variable (Duncan-Jones and Henderson, 1978; Henderson et al., 1979). The population studied was the residents of Canberra, the federal capital of Australia. A systematic sample from the electoral roll was drawn, out of which 756 adults were successfully interviewed, to yield a contact rate of 85 percent. These interviews were conducted mainly in respondents' homes by specially trained interviewers. After being carefully selected by us for their comportment, experience, and interviewing skills, these interviewers spent a week in the Unit being trained, with special emphasis on the ISSI and the List of Recent Experiences. The latter was our instrument for measuring exposure to adversity in the previous twelve months. Its design and performance have been described by Henderson, Byrne, and Duncan-Jones (1981). Steele, Henderson, and Duncan-Jones (1980) found it to have acceptable reliability for total scores but not for individual events.

In their first interview, respondents were administered the thirty-item General Health Questionnaire (GHQ; Goldberg, 1972), an instrument of established sensitivity and specificity for the detection of nonpsychotic psychiatric morbidity. It has been validated for an Australian population (Tennant, 1977). On the basis of their score on the GHQ, respondents were then selected to form a weighted subsample for much more detailed examination with the Present State Examination (Wing, 1976; Wing, Cooper, and Sartorius, 1974; Wing et al., 1977; Wing, Henderson, and Winckle, 1977). This allowed estimates to be calculated of the prevalence of morbidity within CATEGO diagnoses; the estimates were not just for this subsample ($n = 157$) but for the whole sample and therefore for the total population. Furthermore, a method was developed to estimate the probability that an individual was a case, in the PSE sense of being at Index of Definition (ID) levels 5 or 6, given that one knew his score on the GHQ (Duncan-Jones and Henderson, 1978). This has been used as the dependent variable in a number of our analyses.

217

It was important to obtain this description of the pattern of morbidity being studied, and to do so in an internationally standardized way, before going ahead with the testing of etiological hypotheses. This point has been emphasized by Wing, Cooper, and Sartorius (1974) and Orley and Wing (1979). The prevalence of psychiatric disorder in Canberra, at the level of case and threshold case (ID levels of 5 and 6), was 9.0 percent (s.d. 3.2). Most of the morbidity, as expected, was anxiety neurosis and neurotic depression. A full account of this aspect of the survey has been given elsewhere (Henderson et al., 1979).

THE ISSI IN A GENERAL POPULATION SAMPLE

Because the ISSI was administered to a representative sample of a general population, we are in a position to describe the pattern of social relationships experienced by individuals in this one city. At the same time, we did not feel it would have been right to use the ISSI results as an expression of the principal independent variable without first making some assessment of the reliability and validity of the instrument.

Reliability The internal consistency of the instrument was examined on the data from the total cross-sectional sample ($n = 756$). The test-retest reliability was examined in a small random subsample ($n = 51$) of the total sample, visited about eighteen days (s.d. 4.6) after the first interview. As is described in our paper on the development and performance of the instrument (Henderson, Duncan-Jones, Byrne, and Scott, 1980), these reliability coefficients were entirely acceptable, most being over 0.7. We were able to go on to examine the long-term stability of these indices of social relationships. In the panel study that followed the cross-sectional survey, a random subsample of 221 persons was interviewed again at four, eight, and twelve months from the time of the initial examination. The long-term stability of scores was impressive. Duncan-Jones's estimates of correlations between the true scores at the first and the twelve-month interviews were as follows: AVAT .85; ADAT .69; AVSI .85; ADSI .66. These figures were estimated by confirmatory factor analysis.

Validity Validity has been investigated at some length. Face validity was judged on the content of the scales in relation to what they purport to measure. Inspection of the items for, say, the availability of attachment, or the adequacy of social integration, will allow the reader to make his own judgment of this. The items have been carefully constructed to tap those attitudes and behaviors that characterize the en-

218

tire range of social relationships, from the emotionally close and highly person-specific to the more diffuse. Next scores were compared in several sociodemographic groups, such as the widowed, the elderly, and those only recently arrived to live in Canberra. The expected differences were confirmed for both attachment and social integration.

As we indicate below, the study was conducted in two parts. The first was the cross-sectional examination of the total sample ($n = 756$). This is referred to as Wave 1. A random subsample was reexamined three more times at four-month intervals. These examinations are referred to as Waves 2, 3, and 4. Extraversion and neuroticism were measured by the Eysenck Personality Inventory (EPI; Eysenck and Eysenck, 1964) in Waves 2 and 4 of the panel study, along with repeated ISSI interviews. This allows the association between extraversion and the ISSI indices to be examined. There was a correlation of .31 between extraversion and the score for availability of social integration, but no significant correlation with attachment. This is very much in keeping with what one might reasonably predict. Neuroticism, though, has a modest negative correlation with the availability and the adequacy of both attachment and social integration.

In the fourth and last Wave of the panel study, a random half were asked to nominate someone who would be well informed about their social relationships. Successful interviews were completed with nearly all of these people, giving collateral information for 114 respondents. An amended version of the ISSI was used for this, appropriately adapted by Ruth Scott and others for inquiry about the respondent in the eyes of this informant. Correlations between the pairs of scores were: AVAT .42; ADAT .39; AVSI .59; ADSI .26. Such correlations, which are all significant beyond the 1 percent level, are satisfactory for such an exercise, as they are within the range to be expected when one person rates another on such attributes, as shown by Scott and Scott (1979).

Last, we considered the possibility that social desirability might materially affect the responses on the ISSI interview. The Crowne-Marlowe measure of need for approval (Crowne and Marlowe, 1964), derived from the positively and reverse-scored items (Rump and Court, 1971), was administered within the course of the panel study. To these two scores was added the Lie Score from the Eysenck Personality Inventory. The percentages of the variance in ISSI scores explained by these three sets of scores were: AVAT 5.8; ADAT 8.4; AVSI 5.7; ADSI 10.6. Bearing in mind the nature of the constructs the ISSI explores, these are low values. The conclusion was that the ISSI carried an acceptable level of validity.

219

THE ISSI AS A TOOL FOR CLINICAL OR EPIDEMIOLOGICAL RESEARCH

The development of the Interview Schedule for Social Interaction has been described here in some detail to show how such work was prompted by a clinically derived hypothesis, to try to make a contribution to an area of social psychiatry hitherto neglected. The ISSI takes an investigator rather closer to conditions in an individual's day-to-day life. We believe it should continue to be used only in an interview, although some workers would doubtless find a self-completion instrument quicker and more convenient. A more detailed description of the ISSI is given in Henderson, Duncan-Jones, Byrne, and Scott (1980), together with an account of the pattern of social relationships observed in one population.

Findings

CROSS-SECTIONAL ASSOCIATION BETWEEN NEUROSIS AND
DEFICIENCIES IN SOCIAL RELATIONSHIPS

Our findings, described elsewhere in detail (Henderson, Byrne, Duncan-Jones, Adcock, and Scott, 1980), can only be summarized here. The thirty-item General Health Questionnaire was used as the principal measure of the dependent variable in most of our analyses of these data. This is adequate for an initial exploration of the association with deficiencies in social relationships, although we recognize that a much more precise and clinically more realistic examination can be made with data such as the Present State Examination provides. We shall describe here the association between GHQ scores and the summary ISSI scores. These are shown as product-moment correlations in table 11-1.

These correlation coefficients show that, for women, a modest negative association is present between neurotic symptoms and the availability of both attachment and social integration. This is not the case for men. But for both sexes there is a substantial association with the perceived adequacy of both types of relationship. Taken together, these ISSI measures account for 7.8 percent of the variance in GHQ score in men and 15.4 percent in women. (Arguments and adverse experiences, which were included in the analysis described in Henderson, Byrne, Duncan-Jones, Adcock, and Scott [1980], have not been

TABLE 11-1

Correlations between GHQ and ISSI Scores, by Sex, in a
General Population Sample: Cross-Sectional Data

Correlation with	Men (n = 357)	Women (n = 393)
AVAT	−.04	−.16
(Availability of close relationships)		
ADAT%	−.23	−.35
(Perceived adequacy of close relationships)		
NONAT	−.06	−.03
(Acceptance of not having close relationships)		
AVSI	−.04	−.14
(Availability of more diffuse relationships)		
ADSI	−.24	−.32
(Perceived adequacy of more diffuse relationships)		

brought into the equation here; they raise the total explained variance to 16 percent and 22 percent respectively.)

When one goes on to consider the same association according to whether the respondents have been having high or low levels of adversity, as measured by the List of Recent Experiences, the findings are that, for women, a deficiency of ADAT% in the presence of adversity is associated with an increased level of morbidity. This does not hold for men. By contrast, a deficiency of social integration (ADSI) in the presence of adversity is associated with increased morbidity in men, but not in women. The former observation is in line with those of Brown and his colleagues (Brown, Bhrolcháin, and Harris, 1975; Brown and Harris, 1978) that a confiding relationship had a protective effect on women in adversity.

There are a number of reasons why one cannot be satisfied with such cross-sectional observations. Persons who have already established neurotic symptoms may perceive their social relationships as deficient because of their affective state, or their symptoms and behavior may have had a repelling effect on those around them. Another possibility is that an underlying variable, such as certain personality traits, may have rendered such persons vulnerable to neurosis on the one hand and, at the same time, less competent in establishing or maintaining mutually satisfying personal relationships. This is in accord with the deep-thinking work of Foulds (1965, 1976). Accordingly,

221

we saw the necessity for having longitudinal observations on a representative subsample of those examined in the cross-sectional study. This, we hoped, would allow the causality problem to be tackled. A lack of social relationships was postulated to have a causal effect in its own right, and not only through providing a cushion or buffer, as had been proposed by Cassel (1976) and by Brown and his colleagues for close, confiding relationships (Brown, Bhrolcháin, and Harris, 1975; Brown and Harris, 1978). The design and analysis of the findings have been reported in some detail elsewhere (Henderson, Byrne, Duncan-Jones, Adcock, and Scott, 1980; Henderson et al., 1981).

The Panel Study

From the 756 respondents examined in the cross-sectional survey (Wave 1), a random subsample (n = 323) was drawn and an attempt made to interview each of them, usually in their homes, at four-month intervals, on three further occasions, Waves 2, 3, and 4. This is called the panel study. Of this subsample of 323, 220 had completed all four interviews one year later. Those who were not examined were found not to have differed on relevant variables from those who were maintained in the cohort.

The measures made at each Wave that will be considered here were the thirty-item GHQ, the ISSI, and the List of Recent Experiences for the year prior to Wave 1 or since the last interview in Waves 2, 3, and 4.

FINDINGS

To avoid the problem of contamination between neurotic symptoms and the predictor variables, only persons in the panel sample who were well at Wave 1 were considered (*n* = 177). A GHQ score of less than 6 was taken as the criterion. Their ISSI and life event measures were likely to be free of the various forms of contamination that having neurotic symptoms could bring. We then calculated the correlations between their ISSI and adversity indices at Wave 1 and their GHQ scores in Waves 2, 3, and 4. According to this first hypothesis, the ISSI indices should be statistically significantly correlated (negatively) with these GHQ scores. This was confirmed, with the ADAT% and ADSI indices being correlated with the Wave 2 GHQ scores at the .003 and .001 levels of significance. The correlations with other indices were weaker. All the correlations were strongest for Wave 2 and tended to decline in subsequent Waves. We therefore focused our attention on the ISSI indices measured at Wave 1 with the GHQ scores four months later, namely at Wave 2. Collectively, they explained 12.7 percent of the variance in the onset of morbidity. By contrast, our adversity measure, again made at Wave 1, explained only 4.0 percent of variance. We concluded that the evidence was in favor of the first hypothesis, that a lack of social relationships is a causal factor in the onset of neurosis. What was not expected, though, was that the self-reported adequacy would be more important than the availability of social relationships. We recognize that this called for careful interpretation.

SOCIAL RELATIONSHIPS IN THE PRESENCE OF ADVERSITY

To test the second hypothesis—that a deficiency in social relationships is a causal factor independent of the amount of adversity—we divided the 177 respondents who were well at Wave 1 into those who reported having had high and low levels of adversity in the previous twelve months (n = 115 and 62 respectively). The adversity score was cut at its mean for this purpose ($\bar{X}$ = 89, s.d. = 62.4, range 0 to 320). The results were striking: For those with the lower level of adversity, the ISSI indices collectively explained only 4.1 percent of the variance; by contrast, they explained 30.0 percent in those who had the higher level of adversity. The individual correlations are shown in table 11–2, where it can be seen that for those with low adversity, the correlation between each ISSI index and the GHQ score four months later is only trifling. By contrast, for those persons with high adversity, some correlations are substantial. It is important to note too that the highest correlations are with the adequacy measures, ADAT% and ADSI. The availability of attachment does not produce a statistically significant correlation, while the availability of social integration (more diffuse relationships) does so only at the 5 percent level. We shall shortly return to an examination of why it is the adequacy indices that have by far the stronger association with subsequent symptoms.

These results suggest that there is an interaction effect between social relationships and adversity in the onset of neurotic symptoms. This interaction was further investigated by calculating the regressions of the Wave 2 GHQ scores on the ADAT% score and on the ADSI scores, but doing so separately for those respondents with the higher and with the lower levels of adversity. The differences are statistically significant at the .001 and .0005 levels respectively. These findings re-

223

TABLE 11-2

Social Relationships as Predictors of Symptom Onset

Sample well at Wave 1. Correlations between ISSI indices at Wave 1 and GHQ score at Wave 2, by level of adversity at Wave 1.

	Low Adversity ($n = 115$)	High Adversity ($n = 62$)
AVAT (Availability of close relationships)	.07	−.16
ADAT% (Perceived adequacy of close relationships)	.04	−.45[b]
NONAT (Acceptance of not having close relationships)	−.07	−.26[a]
AVSI (Availability of diffuse relationships)	.06	−.29[a]
ADSI (Perceived adequacy of diffuse relationships)	−.14	−.44[b]
ATTROWN (Rows with close others)	−.04	−.16

SOURCE: From Henderson (1981). Reproduced by kind permission of the Editor, *British Journal of Psychiatry.*
[a] $p < .05$ (one-tailed)
[b] $p < .001$

quire the second hypothesis to be rejected. Instead, they are powerful evidence in support of its converse, that a lack of social relationships is pathogenic only when adversity is also present.

INTERPRETATION OF THE LONGITUDINAL DATA

To interpret such findings, it is first necessary to consider the strengths and weaknesses of the study. Prospective data of this type are expensive and laborious to gather. The strengths are that the study was conducted in a general population sample, so that the data were free from the selection effects inherent in samples of those who have sought professional help (Mechanic, 1968); it was prospective in design so that contamination by the outcome variables is avoided; and it has employed a recently developed method for systematically examining an individual's personal network and the Weiss provisions derived from it. The instrument used to measure adverse experiences was of demonstrated reliability. It is more comprehensive than other life event inventories, in that it includes longstanding difficulties as well as temporally discrete events.

The main deficiency of the study is the measure of neurosis. The GHQ, although a well-established instrument for the detection of nonpsychotic disorder, cannot be a satisfactory substitute for a standardized psychiatric interview. Ideally, therefore, the cohort should have been examined with an instrument such as the Present State Examination, at least at Waves 1 and 2. Regrettably, this was beyond our manpower resources. A second deficiency was the sample size: The panel subsample of 220 naturally yielded only a modest amount of morbidity during the period of study. Nevertheless, there was a sufficient amount of fresh morbidity to give results of high statistical significance. The findings may be accepted as support for the first hypothesis and for the converse of the second, but other interpretations must be considered.

The possibility was considered that those who had high adversity by Wave 1 had continued to have higher adversity through to Wave 2. In fact, this was found to be the case, but it applies as much to those with low as with high ISSI measures. This interpretation can therefore be discounted.

A second possibility, and one of considerable clinical interest, is that the cohort of mentally healthy persons, considered prospectively from Wave 1, contained some who were "incubating" neurotic symptoms and who had already damaged their social relationships by Wave 1. They may not have had raised GHQ scores at that stage. Such an interpretation is plausible but has not yet been further investigated on the present data. Furthermore, it would call for a method to identify latent neurosis, which is not a feasible proposition in epidemiological studies.

A third interpretation is that both neurotic symptoms and deficiencies in social relationships are the product of a third variable, in the form of some attribute of personality; and that this effect is stronger under the challenge of adverse experiences. Neuroticism as measured by the Eysenck Personality Inventory (Eysenck and Eysenck, 1964) is generally accepted as an index of vulnerability to neurotic illness. Foulds (1965) has argued that one should distinguish between these two quite distinct universes of discourse. It is unfortunate that the EPI was not used as a measure in Wave 1, before some respondents developed symptoms. Instead it was administered to the cohort only in Waves 2 and 4. Taking the latter, which is less likely to be contaminated by neurotic symptoms, it was found that the mean neuroticism score for the twelve persons who became symptomatic by Wave 2 was indeed significantly different statistically from the 165 respondents who were still well at Wave 2 ($p < .01$). The conclusion is that neuroticism may have been a common precursor of both symptoms and deficiencies in social relationships.

Of course, it is to be expected on theoretical grounds that there would be an association between neuroticism and the perceived inadequacy of social relationships. Presumably it would run in either direction in such an association. This phenomenon is likely to be fairly complex in the development of the individual. Both could be expressions of "dependency" or of anxious attachment, as described by Bowlby (1973). In looking for this, it was necessary for us first to exclude symptomatic persons, because their affective state could have distorted both their neuroticism and ISSI scores. For those respondents who had a GHQ score of less than 6 in Wave 4 ($n = 206$), the correlation between neuroticism and the ADAT% and the ADSI scores in Wave 4 were $-.26$ and $-.18$ respectively. These are statistically significant at the .001 and .004 levels. The two sets of variables are therefore by no means independent. When the neuroticism score in Wave 4 is entered as the last variable in an equation for the regression of the GHQ score in Wave 2 on the collective ISSI indices measured on well people in Wave 1, neuroticism raises the explained variance to 6.7 percent and 42.2 percent for those experiencing low and high adversity. We may conclude that neuroticism has an effect in its own right, in addition to the ISSI indices. It is nevertheless possible that a trait such as neuroticism has the dual effect suggested—it leads both to neurosis and to deficiencies in social relationships. Furthermore, there may be some interaction, or compounding effect, of neuroticism and social relationships where the latter are deficient. This issue has not been further investigated on the present data.

PLAINTIVE SET

We have been interested in another attribute of the individual that might be invoked to explain the present findings. Ernest Gruenberg[2] has described a phenomenon he calls "plaintive set," in which the individual has a conspicuous tendency to complain and to be dissatisfied. In Yiddish it is to "kvetch"; in Scottish dialect it is to "girn"; and in English, to "winge." Whether this is taken to be a trait or a state, an

2. E. M. Gruenberg, personal communication.

attribute such as this could lead to the individual's reporting both the experience of adversity and deficiencies in satisfying personal relationships. It might also be associated with an increased vulnerability to develop neurotic symptoms, or at least to endorse items on an instrument such as the GHQ. Such persons, however, are likely to have been excluded when we removed symptomatic persons from the cohort at Wave 1. Despite this, one cannot avoid being impressed with the prominence of the adequacy as opposed to the availability items in the correlations with subsequent morbidity. Plaintive set, we believe, remains a legitimate interpretation. To look at this issue further would require an instrument designed specifically to tap this construct.

Finally, it seemed possible that good social relationships might only postpone the effects of adversity, lengthening the incubation period, as it were. This interpretation was examined by calculating the mean GHQ scores in Waves 2, 3, and 4 for those with high and those with low levels for the adequacy of social relationships. It was found that the peak GHQ scores were indeed in Wave 2 for both these groups. Therefore, this lag interpretation can be discounted.

Conclusions

This study set out to identify elements in the individual's social environment which, when deficient, may contribute to the causes of neurosis. On the basis of fairly impressive pointers from other studies, we set up two hypotheses about social relationships and nonpsychotic morbidity. Testing these hypotheses has required the development of an instrument to measure social relationships.

The crucial property of social relationships, insofar as neurosis is concerned, is not their availability, as we had expected, but how adequate they are perceived to be when individuals are under adversity. The reported level of adequacy may be considered to have two components, which cannot be teased apart in the present data: first, an objective judgment of adequacy, taking the context into account, so that the individual's personal network is assessed on how well it actually performs when called upon to do so; and second, the intrapsychic needs of the respondent, in terms of "dependency" or anxious attachment.

If the low adequacy scores in those who subsequently develop neurotic symptoms are due to the respondent's intrapsychic needs rather than to an actual failure of the individual's primary group to perform adequately, this would be evidence that social factors, as measured here, are of little importance in neurosis. The data say that it is not the supportiveness of the actual social environment, but the way it is construed that is likely to be causally powerful. The significance of this finding is that it is epidemiological evidence for psychological concepts formulated by Fairbairn (1952), Rado (1956), and Bowlby (1973). In essence, these concepts tell us that it is not the *real* social world but how it is *construed* that matters in the formation of neurotic symptoms. The adequacy indices in the ISSI are likely to tap attributes of personality, not actual conditions in the individual's personal network. By personality one means certain enduring intrapsychic attributes that determine attitudes and behavior. In keeping with recent developments in personality theory (Hunt, 1965; Bem and Allen, 1974), the predictive effect lies not so much in these personality attributes themselves as in their interaction with current contextual factors. The latter are provided here by the adversity measure.

The conclusion, then, is that the actual social environment has little effect on the development of neurotic symptoms; but when faced with adversity, those people who view their social relationships as inadequate have a substantially increased risk of developing neurotic symptoms.

We find these results and the conclusions made from them most stimulating because they have to be seen as a clear lead for further studies of the causes of neurosis. Attributes of the individual which are biological or constitutional are likely to be more powerful than properties of the immediate social environment or other ecological variables. But just as Adolf Meyer (1951) taught, these constitutional factors, which reside within the individual, interact strikingly with his recent experience of life stresses.

REFERENCES

Beach, H. D., and Lucas, R. A., eds. 1960. *Individual group behavior in a coal mine disaster,* Disaster Study no. 13, Publication 834. Washington, D.C.: National Academy of Sciences, National Research Council.

Bem, D. J., and Allen, A. 1974. On predicting some of the people some of the time: The search for cross-situational consistencies in behavior. *Psychological Review* 81:506–520.

Berkman, L. F., and Syme, S. L. 1979. Social networks, host resistance and mortality: A nine-year follow-up study of Alameda County residents. *American Journal of Epidemiology* 109(2):186–204.

Bowlby, J. 1973. *Attachment and loss. Vol. 2: Separation: Anxiety and anger.* New York: Basic Books.

————. 1977. The making and breaking of affectional bonds: Aetiology and psychopathology in the light of attachment theory. *British Journal of Psychiatry* 130:201–210.

Broom, L., and Selznick, P. 1973. *Sociology.* New York: Harper & Row.

Brown, G. W., Bhrolcháin, M. N., and Harris, T. 1975. Social class and psychiatric disturbance among women in an urban population. *Sociology* 9(2):225–254.

Brown, G. W., and Harris, T. 1978. *Social origins of depression: A study of psychiatric disorder in women.* London: Tavistock.

Carstairs, M., and Kapur, R. 1976. *The great universe of Kota.* London: Hogarth Press.

Cassel, J. 1974. An epidemiological perspective of psychosocial factors in disease etiology. *American Journal of Public Health* 64:1040–1043.

————. 1976. The contribution of the social environment to host resistance. The fourth Wade Hampton Frost lecture. *American Journal of Epidemiology* 104(2):107–123.

Cooley, C. H. 1909. *Social organization: A study of the larger mind.* New York: Charles Scribner's Sons.

Crowne, D. P., and Marlowe, D. 1964. *The approval motive: Studies in evaluative dependence.* New York: Wiley.

Dean, A., and Lin, N. 1977. The stress-buffering role of social support: Problems and prospects for systematic investigation. *Journal of Nervous and Mental Disease* 165: 403–417.

Dohrenwend, B. P., and Dohrenwend, B. S. 1969. Etiological leads from epidemiological studies. In *Social status and psychological disorder: A causal inquiry,* ed. B. P. Dohrenwend and B. S. Dohrenwend. New York: Wiley Interscience.

Duncan-Jones, P. 1981a. The structure of social relationships: Analysis of a survey instrument, part I. *Social Psychiatry* 16:55–61.

————. 1981b. The structure of social relationships: Analysis of a survey instrument, part 2. *Social Psychiatry* 16:143–149.

————, and Henderson, A. S. 1978. The use of a two-phase design in a population study. *Social Psychiatry* 13:231–237.

El-Islam, M. F. 1975. Culture-bound neurosis in Qatari women. *Social Psychiatry* 10:25–29.

Eysenck, H. J., and Eysenck, S. B. G. 1964. *Manual of the Eysenck Personality Inventory.* London: London University Press.

Fairbairn, R. 1952. *Object relations theory of the personality.* New York: Basic Books.

Foulds, G. A. 1965. *Personality and personal illness.* London: Tavistock.

————. 1976. *The hierarchical nature of personal illness.* London: Academic Press.

Goldberg, D. P. 1972. *The detection of psychiatric illness by questionnaire.* Institute of Psychiatry Maudsley Monographs no. 21. London: Oxford University Press.

Goldschmidt, W. 1959. *Man's way,* Cleveland: World Publishing Company.

Hamburg, D. A. 1968a. Emotions in the perspective of human evolution. In *Perspectives on human evolution,* ed. S. L. Washburn and P. C. Jay. New York: Holt.

————. 1968b. Evolution of emotional responses: Evidence from recent research on nonhuman primates. *Science & Psychoanalysis* 12:39–54.

Henderson, S. 1974. Care-eliciting behavior in man. *Journal of Nervous and Mental Disease* 159(3):172–181.

————. 1977. The social network, support and neurosis: The function of attachment in adult life. *British Journal of Psychiatry* 131:185–191.

————. 1981. Social relationships, adversity and neurosis: An analysis of prospective observations. *British Journal of Psychiatry* 138:391–398.

————, and Bostock, T. 1977. Coping behaviour after shipwreck. *British Journal of Psychiatry* 131:15–20.

Henderson, S.; Ritchie, K.; McAuley, H.; and Duncan-Jones, P. 1978. The patient's primary group. *British Journal of Psychiatry* 132:74–86.

Henderson, S.; Byrne, D. G.; Duncan-Jones, P.; Adcock, S.; Scott, R.; and Steele, G. 1978. Social bonds in the epidemiology of neurosis: A preliminary communication. *British Journal of Psychiatry* 132:463–469.

Henderson, S.; Duncan-Jones, P.; Byrne, D. G.; Scott, R.; and Adcock, S. 1979. Psychiatric disorder in Canberra. A standardised study of prevalence. *Acta Psychiatrica Scandinavica* 60:355–374.

Henderson, S.; Duncan-Jones, P.; Byrne, D. G.; and Scott, R. 1980. Measuring social relationships. *Psychological Medicine* 10:723-734.

Henderson, S.; Byrne, D. G.; Duncan-Jones, P.; Adcock, S.; and Scott, R. 1980. Social relationships, adversity and neurosis: A study of associations in a general population sample. *British Journal of Psychiatry* 136: 574-583.

Henderson, S., Byrne, D. G., and Duncan-Jones, P. 1981. *Neurosis and the social environment.* Sydney, Australia: Academic Press.

Holmes, T., and Rahe. R. H. 1967. The social readjustment rating scale. *Journal of Psychosomatic Research* 11:213-218.

Hunt, J. McV. 1965. Traditional personality theory in the light of recent evidence. *American Scientist* 53:80-96.

Killian, L. M. 1952. The significance of multiple group membership in disaster. *American Journal of Sociology* 57:309-314.

Leighton, D. C.; Harding, J. S.; Macklin, D. B.; Macmillan, A. M.; and Leighton, A. 1963. *The character of danger.* New York: Basic Books.

Leighton, A. H.; Lambo, T. A.; Hughes, C. C.; Leighton, D. C.; Murphy, J. M.; and Macklin, D. B. 1963. *Psychiatric disorder among the Yoruba.* New York: Cornell University Press.

Lin, N.; Ensel, W. M.; Simeone, R. S.; and Kuo, W. 1979. Social support, stressful life events and illness: A model and an empirical test. *Journal of Health and Social Behavior* 20:108-119.

Malzberg, B. 1964. Marital status and the incidence of mental disease. *International Journal of Social Psychiatry* 10:19-26.

Maslow, A. H. 1968. *Toward a psychology of being.* New York: Van Nostrand.

Mechanic, D. 1968. *Medical sociology: A selective view.* New York: Free Press.

Meyer, A. 1951. *The collected papers of Adolf Meyer,* ed. E. E. Winters. Baltimore, Md.: Johns Hopkins University Press.

Miller, P. McC.; and Ingham, J. G. 1976. Friends, confidants and symptoms. *Social Psychiatry* 11:51-58.

Orley, J., and Wing, J. K. 1979. Psychiatric disorders in two African villages. *Archives of General Psychiatry* 36:513-520.

Paykel, E. S., Prusoff, B. A., and Uhlenhuth, E. H. 1971. Scaling of life events. *Archives of General Psychiatry* 25:340-347.

Pearlin, L. I., and Johnson, J. S. 1977. Marital status, life strains and depression. *American Sociological Review* 42:704-715.

Pilowsky, I. 1969. Abnormal illness behaviour. *British Journal of Medical Psychology* 42:347-351.

———. 1978. A general classification of abnormal illness behaviours. *British Journal of Medical Psychology* 51:131-137.

Post, F. 1962. The social orbit of psychiatric patients. *Journal of Mental Science* 108:759-771.

Rabkin, J. G., and Struening, E. L. 1976. Life events, stress and illness. *Science* 194:1013-1020.

Rado, S., ed. 1956. Psychodynamics of depression from the etiological point of view. In *Psychoanalysis of Behavior, Collected Papers,* vol. I. New York: Grune & Stratton.

Robins, L. N. 1978. Psychiatric epidemiology. *Archives of General Psychiatry* 35: 697-702.

Rump, E. E., and Court, J. 1971. The Eysenck Personality Inventory and social desirability response set with student and clinical groups. *British Journal of Clinical and Social Psychology* 10:42-54.

Sartorius, N. 1977. Priorities for research likely to contribute to better provisions of mental health care. *Social Psychiatry* 12:171-184.

Scott, J. P. 1969. The emotional basis of social behavior. *Annals of the New York Academy of Science* 159(3):777-790.

Scott, W. A., and Scott, R. 1979. Acquaintance ratings as criteria of adjustment. *Australian Psychologist* 14(2): 155-167.

Steele, G. P., Henderson, S., and Duncan-Jones, P. 1980. The reliability of reporting adverse experiences. *Psychological Medicine* 10:301-306.

Tennant, C. 1977. The general health questionnaire: A valid index of psychological impairment in Australian populations. *Medical Journal of Australia* 2:392-394.

Washburn, S. L., and Harding, R. S. D. 1976. Evolution and human nature. In *The American handbook of psychiatry*, ed. S. Arieti, vol. 6. New York: Basic Books.

Washburn, S. L. and Jay, P. C., eds. 1968. *Perspectives on human evolution.* New York: Holt.

Weiss, R. S. 1973. *Loneliness: The experience of emotional and social isolation.* Cambridge, Mass: MIT Press.

——— . 1974. The provisions of social relationships. In *Doing unto others,* ed. Z. Rubin. Englewood Cliffs, N.J.: Prentice-Hall.

Wing, J. K. 1976. A technique for studying psychiatric morbidity in in-patient and out-patient series and in general population samples. *Psychological Medicine* 6: 665–671.

——— , Cooper, J. E., and Sartorius, N. 1974. *The measurement and classification of psychiatric symptoms.* Cambridge, England: Cambridge University Press.

Wing, J. K., Henderson, A. S., and Winckle, M. 1977. The rating of symptoms by a psychiatrist and a non-psychiatrist: A study of patients referred from general practice. *Psychological Medicine* 7:713–715.

Wing, J. K.; Nixon, J. M.; Mann, S. A.; and Leff, J. P. 1977. Reliability of the PSE (ninth edition) used in a population study. *Psychological Medicine* 7:505–516.

12

George W. Brown

EARLY LOSS AND DEPRESSION

ONE OF THE REWARDS of being asked to contribute to this volume is that it is possible to express publicly something of my admiration for John Bowlby's work. High on my list of his virtues has been his pursuit of a problem no matter where it goes; and his ability to do this and not lose his allegiance to his own discipline.

> Our interest's on the dangerous edge of things
> The honest thief, the tender murderer,
> The superstitious atheist, demireps
> That love and save their souls in new French books—
> We watch while these in equilibrium keep
> The giddy life midway: one step aside,
> They're classed and done with. . . .
>
> Robert Browning
> "Bishop Blougham's Apology"

To this list I would add the scientific psychoanalyst.

But Bowlby exemplifies an approach to research, as Robert Browning conveys, that is not without its perils. In the research I will be describing on the loss of a parent in childhood or adolescence, I have strayed a good deal from the concerns of most of my colleagues in sociology; in doing so I have gained confidence from John Bowlby's

The research in Camberwell was supported by the Social Science Research Council, the Medical Research Council, and the Foundation Fund for Research in Psychiatry, and that in Walthamstow by the Medical Research Council. Tirril Harris made invaluable comments regarding this chapter, has played a major part in collecting the material in the two populations, and has contributed very greatly to my ideas about early loss and depression.

example. For those who are still wary of such ventures, it should perhaps be added that there are ways of limiting its perils. To follow a problem where it goes is compatible with taking soundings of the terrain to be traveled, and the work I will describe is largely of this cartographic kind. Indeed, I will be principally concerned to settle whether there are grounds for taking seriously the possibility of a causal link between early loss of a parent and increased risk of depression in adulthood. Many would claim the research has not provided support for the proposition.

Two things are needed, I believe, if we are going to produce research capable of giving us the necessary confidence that there is an issue worth investigating. First, methodological shortcomings found in published research must be corrected; second, the etiological role of early loss of a parent by death or separation should be placed in the context of a more *general* causal model of depression that concentrates on the present. The effects of early loss of a parent, although perhaps real enough, may be missed if possible "counterbalancing" influences in the current environment are ignored. If early loss is significant, almost certainly it only plays a role in conjunction with more recent experience.

In its simplest form, the model I will use in this chapter is:

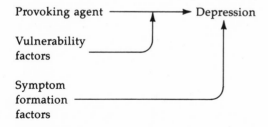

The *provoking agent* factor covers experience such as important loss or disappointment in the current environment that is capable of bringing about a depressive disorder. Such experience must, of course, occur before the onset of the depressive disorder in question (research at present indicates that it will usually not predate onset by much more than six months). However, the chance of such experience bringing about depression is influenced by the presence of certain *vulnerability factors,* such as lack of social support. The indirect arrow in the diagram pointing from vulnerability factors represents the fact that these factors increase risk only in the presence of a provoking agent. The actual experiences leading to vulnerability might stem from childhood, adolescence, or adulthood. The third, *symptom-formation* factor, is different from the others in that rather than increasing risk of depression, it influences its form once it occurs—say in terms of the degree to which it is "psychotic" rather than "neurotic." The relevant experience leading to such an effect may come from any point in a person's life.

For a causal model to be effective one must be able to rule out that associations or lack thereof between its components are merely due to artifacts of measurement or faults in design. As long as this can be done, measurement does not necessarily have to be particularly sophisticated in order to be useful. For instance, it is difficult to believe that the experience of loss of a parent *as such* increases risk of depression in adult life. If it has an effect, it must surely be via something associated with the loss—say, failure to carry out appropriate mourning. Merely to record the presence of early loss of a parent therefore means dealing with an irredeemably crude measure, but one that, nevertheless, may still be able to achieve a clear-cut result when used in the context of an adequate model of depression.

However, as I have already indicated, confidence that early loss plays any role at all has not been easy to achieve. There have been serious methodological weaknesses in most published studies. Inconsistent and negative findings have been common, and, since negative findings have tended to be produced by the studies with the fewest obvious methodological shortcomings, it has been possible to doubt whether early loss of a parent plays *any* etiological role. In an authoritative review Granville-Grossman (1968) concludes that no consistent evidence has been found to support the view that the early environment is of etiological importance in the affective disorders. A major problem has been the great practical difficulty of obtaining adequate comparison series concerning the rate of loss in the general population. For instance, few studies appear to have paid adequate attention to the fact that loss of parent is probably more common among working-class children. Since Granville-Grossman's review there has been further research, and persuasive clinical reports about the importance of early loss continue to accumulate, but a recent review in *Psychological Bulletin* states that "parental death during childhood has not been established as a factor of etiological significance in adult depression or any subtype of adult depression studied to date" (Crook and Eliot, 1980, p. 259). The same conclusion is reached in another recent review in *Psychological Medicine* (Tennant, Bebbington, and Hurry, 1980).

234

By contrast I will argue that there is now quite convincing evidence that early loss of a parent does increase risk of depression in adult life. I will not try to support this assertion by using data from other research centers, as I think it is possible to make convincing methodological objections to such work at least in its published form. Instead I will review research I have carried out with Tirril Harris, which I think can be defended from such criticism and also linked to the model of depression I outlined earlier.

Meaning and Measurement

The research consists of two studies carried out in London. Unlike most previous research it has considered not only parental death but loss by separation as long as this lasted at least one year. The results of the first study in Camberwell in South London have already been published (Brown, Harris, and Copeland, 1977), although here I will place a somewhat different emphasis on the findings. The second study in Walthamstow in North London, carried out in conjunction with Tirril Harris and Toni Bifulco, is so far unpublished. Here I will present only a preliminary account of it.

Both studies were based on the assumption that affective disorders are in some way complications of the ordinary emotions of depression and anxiety. Before I outline any results I will deal with some of the implications of this view. We believe that such complications, like ordinary emotions themselves, are usually reactions to happenings in our lives. It follows that if such reactions play a central etiological role in affective disorders, it is essential to take into account the meaning for the person of experiences of potential etiological importance. After all, it is the meaning of experience that is usually responsible for producing emotion.

Although the experiences producing such complicated reactions are akin to the etiological agents of traditional epidemiological inquiry, the question of meaning has not been even remotely considered by such research. There are good reasons, of course, for such an omission. An obvious difficulty is the way the various emotions are capable of being produced by an extremely wide range of stimuli, including other emotions (Tomkins, 1963). Fortunately there also appears to be a

235

certain underlying logic to this plasticity. The ordinary emotion of depression, for instance, tends to be provoked by situations of loss and disappointment, and anxiety by threat of something yet to occur.

> Depression, like anxiety, puts a temporary brake on behaviour because of a mismatch between environmental changes and one's repertoire of behaviours. But now it is not because of a mismatch between the behaviours and some anticipated event but because of the mismatch between the behaviours and the environment that has already been altered because of a change that has already occurred. (Costello, 1976, p. 49)

This match between stimulus and particular emotions, however, is only a rough one. Just what is seen as an important loss or danger will also be influenced by cultural and personal factors.

There have been interesting speculations along evolutionary lines about what specific functions emotions may have served. Charles Costello, from whose argument I have just quoted, suggests that the ordinary mood of depression encourages conservatism. It protects against the fragmentation of our lives by making separation from the group a stressful, sometimes extremely stressful, event. But such views, however stimulating, are not a great deal of help for establishing the meaning of a situation for a particular person. There is, nevertheless, a way forward that enables a useful estimate to be made and that allows some account to be taken of unique cultural and personal determinants of meaning *and* the broad logic concerning themes such as loss and danger that underlie much of our emotional experience.

This can be done by building on the link that usually exists between the meaning of an incident and our plans and purposes. We usually find it essential to make out the meaning of an occurrence vis-à-vis our plans before we can find our bearings (McCall and Simmons, 1966; Marris, 1974 and chapter 10 herein). Therefore, one way of finding out something of the likely meaning of an event is to relate it to a person's plans and purposes. The point is a straightforward one. If we know that a woman has, with her lover's encouragement, been planning to live with him once he has left his wife and child, then it follows that she is likely to feel distressed and depressed by his announcement that he realizes that he can never leave his wife.

It is also obvious that our plans will often arise from role identities, the imaginative view we have of ourselves as an occupant of a particular social position. And these, of course, are closely related to our attachment to persons, although it is necessary to emphasize that the "events" arousing emotion frequently have nothing directly to do with another person. For example, learning that the hope of moving from a slum dwelling has been dashed may have a powerful emotional impact on a woman, but involve other persons only in the sense that she is living with her husband and children.

Such identities and attachments will usually be the result of a long history of past actions; the person just mentioned may have hoped and schemed for a change of residence for several years. Identities and attachments therefore cannot usually be changed as we might change arrangements for a weekend outing; this is one of the reasons why there is more stability to our emotional lives than might at first appear possible in light of the great variety of ways emotions can be called forth by objects. Of course, we can readily make new plans and even carry them out—say, to leave a husband—but this will usually not be enough in itself to settle the meaning of subsequent events. As Weiss has pointed out in chapter 9, a woman who has longed to leave her husband may, once a separation has been made, experience profound loneliness and purposelessness and a strong need to return to him. If we are to understand such a response in terms of meaning, it cannot be done solely in terms of the woman's latest plan, for she will probably find her reaction inexplicable in terms of what she knows she wants to do. Another woman may be surprised at the strength of her distress and depression after she has been unexpectedly reunited with a son who had been adopted many years before and whom she has longed to see again.

Perhaps all that is necessary to make sense of such apparently unintelligible responses is to recognize that we cannot easily escape from *past* plans and actions. A woman who has centered her actions on her husband for a decade and who, however unhappy, has gained personal significance from such activity, loses this source of self-validation with a separation. A woman who unexpectedly reacts with distress to a long-awaited reunion with her son may have been led by it to recognize how much of the past that she could have spent with him has been irretrievably lost.

It is clear from these instances that, when the meaning of events arises from past activity in this way, what is happening to oneself in emotional terms may not be readily formulated in words. Ernest Becker (1964) has argued that a person can be divided against himself in terms of the varying explicitness of vocabularies of motive; he particularly emphasizes the importance of different voices that can arise

237

from early childhood experiences. I do not argue that the particular meanings I have suggested are the only plausible ones; for instance, the woman who was reunited with her son may in fact have been disappointed at the way he had turned out. All I suggest is that explanation of such responses in terms of their *likely* meaning should be given as much serious consideration as explanations not involving conscious meaning—that, for example, the separated woman reacted the way she did simply because of the major changes it brought in her habitual activities and the other woman because of the event's arousal of unconscious guilt.

Fortunately the link between the meaning of events and emotional response is in most instances less complicated than what these examples suggest. After all, our plans will often reflect in a fairly straightforward way what actions have gone before, and new plans can at times arise unencumbered by the past. However, the examples are enough to illustrate the need to take account of the possibility that the dominant meaning provoked by an event may be the result of past actions (in the first case, a marriage) or past fantasies (in the second, longing to be reunited with an adopted son).

In the light of this kind of argument, and spurred by the need to deal with methodological problems, my colleagues and I have developed a contextual method for rating the meaning of events. We argued that if enough is known about a person's way of life, plans, and activities, then it will be possible to make a reasonable estimate of the meaning of an event *without knowing or even asking about his or her actual response to it*. The approach, while based on intuitive assessments, has been systematized a good deal by the listing of several thousand examples of ratings. It has also enabled us to avoid being paralyzed by doubt about the possibility of circularity in our arguments about causality. A person who now says some earlier event had been very upsetting may do so as a means of explaining a depressive illness that followed quite soon after the event. The use of contextual ratings of threat avoids the possibility that any apparent causal association between the threat of some recent incident and onset of depression is due to such reconstruction of meaning (Brown and Harris, 1978a).

But this approach to meaning appears to have been equally successful in tackling the kind of substantive question that I have been discussing: something that may seem surprising, given that the method claims no more than that a person is *likely* to have experienced an event in the way stated. The approach has been used to demonstrate that the majority of depressive and anxiety disorders appear to be brought about by a certain class of relatively rare threatening events—what we have called severe events. (A woman in an urban setting may expect on average to experience one such event about every three years.) One of its most notable achievements has been to show that different types of severe events tend to produce depressive disorders and anxiety states (Finlay-Jones and Brown, 1981).

Events provoking depression concern for the most part significant loss and disappointment, if this is understood to involve not only loss of person but of a role or even an idea. (Loss in the sense of bereavement forms only a small minority of such severe events occurring to women in London.) By contrast, the onsets of anxiety states tend to be preceded by severely threatening events involving danger; that is, by an event that suggests that some other threatening event may well occur as a consequence of the first. Mixed depressive and anxiety conditions have a raised rate of both types of severe event or of an event involving both loss *and* danger. Thus a mother learning that her daughter had been systematically stealing from her would be an example of a severe loss event in the sense the woman has probably lost an important conception of her daughter and perhaps of herself as an effective parent. A woman told that her husband may have cancer has not lost anything in the strict sense, but she has experienced an event intimating future loss, that is, danger. I will refer to a person's understanding of events in these broad terms as *primary meaning;* that is the person's fairly immediate response to the event (or, in terms of contextual meaning, what the person probably felt as an immediate response to the event).

Therefore, although the contextual measures were developed largely for methodological reasons, they have proved to be important in differentiating the broad types of response involved in reaction to loss and danger that are clearly based on very long-term evolutionary development. Particularly welcome has been their help in tapping "hidden" meanings where, as in my two examples, past commitments have been involved. Because we take no notice of what a person said he felt about the event—that is, its immediate meaning—in making contextual ratings, we are likely to place as much importance on past activities and commitments as on current plans. A woman leaving a man with whom she has been living for several years would be given a high rating on contextual threat, irrespective of how she might report her immediate response and of what role she had played in the separation.

239

Certain variations to this basic theme have been added but this review is sufficient to allow me to deal with the etiological role of early loss of a parent.

Depression and Early Loss of Parent

Early loss of parent has been studied in relation to a wide range of psychiatric conditions, and it is first necessary to make clear what I mean by a depressive disorder. All those who have been studied were asked in detail about psychiatric symptomatology occurring in the twelve months before interview (or contact with psychiatric services), using the shortened version of the Present State Examination (PSE), a clinical-type interview (Wing, Cooper, and Sartorious, 1974). Three kinds of decisions were made about psychiatric symptoms: (1) what should count as presence of psychiatric symptoms; (2) what degree of intensity, frequency, and duration of symptoms were necessary for a person to be termed a case; and (3) into what recognizable psychiatric syndromes the symptoms fell. The PSE has as its core a glossary of terms and definitions about specific symptoms, and it has been established that medical and nonmedical interviewers can reach satisfactory reliability in rating specific items (Cooper et al., 1977; Wing et al., 1977). We have added a number of further stages to these initial ratings. One of these is to rate women considered to have experienced a definite psychiatric syndrome in the year before interview as *cases* and those with lower disturbance as *borderline cases*.

In order to make the judgment about whether or not a person was a case, we have attempted to define a group of women whose psychiatric symptoms are at a level of severity such that, if they presented themselves for psychiatric care, they would almost certainly be seen as psychiatrically ill and accepted for treatment. Essential to the whole procedure has been the development of reference examples of cases in each diagnostic group. The large majority of women living in Camberwell who were cases were suffering from depression. Both numbers 1 and 2 in the following checklist must be present for a person to be considered a case. These items have been shown statistically to underlie the clinical criteria we have developed and give a quick guide to our diagnosis of depression (Finlay-Jones et al., 1980).

1. Depressed mood.

240

2. Four or more of the following ten symptoms: hopelessness, suicidal ideas or actions, weight loss, early waking, delayed sleep, poor concentration, neglect due to brooding, loss of interest, self-depreciation, and anergia.

Usually many other PSE symptoms are also present.

I have already outlined the three main factors of our etiological model of depression. In fact, two types of experience have been shown to act as provoking agents capable of bringing about such a depressive disorder. The most important are the severe events described earlier, which for the most part involve important losses and disappointments. A second and somewhat less important agent concerns ongoing major difficulties such as might be brought about by overcrowded and poor housing or by a husband who drinks heavily. (Methods of measuring the unpleasantness of such difficulties have broadly followed those I have already outlined for events.) Turning to the second factor of the etiological model, research so far has produced reasonably good evidence that lack of an intimate tie with a husband or boyfriend and having three or more children under the age of fourteen living at home act as vulnerability factors—that is, that risk of depression is increased in their presence once a provoking agent occurs. There is some suggestion that lack of employment may play this role, under certain circumstances, but evidence is less convincing. Rather than dealing with these factors in more detail, I will turn to my main proposition that for a woman loss of a mother in childhood can act as a vulnerability factor. If this is so it follows, of course, that early loss should be associated with a raised prevalence of depression.

CAMBERWELL GENERAL POPULATION

The research was carried out among women living in Camberwell, an inner-city area of London with the well-recognized social problems of such areas, although it also contains a substantial middle-class population, particularly in the southern suburban parts of the borough. This research differs from previous work on early loss by concentrating on women developing depression in a defined geographical area irrespective of whether they were receiving treatment from a psychiatrist or, indeed, from any medical practitioner. The advantage of a dual design involving patients and nonpatients will become clear as I proceed.

There was in fact a sizable association between early loss of a parent and whether or not the woman could be considered a psychiatric case in the year before our inquiry; the great majority of these conditions

241

TABLE 12-1

Women with a Loss of Parent before Age 17 among Psychiatric
Cases (n = 76) and Other Women (n = 382)

Age at Loss	Loss of Mother		Loss of Father		Loss of Either Parent	
	Cases (%)	Others (%)	Cases (%)	Others (%)	Cases (%)	Others (%)
0 to 10	22.4	6.0[a]	17.1	11.5	34.2	13.6[a]
11 to 16	0.0	2.1	2.6	5.0	2.6	6.0

NOTE: Two-tailed X^2 tests based on frequencies have been used throughout the chapter.
[a] $p < .01$ Other differences are not significant at the .05 level.

involved an important depressive component (table 12-1). (All new onsets of disorder occurring in the year were in fact of depression and the results to be reported while covering all affective disorders remain unchanged if only those with depression are considered.)

When the type of loss is considered, only that of a mother before age eleven by either death or separation has a clear association with the chance of being a case in the year; the proportion with an early loss of a father is not statistically significantly different from other women. We did not include a father's war service or separation due to the subject's wartime evacuation. It was only after our first study that we became aware that early separation could play a role similar to early death. Since we lacked the resources to deal with such a special group of experiences, such separations were not included in our later, more intensive, study of early loss of parents. However, we believe that research into their potential role would be valuable. Twenty-two percent of cases had a loss of mother before age eleven compared with 6 percent of other women. Figures for loss of a father before age eleven are 17 and 12 percent respectively. Therefore, while the presence of some increased risk for those with loss of a father cannot be ruled out entirely, from these results only loss of a mother before age eleven gains clear-cut support as having an etiological role.[1]

1. One of the recent reviews on the relationship of parental death in childhood to adult psychiatric morbidity concluded that there has been no evidence to support such a connection, but the authors felt they could not discuss the Camberwell findings at all since they had not presented the figures for deaths separately from those for separations (Tennant, Bebbington, and Hurry, 1980). The Camberwell material, in fact, showed that the relationship between early loss of mother and rate of depression holds equally for death and for separation; for losses before the age of 11 the rate of death was 15.8 percent for cases and 3.9 percent for other women, and the rate of separation 6.6 percent and 2.1 percent respectively.

The only other population survey of which I am aware that has considered the long-term effect of losing a parent is the Midtown survey in New York (Langner and Michael, 1963). Unfortunately, it used a suspect measure of psychiatric disorder based on a standardized questionnaire. However, it is of interest that this study also showed an increased risk of current psychiatric disorder for those with loss of a mother by death before the age of sixteen. (A broken home only related to an increased risk for those less than seven years old at the time of the crisis.) This result concerning loss of mother by death held only for "lower-class" women. Our own result also held most strongly for working-class women; but since the relevance of this apparent link with social class can only be understood in the light of our full causal model of depression, I will delay discussion of this link with class until later.

For a test of early loss of a parent as a vulnerability factor such prevalence data is not enough. Such a raised rate might be the result of quite different processes and might have nothing to do with increased risk—for instance, because psychiatric disorder tends to take a chronic course in those with early loss. In order to test whether early loss acts as a vulnerability factor, it is essential to consider whether risk is increased among those with early loss only when it occurs together with a provoking agent in the year before any onset of disorder. (Persons suffering from chronic conditions arising outside the year of inquiry therefore had to be excluded, as information about provoking agents was only collected for the year before we interviewed each woman, and by definition such chronic cases had become disturbed before this.) The proposition is supported: There is a much-increased risk of depression in the year of the inquiry among those who lost their mothers before the age of eleven in the presence of a provoking agent (47 percent) but *no* raised risk without a provoking agent. In fact, none of the fifteen women in the general population with early loss of a mother but without a provoking agent developed depression compared with seven of the fifteen with such an agent (see table 12-2A). Loss of mother before age eleven therefore does appear to act as a vulnerability factor.

But we did not restrict ourselves to loss of a parent. A more general measure of early loss called *past loss* was created by taking (1) loss by death or separation of one year or more of a parent before the age of seventeen; (2) loss of a sibling between the ages of one and seventeen; (3) loss due to death or permanent separation from a child; or (4) loss of a husband by death at any age. The first two categories were by far

243

TABLE 12-2
Women in Camberwell Developing a Psychiatric Disorder
in the Year of Study by Whether They Had a Severe Event
or Major Difficulty and Loss of Parent (chronic cases excluded)

	A. Loss of Mother before Age 11		B. Loss of Father before Age 11 (excluding 30 women with a loss of mother before age 11)	
	Yes (%)	No (%)	Yes (%)	No (%)
Severe event or major difficulty	47 (7/15)	17[a] (26/150)	20 (3/15)	17 (23/135)
None	0 (0/15)	2 (4/239)	0 (0/17)	2 (4/222)

	C. Other Past Loss (excluding 30 women with loss of mother before age 11)	
	Yes (%)	No (%)
Severe event or major difficulty	15 (8/53)	19 (18/97)
None	3 (2/60)	1 (2/179)

[a] $p < .01$. Other differences are not significant at the 0.05 level.

the most common. No loss was included unless it occurred more than two years before the onset of the current episode. Neither past loss in general (table 12-2C) nor loss of father before the age of eleven (table 12-2B) related to increased risk of depression when those with a loss of mother before the age of eleven were excluded.

At this point it is also possible to consider the question of social class. The fact that the effect of a vulnerability factor such as early loss depends on the presence of a provoking agent means that it will be bound to show a relatively low association with prevalence of depression in any population with a low rate of provoking agents. This must be so even though there is no difference between populations in the way early loss predisposes a person to depression. This lack of an association, of course, would be expected to occur in a predominately "middle-class" population. Furthermore, since risk of depression increases with the *number* of vulnerability factors, early loss of mother will be more highly associated with depression in any population in which such loss is correlated with other vulnerability factors. In Camberwell, at least, both points hold for working-class women—they more often experience provoking agents and vulnerability factors, and among them early loss of mother is more highly correlated with the other vulnerability factors. It is therefore understandable that they have in general a higher risk of developing depressive disorder than middle-class women (Brown and Harris, 1978a). For my immediate argument the important point is that, given these correlations, it follows that early loss of mother should be more often associated with depression among working-class women. As noted earlier when discussing the Midtown survey, this is indeed just what occurs.[2]

This general argument may also be enough to explain the lack of an association between early loss and psychiatric disorder among middle-class women in the Midtown survey. Equally significantly, it serves to make the general point that findings concerning early loss of a parent will probably prove to be highly dependent on the social composition of a population—in general, the lower the rate of provoking agents and vulnerability factors in a population, the lower the association between early loss and depression. However, it is also worth noting that this variability can be overcome by a *full* test of the model I have outlined. If onset of depression is considered in the context of provoking agents and all the other vulnerability factors, the question of social class is in one sense bypassed. This is due to the fact that the presence or absence of vulnerability factors and provoking agents is controlled and social-class differences in risk associated with early loss should disappear. In fact, something like this does appear to occur in the Camberwell material (Brown and Harris, 1978a, p. 359, footnote 8).

Any broader interpretation of the Camberwell results concerning early loss of mother must take into account the fact that three other vulnerability factors exist and there is a tendency for them to be correlated. Further, the risk of depression increases with the number of vulnerability factors.[3] Among women with a child living at home, loss of mother before the age of eleven was correlated with two of the three vulnerability factors—having three or more children under fourteen at home and low intimacy with a husband (see figure 12-1). It is therefore significant that loss of a mother before the age of eleven still

2. Fifty-eight percent (15/26) of working-class women in Camberwell with an early loss of mother were cases compared with 20 percent (43/214) without such loss ($p<.001$); figures for middle-class women were 14 percent (2/14) and 8 percent (16/206), respectively (n.s.)

3. The presence of a confiding relationship with a husband appears to neutralize the effect of the other three vulnerability factors. However, the statement that there is an association between risk of depression and number of vulnerability factors is correct enough for the present argument (Brown and Harris, 1978a, p. 181).

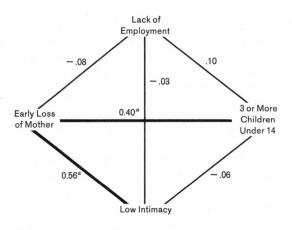

^{a}p < .05

FIGURE 12-1
Associations between Vulnerability Factors Expressed in Terms of Gamma

TABLE 12-3
*Women in Camberwell Developing Depression by Whether They Had (1) Low
Intimacy with Husband/Boyfriend or 3 or More Children Under 14, (2) Lost a
Mother before Age 11, and (3) a Severe Event or Major Difficulty*

	A Low intimacy with husband *or* three or more children under 14			B High intimacy with husband *and* fewer than three children under 14		
Severe event or major difficulty	Loss of mother before age 11			Loss of mother before age 11		
	Yes (%)	No (%)		Yes (%)	No (%)	
Yes	64 (7/11)	23 (18/78)	*p* <.05	0 (0/4)	11 (8/71)	n.s.
No	0 (0/6)	3 (2/71)	n.s.	0 (0/9)	1 (2/169)	n.s.

increases the risk of depression in the presence of a provoking agent
among women with one or other of these two vulnerability factors
(see table 12-3).[4]

The correlation of early loss with low intimacy with husband and
having three or more children under fourteen raises a further ques-

4. Unfortunately, the number of women with a loss of mother who also had a provoking agent is too small to see whether there is a difference when there is high intimacy and the woman is without three children under fourteen. There is a possibility that
this may be enough to "neutralize" the affect of early loss of mother (see table 12-3B).

246

tion. How far does such loss increase the risk of depression because of its link with experiences in adult life? To put the issue in crude terms, are certain long-term consequences of early loss, such as marrying early, critical, or is there some direct change in "personality" stemming from the loss itself? (A third possibility is, of course, that both may be involved. Feelings of insecurity, for example, may lead to a tendency to earlier and less successful marriage.) Before I consider these questions it is necessary to complicate the results I have presented so far by discussing the patient series.

CAMBERWELL PATIENTS

We collected comparable material for 114 women living in Camberwell and treated by psychiatrists as in-patients (73) and outpatients (41) who had had a recent onset of depression. Unfortunately, findings concerning early loss of a parent were less clear-cut, a result that at least conforms to the generally inconsistent findings of studies based on patient populations. There was only a very small association between early loss and depression among both groups when judged by the occurrence of early loss among the women sampled at random from the same Camberwell population. (The two groups of women were of much the same age and social class background.) However, I believe there is a straightforward reason for this lack of association and that it should not be seen as a refutation of the results obtained from the study of depression in the general Camberwell population. It is easily overlooked that all comparison groups so far used in conjunction with studies of patient populations have included women who are themselves suffering from depression. As we have seen, since such women also have a high rate of early loss of a parent, their inclusion is bound to attenuate any association between early loss and depression. To my knowledge no one has made an adequate allowance for this, and this is likely to go some way in explaining the negative findings in the published literature. Failure to exclude such women is probably related to a fairly general lack of appreciation of how common the experience of depression can be in the general population—during the three months before the interview, 15 percent of women in Camberwell suffered from a definite psychiatric disorder, which usually involved an important depressive component. Only a small number of the women were receiving care from a psychiatrist.

Therefore, it is not surprising that when patient results are reexamined after women who had been cases in the year before interview have been excluded from the comparison group, a difference *does* emerge in the Camberwell material. Almost double the proportion of patients had a loss of mother before the age of eleven when compared with women in Camberwell who were not cases (table 12-4). Nonetheless, this difference is still smaller than that obtained from women within the general population and, indeed, does not reach statistical significance. However, whether a difference is statistically significant is, of course, a function of the size of the sample. Given the order of the difference obtained, only a small increase in numbers would produce a significant result. Indeed, if loss by death or separation of a mother or father before the age of seventeen is considered, the difference in the experience of loss between patient and comparison group does reach statistical significance. Therefore it seems reasonable to conclude that results for the Camberwell patients confirm the etiological importance of early loss of a parent and also confirm, at least for women, the overriding significance of loss of a mother. However, it is also necessary to recognize that the increased risk of depression associated with such loss among patients is still a good deal smaller than that found when women with depression in the general Camberwell population are considered—that is, it is approximately double compared with four times the risk.

TABLE 12-4

Women with Loss of Parents before Age 17 among Patients and the General Population

Age at loss	Patients (%) ($n = 114$)	General population (%) ($n = 458$)	General population excluding cases (%) ($n = 382$)
A. *Loss of Mother*			
0 to 10	10.5	8.7	6.0
11 to 16	3.5	1.7	2.1
B. *Loss of Father*			
0 to 10	15.8	12.4	11.5
11 to 16	5.3	4.3	5.0

No differences are significant at the .05 level.

Two Kinds of Selective Bias

SELECTION DUE TO TREATMENT

One possible explanation for the fact that results concerning early loss of a parent are less clear-cut when studying patients is that vulnerability factors may increase risk of depression but, once depression has occurred, decrease chances of contacting a psychiatrist. This is not as far-fetched a possibility as it might at first appear.[5] Evidence is twofold. First, while having three or more children under the age of fourteen clearly increases risk of depression among women in the general population, having young children was *not* more common among depressed patients. Furthermore, the presence of young children at home was associated among the cases in the general population with a reduced chance of being treated by a general practitioner for a depressive condition (Brown and Harris, 1978a, p. 188). Second, while there was a much greater frequency of depression among working-class women in the general Camberwell population, this characteristic almost disappeared when women receiving psychiatric treatment were considered (Brown and Harris, 1978a). Although indirect, these findings do suggest that there may be selective factors influencing those who receive psychiatric care, and that since early loss of mother relates both to having three or more children under fourteen living at home and to a working-class status, it is possible that some of the inconsistency of published research has been the result of studying only psychiatric patients. Patients may show a lower rate of early loss of parent than would be expected from population surveys because, once depressed, women with such loss are less likely to receive psychiatric care. I have emphasized this possibility although the evidence is provisional, because, together with the general failure to select an appropriate comparison group, it might well explain the puzzling inconsistency of published research.

5. Such reversals of causal influence at different "stages" of a process may well be quite common. For instance, in a study of infectious mononucleosis among cadets at the West Point Military Academy, it has been shown that the same variable, low social class of father, relates to a lower chance of becoming infected with mononucleosis (as measured by acquisition of a specific antibody), but once infected, it relates to a higher chance of developing a clinical form of the disorder (Kasl, Evans, and Niederman, 1980).

SYMPTOM FORMATION

I have yet to discuss the third component of our model, *symptom formation* factors that influence the form taken by depression rather than increasing risk of its occurrence. In our own research a psychiatrist trained at the Institute of Psychiatry in London classified the 114 patients living in Camberwell in general clinical terms as psychotically or neurotically depressed. The diagnosis was made purely on the symptoms and impairment presented at interview. Sixty-three patients were rated as suffering from psychotic depression and forty-nine from neurotic depression. (Two with definite manic symptoms were excluded and clinical data about one was lost at this stage; Brown, Harris, and Copeland, 1977.)

I have already defined past loss; loss of this kind had occurred more frequently among the psychotic than neurotic depressives (66 percent vs. 39 percent, $p<.01$), the majority of losses occurring in childhood and adolescence. Psychotics experienced significantly more losses through death than neurotic depressives (60 percent vs. 16 percent, $p<.001$), while neurotics experienced more through separation than psychotics (22 percent vs. 6 percent, $p<.02$). The differences remain when age of the patient is controlled. Much the same results were obtained when we looked at a second group of depressed patients whose clinical state had been evaluated by a research psychiatrist unconnected with our research (Professor Robert Kendell) and made several years before we carried out our study (table 12-5).

In contrast to the issue of increased risk, there is considerable consistency in published research for an association between early loss of

TABLE 12-5

Patients by Type of Past Loss and Degree of Psychotic/Neurotic Depressive Features According to Discriminant Function Scores

	Present Series (n = 111)		Second Series (n = 70) (Kendell)	
	Loss by death (%)	Other loss (%)	Loss by death (%)	Other loss (%)
Top third (most psychotic)	68 (25/37)	1 (1/37)	48 (12/25)	0 (0/25)
Middle third	43 (16/37)	16 (6/37)	39 (9/23)	17 (4/23)
Bottom third (most neurotic)	11 (4/37)	22 (8/37)	14 (3/22)	32 (7/22)
	41 (45/111)	14 (15/111)	34 (24/70)	16 (11/70)
	$p<0.01$	$p<0.05$	$p<0.05$	$p<0.01$

parent and some kind of severity of depression. Our own finding of a large association between past loss and type and severity of depressive symptoms only emerged when we distinguished (1) severity of the depression at admission, (2) the predominance of neurotic and psychotic features, (3) four kinds of loss (of siblings, child, and husband and not just of parents), and (4) whether loss was due to death or other reasons. While this type of analysis has not been done before, five studies have looked at loss of a parent during childhood and adolescence and severity of depression.[6] Since these studies ignored the other three distinctions, only a modest association between loss and severity could be expected. Birtchnell (1970) provides results for women with a loss before the age of twenty, and there is a close similarity with our material when the same simple twofold distinction is made: 38 percent of the most and 22 percent of the least depressed patients had lost a parent in childhood or adolescence compared with 37 and 23 percent in our series (29/77, 21/94, 30/81, and 7/30 respectively).

The four other studies do not separate data for men and women. Three (Beck, Sethi, and Tuthill, 1963; Sethi, 1964; Munro, 1966) give results similar to those just quoted, and one (Abrahams and Whitlock, 1969) does not show a difference, although a measure of unsatisfactory family relationships in childhood does relate. Similar to our study when we used the total community series as a comparison group, none of the five studies obtained an association between early loss of a mother or father and the occurrence of depression as such. Two other studies are relevant. Wilson, Alltop, and Buffaloe (1967) found that depressed patients who had lost either parent by death before the age of sixteen had an elevated score on the psychotic but not the neurotic scales of the Minnesota Multiphasic Personality Inventory. A study by Forrest, Fraser, and Priest (1965) did not find any differences in childhood bereavement before the age of fifteen between a neurotic and psychotic depressed group. The fact that they were a highly selected group of patients taking part in a drug trial may have some bearing on the results. A comparison group from the general population is, of course, unnecessary for testing for such effects. A contrast of these results with studies concerning early loss and later risk of depression where use of a comparison group is essential, perhaps can be seen as some support for what I argued earlier—that shortcomings in the se-

6. Beck, Sethi and Tuthill, 1963; Sethi, 1964; Munro, 1966; Abrahams and Whitlock, 1969; Birtchnell, 1970. The study by Sethi (1964) includes loss of a sibling. However, the inclusion of nondepressed patients in his "no or low-depression" group confuses the issue of the role of loss in symptom formation in depression.

lection of suitable comparison series from the general population largely explains the inconsistency of results concerning early loss of parent and risk of depression in adulthood.

SELECTION DUE TO SEVERITY

However, this result concerning symptom formation was not repeated in the general population, although there was a certain hint of the effect. Therefore we have to face a second instance of failure to replicate, this time in the general population. One obvious explanation is the relative rarity of severe psychotic-like signs of depression such as delusions and severe retardation in the general population. The patient sample consisted mainly of in-patients who by and large were probably receiving this particular form of care because of the severity of their depressive symptoms. Given this, a second kind of selection may be enough to explain this latest inconsistency in results. I will call it *severity* selection in contrast to the *treatment* selection already discussed. While treatment selection is concerned with the factors correlated with early loss of a parent that lower chances of receiving psychiatric care, severity selection concerns the fact that a measure such as past loss may be more valid among a group such as patients selected because of the overall tendency for their symptoms to be more severe. The argument is as follows: An index such as past loss is bound to be a crude and indirect measure of whatever is causally important. Loss of a close relative is not uncommon, and it is certainly not *any* such loss that is relevant, but one occurring under particular circumstances—say in the context of ineffective mourning or when the impact on the usual pattern of activities has been particularly severe. It is therefore likely that only a small proportion of "past losses" are capable of playing a role in symptom formation. And yet we have seen that a crude index based on *all* such losses has a very large association with type and severity of depression in two series of patients. Selective processes involving severity of the condition may well be enough to explain this paradox. Severely depressed women almost certainly have a greater chance of receiving psychiatric treatment; it follows that, given that past losses of a certain kind are capable of increasing severity, losses experienced by such patients will tend to be a kind that are *effective* in increasing severity of depression. Therefore, by studying a patient group, particularly as the great majority were in-patients, we may well have stood a greater chance of selecting certain kinds of past loss for study.

Such selection may therefore greatly increase the usefulness of a crude indicator, but only for the particular subsample of persons involved in the selective process. There is no question here of a sampling bias leading to invalid conclusions. Indeed, if this argument is correct, such severity selection provides a useful first step in improving the measurement of past loss; analysis of losses in a patient series may give us important clues of just what it is about past loss that influences the form of depressive disorder. While such bootstrap operations are a perfectly legitimate research exercise, it does follow that we must live with uncertainty about whether the original finding is replicable in a population not subject to such selection. The answer will have to wait until more detailed research has been able to isolate just what it is about such losses that is important.

NEGATIVE FINDINGS

My discussion of possible selective processes as means of explaining away two negative results may strike some as ill judged. Should not the negative findings just be accepted? After all, it is an area of research where failure to replicate findings has been the rule. I think this view mistaken—it is the very inconsistency of previous research that demands explanation. Scientifically it is just as unsatisfactory to accept lack of an association as correct when there is one as to accept the presence of an association when there is not one.

The question of the role of selection can be usefully extended to a more general question of the measurement of the factors in our model. A factor may have different and even "reverse" effects at different points of the processes outlined by a causal model. In the model of depression, loss of mother before the age of eleven acts as both a vulnerability factor increasing risk of depression and as a symptom-formation factor influencing the form it takes and its severity. There is nothing necessarily misleading in this—loss of a mother merely represents more than one "thing." As with the index of "past loss," it is necessary to push toward a closer specification of just what is involved. However, it is perhaps worth noting that it may in time prove possible to amalgamate vulnerability and symptom-formation factors. So far I have emphasized that the latter do not increase risk of depression, but only its form. But it is obvious that there is likely to be some link between increasing severity and increasing risk. Indeed, this can already be seen in one of the Camberwell results: In the presence of a provoking agent lack of a vulnerability factor increases the chance of a woman developing a borderline case rather than a case condition (Brown and Harris, 1978a). In other words, when there is a provoking agent those women without a vulnerability factor will tend to develop mild symptoms rather than a definite psychiatric disorder. However, in spite of the possibility of viewing symptom-formation factors as a special instance of processes that increase risk of severity of depression, I think it important to continue to distinguish the two factors in future research in order to establish just how closely they can be brought together.

At this point I should note that in their current review of research on parental death in childhood, Crook and Eliot (1980), do not exempt the research I have just reviewed from their general criticism. However, in doing so they ignore the clear-cut results concerning loss of mother before the age of eleven in the Camberwell population survey and deal only with the fact that loss of mother was unrelated (in the sense of statistical significance) to risk of depression in the patient series. Even here I have shown that when loss of *either* parent before the age of seventeen is considered, the results do reach statistical significance.[7]

They also refer to earlier criticisms made by Tennant and Bebbington (1978) as a reason for dismissing the results of the Camberwell survey but fail to note our reply, which makes clear that these criticisms were based on a misinterpretation of what had been done (Brown and Harris, 1978b). While the Camberwell findings as a whole require replication, they make a reasonably convincing case that loss of a parent in childhood, and perhaps in adolescence, increases later risk of depression and that such loss also influences the severity of any disorder that does develop. The results certainly should not be accepted less willingly because of the negative findings of any number of poorly designed inquiries. There often appears to be an assumption in review papers that the results of one poorly designed inquiry are made more secure when the results of equally poorly designed inquiries are added to it. This, of course, is a fallacy; the latter alter not a jot the insecurity of the findings of the first survey. A wider recognition

---

7. I do not place any particular weight on the age of seventeen in this result; it probably reflects the fact that when a finding is just short of a particular level of statistical significance, quite small changes in the arrangement of the numbers involved may make the result statistically significant. (However, it is of interest that the Walthamstow survey that I will discuss and that involved larger numbers does suggest that losses between the ages of eleven and seventeen can raise risk of depression.) Results for death alone also show the same twofold difference for the patient series, but given the smaller numbers involved they do not approach statistical significance: 12 percent (14/114) of patients and 6 percent (24/382) of women who were not cases in the general population experienced a death of mother before the age of seventeen.

of this fallacy might lessen some of the burdens of reviewers and readers.

Some Theoretical Interpretations

I have already said something of one possible theoretical interpretation of these results. We have speculated that the importance of major loss and disappointment is that they deprive women of sources of value and reward, of good thoughts about themselves, their lives, and those close to them, and it is a feeling of hopelessness associated with such deprivation that is critical. Particularly significant, as Melges and Bowlby (1969) have argued, is loss of faith in one's ability to obtain an important and valued goal. But such hopelessness is doubtless quite a common response to adversity and is not enough to produce clinical depression (in contrast to a depressed mood). We have speculated that it is only when it leads to thoughts about the hopelessness of one's life as a whole, when the hopelessness generalizes, that the central core of a depressive disorder can be set in train; and it is from such generalization of hopelessness that the characteristic bodily and psychological symptoms of depression arise.

We believe that relatively few people develop such *generalized* hopelessness in response to loss and disappointment because of the key role played by ongoing feelings of self-esteem or self-worth.[8] If these are low before a major loss or disappointment, a person is less able to imagine emerging from the privation. This change from specific to generalized hopelessness can be seen in terms of a secondary level of meaning developing from the primary meaning of an occurrence. It is here, with secondary meanings, that the vulnerability factors play a vital role, although I do not suggest they are the only way such generalization can occur. We have suggested that low self-esteem tends to be the common feature behind the four disparate vulnerability factors and it is this that gives some theoretical sense to them. The formulation concentrates on the present: on low intimacy with a husband, having three or more children under the age of fourteen, and lack of

8. I have somewhat simplified the case here. I do not rule out altogether some role for genetic and constitutional factors that can easily be fit into the model, nor the fact that at times bodily factors may play a crucial etiological role on their own.

employment outside the home. It is easy to see how these might, in an urban setting at least, relate to enduring feelings of failure and low self-worth. But early loss of a mother is more difficult to explain in such terms. There are two obvious possibilities. Such loss may lead to changes in "personality," say in doubts about how lovable one is, and this leads to a particular reaction to current losses and disappointments. Alternatively early loss may increase the chance of certain experiences occurring in adulthood. In turn these may increase the chance of experiencing one of the vulnerability factors and perhaps also subject a person to a greater risk of experiencing a provoking agent. There is, of course, no reason why both possibilities should not play a role.

Obviously relevant here is John Bowlby's masterly recent review of evidence concerning childhood antecedents of disordered mourning and of clinical depression and anxiety (Bowlby, 1980; see also Bowlby, 1969, 1973, and 1979). As I have already noted, he considers a sense of helplessness or hopelessness the key characteristic of clinical depression and sees both as related to three kinds of experience in childhood: never attaining a stable and secure relationship with parents; being told repeatedly about being unlovable, inadequate, or incompetent; and experiencing loss of a parent with disagreeable consequences that are not easily changed. Such experiences are important insofar as they impart "cognitive biases" of a kind that lead to seeing later loss in terms of personal failure or in which the person sees himself as doomed to frustration in restoring or replacing what has been lost, processes I have discussed in terms of secondary meaning.

Bowlby's view is close to the one I have outlined, although it goes much further in detailing intervening cognitive processes. I will therefore note possible points of disagreement. Bowlby places most emphasis on early childhood experiences and later bereavement in explaining depression, whereas we have taken the view that such experiences are only one way, and not necessarily the most important, of increasing vulnerability to depression. He does emphasize the important role later experience can play in modifying the baleful affects of early experience, but this is not quite the same as emphasizing that experience in adulthood may be enough in itself to increase vulnerability to depression. However, it is not known how far our indicators of vulnerability, such as low intimacy with a husband, are in some way consequences of early experience. If this relationship were a close one, the difference between the two views might not be as significant as it might at first appear.

The greater emphasis the Camberwell research gives to the role in adulthood of experiences other than bereavement is almost certainly correct in the sense that only a small minority of the provoking agents in Camberwell involved the death of someone close. (The proportion is rather greater in the Outer Hebrides. See Prudo et al., 1981.) Furthermore, only about half of the provoking agents involved trouble with an affectional relationship—something that Bowlby sees as critical: "the principal issue about which a person feels helpless is his ability to make or maintain affectional relationships" (1980, p. 247). However, here again the difference may prove less than might at first appear; the difficulties and crises involving housing, financial problems, and employment that loomed so large as provoking agents might have their impact through an assessment on the woman's part of their likely deleterious effect on her affectional ties. Because of its likely impact on an already difficult marriage or strained relationships with children, knowledge of yet another pregnancy may be profoundly disappointing to a woman living in overcrowded and poor housing.

One other possible difference between Bowlby and myself may lie in the degree to which the basic cognitive and behavioral dispositions that he outlines are seen as necessarily increasing risk of depression. My colleagues and I feel we are often able to recognize such basic dispositions in women who have had an early loss of parent, but we are not convinced that they necessarily increase risk of depression. It is not uncommon, for instance, to find behavior that appears to approximate to the "compulsive caregiving" that Bowlby sees as predisposing to chronic mourning: One woman who had two children of her own took on as a foster parent a series of children and had adopted two of them. She was much valued by the local Social Services Department and had frequent friendly contacts with social workers. Through these experiences she had decided, despite leaving school at fifteen, to obtain some training herself in "social work." She obtained an impressive range of "rewards," both through the care she gave and friendships she had developed in connection with her foster mothering, and it is difficult to see her behavior as in any way maladaptive or increasing basic vulnerability to depression. (She showed other features of "caregiving" that I have not mentioned here.) Although her drive to care for others could be seen as compulsive, her behavior lacked the anxious quality that emerges in the descriptions of Bowlby's cases. It may be the insecurity in attachment that often goes with such caregiving rather than the compulsion to give care itself that is the crucial determinant as to whether people become depressive cases rather than just grief stricken when they lose the person for whom they were caring (cf. Prudo et al., 1981, for further discussion about chronic psychiatric disorder following a death of a close relative). I suspect that Bowlby may in fact agree with this point, and I make it really to emphasize the need for future research to "fill in" relevant experiences for the whole period between early loss and the occurrence of crises, whether bereavement or other events taking place in adulthood; and to emphasize the importance of doing this for women who have *and* have not developed psychiatric disorder following crises in their adult lives. It is possible, for instance, that the most relevant aspect of compulsive caregiving is simply that it increases the risks of important losses: Those who give less have less to lose.

Current Walthamstow Study

With this last point in mind, my colleagues Tirril Harris and Toni Bifulco carried out a more detailed study of the consequences of early loss of a parent that has involved screening 2,000 women living in Walthamstow by means of a postal questionnaire asking about various kinds of early loss and separation in childhood. On the basis of their other answers we selected for special study women with:

1. Loss of mother before the age of seventeen either by death or by separation for one year or more (excluding wartime evacuations).

2. Loss of a father in a similar way before the age of eleven (excluding war service).

3. No loss of a parent before the age of seventeen (not even evacuation or war service).

Table 12–6 summarizes the basic results for various kinds of loss of parent. As expected, those without any loss had a much lower rate of currently being a case—4 percent. I will summarize results by beginning with any loss of a parent before the age of seventeen. The highest rate was 24 percent among those with a loss of mother by death. The rate for women with a separation from a mother was rather lower (16 percent) and was not quite statistically significantly different from that of the comparison group. Ten of the separations were due to illness of the subject or the mother—in other words, they were not permanent. If these are excluded the rate of being a case in the "separat-

TABLE 12-6

*Cases of Affective Disorder in the Twelve Months before Interview
Walthamstow 1977–1979*

	Age at Loss of Parent		
	0–10 (%)	11–17 (%)	0–17 (%)
A. *No loss*			4 (2/45)
B. *Loss of mother*			
Death of mother	29 (14/49)[a]	17 (5/30)[a]	24 (19/79)
Separation from mother (excluding illness)	17 (4/23)	18 (2/11)	18 (6/34)
Separation from mother due to illness	10 (1/10)		10 (1/10)
Total for mother	23 (19/82)	17 (7/41)	21 (26/123)
C. *Loss of father*			
Death of father[a]	9 (2/23)	Not studied	9 (2/23)
Separation from father[a]	18 (4/22)	Not studied	18 (4/22)
Total for father	13 (6/45)	Not studied	13 (6/45)

[a] The total number of subjects in this table is four more than we quote later because some subjects filled in the initial postal questionnaire erroneously—they had in fact lost both parents but only told us about one. We debated whether to exclude them from this part of the research (we have since interviewed a special sample with multiple losses) but decided to leave them in and include them under "mother" *and* "father." Two of the three with a death of mother and of father before age eleven were current cases of depression, the one with a separation from her father at age two and a death of mother at age eleven was not a current case. Only one of the separations from father was due to illness—a fact that suggests that fathers with long-term illnesses (over a year) were more often nursed at home (by the mother) than were mothers with long-term illnesses.

ed" group increases to 18 percent but the difference still does not quite reach statistical significance.

Death of a father was unrelated to the rate of being a case, but there is some hint that there may have been an increased rate among those who separated from a father.

When those who lost a mother between the ages of eleven and seventeen are considered, results remain essentially the same except for those who lost a mother by death before the age of eleven. These women had approximately double the chance of being a case compared with those with such a loss between the ages of eleven and seventeen (29 percent and 17 percent respectively—n.s.).

Interpretation of the results is handicapped by the small numbers in the comparison group. If they were larger, a number of these individual results would probably reach statistical significance.

259

Clearly the original Camberwell finding covering loss of mother before the age of eleven is confirmed; but this new and larger series now suggests that the influence of maternal loss on depression can extend until the age of seventeen although the impact may be somewhat less than before the age of eleven. There is also some suggestion that loss of a mother by death leads to a greater risk of subsequent disorder than loss by separation.

Once again, loss of a father is very much less important than loss of a mother, although there is some hint that at times it can have an influence, particularly if it is the result of a separation. This should perhaps be taken seriously as there are now several studies that suggest that loss of father is linked to an increased risk of suicide and attempted suicide (Adam, chapter 13 herein).

As in the research in Camberwell, chances of being a case were higher for working-class women, but since we had insured that there were comparable numbers of working-class women in each of the loss groups there is no possibility that the different rates of being a case in the various loss groups were brought about by differences in social class.[9] Since social class was also controlled in an earlier Camberwell study, it is possible to see the results as the confirmation of the importance of a genuine rather than a spurious causal link between early loss of parent and later depression mediated by social class. That this possibility has not been ruled out is one of the major reasons recent reviews have given for rejecting the results of previous research.

Much the same pattern of differences occurs when *any* episode of being a case during a woman's life is considered (table 12–7). (We refer to "probable cases," since with the time period involved and the resulting problems of recall we have less confidence in our data on symptoms than for the current year. However, since we have been cautious in rating a woman as a case in the past, the figures for lifetime prevalence are, in fact, likely to be underestimates. But there is no reason why the amount of underestimation should vary systematically between the groups; it is likely to be the same for all, and the between-group differences would be expected to remain with more accurate estimates of the experience of being a case in the past.)

In designing this latest study we had not anticipated the recent spate of doubt about whether early loss can have *any* effect on later chances of developing depression. We had seen it primarily as a vehicle for exploring the processes at work in bringing about an increased

---

9. For details of the occupational class measure see Brown and Harris, 1978a.

TABLE 12-7

Probable Cases of Affective Disorder at Any Time
(lifetime prevalence): Walthamstow Loss of Parent Sample

	Age at Loss of Parent		
	0–10 (%)	11–17 (%)	0–17 (%)
A. *No loss*			24 (11/45)
B. *Loss of mother*			
Death of mother[a]	57 (28/49)	60 (18/30)	58 (46/79)
Separation from mother (excluding illness)	43 (10/23)	36 (4/11)	41 (14/34)
Separation from mother due to illness	50 (5/10)		50 (5/10)
Total for mother	52 (43/82)	54 (22/41)	53 (65/123)
C. *Loss of father*			
Death of father[a]	17 (4/23)	Not studied	17 (4/23)
Separation from father[a]	36 (8/22)	Not studied	36 (8/22)
Total for father	26 (12/45)	Not studied	26 (12/45)

[a]Four women had lost both parents. Two of the three who suffered the death of both parents had been probable cases of affective disorder at some time. One woman was separated from her father at age two and her mother died when she was eleven, and she had never been a probable case.

risk following such loss. One possible objection to the results I have reviewed therefore stems from the size of the comparison series, which we had deliberately kept small. Moreover, the rate of psychiatric disorder in the comparison group is particularly low compared with that found in the earlier research in Camberwell.[10] Fortunately, it has been possible to make a second, albeit somewhat untidy, test of these differences, which, I believe, provides a convincing confirmation of the results.

In the course of developing a family interview in a different project, we interviewed married women selected at random, aged between eighteen and forty-five and also living in Walthamstow. They can be used as an additional comparison series. When women in our original series who had lost a mother before the age of seventeen are matched with these women in terms of social class, age, marital status, and stage of family development, their rate of affective disorder is again

10. Walthamstow does not appear to have as many social problems as the inner London borough of Camberwell, and other research we have been carrying out in Walthamstow suggests that the overall prevalence of psychiatric disorder in Walthamstow may be lower than in Camberwell (e.g., Murphy and Brown, 1980).

261

much higher—37 percent (7/19) compared with 10 percent (6/59), *p* <.01. The matching decreases the number of women who lost a mother by death from 79 to 19 (many in the original early-loss series could not be matched as they were over forty-five years of age or unmarried), but the result is a clear confirmation with a second comparison series of the importance of early loss of mother by death in increasing later risk of depression. (The number of women who could be matched with those with a loss of father was too small for comparison concerning loss of a father to be made.)

Final Theoretical Interpretations

Given that a general case has been made for the significance of early loss of mother, it is possible to turn to the main object of the Walthamstow inquiry—a search for "intervening" variables that help to explain why it increases later risk of depression. Unfortunately, we have only begun the necessary analysis of our material and I am able to present just one set of findings, which should be seen as an illustration of the kind of analysis that will be possible.

Premarital pregnancy is of interest because it is known that there is a tendency for women from broken homes to have a higher rate of conception outside marriage—although the size of the association found in large-scale epidemiological inquiries has been modest (e.g., Illsley and Thompson, 1961; Wadsworth, 1979). The association was confirmed in the present inquiry: 20 percent (25/123) of the women with a loss of mother by death or separation before the age of seventeen had a premarital pregnancy compared with 10 percent (9/86) of those without any loss of a parent or only the loss of a father before the age of seventeen—*p* <.05.

Since there is a marked association in the Walthamstow series as a whole between being considered a case and premarital pregnancy, such pregnancy may be an important mediating experience between early loss and later disturbance. Of those who had a premarital pregnancy, 44 percent (15/34) were current cases compared with 10 percent (17/175) of those who had not—*p* <.001.

The results shown in table 12-8 do not rule out this possibility. Premarital pregnancy is very highly associated with being a case whether or not it is linked to early loss of mother: Just under half the women

262

TABLE 12-8

Premarital Pregnancy, Loss of Mother before Age 17, Intimate Relationship with Husband and Whether Currently a Case

	Loss of Mother before Age 17									No Loss of Mother before Age 17								
	Nonintimate			Intimate			Total			Nonintimate			Intimate			Total		
	Case	Not case	% case	Case	Not case	% case	Case	Not case	% case	Case	Not case	% case	Case	Not case	% case	Case	Not case	% case
Premarital pregnancy	8	6	57	4	7	36	12	13	48	1	1	50	2	5	29	3	6	33
None	7	26	21	7	58	11	14	84	14	2	17	11	1	57	2	3	74	4
Total	15	32	30	11	65	14	26	97	20	3	18	14	3	62	5	6	80	6

with such a pregnancy were current cases. Early loss of mother *without* such a pregnancy is also linked to a raised chance of being a case, but the average risk is far less than that when it is associated with premarital pregnancy (14 percent vs. 48 percent, $p < .01$). Perhaps the most plausible model is:

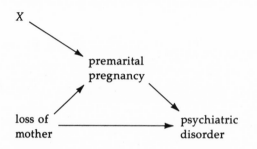

where the unknown X factor influencing the rate of premarital pregnancy might well include other experiences associated with childhood. However, for us perhaps the most important implication of the apparent importance of premarital pregnancy and its link with early loss is that the effects of the latter can be mediated in some way by its impact on *current* experience. Such an interpretation would be strengthened if it were possible to show that the influence of premarital pregnancy was associated with a greater tendency for lack of intimacy in marriages following such pregnancies, since the role of lack of intimacy in vulnerability to depressive disorders is established. In fact, premarital pregnancy did relate to the lack of a confiding relationship with a husband—among those with loss of mother, 56 percent (14/25) compared with 34 percent (33/98) who had one, $p < .05$—where for those without loss of mother the figures were 22 percent (2/9) compared with 12 percent (9/77). This might suggest that lack of maternal care, by leading in some way to a raised rate of premarital pregancies, forces women to marry before they may be ready to decide whether they can establish a truly intimate, confiding relationship with the putative father—in other words, it traps them in relationships which will make them vulnerable to depression after a provoking agent. It may be of interest that the only two of these pregnancies to be ended by a termination were not current cases, both in the loss of mother group.

However, the data also suggest that the final explanation of what occurs with regard to premarital pregnancy is likely to be a complex one. The tendency for women with a premarital pregnancy to lack a confiding relationship with their husbands is not enough to explain their increased risk of depression. Among women with early loss of mother, even those in the premarital pregnancy group *with* an intimate relationship with their husbands have a higher rate of depression than those without premarital pregnancy with such a relationship—36 percent (4/11) vs. 11 percent (7/65), $p < 0.05$. Indeed, table 12-8 indicates that lack of an intimate tie with a husband and premarital pregnancy independently contribute to raising the risk of depression. Premarital pregnancy and intimacy are linked in that those with such a pregnancy are more likely to lack an intimate tie with a husband; however, given this, both contribute independently to raising the risk of depression.

Why, we must therefore ask, are women with early loss of mother and premarital pregnancy particularly predisposed to later depression? The kind of relationship they develop with their husbands certainly appears to play a part, but, as we have just seen, women with a close relationship with a husband (or indeed without three or more children at home, another vulnerability factor) are still at higher risk. The result is consistent with the presence among some of the women of a long-term predisposition along the lines of John Bowlby's "cognitive biases." One of the cognitive biases we chose to investigate was that of helplessness, which of course has been the interest of Seligman and his colleagues (Seligman, 1975; Abramsom, Seligman, and Teasdale, 1978). Our measurement of helplessness was based on questioning about behavior in thirteen different types of situations, such as relationships with in-laws, relationships with neighbors, day-to-day practical matters, life plans, and wider affairs. A preliminary examination of the data suggests an association on the one hand between a personality characteristic of "helplessness" prior to onset and being a case currently, and on the other hand between premarital pregnancy and marked helplessness at some point in life. Following the previous diagram, the most important role of the uncertain factor X might be to produce such a cognitive bias of "helplessness." The main causal influence involving early loss of mother and premarital pregnancy would then be:

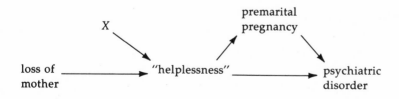

265

Of course, a full model would need extra arrows to take into account, for example, intervening factors between "helplessness" and psychiatric disorder, and premarital pregnancy and psychiatric disorder. Indeed, the latter arrow would only be justified if, as I have suggested, there were experiences such as low intimacy with a husband that raise the risk of an affective disorder over and above that produced by the cognitive set of helplessness.

Another possible explanation of the link between premarital pregnancy, early loss of maternal care, and psychiatric vulnerability will be familiar to those with a psychiatric perspective—the fantasy that becoming pregnant will somehow compensate for the closeness of the mother-child relationship of which the woman herself was deprived.

This possible intervening link between loss in childhood and depression in adulthood is, of course, only one of the many that must be considered. Among the others are some that Bowlby describes, including the woman's experiences with the replacement parent and the degree of support or rejection she received prior to the loss of parent, to name just a few. In our study we shall also look at the degree of discord and disruption in the childhood home(s), for it has been suggested that it is this that is pathogenic rather than the loss itself (Rutter, 1971, 1972; Adam, chapter 13 herein). Nor do we feel confident that the crucial intervening links are necessarily located in childhood itself. We are examining the quality of the women's relationships in adulthood, the women's characteristic coping in terms of hostility and assertiveness, and aspects of their work or careers, for we believe it possible that all or any of these could mitigate or amplify the impact of the earlier loss of parent. The analysis will be complex, but such complexity must be expected. It is most unlikely that there will be simple answers. Even though research of formidable complexity is required, it may be of some comfort that one can start with the reasonable assumption that early loss of mother does *in some way* increase risk of depression in adult life for women. Research attempting to elucidate why this is so is therefore likely to lead to important insights into the etiology of depression. It may still be objected that early loss of a parent is a fairly rare occurrence. This is certainly so, but the importance of studying early loss arises less from the absolute number of instances of depression it can explain than the insights it can give to the fundamental processes involved. John Bowlby has argued that a broad range of experience in childhood and adolescence may increase later risk of depression, not just experience associated with loss of a parent. Given this possibility, the study of early loss of a parent is probably best seen as part of a study on the effect of early relationships in general. In any case the point about the relative infrequency of loss of a parent should not be taken too far, for we have also seen that there is some suggestion that loss of any close relative may influence the form of later depression. And such losses are not uncommon.

REFERENCES

Abrahams, M. J., and Whitlock, F. A. 1969. Childhood experience and depression. *British Journal of Psychiatry* 115:883–888.

Abramsom, L. Y., Seligman, M. E. P., and Teasdale, J. D. 1978. Learned helplessness in humans: Critique and reformulation. *Journal of Abnormal Psychology* 87:49.

Beck, A. T., Sethi, B. B., and Tuthill, R. W. 1963. Childhood bereavement and adult depression. *Archives of General Psychiatry* 9:295–302.

Becker, E. 1964. *The revolution in psychiatry.* New York: Free Press.

Birtchnell, J. 1970. Depression in relation to early and recent parent death. *British Journal of Psychiatry* 116:299–305.

Bowlby, J. 1969. *Attachment and loss. Vol. 1: Attachment.* New York: Basic Books.

————. 1973. *Attachment and loss. Vol. 2: Separation: Anxiety and anger.* New York: Basic Books.

————. 1979. *The making and breaking of affectional bonds.* London: Tavistock.

————. 1980. *Attachment and loss. Vol. 3: Loss: Sadness and depression.* New York: Basic Books.

Brown, G. W., and Harris, T. O. 1978a. *Social origins of depression.* London: Tavistock and New York: Free Press.

————. 1978b. Social origins of depression: A reply. *Psychological Medicine* 8:577–588.

————, and Copeland, J. R. 1977. Depression and loss. *British Journal of Psychiatry* 130:1–18.

Cooper, J. E.; Copeland, J. R. M.; Brown, G. W.; Harris, T. O.; and Gourley, A. J. 1977. Further studies on interviewer training and interrater reliability of the present state examination (P.S.E.). *Psychological Medicine* 7:517–523.

Costello, C. G. 1976. *Anxiety and depression: The adaptive emotions.* Montreal: McGill-Queen's University Press.

Crook, T., and Eliot, J. 1980. Parental death during childhood and adult depression. *Psychological Bulletin* 87:252–259.

Finlay-Jones, R. A.; Duncan-Jones, P.; Brown, G. W.; Harris, T. O.; Murphy, E.; and Prudo, R. 1980. Depression and anxiety in the community: Replicating the diagnosis of a case. *Psychological Medicine* 10:445–454.

Finlay-Jones, R. A., and Brown, G. W. 1981. Life events and the onset of anxiety and depressive disorders. *Psychological Medicine* 11:803–815.

Finlay-Jones, R. A.; Duncan Jones, P.; Brown, G. W.; Harris, T. O.; Murphy, E.; and Prudo, R. 1980. Depression and anxiety in the community: Replicating the diagnosis of a case. *Psychological Medicine* 10:445–454.

Forrest, A. D., Fraser, R. H., and Priest, R. G. 1965. Environmental factors in depressive illness. *British Journal of Psychiatry* 111:243–253.

Granville-Grossman, K. L. 1968. The early environment of affective disorder. In *Recent developments in affective disorders,* ed. A. Copen and A. Walk. London: Headley Brothers.

Illsley, R., and Thompson, B. 1961. Women from broken homes. *Sociological Review* 9: 27–54.

Kasl, S. V., Evans, A. S., and Niederman, J. C. 1980. Psychosocial risk factors in the development of infectious mononucleosis. *Psychosomatic Medicine* 41(6):445–466.

Langner, T. S., and Michael, S. T. 1963. *Life stress and mental health*. London: Collier-MacMillan.

McCall, G. J., and Simmons, J. L. 1966. *Identities and interactions*. New York: Free Press.

Marris, P. 1974. *Loss and change*. London: Routledge & Kegan Paul.

Melges, F. T., and Bowlby, J. 1969. Types of hopelessness in psychopathological process. *Archives of General Psychiatry* 20:690–699.

Munro, A. 1966. Parental deprivation in depressive patients. *British Journal of Psychiatry* 122:443–457.

Murphy, E., and Brown, G. W. 1980. Life events, psychiatric disturbance and physical illness. *British Journal of Psychiatry* 136:326–338.

Prudo, R.; Brown, G. W.; Harris, T. O.; and Dowland, J. 1981. Psychiatric disorder in a rural and an urban population: 2. Sensitivity to loss. *Psychological Medicine* 11:601–616.

Rutter, M. R. 1971. Parent-child separation. Psychological effects on the children. *Journal of Child Psychology and Psychiatry* 12:233–260.

———. 1972. *Maternal deprivation reassessed*. Harmondsworth: Penguin Books.

Seligman, M. E. P. 1975. *Helplessness: On depression, development and death*. San Francisco: W. H. Freeman.

Sethi, B. B. 1964. Relationship of separation to depression. *Archives of General Psychiatry* 10:486–496.

Tennant, C., and Bebbington, P. 1978. The social causation of depression: A critique of Brown and his colleagues. *Psychological Medicine* 8:565–575.

———, and Hurry, J. 1980. Parental death in childhood and risk of adult depressive disorders: A review. *Psychological Medicine* 10:289–299.

Tomkins, S. S. 1963. *Affect, imagery, consciousness. Vol. 2: The negative affects*. London: Tavistock.

Wadsworth, M. 1979. *Roots of delinquency. Infancy, adolescence and crime*. London: Martin Robertson.

Weiss, R. S. 1977. *Marital separation*. New York: Basic Books.

Wilson, I. C., Alltop, L., and Buffaloe, W. J. 1967. Parental bereavement in childhood: MMPI profiles in a depressed population. *British Journal of Psychiatry* 113:761–764.

Wing, J. K., Cooper, J. E., and Sartorious, N. 1974. *The measurement and classification of psychiatric symptoms: An instruction manual for the present state examination and CATEGO programme*. London: Cambridge University Press.

Wing, J. K.; Nixon, J. M.; Mann, S. A.; and Leff, J. P. 1977. Reliability of the PSE (ninth edition) used in a population study. *Psychological Medicine* 7:505–516.

13

Kenneth S. Adam

LOSS, SUICIDE, AND ATTACHMENT

Introduction

The relationship of loss to depression and suicide was first mentioned by Freud in his paper "Mourning and Melancholia" in 1915 (Freud, 1957), and although other analytic writers reported clinical material relating to the theme (Klein, 1948; Hendricks, 1940), it was not until 1937 that Zilboorg suggested that the death of a parent might have a special bearing on the etiology of suicide, particularly when it occurred during childhood or adolescence. Impressionistic studies on larger series of suicidal patients appeared during the 1940s and 1950s, stressing the importance of identification with a dead parent in suicidal behavior, but the major body of systematic research began in direct response to the stimulus of John Bowlby's work on parental deprivation in the 1960s. Bowlby's paper "Childhood Mourning and Its Implications for Psychiatry" (1961) drew attention to a number of studies that examined the relationship of early loss to adult psychiatric disorders, including suicidal behavior. Since that time nearly two dozen papers have been published dealing with the theme of early loss and suicidal behavior, with somewhat inconclusive results.

The Incidence of Parental Loss in Suicidal Behavior

The reported incidence of "parental loss," "parental deprivation," or "broken homes" in different samples of suicidal individuals varies

269

from a low of around 30 percent (Koller and Castanos, 1968) to as high as 76 percent (Walton, 1958), with a wide range of figures in between. Most of the earlier workers defined "loss" rather broadly, often including parental strife, illegitimacy, or separation from siblings as well as parents in their criteria.[1] These studies uniformly reported high incidence figures for "parental deprivation." Later studies, using more restricted definitions of loss, reported lower figures, with the general finding of a higher incidence of loss in suicidal patients than in various comparison groups.[2]

Exceptions to this trend have been the studies of McConaghy, Linane, and Buckle (1966), who found no statistically significant differences between two groups of attempted suicides and general hospital patient controls, and those of Bunch and associates (1971) and Crook and Raskin (1975), both of whom found no difference in the incidence of parental death in suicidal subjects compared to controls.

Factors that have acted to inflate loss figures in some studies are: (1) the inclusion of temporary as well as permanent separations in definitions of "loss"; (2) the inclusion of separations from siblings and the loss of "significant" persons other than parents; and (3) extending the period of childhood during which "early loss" was considered to have occurred. Most studies have examined for loss prior to the age of fifteen or sixteen, although some have expanded the interval to the age of eighteen (Dorpat, Jackson, and Ripley, 1965; Oliver et al., 1971) or even twenty (McConaghy, Linane, and Buckle, 1966).

The selection of control subjects for these studies poses particular difficulties. The presence of suicidal or potentially suicidal subjects in control groups may diminish differences between controls and the suicidal subjects under study, and the use of psychiatric patients as controls may also affect the results because of the more general association of parental deprivation with a number of other adult psychiatric disorders (Gay and Tonge, 1967). In general, the incidence of loss in psychiatric patient controls is higher than among nonpsychiatric patient controls or general population controls, although differences between the latter two are not great.

If one confines the definition of loss to permanent loss by either parental death, divorce, or separation, during approximately the same

1. See Walton, 1958; Palmer, 1941; Reitman, 1942; Batchelor and Napier, 1953; and Moss and Hamilton, 1956.
2. See Koller and Castanos, 1968; Bruhn, 1962; Greer, 1964; Greer, Gunn, and Koller, 1966; Levi et al., 1966; Hill, 1969; Birtchnell, 1970; Oliver et al., 1971; and Werry and Pedder, 1976.

TABLE 13-1

Incidence of Early Loss in Various Studies of Attempted Suicides Corrected for Similar Definition of Loss and Approximate Age at Time of Loss[a]

Author	Adam, Bouckoms, and Scarr, 1980	Batchelor and Napier, 1953	Dorpat, Jackson, and Ripley, 1965	Greer, 1966
Losses to Age Attempted	16	17	18	15
Suicide (%)	31.6	33.0	40.0	41.6
Control 1	16.7% general practice patients			15.3% nonsuicidal psychiatric patients
Control 2	15.0% general population[b]			16.6% medical and surgical patients

[a] Losses from parental death or permanent separation.
[b] From J. Isherwood. Doctoral dissertation, University of Otago, 1980.

period of life, the results are considerably more consistent. Table 13–1 illustrates the incidence of permanent parental loss from death, divorce, or separation in several studies of consecutive attempted suicides some of which contain control comparisons. In some cases the original data has been corrected to remove temporary loss or separation and the authors' figures recalculated for loss within approximately the same period of time. The incidence of permanent loss varies between 32 percent and approximately 42 percent in the various consecutive attempted-suicide samples, with figures for the control groups almost identical at around 16 percent. The results represent data from England, New Zealand, and the United States.

Other Variables in Loss Studies

Whereas one can account in part for wide variations in the incidence figures for loss in attempted suicides on the basis of the previously mentioned methodological differences, this is not so clearly the case when one considers the details surrounding these experiences. For example, regarding the age of the subject at the time of the loss, in two separate studies Greer (1964, 1966) found parental loss before the age

271

of five to be high in his attempted-suicide group. Hill (1969), however, found paternal death in suicidal depressives to be more prominent in the ten- to fourteen-year age period than in nonsuicidal depressive controls, and Dorpat, Jackson, and Ripley (1965) and Koller and Castanos (1968) found no significant difference for loss at any age in their studies. In a similar vein, Greer (1966) and Greer, Gunn, and Koller (1966) reported loss of both parents to be more common in his attempted-suicide subjects than in controls, but Koller and Castanos (1968), studying a similar sample, found maternal loss and single-parent loss in excess of loss of both parents. Batchelor and Napier (1953) and Hill (1969), on the other hand, found an excess of paternal loss over maternal loss in their studies.

Similar inconsistencies have been found in data relating to the type of loss sustained by suicidal subjects compared to controls. The majority of studies have found divorce or separation to be more prominent than parental death in attempted-suicide samples.[3] However, Greer (1966), Greer, Gunn, and Koller (1966), and Batchelor and Napier (1953) have reported an excess of parental death over loss from divorce or separation. Dorpat, Jackson, and Ripley (1965), on the other hand, reported loss from divorce or separation to be associated with attempted suicide and parental death to be associated with successful suicide.

The absence of significant differences in the incidence of actual childhood bereavement between suicidal patients and control subjects in their study led Crook and Raskin to the conclusion that "a childhood characterized by parental discord and intentional separation of parents from the child is associated with attempted suicide in adult life, while a childhood characterized by loss of a parent from natural causes appears unrelated" (1975, p. 277). In an even stronger statement the *Lancet* has stated "the only firm consensus is that parental deprivation is a relatively common experience which most people survive unscathed" (1966, p. 326).

The Montreal Study: Loss and Suicidal Ideation

In an attempt to clarify the role of loss in the predisposition to suicidal behavior, we have undertaken two closely related studies. The first

3. See Koller and Castanos, 1968; Bruhn, 1962; Oliver et al., 1971; Crook and Raskin, 1975; Greer, 1966; and Lukianowicz, 1972.

study differs from most of those that have preceded it in a number of ways. Instead of selecting subjects with demonstrated suicidal behavior and examining them retrospectively for losses in early life, it was decided to select our subjects on the basis of early loss and to examine them with an anterospective view, inquiring about the existence of suicidal tendencies. Since overt suicidal behavior in the form of suicide attempts or suicidal threats occurs relatively infrequently in the population as a whole, we decided to focus in this study primarily on suicidal ideation on the assumption that preoccupation with thoughts of suicide and suicidal behavior were closely related phenomena.

As the method of data collection and characteristics of the sample have been described in detail elsewhere (Adam, Lohrenz, and Harper, 1973; Adam et al., in press), they will just be summarized here. Three groups of university students referred to a student health service over a five-year period were selected for study on the basis of information provided on a routine screening questionnaire. One group consisted of students who reported the loss of one or both parents by death before the age of sixteen, and a second group consisted of students with a history of parental separation or divorce before the age of sixteen. A third group, which consisted of students with both parents alive and living together, served as controls. Detailed information was collected about the frequency, intensity, and duration of past and present suicidal thoughts, and these were scored as either *suicidal* ideation or *no suicidal* ideation according to criteria defined in pilot interviews.[4] Overt suicidal behavior in the form of suicidal attempts was also recorded. A detailed family history was taken with particular emphasis on death, separation, or divorce of parents and the circumstances surrounding these events. The key items relating to suicidal ideation were scored while the interviewer was blind to the family background of the subject. Reliability was checked by independent raters scoring from tape recordings of the interview.

RESULTS

Highly significant differences were found between subjects with parental loss and those from intact homes for both the incidence of

4. Subjects were asked whether they had ever had thoughts of suicide; when reported, detailed information was sought about the thoughts' onset, frequency, intensity, and duration. Responses were rated as being of high, moderate, or low order on each of the dimensions of frequency, intensity, and duration. Ratings of moderate to high on at least two of the three dimensions were rated as *suicidal ideation*. All other subjects were rated as *no suicidal ideation*. Examples illustrating these ratings can be found in Adam (1973).

273

TABLE 13-2
Suicidal Ideation

	Suicidal Ideation	No Ideation	Total
Intact Home	8 (13%)	53 (87%)	61
Parental Death	21 (51%)	20 (49%)	41
Parental Divorce or Separation	15 (43%)	20 (57%)	35
Total	44	93	137

$n = 137$; $x^2 = 18.81$; $p < .001$.

TABLE 13-3
Suicidal Attempts

	Yes	No	Total
Intact Home Subjects	3 (5%)	58 (95%)	61
Parental Loss Subjects	14 (18.5%)	62 (81.5%)	76
Total	17	120	137

$n = 137$; $x^2 = 4.17$; $p < .05$.

suicidal ideation and suicide attempts. These results are set out in tables 13-2 and 13-3.

In the parental-loss sample as a whole, significantly more female than male subjects were recorded as having suicidal ideation (2 to 1 ratio) ($x^2(1) = 6.17$, $p < .02$), and the ratio for those subjects reporting suicide attempts was even greater (3.6 to 1)($x^2(1) = 10.33$, $p < .01$). Loss of father and loss of both parents were significantly greater in subjects with suicidal ideation than in those without ($x^2(2) = 8.15$, $p < .025$), but there were no differences in these variables between females and males. No differences were noted in the incidence of suicidal ideation for loss at particular age periods in childhood.

Although the history of parental loss was strongly associated with suicidal ideation, the absence of such ideas in nearly 50 percent of our parental-loss subjects was equally striking. If loss was a significant variable in the predisposition to suicidal ideation, as it seemed to be, then protective factors must have been operating in those who showed no evidence of suicidal ideation. It occurred to us, therefore, that it would be useful to reexamine our data comparing suicidal-ideation subjects with nonsuicidal-ideation subjects for the consistency and quality of the parental care they actually received both before and after the breakup of the home. Although initial attempts were made to rate individual variables in connection with the family disruption, the multitude of variables involved and the difficulties of assigning them meaningful weightings soon rendered this a futile exercise. Subsequently, global criteria relating to the stability of the home were drawn up and the early family life was rated as either *stable, unstable,* or *chaotic* according to these criteria.[5]

In order to determine whether the unfavorable effects of loss were the result of its immediate experience or due to its long-term consequences, family stability was rated separately for the period prior to the loss, for the immediate period surrounding the loss (approximately one year), and for the long-term period following the loss.

FAMILY STABILITY BEFORE, DURING, AND AFTER LOSS

As can be seen from table 13-4, important differences were found between suicidal-ideation and nonsuicidal-ideation subjects in ratings of family stability. Family stability prior to the loss was not significantly different in the suicidal-ideation subjects compared to nonsuicidal-ideation subjects, although there were numerically more chaotic homes in the suicidal group. The immediate effect of the loss appears to have been unfavorable for most subjects in the suicidal-ideation group, with few having had stable homes during this time and most having had unstable or chaotic homes. The nonsuicidal-ideation group, however, had more stable homes and fewer unstable homes, but a slight increase in the number of chaotic homes. Differences between the two groups for this period were not significant. In the long term, however, the differences were very marked. Only 8 percent of the suicidal-ideation subjects had stable homes in contrast to 65 percent of nonsuicidal-ideation subjects, and the remainder of homes of suicidal-ideation subjects were rated as either unstable or chaotic. Differences between the two groups of subjects were highly significant.

Although these findings were the same whether the loss was due to death of a parent or divorce/separation, close examination of the data suggested, not surprisingly, that the pre-loss environment was more likely to have been stable where parental death had occurred than in cases of divorce/separation.

5. *Family Stability Ratings*
Stable: Consistent availability of adequate parental care without material hardship.
Unstable: Parental figures inconsistently available either for physical or emotional reasons with or without material hardship.
Chaotic: Gross deprivation of adequate parental care associated with prolonged separations from parental figures and often material and emotional deprivation for prolonged periods of time. An environment of constant uncertainty.

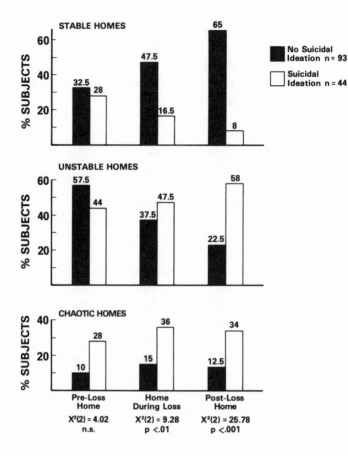

TABLE 13-4
Stability of Home before, during, and after Loss

Several case examples serve to illustrate these findings.

CASE EXAMPLE 1: SUBJECT WITH STABLE HOME FOLLOWING
DIVORCE/SEPARATION

Miss N, a twenty-year-old woman, came to the clinic seeking help with improving her self-confidence and her relationships with men. Although she occasionally experienced mild feelings of depression, she never felt hopeless about life and had never entertained thoughts of suicide, which she regarded as an "inability to face things."

Her parents' marriage broke up when she was three years old after an

276

extensive period of instability during which time her father was reported to have been alcoholic, unfaithful, and a poor provider. Following their separation she, her brother, and her mother went to live with her maternal grandmother, and her mother went to work to support them. The grandmother took over most everyday caretaking functions while mother was working, but these duties were sometimes shared with her mother's brother who lived with his family in the same building. He took a good deal of interest in them, including them in his family's outings and treating them "like his own children."

Although Miss N had no contact whatsoever with her father from the time of the separation until she was fourteen, his parents maintained contact with her mother and provided financial support from time to time. Eventually, when she was fifteen, her mother remarried a stable breadwinner who accepted responsibility for the children, although he did not show them a great deal of interest. This occasionally became a source of conflict in the home, but the mother always made it plain that her primary loyalties were to her children and that she would be prepared to care for them on her own again if necessary.

Following her father's remarriage when Miss N was fourteen, he tried to make amends and reestablish a relationship with the children. Miss N reported feeling sympathy tinged with resentment toward him and has continued to see him occasionally without feeling any deep attachment. She described her relationship with her mother as extremely close and expressed admiration and respect for her.

CASE EXAMPLE 2: SUBJECT WITH CHAOTIC HOME FOLLOWING PARENTAL DIVORCE

JG, a nineteen-year-old science student, sought help at the clinic because of difficulties in communicating with her peers, fears of rejection in interpersonal relationships, and profound feelings of worthlessness. She explained that she had never felt good about herself, had frequent and prolonged bouts of depression, and had thoughts of suicide as far back as she could remember. She often thought about how she would eventually kill herself with pills ("to avoid a mess") and was surprised that more people didn't commit suicide.

Background information revealed that her parents had separated when JG was two years of age following several years of conflictual marriage attributed to father's alcoholism. JG learned from her older sister that her mother had left home suddenly without explanation, leaving her and her three siblings in the care of her father. For a number of years the day-to-day care of the children was provided by her paternal grandmother, the father's mistress, and a succession of maids, none of whom remained in the home for any length of time. This arrangement continued until JG was about ten, with only irregular contact with her mother, who lived on her own.

At the death of her grandmother, one of JG's sisters and a brother went to live with the mother while JG and her older sister remained with the father. Although the father's mistress occasionally "stayed over" and sometimes cooked meals for the family, her sister increasingly assumed the caretaking role. All contact with her mother was actively discouraged by the father, who spoke disparagingly of her, and JG recalls avoiding her on the street.

When she was fifteen, her older sister left home abruptly to escape constant fighting with her father, and for the next year JG became the butt of his violent and unreasonable accusations. Finally, in desperation, she contacted her mother, who eventually agreed to take her in after her older sister interceded on her behalf. This arrangement worked poorly because of her mother's ambivalence toward her, and she moved in to live with her elder sister who, by this time, was working and supported them both.

Throughout the interview JG spoke in negative terms of both parents and all her other transient caretakers, with the exception of her sister, whom she felt genuinely cared for her.

CASE EXAMPLE 3: CHAOTIC OUTCOME FOLLOWING PARENTAL DEATH

MG was a twenty-one-year-old student brought to the clinic by several friends following a dramatic episode of screaming and crying that had ensued on learning that her boyfriend was breaking up their relationship. When seen she was tearful and shaking, and had been sobbing constantly for more than twenty-four hours. She described feelings of unreality, stated "it couldn't be true," and expressed strong suicidal thoughts. She described a previous similar experience two years earlier that had been followed by severe depressive feelings lasting several months.

Background information revealed that her father had died when she was six years old after a prolonged chronic illness that had prevented him from working for many months. She recalled her mother's shock at receiving the telephone call informing her of father's death and remembered herself feeling "confused" and "kind of vacant." She and her three siblings were sent away to different relatives for a period of several months but eventually returned to their mother, who by that time had moved and was working. This arrangement was interrupted again a year later when mother was hospitalized for several weeks with a nervous breakdown. The subject was unable to recall clearly just what arrangements were made for her care during this time, but she remembered that she was again separated from her siblings.

When she was nine years of age, her mother remarried an old school friend. This proved to be a stormy affair, and MG became deeply embroiled in trying to mediate between them. She tried to get along with her stepfather although she had objected to mother remarrying at the time, but found it difficult to be close. When she was about twelve years of age she learned accidentally that her father had actually committed suicide and reacted to this with anger and horror. She felt strongly affected by this news for a long time, began to think a lot about her father, and tried to communicate with him using a variety of spiritualistic techniques. Her preoccupation with thoughts about her father increased throughout her adolescence, and she often had fantasies of "escaping" from her home situation and suicide. When she finally did leave home to go to a university, she quickly became involved in an intense, clinging relationship with a man.

The Christchurch Study: Loss and Attempted Suicide

In view of the promising direction pointed to by the Montreal study, it was decided that a replication of the retrospective approach of previous studies on attempted suicide would be undertaken, this time going beyond the examination of a history of early loss to a detailed examination of family stability using the ratings previously described. We first looked at our sample for the incidence of permanent loss from parental death or divorce/separation, and the timing of these events. Then we applied our family stability criteria for the period before, during, and after the loss, as we had done in the previous study. As it seemed likely that the mere presence of both parents was not always synonymous with a stable family, we took the additional step in this study of applying our family stability ratings to subjects with intact homes as well. Because we felt that to restrict the examination of the family environment only to the earliest years might prejudice the possibility that later events could have been important, we looked at the incidence of parental loss right up until the age of twenty-five and then reexamined our data for smaller age periods within this range.

In order to compare our findings with those of others, we selected for study 100 consecutive attempted-suicide patients admitted to the Emergency Department of Christchurch Hospital, New Zealand, and compared them to matched control subjects from a general practice.[6] Control subjects with a history of suicide attempt were eliminated from the study. All data were recorded during a semistructured clinical interview with the key items scored independently by two raters during a blind review of the interview protocol. Further details about the methodology and findings can be found elsewhere (Adam, Bouckoms, and Scarr, 1980; Adam, Bouckoms, and Streiner, in press).

6. Attempted suicide was defined as any intentional self-destructive act, however minor.

TABLE 13-5
Family Status to Age 25

Status	Attempted Suicide	General Practice Controls	z value[a]
Father dead	12 (12.2%)	4 (3.9%)	2.17[a]
Mother dead	8 (8.2%)	9 (8.8%)	.167
Both dead	3 (3.1%)	2 (2.2%)	.493
Divorced or separated	24 (24.5%)	8 (7.8%)	3.21[b]
Other separation	3 (3.0%)	1 (1.0%)	1.05
Intact home to age 25	48 (49.0%)	78 (76.3%)	4.03[c]
Total	98	102	

[a] $p < .05$
[b] $p < .01$
[c] $p < .001$
Z values refer to the test of independent proportions.

TABLE 13-6
Age of Subject at Time of Parental Loss

Age Period (years)	Attempted Suicide	Controls	z value
0– 5	20 (20.4%)	3 (3.0%)	3.87[c]
6–10	8 (8.2%)	3 (3.0%)	1.62
11–16	5 (5.1%)	12 (11.8%)	1.69
17–20	8 (8.2%)	2 (2.0%)	2.01[a]
21–25	6 (6.1%)	4 (3.8%)	0.714
Over 25	11 (11.2%)	17 (16.6%)	1.11
No disruption	40 (40.8%)	61 (59.8%)	2.68[b]

[a] $p < .05$
[b] $p < .01$
[c] $p < .001$

THE INCIDENCE OF PARENTAL LOSS

Initial examination of the family background data in terms of the incidence of parental loss revealed data similar to that of previous studies reported in the literature. (See tables 13-5 and 13-6.)

The incidence of parental loss overall was significantly higher in the attempted-suicide group than control group, with loss due to death of father and divorce or permanent separation of parents also reaching statistical significance. Loss in the zero- to five-year period and the seventeen- to twenty-year period was significantly higher among attempted suicides, and there was a trend toward a higher number of losses during the six- to ten-year period in this group as well. Loss in the eleven- to sixteen-year age group was greater in control subjects, but this finding did not reach statistical significance.

Separate examination of the two types of loss revealed that earlier losses (before age ten) were much more likely to have been due to divorce or separation of the parents than were later losses (after age ten). This finding suggests that studies restricting their sample to loss in the earliest years might be liable to an overreporting of loss from divorce/separation and an underreporting of loss from parental death. I will return to this point later.

FAMILY STABILITY—ALL SUBJECTS

Although the previous figures showed a higher incidence of early loss in the attempted-suicide group, the etiological significance of this to suicidal behavior could be questioned by the fact that almost as many of the sample were found to have had intact homes up until this age. Examination of the family background data in terms of our family stability categories described earlier clarifies the picture. (See table 13-7.) Only 9 percent of the attempted-suicide group reached the age of twenty-five having had a consistently stable family environment in contrast to 60 percent of our control subjects. Ninety-one percent of the attempted-suicide group were rated as either unstable (53 percent) or chaotic (38 percent), in contrast to 40 percent of our control subjects of whom 34

TABLE 13-7

Stability of Home to Age 25

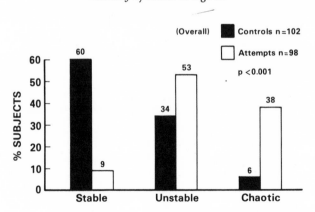

281

TABLE 13-8
Attempted Suicide Subjects n = 98
Long-Term Family Stability

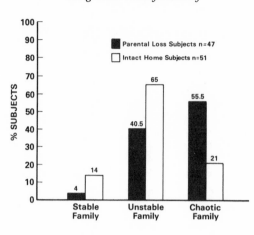

percent were classified as unstable and only 6 percent as chaotic. These differences are highly significant ($x^2(2) = 64.24$, $p < .001$).

Parental-Loss and Intact-Home Subjects Compared Although a high degree of family instability was found overall in the attempted-suicide subjects, those with a history of parental loss showed a greater *degree* of family disorganization than those with intact homes. Fifty-six percent of the loss group were rated as having chaotic homes in the long run, in contrast to 21 percent of the intact home group ($x^2(2) = 12.49$, $p < .01$). These findings are illustrated in table 13-8.

Family Stability before, during, and after Loss Although the most striking differences between the attempted-suicide and control groups were found in the long-term ratings of family stability, examination of the family environment prior to the loss also revealed significant differences between the two groups. (See table 13-9.) Only 8.5 percent of the attempted-suicide parental-loss group had homes rated as stable prior to the loss in contrast to 46 percent of the controls, and twice as many were rated as having had chaotic homes during this period (45 percent vs. 21 percent).

During the period immediately following the loss, a marked deterioration in family stability was noted in control subjects to the point that differences between attempted suicides and controls were not significant.

282

TABLE 13-9

Stability of Home before, during, and after Loss

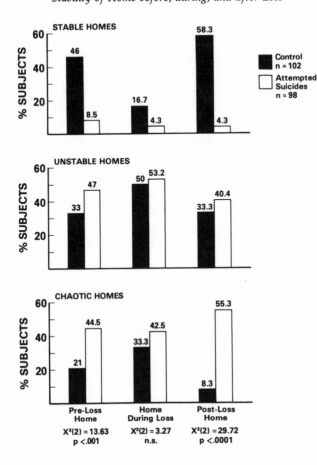

In the long run, however, the findings were nearly identical to those of the Montreal study; attempted-suicide subjects show marked deterioration in levels of family stability post-loss, whereas control subjects show a recovery to pre-loss levels of stability, and even somewhat higher.

Discussion

The findings of the Christchurch study confirm those of a number of other retrospective studies that have found a strong association between early parental loss and attempted suicide. Our review of the literature suggests that when methodological differences are taken into account, there is greater consistency among these findings than immediately meets the eye, at least insofar as the incidence of loss is concerned. In the light of our results, a closer examination of three negative reports raises questions about their findings.

Bunch and associates (1971) and Crook and Raskin (1975) found no significant difference in the incidence of parental death before the ages of sixteen and twelve respectively when they compared suicidal subjects to controls, although the latter study found a higher incidence of parental divorce/separation. Our Christchurch data found loss from divorce/separation to be proportionately greater in the early years of childhood than loss from parental death. Furthermore, we found a second peak for loss, primarily from parental death, in the seventeen- to twenty-year age period. As neither of these two studies examined for loss in this later age period, and neither looked at their data for smaller age periods within the earlier years, it is quite possible that significant differences remain hidden in their data. Many years ago Bowlby (1961) drew attention to the dangers of statistically relevant differences being masked by too superficial an examination of early-loss data.

McConaghy, Linane, and Buckle's study (1966), which has been quoted as not supporting any relationship between early loss and suicidal attempt (*Lancet*, 1966) is more difficult to compare because of the smaller size of his two samples of attempted suicide and because of his unique definition of parental deprivation (separation from either parent for three months or more). If one only considers his figures for loss from parental death, then his findings for attempted-suicide subjects are much the same as ours, although his figures for his controls are much higher. While we cannot account for this higher incidence of loss in his controls, the fact that they were hospital patients and that he failed to screen out those with a history of suicidal attempt may have, in part, been responsible.

Some of the apparent discrepancies of studies that have quoted high incidence figures for "parental deprivation" take on a different light when the larger role of family instability as a measure is considered.

Close reading of these works suggests that at least some of these authors were considering variables of family instability similar to our own in their broad definitions of deprivation, and it is interesting to note that their high figures for such deprivation correspond rather closely to our figures for long-term family instability in suicidal patients. Most of the case histories reported in Palmer's 1941 study, for example, would have been rated on our criteria as having unstable or chaotic early family life.

As early as 1962 Bruhn noted that the circumstances following upon parental loss were likely to be as important as the loss itself, but his suggestion to consider this in planning future studies has largely been ignored. Greer, in both his studies (Greer, 1966; Greer, Gunn, and Koller, 1966), and Koller and Castanos (1968), in their replication of Greer's study, considered the family environment subsequent to loss in their subjects but found no difference between attempted suicides and controls. Their criteria, however, were primarily concerned with whether or not the subject continued to live with his family after the loss and did not consider the *quality* of care given. To our knowledge no study before ours has attempted to compare the quality of the family environment prior to the loss or during the period of the loss with the long-term outcome following loss.

Our finding of a high degree of suicidal preoccupation in a group of students selected for study only on the basis of parental loss adds weight to the retrospective findings of our second study, although the special nature of the sample makes replication in a broader group mandatory. The only other work in the literature that studies patients selected on the basis of early loss is that of Gay and Tonge (1967), who also found suicide attempts to be more frequent in subjects with early parental loss. Their study group, however, consisted of psychiatric patients, and their criteria for loss included any separation of six months or more before the age of fifteen.

Although the relationship between permanent loss of parents and suicidal ideation and attempt appears to be a strong one, the association is more direct if one considers the consequences of these events in terms of the provision of adequate parental care and a secure environment in the ensuing years of the child's development (see also Raphael, chapter 7 herein). The death of a parent, however painful to the child, his siblings, and the surviving parent, need not irreparably disrupt the home, and divorce or separation of parents following years of chronic strife may sometimes result in an improved situation for everyone concerned. Our data indicate that when the family has accommodated successfully to loss or has been adequately reconstituted through remarriage or the presence of alternative surrogate parental figures, suicidal trends are unlikely to develop. On the other hand, when the disruption has resulted in major and longstanding family disorganization, a predisposition to suicidal thinking is very probable and the likelihood that this could result in suicidal behavior later in life is high. When a loss has occurred that results in a chaotic environment, such as we have described in our two studies, suicidal trends seem not only likely but virtually inevitable.

Although we have given a good deal of attention in these studies to families with a history of parental loss, it is clear from our Christchurch data that this is not the only situation leading to suicidal predispostion. Many families technically intact were, on closer examination, inadequate in providing a consistent and secure environment for the child. When these intact families were rated as unstable or chaotic, a significant association was noted with both suicidal ideation and suicidal attempt, as it was in homes with parental loss.

Our finding in the Christchurch study that attempted-suicide and control subjects differed significantly in family stability *prior* to the experience of actual loss is an interesting one and raises the question of whether loss in itself is of direct significance to the development of suicidal trends. Two explanations would appear to be possible. It could be argued that family instability is the primary causal factor and that the experience of loss as such is a coincidental finding, unrelated in any way to etiology of suicidal behavior. Alternatively, one could argue that, although family instability might arise from a variety of circumstances, it is particularly likely to do so following the permanent loss of a parent. Our finding that the long-term family stability of the parental-loss subgroup of attempted suicides was qualitatively worse than that of attempted suicides with intact homes would appear to support the latter explanation.

These conclusions have considerable support in the work of John Bowlby (1980), who has documented extensive evidence to indicate the variety of experiences in childhood that may lead to later psychopathology besides the experience of permanent parental loss. Important among these are those conditions that lead to persistent or recurrent insecurity about the availability of parental figures or their love.

Theoretical Considerations

In an earlier work discussing some preliminary findings of the Montreal study (Adam, 1973), we advanced a hypothesis in which early loss was viewed as a *predisposing factor* leading to a propensity to suicidal preoccupation. Recent loss, or the threat of it, was seen as a specific *precipitating factor* leading to activation of the underlying suicidal proclivity and, in some cases, to acting it out in a suicide attempt or actual suicide. The presence of organic brain disease, serious personality disturbances, and states of intoxication, all statistically correlated with suicidal behavior, were seen as *contributing factors* favoring the emergence of the preexisting suicidal proclivity. This model has much in common with that advanced by Brown and Harris for depression (1978; Brown, chapter 12 herein), which they see as the interaction of specific vulnerability factors (including early loss), current provoking agents (which determine onset), and symptom-formation factors (which influence course).

While the data reported here support several aspects of this earlier theoretical model, our findings regarding the modifying factors that influence the response to loss and the importance of equivalent situations of profound insecurity in families with intact homes suggest it should be altered. In modified form, it may be illustrated thus:

FIGURE 13-1
Etiological Model

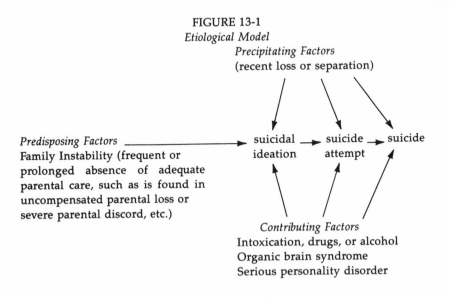

Precipitating Factors
(recent loss or separation)

Predisposing Factors
Family Instability (frequent or prolonged absence of adequate parental care, such as is found in uncompensated parental loss or severe parental discord, etc.)

suicidal ideation → suicide attempt → suicide

Contributing Factors
Intoxication, drugs, or alcohol
Organic brain syndrome
Serious personality disorder

Explanatory hypotheses accounting for the association of loss and suicide have leaned heavily on classical psychoanalytic formulations that have stressed depressive dynamics and the mechanism of identification. According to this hypothesis, suicide is seen as a destructive attack on an internalized lost object that expresses both rage and the wish for retaliation (Freud, 1957). Klein (1948) has suggested that such an attack on the "bad" object may also serve a function in preserving an image of the "good" object, and Hendricks (1940) has pointed out that suicidal impulses may also express a wish to regain an idealized lost object through death.

The suggestion that loss might be more specifically related to suicide when the identification was made with a person already dead, particularly when the death occurred in childhood, was made by Zilboorg (1937). Dorpat, Jackson, and Ripley (1965), who considered that their findings supported Zilboorg's view, suggested that whereas loss of a parent through death was likely to be associated with successful suicide, "lesser" losses such as from divorce or separation were more likely to be associated with suicide attempt. Dorpat's failure to compare either of his study groups with nonsuicidal controls makes these findings hard to assess, and the study has not been replicated elsewhere.

While there is a good deal of evidence from studies of children's reactions to the death of a parent to suggest that identification is often a feature of their mourning process, the relationship of this to suicidal impulses is far from clear. Much confusion appears to exist over the use of the term "identification" to refer to the child assuming characteristics of the dead parent and its use to explain the wish for reunion with the dead parent, which might be better understood in attachment terms (Bowlby, 1980). The data from both of our studies show clearly that suicidal tendencies are at least as likely to be associated with loss from divorce/separation as they are following the death of a parent or, for that matter, where family instability of sufficient degree is present, without an actual physical loss. Furthermore, the emphasis on the wish to die as the primary motivation in suicidal behavior, as suggested by the classical formulation, does not do justice to the well-known fact that the majority of "suicidal" acts are nonlethal in intent and, for the most part, motivated by clearly interpersonal factors. Stengel (1964), writing about attempted suicide, has spoken of the appeal function to significant others in the environment, and Henderson (1974 and chapter 11 herein) describes suicide attempts as one form of "care-eliciting" behavior, which he proposes is an essential part of the phenomenon of attachment.

While we agree with this view, we would extend it considerably, seeing suicidal behavior in more general terms as a manifestation of attachment behavior in adult life emerging in response to the threat of loss of attachment figures and serving important functions in the striving to recover and to maintain proximity to them. Such behavior involves not only an appeal for care and sympathy but, as Bowlby points out, important and urgent expressions of anger and protest directed at an offending attachment figure who is simultaneously appealed to, punished, and implicitly enjoined against further threats to leave. Moreover, we believe that the successful suicidal act more often than not can best be understood as a distorted communication to important attachment figures both past and present. In this case, however, the disillusionment is more chronic, the likelihood of a positive environmental response less, and the degree of hopelessness more pervasive than it is when attempts at suicide are unsuccessful. The final dialogue with the object world in the successful suicide is more deeply internalized, more widely generalized, and more highly symbolized ("good-bye, cruel world").

Clinical observations of the behavior of attempted-suicide patients during their acute presentation suggest striking similarities to the responses of children following brief separations. The sequences of protest, despair, and detachment, so eloquently described by John Bowlby, are often clearly visible in the patients' attitudes to significant family members and caretakers in the clinical setting. Outbursts of anger and aggression intermingled with pleading and clinging are extremely common, as is aloofness and apparent emotional detachment, which contrast sharply with the desperate scenes of a few hours before (Adam and Adam, 1978). Background information typically reveals a history of extreme insecurity in relation to primary attachment figures with chronic difficulties in forming and maintaining close relationships with others later in life. This relationship is supported by a vast epidemiological and sociological literature attesting to the overrepresentation of persons with broken marriages and difficulties in interpersonal relationships among those with suicidal tendencies (Weissman, 1974). In addition, an extensive body of literature is accumulating that points to the association of similar disturbances in the stability of early attachments and depression (Brown and Harris, 1978; Lloyd, 1980), alcoholism (Birtchnell, 1972), excessive dependency

289

(Birtchnell, 1975), and delinquency and antisocial personality disorder (Rutter, 1972), all of which are strongly intercorrelated with suicidal behavior. Brief separations in childhood regularly lead to the psychological response characterized by Bowlby (1973) as separation anxiety, and Keeler (1954) reports a high incidence of suicidal preoccupations among children brought to psychiatric attention following traumatic permanent losses. That such experiences might contribute directly to the existence of the chronic feelings of low self-esteem, hopelessness, and hostility toward others so frequently described in suicidal patients (Weissman, Fox, and Klerman, 1973) seems a reasonable assumption, as is the likelihood that these psychological states contribute to the cycle of interpersonal difficulties that pervade these persons' lives.

The placing of these observations within the context of attachment theory allows for the consideration of much established data on suicide within a developmental context. Furthermore, it serves to clarify some of the more puzzling aspects of the vast epidemiological and sociological data on the subject. For example, nonlethal suicidal behavior, which is well known to be more frequent among younger individuals, is clearly associated with crises in interpersonal relationships, whereas fatal suicidal behavior, which is more frequent in the later years of life, is associated with recent bereavement, social isolation, and diminished personal and social resources (Weissman, 1974; Bunch, 1972). Viewed in attachment terms, the peaking of suicide attempts in the earlier adult years could be seen as a manifestation of more active attachment behavior among a group prone to form insecure attachments but with abundant opportunities for them, whereas the increase in actual suicide in later life may reflect the greater vulnerability to the consequences of loss that is associated with the diminished opportunities to form new relationships. The successful formation of stable attachments throughout the early years may shield many otherwise vulnerable individuals from reexperiencing underlying separation anxiety. Repeated failure to form stable attachments, which is made more likely by associated personality difficulties and excessive demands on attachment figures, may ultimately lead to the extreme social isolation that is such a large part of the context of successful suicide. Viewed in this light, attempted suicide and actual suicide may not represent different but overlapping groups, as has been suggested by the epidemiological data, but rather the same group on different points of a developmental continuum of attachment.

A word must be said about the well-known association of attempted suicide with younger females and successful suicide with older males, a relationship that has defied adequate explanation. In both of our studies we noted a much higher incidence of both suicidal ideation and attempt among female subjects than males, with this ratio being even higher among those with a history of early loss. This would appear to indicate a greater female vulnerability to the effects of loss.

Whether this is due to specific biological and developmental differences between the sexes or to the fact that our culture provides more alternatives to the male, enabling him to buffer the vicissitudes of insecure attachments, is not clear. If the latter case were true, then females might have a greater need to activate attachment behavior than males, particularly in the earlier part of life when work and other diversions are more available to men. Men, however, may subsequently exhibit a greater vulnerability to loss in later life when these alternatives to close attachments are threatened by ill health, bereavement, and retirement. Put another way, women may be more reliant on attachment to others for the maintenance of self-esteem and emotional stability, and this may result in attachments that are more enduring and protective in the long run than those of the male.

Our discussion has taken us well beyond the simple consideration of the role of "early loss" as an etiological variable to a broader consideration of the context in which such losses occur and some of their consequences. In addition, we have attempted to place these findings within the framework of a theoretical model for suicidal behavior and have made some attempt to integrate them with the findings of others. That subjects with a pathological outcome following loss (as defined by the presence of suicidal tendencies) frequently came from homes that were previously unstable and that others with a similar outcome had disorganized homes with no permanent loss argues against the emphasis on early loss as an exclusive variable in the etiology of suicidal behavior. It does not, however, diminish its importance as a variable of great importance leading to fundamental insecurity in relation to primary attachment figures. A good deal more information is needed to elaborate the variety of circumstances determining the consequences described in our global ratings of family stability.

The choice of suicidal behavior as a marker of attachment pathology may be seen as a rather narrow focus in view of the rather extensive data implicating the role of early loss in depression and other psychiatric conditions, but at least it has the virtue of being subject to reliable definition allowing for easier comparison with other research data. Suicidal acts have long attracted the interest of sociologists as an indicator of social pathology, and they are, in addition, statistically

291

correlated with a number of other serious psychiatric conditions. Although our data do not directly add to the body of information about these other conditions, there is obvious overlap between them, and certain aspects of our methodology may have direct application to their study.

In the third volume of his monumental study on attachment and loss, John Bowlby, speaking of some common clinical disorders, states:

> ... although disruptions of bonds, and experiences related to or consequent upon disruption, undoubtedly play a causal role in these and other conditions, we remain ignorant of how large a causal role they play and in precisely what circumstances they play it. In order to find out, continuing research, using a broad range of methods, will be necessary. Only when this is done, and the conceptual framework itself refined, elaborated and tested, shall we know how productive the enquiry described will turn out to be. (1980, p. 441)

It is our hope that the work summarized here, which was directly stimulated by the pioneering work of John Bowlby, has made a contribution toward these ends and offers some directions for further research.

REFERENCES

Adam, K. S. 1973. Childhood parental loss, suicidal ideation and suicidal behavior. In *The child and his family*, ed. E. James Anthony. New York: Wiley.

———, and Adam, G. 1978. Attachment theory and attempted suicide. Paper presented at the Fifteenth Annual Congress of Royal Australian and New Zealand College of Psychiatrists, Singapore.

Adam, K. S., Bouckoms, A., and Scarr, G. 1980. Attempted suicide in Christchurch: A controlled study. *Australian and New Zealand Journal of Psychiatry* 14(4):305–314.

Adam, K. S., Bouckoms, A., and Streiner, D. Parental loss and family stability in attempted suicide. *Archives of General Psychiatry*. (In press.)

Adam, K. S., Lohrenz, J. G., and Harper, D. 1973. Suicidal ideation and parental loss: A preliminary research report. *Canadian Psychiatric Association Journal* 18:95–100.

———, and Streiner, D. Early parental loss and suicidal ideation in university students. *Canadian Journal of Psychiatry*. (In press.)

Batchelor, L. R. C., and Napier, M. C. 1953. Broken homes and attempted suicide. *British Journal of Delinquency* 4:99–108.

Birtchnell, J. 1970. The relationship between attempted suicide, depression and parent death. *British Journal of Psychiatry* 116:307–313.

———. 1972. Early parent death and psychiatric diagnosis. *Social Psychiatry* 7:202–210.

———. 1975. The personality characteristics of early-bereaved psychiatric patients. *Social Psychiatry* 10:97–103.

Bowlby, J. 1961. Childhood mourning and its implications for psychiatry. *American Journal of Psychiatry* 118:481–497.

_____. 1973. *Attachment and loss. Vol. 2: Separation: Anxiety and anger.* New York: Basic Books.

_____. 1980. *Attachment and loss. Vol. 3: Loss: Sadness and depression.:* New York: Basic Books.

Brown, G. W., and Harris, T. 1978. *Social origins of depression: A study of psychiatric disorder in women.* London: Tavistock.

Bruhn, J. G. 1962. Broken homes among attempted suicides and psychiatric outpatients: A comparative study. *Journal of Mental Science* 108:772–779.

Bunch, J. 1972. Recent bereavement in relation to suicide. *Journal of Psychosomatic Research* 16:361–366.

_____, Barraclough, B.; Nelson, B.; and Sainsbury, P. 1971. Early parental bereavement and suicide. *Social Psychiatry* 6(4):200–204.

Crook, T., and Raskin, A. 1975. Association of childhood parental loss with attempted suicide and depression. *Journal of Consulting and Clinical Psychology* 43(2):277.

Dorpat, T. L., Jackson, J. K., and Ripley, H. S. 1965. Broken homes and attempted suicide and completed suicide. *Archives of General Psychiatry* 12:213–216.

Freud, S. 1957. Mourning and melancholia. In *The standard edition of the complete psychological works of Sigmund Freud,* ed. J. Strachey, vol. 19. London: Hogarth Press. (Originally published 1915.)

Gay, M. J., and Tonge, W. L. 1967. The late effects of loss of parents in childhood. *British Journal of Psychiatry* 113:753–759.

Greer, S. 1964. The relationship between parental loss and attempted suicide: A control study. *British Journal of Psychiatry* 110:698–705.

_____. 1966. Parental loss and attempted suicide: A further report. *British Journal of Psychiatry* 112:465–470.

_____, Gunn, J. C., and Koller, K. M. 1966. Aetiological factors in attempted suicide. *British Medical Journal* 2:1352–1355.

Henderson, S. 1974. Care eliciting behavior in man. *Journal of Nervous and Mental Disorders* 159:3, 172–181.

Hendricks, I. 1940. Suicide as wish-fulfillment. *Psychiatric Quarterly* 14:30–42.

Hill, O. W. 1969. The association of childhood bereavement with suicidal attempt in depressive illness. *British Journal of Psychiatry* 115:301–304.

Keeler, W. R. 1954. Children's reaction to death of a parent. In *Depression,* ed. P. Hoch and J. Zubin. New York: Grune & Stratton.

Klein, M. 1948. A contribution to the psychogenesis of manic-depressive states (1934). In *Contributions to psycho-analysis, 1921–1945.* London: Hogarth Press and The Institute of Psycho-Analysis.

Koller, K. M., and Castanos, J. N. 1968. The influence of childhood parental deprivation in attempted suicide. *Medical Journal of Australia* 1:396–399.

Lancet. 1966. Parental deprivation and mental health (editorial). 2:325–326.

Levi, L. D., Fales, C. H.; Stein, M; and Sharp, V. H. 1966. Separation and attempted suicide. *Archives of General Psychiatry* 15:158–164.

Lloyd, C. 1980. Life events and depressive disorder reviewed. I. Events as predisposing factors. *Archives of General Psychiatry* 37:529–535.

Lukianowicz, N. 1972. Suicidal behavior: An attempt to modify the environment. *British Journal of Psychiatry* 121:387–390.

McConaghy, N., Linane, J., and Buckle, R. C. 1966. Parental deprivation and attempted suicide. *Medical Journal of Australia* 1:886–892.

Miller, J. 1971. Children's reactions to the death of a parent: A review of the psychoanalytic literature. *Journal of the American Psychoanalytic Association* 19(4):697–719.

Moss, L. M., and Hamilton, D. M. 1956. Psychotherapy of suicidal patients. *American Journal of Psychiatry* 112:814–820.

Nagera, H. 1970. Children's reactions to the death of important objects. In *The psychoanalytic study of the child,* ed. R. S. Eissler et al., vol. 25. New Haven, Conn.: Yale University Press.

Oliver, R. G., Kaminski, Z.; Tudor, K.; and Hetzel, B. S. 1971. The epidemiology of attempted suicide as seen in the casualty department, Alfred Hospital, Melbourne. *Medical Journal of Australia* 1:833–839.

Palmer, D. M. 1941. Factors in suicidal attempts: A review of 25 consecutive cases. *Journal of Nervous and Mental Disease* 4:421–442.

Reitman, F. 1942. On the predictability of suicide. *Journal of Mental Science* 88:580–582.

Rutter, M. 1972. *Maternal deprivation reassessed.* Baltimore, Md.: Penguin Books.

Stengel, E. 1964. *Suicide and attempted suicide.* New York: Penguin Books.

Walton, H. J. 1958. Suicidal behaviour in depressive illness: A study of aetiological factors in suicide. *Journal of Mental Science* 104:884–891.

Weissman, M. 1974. The epidemiology of suicide attempts. *Archives of General Psychiatry* 30:737–746.

————, Fox, K., and Klerman, G. L. 1973. Hostility and depression associated with suicide attempts. *American Journal of Psychiatry* 130(4):450–455.

Werry, J. S., and Pedder, J. 1976. Self poisoning in Aukland. *New Zealand Medical Journal* 560(83):183–187.

Zilboorg, G. 1937. Considerations on suicide with particular reference to that of the young. *American Journal of Orthopsychiatry* 7:15–31.

14

Colin Murray Parkes

ATTACHMENT AND THE PREVENTION OF MENTAL DISORDERS

DESPITE the fact that the predominant focus in medicine is on cure rather than prevention, it is preventive rather than curative medicine that has been responsible for much of the reduction in the mortality rate and for the improvement in the overall health of the developed countries that has occurred in the last 200 years. These results have been achieved, in most instances, by analyses of the causal chains of events that lead to disease. This enables people at special risk to be identified and measures to be undertaken to reduce that risk.

The complexity and multiplicity of the causal chains of events that precede mental illness are such that preventive psychiatry has lagged behind the rest of preventive medicine, just as clinical psychiatry has lagged behind the rest of clinical medicine. Psychiatrists have been divided into those who espouse theories of psychodynamics, which are rightly criticized as "prescientific," and those who adopt empirical treatments for symptoms without going too deeply into the chains of events that have led up to them.

Nevertheless it would be wrong to say that we are ignorant of the causes of mental disorder. Numerous well-conducted research projects have pointed to genetic inheritance, perinatal influences, childhood environment, and many events and situations in later life, any or all of which can contribute to bring about the types of thinking, feeling, and

295

behaving we term mental illness. The problem is not that we cannot identify causal factors, but that we lack a clear understanding of the intermediate variables, the chains of events that link such factors together.

It is the strength of John Bowlby's trilogy, *Attachment and Loss* (1969, 1973, 1980) that he provides a firmly based and well worked out model that explains some of these chains of events. The study of attachment throws light on many but not all types of mental disorder, and in this chapter I hope to show how some of these can be prevented. The field is large, and we must continue to rely on commonsense and clinical experience to fill some of the gaps in the research.

Attachments and Their Subsequent Effects

Bowlby's work lays great emphasis on the ways in which the interactions between the mother (or mother substitute) and the maturing child give rise to expectations and behavior patterns in the child that may enhance or undermine subsequent personal development. Once they have arisen, interpersonal problems often produce feedback effects that cause them to persist.

Two types of behavior indicative of insecure attachment in infancy are *avoidance behavior* and *clinging*. The former is described by Main in chapter 2, and we may suppose that it predisposes the child to become unusually self-reliant. Having learned that he must not make bids for attention if he is going to be tolerated at all, the young child inhibits attachment behavior. As with all forms of avoidance, once the child has learned to avoid the dangerous or punishing situations that result if he exhibits attachment he has no way of finding out whether or not the danger has passed. Hence his avoidant behavior will tend to persist.

Clinging may be the opposite of avoidance but it too is evidence of insecure attachment (see chapter 1). In this instance the young child learns that in order to keep mother close, he must exhibit frequent and intense attachment behavior. Consequently we should not be surprised to find that he becomes unusually other-reliant.

Clinical studies suggest that both of these behavior patterns are likely to persist into adult life but, whereas they may have proved effective ways of maintaining proximity to mother in childhood, they often

296

have the opposite effect in later life. The compulsively self-reliant person becomes increasingly isolated from others, who naturally interpret his lack of overt affection as a sign of indifference. The excessively clinging person soon finds his behavior evoking the rejection it was intended to prevent, a sequence that only makes him cling the harder and sets up a cycle of clinging/rejection/clinging, and so forth. The former disturbance is seen in its most extreme form in certain psychopaths whose overt indifference to others leads to repeated rejection. (Evidence from several studies was reviewed by Bowlby, 1968). Evidence for the latter sequence was discovered in Lindeman's (1960) study of students attending a university health center. Those students who had suffered loss of or separation from mother in the early years of life were found to have a high incidence of episodes of depression and suicidal ideation (see also Adam, chapter 13 herein). These episodes were found to have followed a predictable cycle of clinging and rejection, which was repeated in the therapy situation when the therapist found himself unable to tolerate the unreasonable demands made by these students. Causal chains of these kinds may well underlie some of the psychiatric disorders discussed in the preceding chapters that have been shown to have a statistical relationship to rejection by or loss of a parent in early childhood.

There is now considerable evidence that the quality of parenting a person receives in childhood is likely to affect the quality of caretaking behavior he or she exhibits as a parent. Those who have experienced insecure attachments to their parents commonly have difficulty in providing a secure base around which their own children can become securely attached to them. Hence it is only too easy for another type of cycle—a cycle of deprivation—to be set up that insures that problems in parenting will be passed from one generation to the next. As we have seen in chapter 5, the woman who was battered as a baby is more likely than others to harm her own children. A major research undertaking in the years to come must be the exploration of means to break such cycles.

But all cycles have to start somewhere, and the work described in this book suggests a number of circumstances that can impair the healthy development of the mother-child bond. Death of or early separation from a parent, nonresponsiveness in the child (e.g., due to drugs or birth trauma), disappointment of the mother in the child, depression in the mother, and other similar problems have all been suggested as capable of interfering with bonding. It follows that any improvement in the provision of good postnatal care and adequate parenting in childhood is likely to reduce the risk of psychiatric disorder in later life.

Autonomy and the Ability to Cope with Change

Attachments may determine how a child reacts to novel situations and other potential threats. A secure attachment provides a secure base from which to explore the world. In the normal course of maturation, as time passes the child tends to exhibit progressively less attachment behavior and more exploratory behavior. This insures that he will build and keep revising an increasingly more accurate internal model of the world (or assumptive world[1]).

With exploration comes self-confidence and relative autonomy. But the aim of exploration is not to produce absolute self-reliance, but to help the individual to make realistic judgments of his own strengths and limitations so that he will know when it is appropriate for him to ask for help. Attachment, on the other hand, may enable him to learn about the strengths of others so that he begins to discover who can be trusted to give help when it is needed and how that help can be obtained.

This view is supported by Heard's findings (chapter 8 herein) that insecure attachments can impair the learning of new skills. Because of the difficulty the insecurely attached child experiences in exploration and thus in building an accurate assumptive world, such children may lack a sense of "fit" between themselves and the world about them.

Similarly the persistence of insecure attachments into adult life may impair a person's ability to modify his assumptive world in the face of change. And failure to cope with change is found to be a precipitating factor in a number of mental illnesses. For example, loss of mother before the age of eleven is a vulnerability factor that increases a woman's susceptibility to depression in the face of emergent life events (see chapter 12 herein).

It seems to me that the loss of a sense of purpose or meaning in life that so commonly follows a major loss results from awareness of a

---

1. I use the term "assumptive world" to imply the world that a person assumes to exist on the basis of his previous experience. It is to be distinguished from other models that can be regarded as "possible worlds," "dreaded worlds," "hoped-for worlds," and so forth (Parkes, 1971).

discrepancy between one's assumptive world and the external situations that impinge. Marris's "structures of meaning" (chapter 10 herein) are bound up with those world models that allow the individual to anticipate and cope with the impinging world.

In the face of major change the person turns first to his assumptive world to provide him with the orientation he hopes will bring about a sense of fit between the world that is and that which should be. Failing to discover such a fit, he turns naturally to attachment figures in the hope that they will protect and help him to cope during the period of transition when he is reviewing and revising his world models. One reason for the peculiarly traumatic quality of the transition that follows loss of a loved person is the fact that this is often the very attachment figure to whom the survivor would normally turn for support at times of change. Hence, perhaps, Henderson's finding that people who have few "available attachments" are at special risk of developing neurotic symptoms under adversity (chapter 11 herein). It follows that any person who is willing to offer support to people who are faced with loss or change and to offer himself as a temporary attachment figure is likely to be perceived as helpful. Such a person will need to provide reassurance of the safety of the person in transition and encourage exploration of the world that is lost and the world that remains. That this is in fact the case is suggested by Raphael's (1977), study to be discussed.

Some Problems in Relearning an Assumptive World

Learning theory throws some interesting light on the processes by which a person unlearns expectations and behavior patterns. In extinction, the repeated occurrence of a response, no longer followed by reinforcement, leads to a decrease in that response. A person who is faced with a major transition can be seen as possessing a set of behavior patterns that can no longer lead to their usual outcomes. For instance, the newly bereaved are repeatedly faced with stimuli that evoke attachment behavior directed toward the lost person. Bowlby and Parkes (1970) have shown how the "searching" behavior characteristic of acute grief is eventually extinguished.

But there are two situations in which the extinction of behavior patterns may be delayed. Anything that removes the stimuli that set the occasion for the behavior will cause it to remain in abeyance but with the potential to appear in full whenever those stimuli occur. And any behavior pattern that has been established in circumstances of intermittent reinforcement will become very difficult to extinguish.

These two situations seem to me to correspond fairly closely to the situations associated with the insecure attachments just described, avoidance and clinging. On the one hand a person may learn to avoid pain or grief by avoiding the circumstances that evoke it. This is seen clearly in people who put away reminders of a dead person and distract themselves by hectic activities—a policy that is thought by clinicians to be a cause of delayed grief. On the other hand we have the chronic grief that commonly follows the dissolution of ambivalent relationships and clinging relationships, two circumstances in which attachment behavior can be expected to have been intermittently reinforced.

The Treatment of Avoided and Chronic Grief

Again from learning theory we expect that any intervention that helps the avoidant person to confront the stimuli that evoke attachment behavior will set in train the work of grieving, as a result of which the obsolete model of the world will be explored and relinquished. This is the method recommended by Lindeman in his classic paper, "The Symptomatology and Management of Grief" (1944). It has become a major part of all services for the bereaved that have been introduced, and it constitutes the rationale for Ramsay's (1979) method of treating pathological grief by forced confrontation. Using a similar technique Mawson and associates (1981) have demonstrated modest improvement in a significant proportion of a mixed group of psychiatric patients with pathological grief reactions compared to a control group.

Unfortunately, the approach cannot be expected to work well when applied to people who, far from avoiding the expression of grief, are already engaged in chronic grieving and are possibly being intermittently reinforced for it as a consequence of the sympathy and other secondary gains evoked by grief. This may explain why Mawson's treatment of a mixed group of "avoiders" and "chronic grievers" was not uniformly successful.

In addition, Lindeman's (1960) and my own work suggest that there is a real risk that the griever will transfer his or her ambivalent and/or clinging behavior onto the therapist. Nevertheless, clinical experience shows that the situation is seldom hopeless, and a planned program of progressive rehabilitation will sometimes succeed. In such cases client and counselor need to agree on clearly specified goals that the client will attempt to reach as a condition of continued support. As in early childhood, "nothing succeeds like success," and it is possible for the other-reliant person to become increasingly autonomous. Such therapy is inevitably time-consuming, and the therapist needs to be aware of the extent of his own commitment when taking on such work.

Other Determinants of Outcome after Loss

In describing the part that insecure attachments arising in childhood play in later life, I do not intend to imply that these are the only factors that determine how an adult will react to loss or change. Just as there is a wide range between adequate and inadequate parenting, so there must be a wide range of vulnerability to subsequent losses, and many other factors have been shown to play a part in deciding how a particular person will respond to a particular change in his life.

Research into the factors that determine the outcome of one type of loss, bereavement, has been carried out prospectively by Maddison and Walker (1967), Raphael (1977), and Parkes (1976). In each of these studies a group of widows and/or widowers were identified at or shortly after bereavement and systematic data collected. This was then intercorrelated with "outcome" measures one or more years later when a second interview was carried out. The outcome measures included systematic counts of symptoms that had occurred for the first time or had become worse during the preceding year; changes in the consumption of drugs, alcohol, and tobacco; replies to "depression" inventories; and systematic assessments of the use of health care services.

Maddison's and Raphael's studies have demonstrated the importance of the family as an influence on grieving, with poorest health outcome in widows who perceive their family as "unhelpful." Multiple losses are also inculpated. Parkes's work confirms the importance of sudden, untimely deaths as a damaging influence in young widows and widowers and suggests that ambivalent relationships and those

301

characterized by clinging are also pathogenic. This work also shows that people from the lower socioeconomic groups who may have few resources in reserve to enable them to cope with stress are also at greater risk after bereavement.

Although these studies were not carried out with a view to confirming or refuting any particular theoretical model, they do provide support for the conceptual framework already outlined. In conjunction with evidence from other sources, it is now possible to subdivide the determinants of outcome into (1) those that predispose to avoidant or delayed responses, (2) those that predispose to clinging or chronic grief, and (3) those that affect the magnitude but not the form of the response.

This subdivision is necessary and will be analyzed in some detail since it seems that different types of preventive intervention are needed if we are to influence the course of the various pathological griefs in a favorable way.

Much of the evidence for the detailed picture is derived from clinical sources and may not be strong in the scientific sense. But the overall picture that emerges is a coherent one, and it seems reasonable to present it here in the hope that further research will fill out the picture and lead to the development of well-founded services aimed at preventing the illnesses that can result from other types of loss.

Postulated Causes of Avoidance of Grief and Their Preventive Implications

The following circumstances are thought to predispose to avoidant responses.

1. Social influences—for example, social pressures that result when a "stiff upper lip" is thought necessary in order to survive the immediate stresses of, for instance, trench warfare (Gorer, 1965) or concentration camps (Cohen, 1953). These responses can be expected to persist after the initial cause has gone.

2. Family influences blocking the expression of grief.

3. Demands of dependents. It is common for mothers with young children to avoid grieving in order to "protect" their children.

Brown's studies (reported in chapter 12) suggest that mothers with young children at home are at special risk following loss and change.

4. The social attribution of "breakdown" to any loss of emotional control. The fear of madness resulting from loss of control over emotional expression may cause some people to inhibit the expression of grief and avoid situations that evoke it.

5. Fear of the physiological accompaniments of distress, which are often interpreted as evidence of incipient breakdown in physical health, may cause some people to avoid the circumstances that give rise to them. A common way of doing this is to take tranquilizers, sedatives, or antidepressants that, by blocking these physiological processes, are expected to "cure" grief. There is some inconclusive evidence, however, that these methods, if they succeed at all, do so only by delaying or distorting the expression of grief.

6. Other environmental demands—such as opportunities for personal advancement or risky adventures—may be real or assumed reasons for avoiding grief.

In all these cases the implications for prevention are clear. A counterculture must be established that recognizes the psychological need for grief and reassures the individual of the normality of the psychological and physiological symptoms that accompany it. This can be done by both public education and by individual and group counseling.

Postulated Causes of Chronic Grief and Their Preventive Implications

Another set of circumstances can be proposed as likely to predispose to the development of chronic as opposed to avoided grief.

1. Social influences may idealize the mourner and perpetuate the process of grieving. Consider the social attitudes to survivors of the Hiroshima bomb, who became identified as "Hibakusha" (Lifton, 1964) or the behavior of children who identify a bereaved parent as a living memorial to the dead person and are shocked by any attempt to achieve autonomy, particularly if it involves sexual behavior.

2. Relationships in which the person who is lost was ambivalently

303

loved. These are common precursors of the chronic self-punitive grief, which is often found in bereaved psychiatric patients (Parkes, 1965) and is predictive of poor outcome following bereavement (Parkes, 1976).[2]

3. Relationships in which the lost person had fostered a sense of inferiority or insecurity in the partner, who is left with little confidence in his capacity to survive the loss (Parkes, 1976).

4. Undue pressure on the survivor to undertake tasks and responsibilities for which he does not believe himself to be qualified or capable. Queen Victoria is an example. Almost from her birth she was told she must become an ideal monarch. Prince Albert had a very similar view, and throughout their marriage Victoria and Albert drove themselves to conform to this ideal. Albert's death left Victoria in an impossible position, and it is not surprising that she grieved severely and that her grief became an excuse for her continued withdrawal from public life. By an interesting paradox it also created the circumstances by which the public, because of the extent of the queen's withdrawal, could begin to project onto her their own needs for an ideal monarch. By the end of her long reign she had become a virtual "faerie" queen (Longford, 1964).

5. The absence of any satisfactory alternative to the mourning role—for example, the person who, by reason of age or disability is, or feels himself to be, on the "scrap-heap." Our society provides few roles for the widow save that of mourner.

The chances of pathological developments can be expected to be reduced if support is given to the bereaved and to those who support them throughout the period of grieving. In particular, the bereaved need to be encouraged to express feelings of guilt and anger, help in finding creative rather than destructive solutions, and guidance in finding a new place in the world. The time will come when they may need reassurance that their duty to the dead has been done and permission to explore new sources of personal service and reward. Experience in Aberfan, the Welsh village where a landslide of waste material from the local coal mine destroyed the village school, showed how the problems of guilt and anger can lead to personal growth and development rather than crippling mental illness. (My account of this work has been published in a postscript to the Allen and Unwin edition of Kaj Erickson's book, *In the Wake of the Flood*, 1979.)

2. Reanalysis of this data indicates that ambivalence can also predispose to avoidance of grief, for example, by providing justification for denial that attachment ever existed.

Other Determinants of Grief and
Their Implications for Prevention

Finally there is a third set of circumstances that may contribute to the magnitude of the grief without necessarily determining what form it will take.

1. Lack of preparation. Evidence from several prospective studies (e.g., Natterson and Knudson, 1960; Ball, 1977; Lundin, 1979; and Parkes, 1976) indicates that the magnitude of grief is greater following deaths that are both unexpected and untimely than when the bereaved have had time to anticipate the loss. Of course, not every sudden death is unanticipated, and in the older age range an association between sudden deaths and pathological grief has not been found (Clayton et al., 1973). It seems reasonable to suppose that anticipation enables people to begin to modify their internal models of the world so that they already have a mental "set," a new set of expectations and plans that will make it easier for them to approach the problems of bereavement. Lacking such a model, the newly bereaved will either defend themselves by avoiding realization of what has happened or be overwhelmed by the disorganization of their psychic world. Either of these consequences can give rise to lasting difficulties.

2. Magnitude of the transition—the amount of change in the assumptive world—is the most obvious difference between the loss of a wife and the loss of an old umbrella. In most instances the former can be expected to be the greater cause for grief. Nevertheless, there is good reason not to confine the word "grief" to the loss of a person. Comparative studies have revealed the numerous similarities in reactions to the loss of objects as diverse as a home, a spouse, and a limb (Parkes, 1972).

3. Multiple losses constitute an extension of this. Sometimes one leads to others, as in the case of the widow who, following her husband's death, clung to friends of her husband who involved her in the disposal of stolen property. As a result of this she was arrested by the police and lost her freedom, self-respect, and friends. The result was an acute agitated depressive reaction and an attempt at suicide.

4. Physical or physiological incapacity—fatigue, physical illness, and other bodily changes which reduce psychophysiological resilience, as in the case of a person who is severely injured in an accident that kills other members of his family.

305

The first of these circumstances has clear implications for prevention. Obviously anything that helps people to anticipate and prepare themselves for a loss can be expected to reduce the impact of that loss when it occurs. When anticipation has not been possible, it is particularly important to insure that those who are responsible for imparting bad news and providing immediate succor recognize that this communication requires sensitivity and will take time and that continuing support needs to be introduced at once. Little systematic research has yet been published in this field, so our guidelines must be those that arise from common sense and clinical experience. Simply by giving the newly bereaved the time to allow news to "sink in" and to begin to talk through its implications we may initiate the preparation that, in other circumstances, would have taken place over a much longer period before the loss. This is particularly important if the loss is a great or multiple one or the individual's resources are low.

There is no space here to give further details of the studies that throw light on these factors, but it is worth pointing out that prospective studies are not only important in pointing to the causes of pathological grief, but they also suggest practical ways of identifying bereaved people who are in need of counseling. A predictive questionnaire has been in use at St. Christopher's Hospice in south London for eight years as an aid to the selection of bereaved people for follow-up support. It is completed by nurses at the time of a patient's death and provides an overall score that is significantly correlated with outcome twenty months after bereavement (Parkes, 1979a). There is a need for further work to develop and refine predictive instruments of this kind.

In addition to questions on family, social, and occupational support, several questions are concerned with the reaction of the subject to the impending loss. Anger, guilt, and pining are easily recognized by nurses and add weight to the predictive score. It seems that they often reflect problems of ambivalence and clinging.

Evidence for the Effectiveness of Bereavement Intervention

Finally we must ask what evidence there is that preventive interventions of the kind just referred to do in fact prevent anything. In recent years seven systematic evaluative studies using randomized control groups and one using carefully matched comparison groups have come to my notice. (These are reviewed in Parkes, 1980.) In view of the depressingly poor results of most well-conducted evaluations of psychological therapies and the difficulties of quantification involved in the measurement of "outcome," we should not be surprised to find little evidence for the effectiveness of preventive intervention in bereavement. In fact this is not the case. Five of the eight studies showed statistically significant differences between helped and unhelped groups favoring the group that had been supported in their bereavement, and even in those studies that showed no such difference some explanation of the results obtained was possible.

Studies that came up with positive findings were those that used the most sensitive indices of health outcome (e.g., measures of health *change* rather than health status), those in which high-risk bereaved were selected for support, and those in which the support was given face to face in the client's home rather than in an office or by telephone. The conclusions reached in my review were:

> It would seem . . . that professional services and professionally supported voluntary and self-help services are capable of reducing the risk of psychiatric and psychosomatic disorders resulting from bereavement. . . . If help can be provided before as well as after bereavement, the chances of success may be further improved. The value of services which lack the support of trained and experienced members of the care-giving professions remains to be established. (Parkes, 1980, p. 9)

It is hard to say which aspects of the bereavement services explain the positive findings obtained in these studies. Was it facilitation of the expression of grief, reassurance of meaning and worth, opportunity for the bereaved person to reexamine and revise his assumptive world, or a combination of these? Or was there some other factor that may have been incidental to these that explains successful counseling?

Raphael's finding (1977) that the group who benefited most from bereavement counseling were the widows who had rated their families as "unhelpful" seems to suggest that the counselor was providing essentially the same help that a helpful family offers.

Implications for Intervention at Other Times of Transition

As we have seen, sensitively responsive caretaking behavior results in the reduction of attachment behavior and the release of exploratory behavior in the young child. It is reasonable to assume that it has similar benefits in adult life. When a person discovers that his assumptive world no longer matches the world he perceives to be at hand, he becomes painfully aware that he can no longer rely on his capacity to predict and behave appropriately. Because of this he feels and often is in a situation of danger or insecurity. The familiar world seems unfamiliar—"My world has been turned upside down." It is appropriate that at such times he should turn to others who are relatively less affected by these changes and who will "take care" of him. Having been given that care, the individual will normally become less apprehensive and begin to explore the world that now confronts him. In doing so he rebuilds his assumptive world in a more appropriate way and completes the psychosocial transition.

The implications of this work are not confined to bereavement counseling. Other forms of help aimed at people who are about to, are undergoing, or have recently undergone other kinds of loss stand a good chance of reducing the risk to mental health that is associated with such life events.[3] Systematic studies have already been carried out to demonstrate the effectiveness of anticipatory guidance in preparation for major surgery, childbirth, and release of recidivists from long prison sentences (recent studies are reviewed in Parkes, 1979*b*). Supportive guidance through the unpredictable circumstances of myocardial infarction has been shown by Rahe, Ward, and Hayes (1979) to reduce subsequent morbidity (an example of midtransition guidance) and posttransition support has also proved effective in speeding recovery following open heart surgery (Lazarus and Hagens, 1968). Other examples of preventive intervention before, during, and after transition that deserve further study include preretirement and postretirement courses; premarriage, marriage, and postmarriage guidance; supportive services for migrants (before, during, and after migration); services for workers who are about to be made redundant; support for elderly or chronic sick before and after they enter institutional care; and support for physically disabled before, during, and after disablement.

In all of these fields the theoretical and practical implications of the work reported in this book are of importance. In fact, it seems very likely that the next decades will see a major advance in the development of support systems aimed at preparing people for and helping them through major changes in their lives.

3. These three forms of help can be termed "anticipatory guidance," "midtransition guidance," and "posttransition support."

REFERENCES

Ball, J. F. 1977. Widow's grief: The impact of age and mode of death. *Omega* 7:307.

Bowlby, J. 1968. Effects on behaviour of disruption of affectional bond. In *Genetic and environmental influences on behaviour,* ed. J. M. Thoday and A. S. Parker, Edinburgh: Oliver and Boyd. Reprinted in *The making and breaking of affectional bonds,* by J. Bowlby. London: Tavistock, 1979.

————. 1969. *Attachment and loss. Vol. 1: Attachment.* New York: Basic Books.

————. 1973. *Attachment and loss. Vol. 2: Separation: Anxiety and anger.* New York: Basic Books.

————. 1980. *Attachment and loss. Vol. 3: Loss: Sadness and depression.* New York: Basic Books.

————, and Parkes, C. M. 1970. Separation and loss. In *The child in his family,* vol. 1 of *International yearbook of child psychiatry and allied professions,* ed. E. J. Anthony and C. Koupernik. New York: Wiley.

Clayton, P. J.; Halikas, J. A.; Maurice, W. L.; and Robins, E. 1973. Anticipatory grief and widowhood. *British Journal of Psychiatry* 122:47–51.

Cohen, E. A. 1953. *Human behavior in the concentration camp.* New York: Norton.

Erikson, K. 1979. *In the wake of the flood.* London: Allen and Unwin.

Gorer, G. 1965. *Death, grief and mourning in contemporary Britain.* London: Gesset.

Lazarus, H. R., and Hagens J. H. 1968. Prevention of psychosis following open heart surgery. *American Journal of Psychiatry* 124:1190.

Lifton, R. J. 1964. On death and death symbolism: The Hiroshima disaster. *Psychiatry* 27:191–210.

Lindeman, E. 1944. The symptomatology and management of acute grief. *American Journal of Psychiatry* 101:141–148.

————. 1960. Psychosocial factors as stress agents. In *Stress and psychiatric disorder,* ed. J. M. Tanner. Oxford: Blackwell.

Longford, E. 1964. *Victoria R. I.* London: Weidenfeld & Nicholson.

Lundin, T. 1979. On crisis theory, reactions to sudden and unexpected death. Proceedings of the Tenth International Conference for Suicide Prevention and Crisis Intervention, Ottawa, Canada.

Maddison, D. C., and Walker, W. L. 1967. Factors affecting the outcome of conjugal bereavement. *British Journal of Psychiatry* 113:1057–1067.

Mawson, D.; Marks, I. M.; Ramm, L.; and Stern, L. S. 1981. Guided mourning for morbid grief: A controlled study. *British Journal of Psychiatry* 138: 185–193.

Natterson, J. M., and Knudson, A. G., Jr. 1960. Observations concerning fear of death in fatally ill children and their mothers. *Psychosomatic Medicine* 22:456–465.

Parkes, C. M. 1965. Bereavement and mental illness. Part I: A clinical study of the grief of bereaved psychiatric patients. *British Journal of Medical Psychology* 38:1–26.

————. 1971. Psycho-social transitions. A field for study. *Social Science and Medicine* 5:101–115.

————. 1972. Components of the reaction to loss of a limb, spouse or home. *Journal of Psychosomatic Research* 16:343–349.

————. 1976. Determinants of outcome following bereavement. *Omega* 6:303–323.

————. 1979a. Evaluation of a bereavement service. In *The dying human,* ed. A. de Vries and A. Carmi. Ramat Gan Israel: Turtledove.

————. 1979b. The use of community care in prevention. In *New methods of mental health care,* ed. M. Meacher. London: Pergamon.

————. 1980. Bereavement counselling: Does it work? *British Medical Journal* 281:9–10.

Rahe, R. H., Ward, W. H., and Hayes, V. 1979. Brief group therapy in myocardial infarction rehabilitation: Three to four year follow-up of a controlled trial. *Psychosomatic Medicine* 41:229–242.

Ramsay, R. W. 1979. Bereavement: A behavioral treatment of pathological grief. In *Trends in behavior therapy,* ed. P. O. Sjoden, S. Bates, and W. S. Dorkens III. New York: Academic Press.

Raphael, B. 1977. Preventive intervention with the recently bereaved. *Archives of General Psychiatry* 34:1450–1454.

Epilogue

John Bowlby

ATTENDING THE STUDY GROUP at which these contributions were first presented and reading the revised versions of them in this book have been heartwarming experiences. For in science, ideas, however promising, are insubstantial until they are tested in further research and fleshed out with empirical data. This is what the foregoing chapters provide for the ideas on attachment that I and other members of the study group have been working on during the past twenty years.

When I first sketched the outline of attachment theory, I was concerned to find a way of explaining certain forms of disturbed personality development that would be better than the explanations offered by the psychological theories then current. Psychoanalysis gave weight to the internal workings of the human mind and recognized the special status of intimate human relationships, but its metapsychology, already obsolescent, was a major handicap, while its fixation on a single, retrospective research method gave no means of resolving differences of opinion. Learning theory had other deficiencies: It refused to concern itself with the human mind as an information processor, to use modern jargon, and failed to appreciate that intimate human relationships play a special, indeed unique, role in personality development and functioning. As a clinician concerned to treat and, if possible, prevent psychological disturbance and suffering, I felt little progress could be made until we had a better conceptual framework. For reasons recorded elsewhere, I started by trying to understand the nature of the child's tie to his mother, moving on from there to problems of separation anxiety, mourning, and defense.

310

The results of these early efforts were different from what I had hoped for. The practicing clinicians to whom my work was addressed showed disappointingly little interest. Having spent long years being trained in certain ways of thinking, they were already fully occupied applying and teaching those ideas and had no time to think afresh. Instead, it was a handful of behavioral scientists, of widely differing backgrounds, who took fire and decided the ideas should be tested in research. Their number included two who were already well known to me. One, Mary Salter Ainsworth, a psychologist, decided to study infant development; the other, Robert Hinde, an ethologist, decided to study rhesus monkeys. The third was a newcomer, Colin Murray Parkes, a psychiatrist, soon to become a colleague, who was already beginning his studies of the psychiatric consequences of bereavement in adult life.

It is unnecessary for me here to emphasize the enormous contributions these researchers have made not only to their own distinctive fields—developmental psychology, ethology, and adult psychiatry, respectively—but to the field as a whole, as their chapters in this volume amply testify. For their early and continuing contributions to my own thinking I remain deeply indebted.

In these widely different fields both the progress of research and appreciation of its potential have been uneven. By 1970, for example, thanks to the work of Mary Salter Ainsworth and her students, few developmental psychologists were unaware of attachment theory, even though it was often misunderstood and remained intensely controversial. On clinicians, however, it had still made little impact. There are many reasons for this. One is the dominant positions of learning theory and traditional psychoanalysis in the psychology taught to psychiatrists, and the near absence of either ethology or developmental psychology. Another is that the field of intimate human relationships is a sensitive and difficult one in which to do research, and any such research is extremely time consuming. As a result, not only are suitable research personnel scarce, but projects are difficult to frame in the tidy and time-limited ways required alike for postgraduate degrees and by funding bodies. Nevertheless, that these problems can be overcome is demonstrated by the clinical contributions to this volume. The work reported I know is no more than the first fruits of a much larger harvest still to come.

In perusing the chapters the reader will perhaps be struck by the diversity of disciplines and approaches represented and, as a consequence, by the very different types of data presented. This diversity I believe to be of the greatest value. No one research method can do more than throw a very narrow beam of light onto any problem area. Yet all too often proponents of one field are contemptuous of the products of another. In psychiatry, for example, an epidemiologist is apt to have no use for the soft data and anecdotes of the therapist, while a therapist, in his turn, is apt to have no use for the colorless statistics, as he sees them, of the epidemiologist. The truth is, of course, as the contributors to this volume are keenly aware, that each method has its own strengths and weaknesses, and that there is always a chance that the strengths of one method may make good at least some of the weaknesses of another. Only by drawing on data produced by a multiplicity of methods is it likely that any complex scientific problem will be solved; and this is more especially the case in fields such as human psychology and psychiatry, where the opportunities for experiment are so limited and the life span of our subjects so long.

It is salutary to remember that comparable problems faced those who, during the last century, were trying to understand the problem of biological species and their distribution, and that it was because Charles Darwin utilized evidence from a great diversity of sources that he was able to make the contributions he did. Many of his sources, moreover, lay far outside the realms of accepted science. Recall, for instance, the many evenings he spent in smoky pubs discussing with pigeon fanciers the methods whereby they produced strains that, had their origin from a single stock not been confirmed, would have been accounted distinct species. For Darwin, the oral traditions of the fanciers and the accounts he found in various old treatises carried great weight. They, and comparable information from plant and stock breeders, showed that systematic breeding, selecting for seemingly trivial variations, could, over the course of generations, produce breeds differing remarkably from one another. This gave him confidence that one of the principal mechanisms of evolution he was proposing had indeed the power he was attributing to it.

The experiences of Darwin illustrate also the converse: that conclusions reached by scientists of the highest repute using methods of the greatest exactitude can nevertheless, when taken in isolation, sometimes prove profoundly mistaken. Lord Kelvin, it will be remembered—the most influential physicist of his day—pronounced that the earth was cooling at such a rate that the eons of geological time the geologists confidently inferred from their observations and that were a necessity for Darwin's theory could not be allowed. Science had spoken and, so it seemed, Darwin's theory was exploded. Not so, of course. At the time of Kelvin's pronouncement the heating effect of the earth's internal radioactivity was unknown. In the course of time, it became clear that geological time was indeed as long as the geologists believed.

Although in this case the conclusions the soft data supported proved true and those drawn from hard data were misleading, no doubt the opposite is more often the case. My reason for recounting the story is that it illustrates that, in a field of great complexity in which useful experimental data are hard to come by, the most reliable conclusions are likely to be those reached when evidence from a multiplicity of sources is drawn upon, and that it is unwise to rely on evidence from any one source, however prestigious that may be.

It would be impracticable as well as inappropriate for me to attempt to comment on the contributions to this book. Let me end therefore where Robert Hinde begins. The tasks for those who use attachment theory to guide their research or their clinical work are to see where the ideas already formulated can aid understanding, to recognize where they need supplementing from elsewhere, and to accept that there are probably many fields on which they shed no light. Attachment theory is still growing: Its potential and its limitations remain unknown.

Name Index

Subject Index